W9-ACG-444

WITHDRAWN

A
Gravity's
Rainbow
Companion

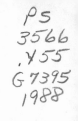

A *Gravity's Rainbow* Companion

Sources and Contexts for Pynchon's Novel

by Steven Weisenburger

The University of Georgia Press

Athens & London

© 1988 by the University of Georgia Press
Athens, Georgia 30602
All rights reserved

Set in Mergenthaler Trump Mediaeval

The paper in this book meets the guidelines for
permanence and durability of the Committee on
Production Guidelines for Book Longevity of the
Council on Library Resources.

Printed in the United States of America
92 91 90 89 88   5 4 3 2 1

Library of Congress Cataloging in Publication Data

Weisenburger, Steven.
    A Gravity's rainbow companion.

    Bibliography: p.
    Includes index.
    1. Pynchon, Thomas. Gravity's rainbow. I. Title
PS3566.Y55G7395 1988   813'.54   87-34321
ISBN 0-8203-1025-5 (alk. paper)
ISBN 0-8203-1026-3 (pbk.: alk. paper)

British Library Cataloging in Publication Data
available

Contents

Acknowledgments

In many ways doing this book was *fun*. It meant readings in American pop and material culture, the occult, varieties of pseudoscience, real science, vernacular geography, and forty-year-old news periodicals—to mention just a few fields I wandered into. A new discovery each week, at the peak of my research. It was sometimes tedious but always enjoyable work, because of friends and colleagues who took an interest. I am grateful to all who helped it along. Roger Sale, for two reasons: for showing that one could enjoy these serendipitous paths of scholarship and for sharing his reading of *Gravity's Rainbow* when the novel was first published. Malcolm Griffith, for suggesting (in 1978) that I should write this book. I put the idea aside for four years, but once under way it was helped by a number of friends and colleagues. Staff members at the M. I. King Library at the University of Kentucky provided invaluable assistance, and I especially want to thank Roxanna Jones and Barbara Wight of Interlibrary Loan, as well as Rob Aken, Dan Barkley, Brad Grissom, and Laura Rein of King Library Reference. Steven Moore, fresh from a similar project on Gaddis's *The Recognitions*, made wise suggestions as I prepared the first draft. Molly Hite gave suggestions and encouragement. To all of Pynchon's scholarly readers, acknowledged in the notes and listed in the bibliography, I owe innumerable debts. Colleagues at the University of Kentucky answered what must have seemed the oddest possible salmagundi of queries and requests. For their help and encouragement I am especially grateful to Tom Adler, Gerald Alvey, Roger Anderson, Tom Blues, Joe Bryant, John Cawelti, Guy Davenport, Joe Gardner, and John Shawcross. Thanks to Bob Hemenway for supporting the work while he was chairman, and in particular for helping me find funds and time off from my departmental responsibilities at a crucial time. The research and preparation of the book were assisted by grants from the University of Kentucky Research Foundation. To complete the final draft, I also managed to steal time from another project that was being assisted by a grant from the National Endowment for the Humanities. Janis Bolster did an epic job of copyediting, down to the last line-number reference. And at the University of Georgia Press, Debra Winter has guided this project with care for all the details that matter. Again, thanks to all.

Finally, to Susan, still my best friend, who knows this project as an oral history: this book's for you.

Lexington, Kentucky   *June 1987*

A
Gravity's
Rainbow
Companion

Introduction

THE first draft of *Gravity's Rainbow* was written out in neat, tiny script on engineers' quadrille paper. The idea had grown, parts of it during a stint in Mexico, from the writing in *V.*, Pynchon's first novel. It had been put aside for a second book, *The Crying of Lot 49* ("in which I seem to have forgotten most of what I thought I'd learned up till then," he would later lament, too harsh a critic of his own work [*Slow Learner* 22]). It was completed in southern California and New York. Visitors to his cavelike rooms perched two blocks up from the Pacific in Manhattan Beach, a Los Angeles suburb, recall only a cot, desk, and some bookshelves. One ruling spirit of the place was a monkish impermanence; another, his warm, nonchalant eccentricity. Arranged on the shelves were an assortment of piggy banks and several books about swine. He delighted in a friend's wife who could parody Shirley Temple singing "On the Good Ship Lollipop." On his desk were deposited, in strata, various letters, miscellanea, and those quadrille sheets. Atop them stood a rocket constructed much like one of Picasso's found objects: a pencil-type eraser (the kind from which you peel off the corkscrew wrapper) with a needle in its nose, and a re-formed paper clip serving as a launching pad.

Gravity's Rainbow was released on February 28, 1973, under the astrological sign of Pisces, the watery house of dreams and dissolution. "Madness spews forth in torrents, Pandora's evils incarnate!" wrote *Publishers Weekly*. Richard M. Nixon, satirized in the novel's final pages as Richard M. Zhlubb, was referring to "the Watergate mess" as an obsessive fabrication of newswriters, and much of the nation still believed him.

Thomas Pynchon's big book quickly confirmed him as one of the few novelists of unprecedented genius to emerge in the postwar era. Here was the Great American Novel at last. The reviewers' favorite comparisons were to *Moby Dick* and *Ulysses*. There was a remarkable flap over the Pulitzer awards, with judges so sharply divided against trustees over the book that no award in fiction was given—the only year it's ever happened. There was also a Howells Medal for the novel, but speaking on Pynchon's behalf stand-up comic Irwin Corey made light of the honor. That early hoopla has long since yielded to more sober assessments of Pynchon's achievement, but scholarly critics have also tended toward superlatives. Tony Tanner (75), for instance, hails the book as "both one of the great historical novels of our time and arguably the most important literary text since *Ulysses*." Translations of the novel attest to its international importance. *Gravity's Rainbow* has been published in French (as *Rainbow*, 1975), German (as *Die Enden der Parabel*, 1981), and Spanish (as *El arco iris de la gravedad*, 1978). Episodes of the book have been translated into Japanese. Through all of this, Pynchon has militantly guarded his privacy. Our glimpses of him are, at best, like brief skyrockets: a few jacket blurbs, letters, introductions to his own and others' work, and a brief (and very crotchety) cover essay for the *New York Times Book Review*. There are persistent rumors of forthcoming work. Still, we know little at all about the author himself; in an age when all manner of novelists are routinely interviewed about their work and composing processes, Pynchon is mum. With *Gravity's Rainbow*, to alter a sentence Pynchon once got from Wittgenstein, "the text" is all that the case is.

ABOUT THIS BOOK

I began this study because a set of basic textual and critical questions needed answers. At a minimum, these questions included: What is the structure of *Gravity's Rainbow*? What are its most persistent and significant stylistic features? The focuses of its satires and parodies? The source texts Pynchon transformed into fiction? The points of connection between (on the one hand) procedures of science and technology and (on the other) the rituals of religion and occultism? Perhaps most basic of all, I wanted a more coherent, readerly idea of the simple when and where of story events. The obvious strategy was to begin annotating the text.

A *"Gravity's Rainbow" Companion* is intended to serve as a comprehensive source book on Pynchon's novel. The following notes were written to ease the demands of the novel's multilanguaged style, its obscure and brilliantly pointed references. They are meant to document sources and to spin readers outside the text itself, into contexts that open the reading in new and unsuspected ways. The *Companion* was conceived as a line-by-line guidebook; indeed, as eight resources in one: a source study, encyclopedia, handbook, motif index, dictionary, explicator, gazeteer, and list of textual errors (nearly twenty-five in the Bantam edition).

On the whole, this commentary is as attentive as I can presently make it, though some items have doubtless escaped notice. For example, Pynchon has a remarkable ear for popular song lyrics—from thirties jazz tunes to sixties rock 'n' roll, from the rhythms of dialogue in *Plasticman* comics to snippets of speech from the film *Casablanca*—and other ears will surely recognize echoes I have missed. My aim was not completion, a desire *Gravity's Rainbow* laughs away by reference to Murphy's law, but comprehension, a sense of the field. The commentary also had to walk a thin line between informative and interpretive notes. I found, for example, that a rare coincidence of the occidental calendar occurred in 1945: Easter Sunday fell on April Fool's Day. Further, the Feast of the Transfiguration fell on Sunday, August 6, when the first atomic bomb was released to the pull of gravity over Hiroshima. For Pynchon, fictions followed from these facts, details that all participate in the stunningly ambiguous cyclical structure of the novel. What Pynchon's critics eventually make of that pattern remains to be seen. For now, however, it would be folly to avoid its interpretive potential.

A brief analogy: Readers familiar with Gifford and Seidman's annotations for *Ulysses*, their *Notes for Joyce* (1974), will remark that I have copied the format, and could as easily have followed their model, of factual, interpretively neutral annotations. But Gifford and Seidman, like their readers, already had access to extensive descriptions of the structure and style of *Ulysses*. Their notes laid a wealth of filigree on an existing model.

I wish this had been the need when I began annotating *Gravity's Rainbow*, but it was not. Indeed, the prevailing impression was that Pynchon's book stood on the landscape like a formless monster with little, if any, organizing skeleton. Amid the current debates over literary theory, this impression is still quite pronounced among many of Pynchon's poststructuralist, deconstructionist readers. They wish to make strong claims for his contemporaneity, and therefore they tend to come out swinging against virtually any hint that a particular signifier might totalize one's reading of the novel. Given this reception of the book, these notes have had to sketch in broad patterns of narrative order, at the same time granting issues of theory involved in doing so. Throughout, I have been guided by the unwritten axiom that textual sources and facts suggest interpretations, and have welcomed such an interplay.

In my view, the most significant discovery of the annotations is that *Gravity's Rainbow* unfolds according to a circular design. Across the novel's four parts, historical events intersect the Christian liturgical calendar, inferring possibilities for return and renewal, but possibilities that Pynchon's satire hopelessly equivocates. This means that readers might have a novel as elegantly modeled as Joyce's *Ulysses* and have their deconstructionism too. Indeed, one might well read *Gravity's Rainbow* as a satire on the very desire for such plots, or metanarratives, a desire the narrative unmasks as the terrible dynamic of a culture huddling on the brink of nuclear winter. I take up these interpretive problems again, briefly, as this introduction ends.

HOW TO USE THIS BOOK

These notes refer to all three American editions of *Gravity's Rainbow*: the Viking (1973), which appeared in both hardcover and as a trade paperback; the Bantam (1974), with its smaller and lengthier format; and the newly released Penguin (1987), which was offset from the last printing of the Viking and so is identical to it (right down to the cover art). Items from the narrative will be listed, in boldface, by page and line numbers for editions—"V" for the Viking/Penguin and "B" for the Bantam, like this:

V592.25–26, B690.32–33   the General Forces Programme features Sandy MacPherson at the Organ   Here, the "distant radio" playing in the background establishes the time of these events. BBC programming schedules in the *Times* of London list Mr. MacPherson on Sunday night, August 5, at 10:15 P.M., and at no other time during the month. See also V13.39–40n.

Sources and contextual references are from items generally listed in the bibliography, and many annotations are cross-referenced using the Viking/Penguin numbers (all that's needed to move around in the *Companion*) and the abbreviation "n." To locate references on their pages of *Gravity's Rainbow* more quickly, it helps to know that uninterrupted pages in the Viking/Penguin editions generally have forty-one lines of text; in the Bantam, forty-two. In these notes, line numbers refer only to actual lines of text; blank lines don't count.

Ideally, one would prefer to have an annotated edition of the novel. One might then "look down at the bottom of the text of the day, where footnotes will explain all," as the narrator remarks (V204.26–27). One solution is simply to put the *Companion* under, or alongside, the novel, and follow an interrupted reading with a more fluent, second turn. Another solution is to read an episode, then the annotations—the best way, in my view, as it more closely approximates the inferential processes of reading. Indeed, the reader soon begins tracking back and forth in the narrative, an activity encouraged by both the cross-referencing and the index. For simplicity, these employ Viking/Penguin numbers *only*. But this poses no problem for Bantam readers. For instance, the discussion of Mr. Pointsman's "Kyprinos Orients" cigarettes (at V55.36) brings out the source of that detail in tiny *Times* of London advertisements but links it to broadly interlinked motifs—of Kyprian Venus, Tannhäuser, and seductive white goddesses of death—at later moments like V88.17 and V690.40. Viking/Penguin and Bantam readers alike can flip to the note for V88.17, B101.42–102.1, and track through the sequence.

One of my ideas in presenting these notes is that scholarly studies can be user-friendly. If *Gravity's Rainbow* sets in motion "the Night's Mad Carnival" (V133.38) of intertextual entertainments, then these annotations succeed if they get more readers aboard more of the rides.

FOR FURTHER STUDY

To open *Gravity's Rainbow* is to step within a shifting field of languages, each with its own spatiotemporal uniqueness. Part 3 represents this field as a horizontal "Zone," an uncertain, skeptical, often violent ground where an old hierarchy of values has been leveled. Everywhere in the novel, words are caught up in the midst of cataclysmic change. Yet the reading must begin with them, and the complexity of that task is apparent from a listing of only those *formal* discourses we encounter, including
  —Hebrew (imaged through Kabbalistic writings)
  —German (through the narrator's references to technical sources
      on rocketry, the poetry of Rainer Maria Rilke, and Teutonic
      mythology)
  —Kazakh (prior to and during its clash with Soviet bureaucracy)
  —Russian (through a score of bureaucratic designations)
  —Spanish (vis-à-vis Argentine literature: Hernandez, Lugones, and
      Borges)
  —French (a source of some conversational puns)
  —Japanese (in references to the kamikaze squadrons and haiku)
  —Herero (as preserved by nineteenth-century German philology,
      then in its fateful clash with German colonialism)
To date, the critical commentary on *Gravity's Rainbow* has mostly side-stepped the implications of this great, encyclopedic heteroglossia, though it is full of possibilities. One line of questions should certainly take up the ways a whole language is represented, or refracted through a specialized jargon or argot: Hebrew, for instance, by way of Kabbalistic mysticism; or Russian, by way of bureaucratic acronyms and the like. Another line of inquiry ought to take up the ways one language is shown being refracted, or even demolished, by another: Kazakh, for example, as it collides with the bureaucratizing needs of Soviet overlords during the twenties; or Herero, under the boot of General von Trotha's colonialist Vernichtungs Befehl (Extermination Order) in 1904. Then there is the larger question of how the novel's "foreign" discourses nuance meanings within its English-language narration. A fine example occurs in episode 4 of part 2, unforgettable (the Pulitzer trustees evidently raged against it) for its depiction of Katje Borgesius as a sable-draped "Domina Nocturna," engaging Brigadier General Pudding in a gut-wrenching act of urolagnia and coprophagia. As the annotations show, two mythologies (the Teutonic and the Kabbalistic) have intersected in this episode, producing a satiric inversion of the Kabbalistic ascent to the Merkabah, or divine throne, a narrative technique that is in fact characteristic of many other moments in the book and hinges here as elsewhere on the means by which a person's profoundest nightmares are colonized and *used* for purposes of control.

Turning next to the variety of *informal* discourses in the narration, one faces a still more uncertain flux. Within the word horde of English there are varieties of pop-cultural and subcultural discourse that include, at a minimum,

— popular slang (picked up from jokes, street ditties, song lyrics, comic books, street speech, and popular cinema)
— ethnic usage (black English, the Hispanic slang of *pachuco* zoot-suiters, others)
— underworld cant (especially as it pertains to black-marketeering in drugs and contraband)
— regional dialects (from the American West, Boston, and Britain)
— service slang (from both the American and the British military services, probably gleaned from Partridge's *Dictionary of Forces' Slang*)
— esoteric cant (by way of astrology, black magic, freemasonry, Rosicrucianism, and the like)
— folk usage (as found in children's lore and games, folktales, material culture, and so on)
— professional jargon (cinematography, ballistics, statistics, chemistry, behavioral and Pavlovian psychology, and many more)

It would be hard to overestimate the importance of these extraliterary languages in *Gravity's Rainbow*. The book's foremost source of surprise, incongruity, bathos, and recognition—in short, of satiric laughter—this heteroglossia nuances every narrative turn. The unofficial side of modern discourse serves as a rich store of curses and excretory and sexual indecencies and fantasies, as well as terms connected with compulsions toward states of inebriation and anesthesia. Such "unauthorized" languages are common to preterite souls everywhere, and in them the narration discovers specific points of view on the world, unsuspected orderings of things and values. Sometimes such views stand in sharp opposition to the official side; just as often they serve up ready-made parodies of it. So these languages may reveal a delightful absence of repression and sublimation, a bluntness that even verges on political aggression: as, for example, in the hard-won sexual intimacy of Roger Mexico and Jessica Swanlake or when Roger and "Pig" Bodine break up the "Krupp wingding" (V711.17) of part 4 with strings of obscene, alliterative epithets. Yet kinds of unofficial discourse may as often be routinized, victimized by other languages: so, for instance, in Brigadier Pudding's humiliating coprophagia or the satirical fantasy of the "Toilet-ship" in part 3.

This unofficial side of ordinary language also supplies the novel with a welter of ready-made folkloric genres: puns, rhyming speech, jokes and ditties, popular lyrics, children's games, and pantomimes. All are integrated into the novel's satirical project. In the closing episode of part 1, Roger Mexico spends Boxing Day at a pantomime of *Hansel and Gretel*, doubtless selected for its harsh judgments against parents, symbolized in the witch whose *Kinderofen* has its analogue in the V-2 rocket used to sacrifice a young boy, Gottfried, in the novel's climactic scene. Or there is the street game popular among children in Berlin, *Himmel und Hölle* (Heaven and Hell), a form of hopscotch involving ten steps, beginning from a zero space called *Erde* (Earth), leading through *Hölle*, and ending in *Himmel* (see V567.24–25n). The game corresponds with a great variety of homewarding, ten-stage motifs in *Gravity's Rainbow*, most notably the countdown preceding a rocket launch.

Whatever their source, these folkloric genres are all redirected by the radical undertaking of Pynchon's novel. Traditionally vital to the acculturation of both children and adults, in *Gravity's Rainbow* they contribute to a vastly articulated defamiliarization of history and culture. This is even the case with the novel's simplest structuring device, its division into four parts, which satirizes a traditional schema from hagiographic and heroic narratives: (1) the disclosure of the hero's miraculous gifts, (2) his education, (3) his testing during a course of travels, and (4) the confirmation of his powers, a *revelation*. This plot is refracted downward; the narration *pulls it down*, not only by inversion but also by means of everyday lore and lingo, those unofficial languages outlined above.

Reading that plot, it quickly becomes apparent that networks of detail are one key aspect of Thomas Pynchon's style, his creative technique. For example, in Marion Cooper's 1933 film *King Kong*, the "giant scapeape" (V275.34) originates from a South Seas place called Skull Island. The V-2 rocket originated from Peenemünde, an island off the Usedom coast of northern Germany glimpsed (on maps from Pynchon's sources) as a skull— for so the narrator remarks. On the fictional page this detail momentarily links both monstrosities, ape and rocket, in a web of narrative inferences. Pynchon is drawn to these possibilities for fictional transformation. The moments that speak most resonantly for him are those when lowly, seemingly preterite stuff is raised, when its hidden signs and broader humanness stand redeemed. The black and evil-smelling coal tars of nineteenth-century organic chemistry are recalled for yielding up a rainbow of colorful dyestuffs. " 'All the shit is transmuted to gold,' " as one of his stoned characters puts it (V440.23). The novel's epigraph puts it another way: "Nature does not know extinction; all it knows is transformation."

In the minutest of the myriad details of its composition, *Gravity's Rainbow* reveals this idea at work. Images on film are transmuted into facts; folk sayings suddenly inspire acts. Characters become the forces signaled from deep in the provenance of their names. And everywhere in the book footnotes (subtexts) are raised from the bottoms of the pages in Pynchon's sources and translated into fictional text. Horsley Gantt, Pavlov's translator, footnotes *gorodki*, a favorite game of Russian peasants; in playing, they lay waste to wood-block "cities" by heaving rough-hewn bats (*gorodki* sticks) over considerable distances. Considering how V-2 rockets were

thrown against London, Pavlov's "old *gorodki* stick" therefore cuts a significant figure in a poem (done after the manner of T. S. Eliot) by the fictional
Pavlovian, Pointsman, as rockets fall about him (V226.33n). It's but one of
many instances where marginal, footnoted material is transmuted into fictional reference and event.

There are several patterns in Pynchon's borrowings that are worth further
attention. The first is that many of the novel's episodes draw their backgrounds, references, even details of plotting, from a central source text: the
two volumes of Pavlov's *Lectures* in several episodes of part 1; a technical
handbook on rocketry by Dutch scientists Kooy and Uytenbogaart in episodes of parts 1 and 2; Richard Sasuly's *IG Farben* on German manufacturing cartels and the dyestuff/chemical industry in particular; an anthropo-
logical dissertation on the Herero for episodes treating South-West Africa;
Thomas Winner on the Kazakhs; General Walter Dornberger on day-to-day
activities and conditions at Peenemünde. A second pattern is that, working
with such texts, Pynchon's eye seems preternaturally alert for moments of
personal testimony, comments often buried in footnotes or beneath heaps
of technical data and objective detail. Pavlov's *gorodki* stick; his use of
himself as subject of study; Dornberger's recollections of local-color detail;
the memories of travelers, anthropologists, wives of rocket engineers, Japanese kamikaze pilots—these and many more were woven into *Gravity's
Rainbow*.

I hope these annotations will help to rebut those impatient Pecksniffs
(the Pulitzer trustees, John Gardner in *On Moral Fiction*, and Gore Vidal, to
name just a few) who have condemned *Gravity's Rainbow* as a careless,
amoral, and malignant book. Pynchon's better readers, too taken by matters
technical and theoretical, have mostly written around the fringes of this
issue. But Pynchon's is no limp, value-free historicism. Everywhere in
Gravity's Rainbow the testimony of his witnesses stands in relation to a
moral vision. For example, in their voluminous recollections ex-Nazis like
Dornberger, Wernher von Braun, and Willy Ley wave aside the issue of slave
labor at Peenemünde with euphemisms like "foreign construction workers"; none of them ever treats the use of death-camp labor at the final assembly plant at Nordhausen. In one of the really chilling ironies of it all,
virtually the only Nazi associated with the rocket program to remember
those death-camp inmates was Albert Speer, sentenced to life imprisonment in Spandau Prison while Dornberger went on to the United States,
where he sat on the board at Bell Helicopter, as von Braun headed up NASA
during the Apollo moon launches. This is the context one is asked to bear in
mind when the narrative infers that Blicero, an embodiment of everything
truly evil and deadly in the German romance of rocketry, has gone on to the
United States, and that to find him readers should "look among the successful academics, the Presidential advisers, the token intellectuals who sit on
boards of directors. He is almost surely there. Look high, not low"

(V749.10–12). At the novel's actual (if not virtual) center, the story of Franz Pökler (episode 11 of part 3) stands against that collective loss of memory. Though composed mainly from Dornberger's testimony, Pökler's struggle with these moral cruxes, including finally his simple act of empathy at the Nordhausen concentration camp, does establish a normative base for Pynchon's satirical aggressions. In their composition, other episodes contribute to such a reading. For the novel's critics, there is thus a great deal more to be said about the politics and morality of its fiction making.

Careful attention to *Gravity's Rainbow* also discloses patterns of structure. Especially in part 1, a number of episodes are composed according to a complex, circular motion. Episode 9, for example, begins with Jessica Swanlake standing at a window and moves through a sequence of analeptic cuts (involving shifts in focalization, all without any of the spatiotemporal markers by which writers conventionally signal them to readers) until it concludes, once more, with Jessica at the window. Again in part 1, episode 14 is a much more complex variant on this cyclical pattern. It opens at Pirate Prentice's London maisonette with Katje Borgesius standing before the lens of Osbie Feel's movie camera; the first analepsis, focalized through Katje, discloses Blicero, Gottfried, and Katje at the rocket battery in Holland; the second, focalized now through Blicero, takes us to South-West Africa during the Herero insurrection of 1922; we return momentarily to the second-order time (at the Holland rocket battery) in order to begin a third analepsis, this time focalized through one of Katje's seventeenth-century ancestors, Frans van der Groov, on the island of Mauritius; and the narration ends by cycling readers back to the original base time, with Katje standing before the camera eye. Other episodes and bits of episodes (the "Tamara/Italo drill" [V261.39–40] of episode 6 in part 2, the circular group-grope of episode 14 in part 3) are similarly shaped. To adopt a term from the narrator's own discussions of organic chemistry, this episodic structuring of *Gravity's Rainbow* is "heterocyclic" (V249.26): rings are looped together in still larger, polymerized rings, looped together in the still larger cycling of its four parts.

In fact, when annotating *Gravity's Rainbow*, one of my greatest surprises came with the discovery that details of story reveal a narrative chronometrics that is concisely plotted. I mean detail of the most unobtrusive sort: images of the moon, remarks about weather, movies playing at London theaters, a song playing over the radio, references to BBC programs and newspaper headlines and saints' days. Many of these were available to Pynchon through one of his main sources, the *Times* of London. Collectively, they enable one to pinpoint the story time of many episodes, sometimes within the hour.

This chronology unfolds according to a carefully drawn circular design. *Gravity's Rainbow* is not arch-shaped, as is commonly supposed. It is plotted like a mandala, its quadrants carefully marked by Christian feast days that happened to coincide, in 1944–45, with key historical dates and ancient pagan festivals. The implications of this design are several, and wonderfully complex.

Part 1 begins on December 18, 1944, in the Advent season, and it ends nine days later on Boxing Day, December 26, when Christmas comes to the British servant classes. A saturnalian office party in episode 20 invokes the pagan counterpart to this Judaeo-Christian feast—Kislev, or Christmas. Part 2 commences around Christmas, with Slothrop newly arrived at Monaco, and it concludes on May 20, 1945—Whitsunday, when Christians celebrate the descent of the Holy Ghost to the disciples, seven weeks after Easter. On that "White-Sunday" in the novel, Pointsman is visited by auditory hallucinations while vacationing at Dover's white cliffs. Part 3 opens with an obscure reference to four saints' days in mid-May and ends on the Feast of the Transfiguration, celebrated on August 6 to mark Christ's final earthly revelation of his divinity—a blaze of illumination followed by a white cloud—witnessed by Peter, James, and John as they stood atop a mountain. But August 6, 1945, was also the day Hiroshima was bombed. Part 4 begins with an analepsis to that day, with Tyrone Slothrop on a mountaintop in central Germany, where he "becomes a cross himself, a crossroads" (V625.3–4), and thereupon begins to disappear from the novel. Transfiguration: Hiroshima. After scattered references to the A-bomb, and narrative inferences of how bomb and rocket are technologies soon to be joined, part 4 ends, nominally, on September 14, 1945, on the Feast of the Exaltation (or "Raising") of the Holy Cross, whose fictional counterpart is the "rocket raising" of V-2 number 00001 by Enzian and his Herero comrades. Figurally, part 4 ends with an almost simultaneous prolepsis and analepsis. The proleptic jump cut takes us to Los Angeles and the Orpheus Theater, circa 1970. The analeptic jump cut reveals, after so much anticipation, the firing of Rocket 00000, with its sacrifice of Gottfried (God's peace), from the Lüneberg Heath, at noon, during Easter of 1945. But in 1945 the Easter holy day fell on April Fool's. Easter: April Fool's. That coincidence had occurred only forty-three times since A.D. 500; it occurred again in 1956 but will not happen again during this century.

This is the shape of *Gravity's Rainbow*: a mandala, its four quadrants marked by crucial dates on the Christian liturgical calendar; a motion in which the circle of redemptive death, or foolishness (read it however you will), is nearly closed; a design that was formed as much by traditional, orderly patterning as by contemporary, purely coincidental event. The liturgical structure seems to focus the novel around a theme of salvation, a redeeming earthly savior. Equally as well, the pagan coincidences suggest that the whole enterprise is a *poisson d'avril*, a red herring, a fool's quest. And one can find nothing in the novel to resolve this antinomy.

Everywhere in *Gravity's Rainbow* the parabolic arch symbolizes disease, dementia, and destruction. Its counterpart is the circular mandala, a symbol of opposites held in delicate equipoise. In the novel drinking games and dances move in circles; the Herero villages used to be arranged mandala-like; and in every episode are windmills, buttons, windows, eyes, Ferris wheels, roulette wheels, rocket insignia, and other cast-down indexes of the novel's grand cycling. Pynchon's lowly, preterite souls come together around such symbols. Indeed, this circular structure is introduced to readers in the opening episode, when Pirate Prentice watches the sunrise blaze through the contrail of a newly launched V-2 and imagines its parabolic trajectory transformed into a rainbow that can only be a perfect circle high over the North Sea (see V6.33–35n). And the narrator reminds us of this event near the close, commenting that the rainbow is: "not, as we might imagine, bounded below by the line of the Earth it 'rises from' and the Earth it 'strikes' No But Then You Never Really Thought It Was Did You Of Course It Begins Infinitely Below The Earth And Goes On Infinitely Back Into The Earth it's only the *peak* that we are allowed to see" (V726.17–21). Put another way, only gravity's rainbow is arch-shaped; the shape of *Gravity's Rainbow* is circular.

The literary precursors of this design, at least those that come most directly to mind, are Joyce's *Ulysses* and Melville's great satire, *The Confidence Man*. Both involve cyclical plots unfolding over exactly three-fourths of a solar day. *Gravity's Rainbow* unfolds over 9 months, three-fourths of a solar year. And like Melville, Pynchon sets the decisive action of his book, the firing of Rocket 00000, on Easter/April Fool's. As in *The Confidence Man*, this one detail hopelessly equivocates any theme of salvation.

Thomas Pynchon ends his great satire on that wholly ambiguous crux. The ninth month of his narrative draws to a close with swarms of characters chasing various red herrings and arriving "too late" at the Holy Center (V752.12). Like the "Holy-Center-Approaching" (V508.35) he satirizes, Pynchon's novel ends on the threshold of a tenth month; the rocket crew runs through its ten-stage countdown; surely, then, some revelation is at hand. Yet the book refuses to dish up that totalizing signifier. It approaches, but avoids, closure. It combines the elegance of a preordained structure and the unintelligibility of pure coincidence. Does it see history as plotted or accidental? Is the rocket descending on the last page a symbol of divinely prefigured salvation or the triumph of an absolute violence? *Gravity's Rainbow* will not say, and neither can the notes in this book. They are offered to fuel that process of transformation which is reading.

Part 1 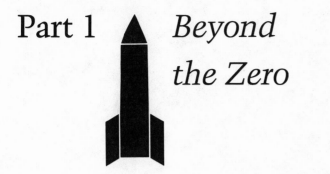 *Beyond the Zero*

PART 1 of *Gravity's Rainbow* (herein abbreviated *GR*), entitled "Beyond the Zero," spans nine days of the Advent and Christmas season, from December 18 through December 26, 1944. There are also a number of carefully orchestrated analepses: to the day several months earlier when the first V-2 rocket fell on England; to an Easter 1942 air raid by Allied bombers on the German city of Lübeck, which first prompted Hitler to warn of the coming *Vergeltungswaffe*, or "revenge-weapons"; to prewar Britain; to the seventeenth-century Dutch colony of Mauritius; and to Puritan America, with all its millennial hopes. Braiding these separate strands of narrative together is a strong theme of anticipated redemption. Characters feel poised at the edge of some sought-after revelation from "Beyond the Zero" of empirical knowledge. The Advent season suggests one form that expectation might assume—in the Nativity story. Yet Pynchon's depictions of technological, psychological, and paranormal research all demonstrate how modern culture secularizes that redemptive hope.

Indeed, Pynchon's satire quickly erases the boundary between sacred and secular. The epigraph to part 1, for example, is taken from the remarks of Wernher von Braun, the Nazi and NASA rocket engineer, before the July 1969 Apollo moon launch. Von Braun's belief in "transformation," his idea that science is another of the means humans use in the attempt to surmount "extinction," will soon correspond with other disciplines represented in the novel. In part 1 Pavlovian psychology is the predominant field of research, but the lexicons of statistics, occult or paranormal literature, organic chemistry, history, and Teutonic mythology all contribute to the narrative's theme of redemption.

Numerological correspondences also shape part 1. Discounting analepses, the narration is carefully plotted through nine winter days; in turn, the novel spans nine months, from mid-December until mid-September of 1945. There are twenty-one episodes in part 1; the Tarot deck has twenty-one numbered cards, if one omits another—the Fool—which is a zero or null card with no assigned place in the Tarot sequence. And this part begins a sequence of astrological correspondences. Events in these episodes unfold beneath the sign of Pisces. Sagittarius, the ninth house on the astrological calendar, would be the *actual* sign; but symbolically, *virtually*, the action everywhere takes on a Piscean aspect because this house, the twelfth, stands for death and dissolution, for contact with the supernatural, as well as for warfare and strife. In part 1 Pisces becomes a sign of endings and anticipations, just as in part 2 Aries will emerge as a sign of renewals and departures.

EPISODE I

The novel opens around dawn in the London cottage of Pirate Prentice. Episodes 1 through 5 all occur on the same day, which subsequent allu-

sions pinpoint as Monday, December 18, 1944. This episode begins with
Pirate dreaming the evacuation from London of its preterite souls, who pass
under "the final arch," symbol of "a judgment from which there is no ap-
peal" (V4.2–4). With the millennial motif thus established in a nightmare
vision, Pirate awakens to the fall of a comrade, whom he manages to save,
and to the impending fall of a V-2 rocket, just launched from Holland,
against which he is powerless. Watching the morning sun illuminate its
vapor trail over the North Sea, Pirate imagines the light refracting into a
rainbow that could only be, not a parabola, but a perfect circle.

V3.3, B3.3–4   The Evacuation still proceeds, but it's all theatre.
Historically, this is a fair analogy. When Germany began its
V-1, or buzz bomb, offensive in June 1944, one and a half million
civilians were evacuated from London. The minister of Home Security,
Herbert Morrison, was also prepared to order an almost total evacuation
if the expected barrage of rockets proved as devastating as he feared.
British intelligence experts had predicted that the rocket would carry a
warhead of seven tons, and Hitler was boasting that Nazi rockets
would deliver five hundred tons of explosives each hour. However,
when the first V-2 dropped on Chiswick in September, British intelligence quickly realized that the weapon would be much weaker (it
carried, not seven tons of amatol explosive, but one) and nowhere near
as prolific (517 hit London during the entire seven months of V-2
assault). Still, the V-2's real strength was as a weapon of terror; and
to calm the populace Home Security proceeded with some of its evacuation plans. Irving (80, 280–81, 287–88) sees them as good public relations with Londoners who needed assurances.

V3.7, B3.8–9   the fall of a crystal palace   A reference to the glass-
and-iron display hall designed by Sir Joseph Paxton for the Great Exhibition of 1851. From 1854 until it was razed by fire in 1936, the
structure stood—a symbol of Victorian progress—in London's Hyde
Park. Two of its towers survived the fire but were dismantled in 1940
to prevent German bomber crews from using them as landmarks.

V3.29, B3.35   naphtha winters   Naphtha is the flammable liquid obtained from the distillation of coal and used to fire gaslights and heaters.
The first of many coal derivatives mentioned in the narrative.

V3.34, B4.3   Absolute Zero   The centigrade temperature of −273.15
degrees, at which matter possesses the least energy; thus a *physically*
inert condition. In Pavlov's neuropsychiatric writings, however, the
term assumes a parallel meaning Pynchon will soon reference: "An un-
reinforced conditioned reflex without any repetitions . . . ends in
every case in extinction, to an absolute zero" (*Lectures* 2:121). Here,
it signifies an absolute lack of response to external stimuli, thus a
psychologically inert condition, the imagined death in Pirate's dream.

V4.36, B5.7–8 un-Hoovered rugs   That is, unvacuumed; after the
popular brand of cleaner manufactured in Ohio. For as ads in the *Times*
of London used to claim, "Post-war as Pre-war for your ideal home,
be it castle or cottage, the world's best cleaner is THE HOOVER."

V5.15, B5.30–31 The Special Operations Executive   Pirate's employer,
the British equivalent of the U.S. Office of Strategic Services
(OSS), was charged with gathering strategic and technical intelligence.
Irving (209) discloses that during March of 1944 eleven SOE commandos
were, like Pirate, parachuted into France and Holland to glean
anything about German V-weapons.

V5.21–22, B5.37–38 a maisonette . . . the Chelsea Embankment
Baedeker's *London* (158–59) describes the Embankment as "a fine
boulevard constructed in 1871–74," extending along the north bank
of the Thames "from Chelsea Bridge to Battersea Bridge, a distance of
over a mile." Corydon Throsp is fictional (as his name, from the pastoral
tradition, suggests), but his "maisonette" (cottage) is characteristic
of the area. Moreover, Pirate's bohemianism extends a tradition: Oscar
Wilde lived at No. 16 Chelsea Embankment from 1884 until his trial
in 1895; and the boulevard also skirts Cheyne Walk, once the home of
Dante Gabriel Rossetti and Algernon Charles Swinburne, whose
drunken carryings-on became legendary stuff.

V6.21, B7.1 A new star   Here, the burst of illumination from a launched
rocket. Soon, though, images of stars will burgeon until a variety
of references is working in *GR*: for example, the stars children put on
their calendars during the Advent season; the star over Bethelehem;
patterns of the zodiac; and the (apparently) fateful stars on Tyrone
Slothrop's map of his sexual conquests throughout London.

V6.26–27, B7.8 it's a vapor trail   Pynchon's source for this detail
is the *Times* of London. V-2 rockets were launched on London from
The Hague, 195 miles distant. Nevertheless, from their rooftops and upper windows Londoners might observe the white star-burst of a
launch and the vapor trail of a rocket climbing over the North Sea.
Many of the missiles were launched at dawn, when the low winter sun
brilliantly illuminated their exhaust. A letter in the *Times* of December
12, 1944 (5, col. 7) describes just such a "bright trace," and it prompted
several letters from others who described similar sights.

V6.30, B7.12 "Incoming mail"   Infantryman's slang for hostile, arriving
ordnance; but see V11.10–11n for an occasion when the metaphor
is literally fulfilled and Pirate receives word of a communiqué sent to
him by V-2 express.

**V6.33–35, B7.17–19 the sun . . . striking the rocket's exhaust . . .
making them blaze clear across the sea**   A fascinating image: the missile's vapor trail would bend the rays of sunlight into a rainbow, not
arch-shaped, as one initially suspects, but perfectly circular. Here are the

details. Later in part 1 (V100.36), Pynchon notes that the rockets
were launched from The Hague on London at a compass bearing of
260 degrees WSW, a detail he found in Kooy and Uytenbogaart (285).
In mid-December, when Pirate observes this dawn firing, the sun
would be nearing its lowest southern latitudes, approximately over
South-West Africa, the topos for many of Pynchon's Herero references.
The sun would be rising at a bearing of about 170 degrees ESE, or
perpendicular to the rocket's line of trajectory and forming, incidentally,
a cross in the sky. Now since a rainbow of illuminated light moves
in a direction opposite to that of its source—that is, since the rainbow
falls as the sun rises—then this imagined rainbow would be high
overhead relative to any observer who might be standing the requisite
one-half to one mile ESE of the rocket's airborne vapor trail. Such
an imaginary observer would see a circular rainbow and not the arch
we normally witness, one-half of which plunges into the earth. Pynchon
reminds us of this fact as *GR* draws to a close: "Of Course It Begins
Infinitely Below The Earth and Goes On Infinitely Back Into the Earth"
(V726.19–20). Note that Pirate's rainbow is *imagined*: to observe
it under these circumstances one would have to be perched high over
the North Sea.

V6.37, B7.22   Brennschluss   Available to Pynchon from a variety
of his technical source books, but most notably Dornberger (9n), who
explains: "*Brennschluss*, the 'end of burning'; the German word is
preferred to the form 'all-burnt,' which is used in England, because at
Brennschluss considerable quantities of fuel may still be left in the
tanks." In the V-2 this stage occurred at an altitude of 20 kilometers
(12.3 miles).

V6.39, B7.24   But the rocket will be here   A typographical error in
the Bantam (and the first of many); misprinted as "But the racket will
be here."

V7.3–4, B7.29–30   the operations room at Stanmore   Thirteen miles
northwest of London; home of the Special Operations Executive.

V7.5, B7.31–32   Less than five minutes Hague to here   Dornberger
(14) gives the flight time as "two-ninety-six seconds."

EPISODE 2

The time is later the same morning; the scene, still Pirate's maisonette,
then greater London. Pirate prepares a lavish "Banana Breakfast"
(V8.28–29) before superiors call him away to retrieve a message come down
by rocket. His departure for Greenwich triggers a lengthy analepsis concerned with the "Eastern Question" of 1914. This spins into one of the

novel's more eccentric nightmares: a monstrous Adenoid poised to swallow the city of London. Pirate's duty as "fantasist-surrogate" (V12.38–39) holds these strands together.

V7.36, B8.25 table stakes, B.O.Q. In poker-playing jargon, "table stakes" is a variable wagering limit fixed by the amount of money on the table at the time of any one bet. "B.O.Q.": a military acronym for a Bachelor Officers' Quarters.

V8.11, B9.2 A4 For *Aggregat-4*: Pirate uses a German cognomen for the V-2 rocket in its operational configuration (or *Aggregat*).

V9.3, B9.38 Miss Grable With her virtuoso display of legs in the 1944 film *Pin-up Girl*, American actress Betty Grable (1916–73) became *the* serviceman's heartthrob of World War II.

V9.4, B9.39 V-E Day Allied acronym for "Victory in Europe," officially declared on May 8, 1945: Pynchon's eighth birthday, President Harry Truman's sixty-first, and a day of increasing significance as *GR* continues (see V269.32n and V628.4n). The Allies began using the term in August 1944.

V9.26, B10.22 Vat 69 As *Times* of London advertisements used to note, "A Luxury Blend Scotch Whiskey, 25/9 per bottle."

V9.29, B10.24–25 the Jungfrau German for "young wife." Here, a mountain located in the Interlaken region of Switzerland, outside Zurich; elevation 4,158 meters (13,514 feet).

V9.40, B10.39 Sam Brownes A type of belt, with diagonal shoulder strap, designed by one-armed British Gen. Sir Samuel Browne (d. 1901).

V10.28, B11.33 *C'est magnifique, mais ce n'est pas la guerre* An exclamation ("It's magnificent, but it's not war!") widely attributed to French general Bosquet as he observed the Battle of Balaclava, October 25, 1854. The occasion was the brief but bloody Charge of the Light Brigade under Lord Cardigan, whose light-horse company charged across the valley at Balaclava, outside Sevastopol (then under siege by English, French, and Turkish troops), against greatly superior Russian troops. General Bosquet observed the charge from a hillside on the left flank. Tennyson's well-known ballad (see V270.14–15n) expresses the popular sense of it as a moral victory in the face of certain defeat.

V11.10–11, B12.18 waiting at Greenwich The mail-carrying rocket has impacted near the Royal Observatory near Greenwich, landmark of the zero degree of longitude.

V11.24–25, B12.34–35 east over Vauxhall Bridge . . . green Lagonda . . . his batman Pirate's route, from the Chelsea Embankment to Greenwich, takes him eastward over the Thames River via the Vauxhall

Bridge. The Lagonda was a luxury sedan with separate driver's compartment; its color, green, will be Pirate's once again in part 4. A batman is the traditional soldier-aide assigned to a British officer.

V11.27, B12.38 sappers Military engineers, those who dig (or "sap") fortifications.

V11.34, B13.4 narodnik Soules (104) points out that the term derives from "the Russian *narod*, 'people.' Intellectual trying to metamorphose peasants into revolutionaries. The *narodniki* flourished in the late 1860s. In the late 1960s, Student Nonviolent Coordinating Committee activists were referred to as *narodniks*. By show-offs."

V11.35, B13.5 Iasi . . . men of the League During the 1930s Romania found itself caught between Germany and Russia, with their crumbling Nazi-Soviet Pact. Corneliu Codreanu organized his League of the Archangel Michael and its military wing, the Iron Guard, a Fascist brotherhood based in the city of Iasi. Iron Guardsmen wore green shirts and carried little bags of Romanian soil, symbolizing their love of the fatherland, tied to thongs around their necks. Behind Codreanu, Romania maintained an alliance with Hitler through August 1944, when Britain and France assisted the deposed young king, Michael, in a successful coup. Still, the political situation remained unstable and was a frequent topic of discussion in the *Times* of London throughout the fall and winter of 1944–45. The Russians had been fomenting an underground struggle, and in March 1945 a Communist faction directed by the Russian commissar Andrei Vyshinski seized control. Here, the significant points are that in 1936 Pirate was having, or "*managing*" (V12.3), the fantasies of a fictional Romanian anti-Fascist and royalist and that it all satirizes those in the British Foreign Office who, as Hitler's power grew, kept applying scenarios from the previous war.

V12.7, B13.18 cup and bleed The archaic medical practice of "drawing blood by scarifying the skin and applying a 'cup' or cupping-glass, the air in which is rarefied by heat or otherwise" (*OED*).

V12.14–15, B13.28 the words of P. M. S. Blackett Javaid Qazi (9) identifies the source of this quotation: a book by Nobel laureate (in physics) Blackett, entitled *Fear, War and the Bomb* (New York, 1948).

V12.22, B13.36 I don't even get to ask for whom the bell's Recalls Ernest Hemingway's best-selling novel of the Spanish civil war, *For Whom the Bell Tolls* (1940), the title of which referenced John Donne's "Meditation XVII" from the *Devotions on Divergent Occasions* (1623): "Any man's death diminishes me because I am involved in mankind, and therefore never send to know for whom the bell tolls; it tolls for thee."

V12.30, B14.5 a walking stick with W. C. Fields' head Note the pun with "Joaquin Stick" (V9.28). Fields (d. 1946) was the irascible, bibulous, strawberry-nosed dandy of American comic cinema.

V13.1, B14.17—18   the mark of Youthful Folly   This is *Meng*, fourth hexagram of the *I Ching*, or "Book of Changes." The upper trigram of this figure depicts a mountain, the lower one a pool of water. Here is Richard Wilhelm's interpretation(20): "Keeping still is the attribute of the upper trigram; that of the lower is the abyss. Stopping in perplexity at the brink of a dangerous abyss is a symbol of the folly of youth. However, the two trigrams can also show a way of overcoming the follies of youth. Water is something that of necessity flows on. When the spring gushes forth, it does not know at first where it will go. But its steady flow fills up the deep place blocking its progress, and success is attained." The figure of this hexagram, and its symbolism, will later apply to Tyrone Slothrop (V378.12n).

V13.11, B14.30   Girl Guides   British version of the Girl Scouts, founded in 1910 by Robert Baden-Powell and his sister Agnes.

V13.14, B14.34   pixilated   Slang for inebriated, as if led by pixies.

V13.26—27, B15.8—9   rather a Eugène Sue melodrama   Perhaps one of his novels about pirate exploits, such as *Plik et plok* or *La salamandre*, which brought critics to call Sue (1804—57) the French Fenimore Cooper.

V13.28, B15.10   dacoits   Members of a robber band from nineteenth-century Burma. In the twelve Fu-Manchu novels by Sax Rohmer (Arthur Sarsfield Ward), dacoits serve as bodyguards and assassins of the megalomaniacal oriental genius, Dr. Fu-Manchu.

V13.30—31, B15.13—14   during his Kipling Period, beastly Fuzzy-Wuzzies . . . Oriental sore   The term "Fuzzy Wuzzy" was British military slang for the Sudanese soldier-conscript, so called because of his hair. Dracunculiasis: swelling caused by an infestation of Dracunculus worms in the leg and arm muscles of those living in tropical environments, like the Indies. Oriental sore: a skin ulcer occurring in the Indies, also known as the Aleppo boil. In 1935, the time of these oriental fantasies, British writer Rudyard Kipling (b. 1865) was a year away from his death; Pirate's "Kipling Period" probably has to do with his reading some of the author's books, like *The Jungle Books* (1894—96), *The Captains Courageous* (1897), or *Kim* (1901).

V13.34—35, B15.18—19   no Cary Grant . . . medicine in the punchbowls   A reference to the 1952 Ben Hecht and Howard Hawks comedy *Monkey Business*, in which Cary Grant, as chemist Barnaby Fulton, develops a marvelous elixir, a kind of psychedelic. When they accidentally ingest it, Barnaby and his co-workers regress to a zany, playful childhood.

V13.39—40, B15.25   Sandy MacPherson playing   The source for this snippet of local texture is the BBC broadcasting schedules listed in the *Times* of London. MacPherson, "on his organ," was occasionally featured in the evenings.

V14.4, B15.31–32 John the Baptist . . . Nathan of Gaza Respectively, the prophet and precursor of Jesus (see Matt. 3:1–16) and the prophet to David (see 2 Sam. 12:1–15). Nathan of Gaza was also the name adopted by a seventeenth-century Jewish mystic and Kabbalist, a forerunner to the famed mystic Sabbatai Zvi (see V639.18–19n).

V14.12, B15.42 the red-cap section A platoon of Sudanese troops (see V13.30–31n), so called for their near-cylindrical red caps.

V14.22–23, B16.13 proper Sherlock Holmes London evening Fog and preternatural quiet are the usual conditions in Conan Doyle's detective novels.

V14.30–31, B16.23 *It was a giant Adenoid* The fantastic creature disappears from *GR* after this analeptic appearance, but a thinly disguised Richard M. Nixon, as "adenoidal" theater manager Richard M. Zhlubb, will reappear in the final, proleptic moments of the narrative (see V754.34). In typical monster-movie fashion, this creature is "as big as St. Paul's," the London cathedral atop Ludgate Hill measuring 250 by 515 feet. Lodged as he also is in the pharynx of Lord Blatherard Osmo, the Adenoid satirizes the nasal characteristics of upper-crust British speech; at least, he satirizes how that speech sounds to preterite ears.

V14.34–36, B16.28–30 Novi Pazar . . . this obscure sanjak Before World War I, Novi Pazar existed as a small "sanjak," or principality, sandwiched between Serbia and Montenegro in a mountainous region with few passes. The 1878 Treaty of Berlin empowered Austria-Hungary to garrison the area, while civil administration was to remain in Turkish hands. In 1908 Austria-Hungary announced plans to run a rail line through the pass at Novi Pazar. It would have been commercially insignificant but far more important as a crucial land bridge to Macedonia and Bulgaria, completing the encirclement of Serbia. These strategic problems were central to the "Eastern Question" occupying the major European powers from 1908 until the outbreak of war in August 1914. Then plans for the railway were shelved, so Pirate's image of getting to the sanjak via the legendary Orient Express is romantic fancy.

V15.2, B16.36 Pack up my Glad-stone A light luggage piece, usually of leather, hinged to open on two compartments; named for William Ewart Gladstone, British prime minister repeatedly from 1868 to 1894.

V15.7, B16.42 Busbies Tall fur caps with cloth bags hanging out the top right-hand side; part of the ceremonial dress for artillerymen, hussars, and engineers of the British army.

V15.12–13, B17.5–6 Mayfair ... East End First the Adenoid moves due east and with no regard to social classes. Mayfair, once the most fashionable residential quarter of London, by 1944 was mostly home to retail businesses, especially the city's better clothiers (hence the "tophats" strewn about the Adenoid's path). The East End includes not only London's "Bloody Tower" and the docks but also the densely populated boroughs of Shoreditch, Whitechapel, and Stepney. East End is London's haven for the preterite: diaspora Jews moved in during the late nineteenth century, and the Salvation Army was instituted there in 1865. In Rohmer's Fu-Manchu novels, it is a warren of opium dens and "the Yellow Peril"—a criminal underground of inscrutable Asians.

V15.20–21, B17.16 in Hampstead Heath The Adenoid has circled counterclockwise, moving north and west into this upper-class borough.

V15.26, B17.22 the Cavendish Laboratory At Cambridge University, the scientific institute named for classical physicist Henry Cavendish (1731–1810). Before World War II it was home to nuclear physicists Rutherford and Bohr, who first proposed the planetary model of the atom and later made the discoveries that enabled researchers to split atoms of uranium.

V15.38, B17.36–37 occupies all of St. James's The Adenoid has closed the circle. St. James Park borders on Whitehall, home of the British War Office, the Admiralty, the Treasury, and Scotland Yard.

V16.5, B18.2 daily *démarche* Diplomatic plan of action or strategic update.

V16.15–16, B18.14–15 a *croix mystique* on the palm of Europe In palmistry, two lines that intersect, crosslike, on the Lunar Mound; symbolic of great clairvoyant power, of contact with the Other Side and therefore perhaps of death.

EPISODE 3

The time is noon of the same "dripping winter" day (V17.9); the scene, headquarters of ACHTUNG, just off Grosvenor Square. Teddy Bloat, spared a broken neck by Pirate's quick reflexes in episode 1, photographs the cubicle of his American co-worker, Lt. Tyrone Slothrop. Thus, before meeting the character himself in episode 4, we are first introduced to Slothrop's possessions. To Bloat, the main item of interest is the map, speckled rainbow-like with colored stars, of Slothrop's London sexual conquests.

V17.7, B19.8–9 flaming SHAEF sword, which Mother had Garrard's make up All servicemen connected with SHAEF, the Supreme Headquarters, Allied Expeditionary Force, wore a shoulder patch depicting a flaming sword with a rainbow arching over it. Garrard and Company, Ltd., are the Crown Jewelers located on Regent Street, *the* place to have such insignia embossed on one's "twin silver hairbrushes."

V17.9, B19.11   this dripping winter noon   From the eleventh until the eighteenth of December 1944, London was held in the grip of a cold fog that blew in from the south. Temperatures held in the upper thirties. "Bleak in the Streets" is how the *Times* described it on December 15. The afternoon of December 18, the fog broke and a cold drizzle began falling (see also V20.1–3n).

V17.11, B19.13–14   Grosvenor Square   Located in the Mayfair district, the square is the London home of the American Embassy and Consulate General and thus the residence and workplace for numerous Americans connected with the diplomatic corps. Oxford Street (V17.14–15): the major thoroughfare two blocks north.

V17.26, B19.31   ATS   Auxilliary Territorial Services, one of many British wartime support groups, such as the WRENS (Women's Royal Naval Service), WAAFS (Women's Auxilliary Air Force), WRACS (Women's Royal Air Corps), and NAAFI (Navy, Army, Air Forces Institute), an "Official Canteen Organization for His Majesty's Forces" comparable to the American USO clubs.

V17.34, B20.3   lino   British slang for "linoleum."

V17.36, B20.5   Jesus College   Of Oxford University.

V17.36–37, B20.6   Lt. Oliver ("Tantivy") Mucker-Maffick   T. S. Soules has pinned down two sources for this monicker: the adjective "tantivy," for a galloping gait; and the verb "maffick," coined to describe the jubilant celebrating after British troops successfully defended Mafeking, during the Boer War. A "mucker" is British slang for one who employs himself in low pursuits, as in the midst of wastes and excrements.

V18.3, B20.10   the ETO   European Theatre of Operations.

V18.8–38, B20.17–21.11   Things have fallen roughly into layers . . . a *News of the World*   Among this list of objects on Slothrop's desk are items, allusions, and brand names left in his wake throughout the novel. He began "chain-smoking," we are told, with the first rocket strikes (V21.22); so the flints for his Zippo brand lighter are a must. Mother Nalline would have to mail him Thayer's Slippery Elm Throat Lozenges because the Henry Thayer Company (formerly of Cambridge, now of Concord, Massachusetts) marketed the product only in New England. The box still stresses how a lozenge "Eases Smoker's Throat." Incidentally, "Nalline" is itself the proprietary name of a pharmaceutical product, Nalorphine, once widely employed in police work as a diagnostic test for the presence of opiates, especially heroin, in a suspect's blood. Slothrop will eventually give up ukelele for harmonica, but Tantivy's comparing him to George Formby (1904–61), ukelele-strumming British screen comic of the forties, may tell us something about Slothrop's singing voice: Formby's was a high screech. Kreml Hair Tonic is a bygone product, but the countless advertisements for it in American magazines from the period (see *Time* or *Life*) all stress the Lothario factor: a Kreml man was a "love-pirate," as one ad put it, because "he always steals away the loveliest looking girls."

Some of these objects exercise a proleptic force. Among the "lost pieces to different jigsaw puzzles," the eye of the "Weimaraner" will reappear in Ned Pointsman's dream as a 1941 champion Weimaraner named Reichsseiger von Thanatz Alpdrücken (V144.32), then again as *Alpdrücken*, a film by the character Gerhardt von Göll (V395.6). Similarly, the "orange nimbus of an explosion" anticipates the news photo Slothrop finds in part 4, of the atomic bomb exploding over Hiroshima after being dropped from a "Flying Fortress" like that in this passage. The can of "Nugget shoe polish" anticipates the analepsis to rag-popping shoeshine boy Malcolm X, working the Roseland Ballroom lavatory in 1939 (see V63.3n), which by circuitous routes will lead to the semantic meditation on "Shit 'n' Shinola" (V687.5). At the end of this catalog we also glimpse Slothrop's reading materials: pamphlets and guidebooks distributed to servicemen by the "F.O.," or Foreign Office; the London daily paper *News of the World*; and reports from "G-2," or army intelligence.

V19.5, B21.21 G-loads Engineers' argot for the gravitational "load," or stress, on an object.

V19.12–14, B21.29–32 near Tower Hill . . . up to Hampstead Heath The mapping of Slothrop's sexual delights and V-2 rocket strikes shows a pattern flowing westward. The idea for this map probably came from Irving. One map in *The Mare's Nest* (228) shows the "number of flying bombs per square kilometer"; another (262), the distribution of rocket strikes around the city, with the strongest concentrations in the east and a thinning pattern as the flow works west.

V19.30, B22.9 the pantechnicon A bazaar in Victorian London, offering for sale various *objets d'art*.

V19.31–32, B22.11 quid wager on the Blackpool-Preston North End game A "quid" is British slang for the monetary denomination of one pound sterling; the game is British football, results of which were posted in each Monday's *Times* of London, after Saturday's games. Blackpool and Preston North End competed in the North League of London's Football Association. As was customary, the two teams played each other twice, on successive weekends: on October 7, 1944, the match produced a 1–1 tie, in a game broadcast over the BBC General Forces Programme at 4:15 P.M.; the next Saturday, the fourteenth, Preston North End narrowly beat Blackpool, 1–0. The dates establish the time of Bloat's analeptic memories in this passage.

EPISODE 4

The time, afternoon of the "dripping winter" day of episode 3; events unfold on the road back from Greenwich, where Pirate's "incoming mail" arrived. Slothrop has also visited the bomb site, and we finally meet him. Most of the narrative consists of analepses to incidents of Slothrop's girl-chasing about London, his childhood in western Massachusetts, his nine generations of Puritan ancestors, and their slowly wasted fortunes as the New World grew older.

V20.1–3, B22.22–24   Wind has shifted . . . rainclouds.   Consistent with the *Times* weather information for December 18.

V20.4, B22.26   out to zero longitude   Again, the Royal Observatory.

V20.10, B22.33   Mark III Stens set on automatic   The Mark III was a silenced version of the British Sten machine gun, a weapon designed especially for commandos: lightweight, mechanically simple, and very deadly.

V20.15, B22.38   T.I.   Acronym for the Technical Intelligence wing of the British army.

V20.16, B23.2   a '37 Wolseley Wasp   Inexpensive two-door sedan, first produced by the Wolseley Automobile Company in 1935.

V20.18–19, B23.5   Lucky Strikes   An American cigarette brand.

V20.36–37, B23.26–27   sending him TDY some hospital   That is, sending him on a "tour of duty" to the (fictional) St. Veronica's Hospital for Respiratory and Colonic Diseases, locus of episode 10.

V21.3–4, B23.31–32   Some more of that Minnesota Multiphasic shit   On the Minnesota Multiphasic Personality Inventory and Slothrop's character as measured by such tests, see V81.22, V81.23–24, V90.8n.

V21.9–10, B23.40   those buzzbombs   The V-1, also known in Allied circles as the "doodlebug," was a pilotless aircraft propelled by a pulse-jet engine (hence the "farting sound" Slothrop hears) and fitted with a one-ton amatol warhead. Irving (23–25), Pynchon's likely source, explains that V-1s were either launched from a ramp or dropped from a bomber. In flight, they reached subsonic velocities of around 470 mph, over a maximum range of 160 miles. Ten seconds after a preset engine cutoff, the V-1 dove toward earth, as described here. The initial attack of V-1s on London commenced just before midnight on June 15, 1944, and by 5 A.M. the following day 244 had been launched, 73 falling directly on London.

V21.19, B24.9   then last September the rockets came   Specifically, at 6:43 P.M. on September 8, 1944, at Chiswick, killing three people and seriously injuring seventeen more (see V26.23n).

V21.36, B24.29   86'd   A rhyming synonym for the slang verb "nix," meaning "to deny" or "to reject." For example, one might be "86'd" from a bar or club, as are Slothrop and Mr. Pox from the Junior Atheneum.

V22.2, B24.39 subdeb legs The legs of a "subdebutante," designating girls generally less than sixteen years old.

V22.4, B24.41 the Frick Frack Club in Soho London's Soho district, now known as the hub of London film making, once was home to clubs of low repute and numerous secondhand shops; the Frick Frack is unknown.

V22.12, B25.8–9 a lindy-hopping girl The lindy hop, named for aviator Charles Lindbergh, was a popular dance of the thirties. Malcolm X describes the wild abandon (the windmilling arms and hopping step) of it in the "Homeboy" chapter of his *Autobiography*, a principal source for episode 10.

V22.24–27, B25.23–26 "I know there is wilde love . . . of God's owne planting" David Seed has identified this obscure passage from Thomas Hooker as deriving from a 1637 sequence of sermons, *The Soules Implantation into the Natural Olive*. The general context is Christian redemptive hope, in which "Adam was the old and wild Olive, Christ the true Vine, and the new Olive" (180). Fallen man must therefore be severed from his unregenerate root and grafted onto, "implanted in," Christ; and the last sermon, "Spirituall Love and Joy," sets worldly love against the fulfillment that stems from this humbling, enlightening influence of the Divinity. Hooker (180) acknowledges mundane passion in the passage Pynchon quotes: "I know there is wilde love and joy enough in the world, as there is wilde Thyme and other herbes, but wee would have garden-love and garden-joy, of Gods own planting, for such hypocriticall love and joy we will not meddle her." Seed's commentary ("Thomas Hooker") is useful: "Pynchon cuts out the dismissive comment at the end of the passage and renders Hooker's whole distinction ironic by quoting it within such a profane context. Indeed Tyrone Slothrop, the novel's closest candidate for protagonist, embodies two of the sins that Hooker rails against—drunkenness and adultery."

V22.27–29, B25.27–29 Teems with virgin's-bower . . . love-in-idleness. Slothrop's mapped garden of earthly delights further ironizes Hooker's image of the divine garden. The virgin's bower (genus *Clematis*) is an American plant with white flowers; the forget-me-not (*Myosotis*), a European plant with clusters of small blue or purple flowers; and rue (*Ruta*), also known as "herb of grace," a Eurasian plant with red flowers. Note the eastwarding progress of these three, for in a sense it summarizes "Slothrop's [eastward] Progress" from the United States back to the longitudes his forefathers left behind. As for the fourth herb, love-in-idleness (*Viola*), Pynchon correctly identifies

this common pansy as growing "all over the place." It summarizes
the three previous plants: pansies come in all colors.

V23.10, B26.14 cup of Bovril Brand of English beef tea (broth).

V23.19, B26.27 Wrens See V17.26n.

V24.13–14, B27.24 the same aging Humber According to Georgano,
"the company's staple products were upper-middle-class family sedans,"
and Humbers "served the Allied forces with distinction in World
War 2" as the standard of British motor poo' .

V24.14–15, B27.25–26 a Saint George after the fact St. George is
the patron saint and romance hero of Britain. Slothrop's dragon is the
rocket, "the Beast" whose "droppings," or exploded parts, lie scattered
over the bomb site; a further point is that Slothrop, no hero, arrives
too late to battle it.

V24.19, B27.31 RAF The Royal Air Force.

V24.30, B28.1–2 a Morrison shelter Named for Minister of Home
Security Herbert Morrison, these "crushproof steel tables" were designed
to double as bomb shelters (Irving 80) but proved useless against
V-2s.

V24.34, B28.6–7 a Thayer's Slippery Elm See V18.8–38n.

V24.39, B28.13 a Shirley Temple smile After the cute, innocent
child star of American pre-World War II cinema (see also V466.4n).

V25.28, B29.7 Bond Street Underground station Getting off work,
Slothrop would walk from his Grosvenor Square office to the intersection of Oxford and Bond streets, then into the underground station
of London's Central Line. Chiswick, where the first V-2 falls, is just over
two miles away.

V25.31–32, B29.12 *memento-mori* A "remembrance of death"; a
death's-head or skull.

V25.32–37, B29.12–18 a sharp crack. . . . "Some bloody gas main" The
source for these impressions of the first V-2 (the "crack," the double
"thunder," the possibility of it being a buzz bomb or an exploded "gas
main") is Irving (285–86).

V26.23, B30.8 6:43:16 British Double Summer Time Again, the
source is Irving (286).

V26.30, B30.17 back home in Mingeborough, Massachusetts A fictional
locale, though Pynchon will soon (V28.21–39) situate it in the
Berkshire mountains, near the actual towns of Stockbridge, Pittsfield,
and Lenox.

**V26.37–38, B30.25–26 *Death is a debt to nature due . . . so must
you*** To Puritan ears, there is heresy in Constant Slothrop's epitaph.
The debt, as Hooker and other Puritan divines would insist, is due
not nature but God—a crucial difference.

V27.5–6, B30.32–33 the nine or ten generations tumbling back The first of many instances of *hysteron proteron*: a trope of backward motion, regression, and reversals of cause and effect. Also, in a similar way Thomas Ruggles Pynchon, Jr., is "nine or ten generations" removed from *his* ancestors, John Pynchon (1626–1702) of Springfield, Massachusetts, and William Pynchon (1590–1662), founder of Springfield and Roxbury. William was a patentee and treasurer of the Massachusetts Bay Company and author of theological treatises ruled heretical by Puritan divines.

V27.11, B30.39 Masonic emblems Perhaps the square, Masonic symbol of this earth, or the compass, symbol of the heavens; also likely are a gavel, a sign of force, and a twelve-inch ruler, sign of reason.

V27.26, B31.15–16 bagged his epitaph from Emily Dickinson Frederick Slothrop's epitaph is lifted from poem 712 in the Dickinson canon, lines written in 1863 and originally published (in 1890) as "The Chariot."

V28.12–13, B32.2–3 around the time Emily Dickinson . . . was writing This next poem is 997 in the Dickinson canon, written during 1865 as the Civil War was winding down but not published until 1945 in *Bolts of Melody*. Pynchon quotes the final stanza.

V28.26, B32.18 in long rallentando The musical term signifies a gradual slowdown of tempo. In this context, another instance of *hysteron proteron*.

V28.33–34, B32.26–27 Harrimans and Whitneys gone The Aspinwall Hotel fire (see below) destroyed the last great summer watering place in the Berkshires. By then, the wealthy John Hay Whitneys and W. Averill Harrimans had already transformed Saratoga, sixty miles northwest in New York, into their summer hideout.

V28.38, B32.32–33 1931 . . . year of the Great Aspinwall Hotel Fire Located outside Lenox, the Aspinwall was a four-story wooden structure of four hundred rooms. Reporting the spectacular blaze in its late edition of April 25, 1931, the *New York Times* described the building (in a front-page story) as "one of the most fashionable hostelries in the Berkshires and a social center for summer activities." John D. Rockefeller and Chauncey Depew were once regular guests; other wealthy financiers and robber barons had drifted through. The fire began at 1:00 A.M. on the morning of the twenty-fifth and was thought to have started when several drunken youths left behind a lighted cigarette. Here is the *Times*: "The blaze spread to the woodland and did widespread damage before finally gotten under control. The burning hotel made a spectacular blaze, the flames rising high and being visible over the mountains for many miles around. Hundreds of residents left their beds and drove to the scene. . . . By 3 o'clock the hotel was reduced to a heap of smoldering ruins."

EPISODE 5

Still December 18, but evening now; the location, someplace vaguely identified as "Snoxall's" (V32.29), where Roger Mexico and Jessica Swanlake attend a séance. These moments of occult contact with the Other Side introduce us to Blicero, the Teutonic deity of death soon to be revealed in an actual character. Like many episodes, this one begins in what seems a traditional omniscient third-person narration, focusing on Roger and Jessica; then the seance is focalized through Pirate Prentice, whose memories take us analeptically back to his tour of duty in the Persian Gulf, in the thirties, and to a woman he loved and lost. Pirate senses a similar loss approaching in Roger's life, and glimpses of a snuggling Roger and Jessica thus bring the episode back full circle in both point of view and time.

V29.31, B33.29–30   a "sensitive flame"   So called because such a
flame appears to serve as a check against hoaxes. In his 1972 study
of Victorian spiritualism, Ronald Pearsall (42–43) summarizes the
"rules" for a séance: "The people who composed the circles should be
of opposite temperaments, 'as positive and negative,' not marked
by any repulsive disease, not obviously struggling under mental hand-
icap. The number of persons should not be less than three, nor more
than twelve, eight being the ideal number. No person of strong magnetic
temperament should be present, as he or she would quash the power
of the spirits. The room should not be overheated, and should be
well ventilated; bright light was anathema to successful dealings with
spirits." Pearsall also describes some of the hoaxes characteristic
of the period: gloves sprayed with phosphorescent powder, to give the
appearance of a materialized hand, and musical instruments that
leapt into action as spirits "played" them. But Snoxall's runs a respect-
able séance: "None of your white hands or luminous trumpets here"
(V29.36–37), as Pynchon notes. The "sensitive flame" would reveal any
shenanigans by registering the movement of air. The "spirit" who
speaks on the following pages is Roland Feldspath (from "feldspar,"
a mineral that forms in rock), whose "medium" is Carroll Eventyr (from
the Danish *eventyr*, "adventure"). Selena (for the ancient moon
goddess) is the surviving wife of Feldspath, and she would be seated
opposite Eventyr. The "control" in a séance is another name for the
spirit of a deceased who speaks for, or about, the spirit in question;
here it is Peter Sachsa, a German Communist and lover of Leni Pökler;
we subsequently learn that he was killed during a Berlin street demonstration of 1930 (on the etymology of his name, see V218.10n). These
constitute the "basic, four-way entente" (V31.27) of the evening's adventure into the Other Side.

V30.1, B33.38 Camerons officers Also known as the Scottish Rifles, a British army regiment; the "trews"—their parade kilts.

V30.12, B34.13 Dominus Blicero Pynchon's source is Grimm's *Teutonic Mythology* (849–50). *Blicero* is one of the many Germanic nicknames for death. Grimm traces the etymology from *bleich* (pale) and *blechend* (grinning), and from these he derives other nicknames, such as *Der Blecker* (The Grinning Death) and *Der Bleicher* (The Bleacher, for what death does to bones). *Dominus* (Lord), from the Latin, recalls the appellation accorded both to Roman emperors by their underlings and to Christ in Latin translations of the Gospels.

V30.30, B34.34–35 "A market needed no longer . . . the Invisible Hand" An allusion to Adam Smith's famous metaphor in *The Wealth of Nations*. Arguing for the beneficial prospects of a true laissez faire economy, Smith reasons that anyone seeking his own benefit will also be guided, as though by an unseen force, to benefit his society. Such a person, he claims, "neither intends to promote the public interest, nor knows how much he is promoting it. By preferring the support of domestick to that of foreign industry, he intends only his own security; and by directing that industry in such a manner as its product may be of the greatest value, he intends only his own gain, and he is in this, as in many other cases, *led by an invisible hand* to promote an end which was no part of his intention" (456; my emphasis). A large vein of Protestant belief in Providence and election lies beneath Smith's metaphor, and Pynchon has already mined it with the image of the "hand of God" (V26.30) emerging from a cloud on Constant Slothrop's headstone. But the war economy has "dispensed with God" (V30.33), as Roland Feldspath claims. As the narrative will frequently suggest, the new industrial cartels erased any distinction between Smith's "foreign" and "domestic" manufacturers.

V30.37, B35.1 "More Ouspenskian nonsense" That is, from a follower of Petr Demianovich Ouspensky (1878–1947), the Russian esoteric and occult philosopher who was a student of Gurdjieff for nine years before a disagreement caused their split and brought Ouspensky to London, where he lectured until war broke out in 1939. His philosophical writings sought to synthesize everything from Neitzsche's Superman to the Tarot, yoga, astrology, the Kabbala, Jungian dream analysis, and Christian iconography. *Tertium Organum: The Third Canon of Thought, a Key to the Enigmas of the World* (1920) is his best-known version of these attempts.

V30.38, B35.3 Sous le Vent A French perfume ("On the Wind"), appropriately selected, considering the "secular . . . personal wind" (V30.20) blowing through this séance.

V31.2, B35.7 Harrods As their *Times* of London ads used to boast, a department store with "the finest selection of quality goods in the world."

V31.17, B35.26–27 achieved perfect tripos At Cambridge University the tripos are any of the examinations for a baccalaureate degree; a perfect score constitutes the highest academic achievement.

V32.5–11, B36.18–26 "Well. Recall Zipf's Principle of Least Effort ... a sort of bow shape" The reference is not to George Kingsley Zipf's 1949 book, *Human Behavior and the Principle of Least Effort.* Instead, the text for this complex, arresting reference is his 1935 study, *The Psycho-Biology of Language.* Zipf was a professor of philology and linguistics at Harvard during the time of Slothrop's fictional attendance there. In the 1935 book he studied language as "a natural psychological and biological phenomenon to be investigated in the spirit of the exact sciences" (v). Examining everyday speech, he found patterns of abbreviation—the linguistic trace of his "Principle of Least Effort"— to be important in unlocking the dynamics of language. Much of his work relies on various statistical and probabilistic tests applied to recorded samples of ordinary discourse, and the text is chockfull of "word-frequency graphs" plotting on double-logarithmic charts the frequency of occurrence of a word, with abscissas indicating the number of words in the sample and ordinates the number of occurrences of the word. These are the "axes" Milton Gloaming describes to a perplexed Jessica Swanlake. The arresting thing, however, is that Zipf (*Psycho-Biology* 224) found natural speech always yielding a straight line in the graphs, a line that could be described by a simple mathematical formula concisely homologous to that "for gravity." In pathological and artistic usage, this law no longer holds. As Gloaming explains to Jessica, the graphs of schizophrenic speech yield, instead of a straight line, "a sort of bow shape." This appropriation of Zipf's data thus tallies with numerous other images in *GR*, where the arch, the parabola, and the bow are all signs of disturbance and pathology. For useful background on Gloaming's comments see Zipf on "Pathological Language" (*Psycho-Biology* 216–18).

V32.26, B37.2 Falkman and His Apache Band Another band name derived from the *Times* of London BBC broadcasting schedules. Only once in December was Falkman the featured, live act (at 7:30 P.M. on December 26), but his recordings might have appeared on the "Top Ten" or "Forces Favorites" shows featured every evening, ten to midnight.

V32.29, B37.6 at here at Snoxall's Corrected in the Bantam to read "as here at Snoxall's."

V32.36, B37.13–14 your Dennis Morgan chap One of Warner Brothers' highest-paid stars of the forties, Dennis Morgan (b. 1910) was noted for his wise-guy grin. During the war, Morgan played a pilot in four different films; here the reference is to *God Is My Co-Pilot* (1944), featuring Morgan as a daring ace with the Flying Tigers of the Far East—hence the image of his grinning at "every little bucktooth yellow rat he shoots down."

V33.17, B37.38   sitreps   Military jargon for "situation reports."

V33.26, B38.7–8   the Witchcraft Act's more than 200 years old   Pynchon means the 1736 act of Parliament that repealed statutes against witchcraft in England and Scotland, the last witchcraft trial having occurred in 1712.

V33.31–32, B38.14   "away to the Scrubs"   London's Wormwood Scrubs prison, completed in 1890 and home to some fifteen hundred felons.

V34.6, B38.31   "EEG"   Electroencephalogram, the graphic representation of a patient's brain-wave activity, developed in 1929 by German neurophysiologist Hans Berger.

V34.21–22, B39.8   agency known as PISCES   A fictional acronym. The twelfth house on the astrological calendar (February 19–March 20), symbolizing confinement, life reigned in by institutions, social responsibilities, and death. Under its influence one also expects contact with unknown forces in the universe. A water sign (the Fishes), and the ruler of narrative action in part 1.

V34.28–30, B39.16–18   Free French plotting ... ELAS Greeks stalking royalists   A brief catalog of some principal struggles and realignments of European power occurring at this time. By December of 1944 the Free French under Charles de Gaulle were not only "plotting" revenge but trying those who collaborated with the Nazis. During late 1944 and into 1945 the Polish Committee of National Liberation based at Lublin carried out the overthrow of a "Varsovian" (that is, Warsaw-based) puppet government. These developments all received daily treatment in the *Times* of London, Pynchon's main source; but throughout December only the German counterattack in Holland took more newsprint than the struggles in Greece. The ELAS Greeks were a Communist-led faction who took to their side various captured Nazis and, mounting a mid-December attack against Athens, attempted to remove Allied forces led by British general Scobie, who was under the strictest orders to keep the Greek royalist faction in power.

V35.3, B39.35–36   a Behaviorist here, a Pavlovian there   The Pavlovian is Dr. E. W. A. Pointsman, who, with the full baggage of his theories, will be introduced to us in coming episodes. Behaviorist psychology dates from the work of John and Rosalie Watson in the twenties; a reference to their work will soon occur in the general context of Tyrone Slothrop's conditioning, in 1920, when he was an infant or toddler (see V84.39–85.3n).

V35.21, B40.16   mixed AA battery   Once again Pynchon's source was the *Times* of London, here the issue of December 21 and its story entitled "Improper Conduct in Mixed Battery." The "mixed" anti-aircraft batteries were necessary because of manpower shortages, and fraternization between the men and women during long winter nights had evidently become a concern. On the NAAFI see V17.26n.

V35.26, B40.22   "a T. S. Eliot April"   Because "April is the cruelest month," as Eliot writes in his opening lines of *The Waste Land*.

V35.32–34, B40.30–31   Bahrein . . . Muharraq   Cities on the Persian Gulf, where Pirate was stationed when oil development was still just beginning in that quarter of the globe.

V36.11–12, B41.12–3   what the lyrics to "Dancing in the Dark" are *really* about   About epigonal love? Last days? Death? The song was written by Howard Deitz and Arthur Schwartz in 1931; in 1941 it was recorded by Artie Shaw and the Gramercy Five, a disk that sold over a million copies. Here are the lyrics:

> Dancing in the dark,
> Till the tune ends,
> We're dancing in the dark,
> And it soon ends—
>
> We're waltzing in the wonder of why we're here—
> Time hurries by,
> We're here and gone,
> Looking for the light
> Of a new love, to brighten up the night—
> I have you, love,
> And we can face the music together . . .
> Dancing in the dark.
>
> What though love is old?
> What though song is old?
> Through them we can be young—
> Hear this heart of mine,
> Make yours part of mine—
> Dear one, tell me that we're one,
> Dancing in the dark!

V37.10–11, B42.19   Fred Roper's Company of Wonder Midgets   An unknown wonder.

EPISODE 6

The time is midnight and early morning of the nineteenth as Roger Mexico and Jessica Swanlake drive southeast out of London, through a light rain, for a rendezvous with Dr. Pointsman. A short episode, analeptically revealing Roger and Jessica's "'cute meet'" (V38.36) and their wordless retreats to an empty house in one of London's evacuated zones, it foreshadows romantic complications: Jessica is attached to a battery mate named Jeremy, Roger to his "mother" (V39.15), the war.

V37.19–20, B42.30   hunched Dracula-style inside his Burberry   The Burberry is the British (luxury) brand of woolen overcoat, here in black with its wide lapels turned up, in the style of Bela Lugosi acting the lead in director Tod Browning's 1931 film version of Bram Stoker's *Dracula*.

V37.32, B43.5–6   "he's a Pavlovian . . . a Royal Fellow"   On Pointsman's institutional connections see V47.3n and V42.15n, respectively.

V38.6, B43.18   "dear old Nutria"   Roger mocks Jessica's nickname for Jeremy. Instead of "Beaver" he uses the noun for a cheap, ersatz beaver pelt that is derived from a South American rodent, the coypu, and that the British call "nutria."

V38.19, B43.33   that awful *Going My Way*   Awful because of its sentimental depiction of Father Chuck O'Malley (played by Bing Crosby), a witty, optimistic, young Catholic priest matched against the cynical, opinionated old pastor of a poor, inner-city parish. Crosby won an Oscar for this 1944 role.

V38.37, B44.12   Tunbridge Wells   Town located twenty-seven miles south of London.

V38.38, B44.13   the vintage Jaguar   Vintage indeed. From 1936 until 1945, the Jaguar was one of nine *models* produced at the S. S. Cars factory of Coventry. Few were made, but their reputation for speed and handling, at fairly affordable prices, won them a small following. After V-E Day, Jaguar became the *make* name of a new motorcar line.

V39.1–2, B44.18–19   "backstage at the old Windmill"   One of the "Non-Stop Revues" listed daily on the *Times* of London entertainments page. Located on Picadilly Circle, the Windmill featured dancing girls "cont. dly. 12:15–9:30," in something called "Revudeville."

V39.7, B44.25   "called up the Girl Guides"   See V13.11n.

V39.11, B44.30   "Nearly to Battle"   A town located twenty miles south of Tunbridge, on the trunk road from London to Hastings.

V40.9, B45.35   Roger's only a statistician.   The Bantam misprints this as "satistician."

V40.13–14, B45.41   the definitely 3-sigma lot   In statistics, sigma is the designation for a standard deviation. On a normal distribution, graphed in parabolic section, plus or minus sigma on either side of the vertical axis amounts to about one-half of the statistical range; plus or minus 2-sigma, about three-fourths of the range; and plus or minus

3-sigma, or three standard deviations, over 99 percent. Thus, 3-sigma: a wildly divergent "lot" of people, with a hodgepodge of interests. See later references at V523.39 and V635.35.

V40.18, B46.3–4 chi-square calculations . . . the Zener cards A Zener deck contains twenty-five cards, with five symbols (cross, wave, rectangle, circle, and star) depicted on them. They are commonly used while testing subjects for extrasensory abilities. Afterward, the data might be subjected to a chi-square test to determine if the statistically expected frequencies of successful guessing matched the observed frequencies.

V40.36, B46.26 a coal-black Packard In the United States, a moderately priced sedan, but exported to England, a luxury-grade sedan for American military brass and the diplomatic corps.

EPISODE 7

Another short episode, placed somewhere to the southeast of London, around 1:00 A.M. on December 19. Roger and Jessica have found Dr. Pointsman at the site of a house smashed earlier that day in a rocket blast. Roger assists him in a slapstick chase after a shell-shocked dog prowling the ruins; during it Pointsman gets his foot stuck in a toilet bowl.

V42.15, B48.17 F.R.C.S. Dr. Pointsman is a Fellow in the Royal College of Surgeons.

V42.24, B48.29 fumed-oak Oak that has been artificially aged by curing in an atmosphere of ammonia.

V42.36, B49.4–5 the electric lantern British nomenclature for a flashlight, also known in Britain as a torch.

V43.12–13, B49.21–22 some woman's long-gathered nest, taken back to separate straws Another instance of *hysteron proteron*.

V43.18–19, B49.29 the boot of the car British nomenclature for the trunk.

V43.28, B49.41 "this *gillie*" In Scotland, the attendant who caters to wealthy hunters and fishermen; he portages and maintains the equipment.

V44.4, B50.20 fumbling a flashlight After such care for proper British nomenclature, above, Pynchon slips back into his American idiom.

V44.17–18, B50.36–37 "Why it's Mrs. Nussbaum!" That is, Mrs. Pansy Nussbaum (pronounced "Noose-bomb") of "Allen's Alley," the American radio program that played over the CBS network beginning in 1943. The format centered on Fred Allen, who used to walk down his back alley, pausing to knock on the neighbors' doors. The comedy stemmed from the resulting exchanges—for example, with Mrs.

Nussbaum, played by Minerva Pious, remembered for her Jewish accent and her phonetic errors and grammatical inversions. Harmon records a typical exchange (169–70): "Why it's Mrs. Nussbaum!" Allen exclaims, and she replies: "You were expecting maybe the Fink Spots?" Despite Pynchon's claim, "Allen's Alley" did not appear over BBC channels on Wednesday nights, or on any other night. *Some* Wednesday evenings brought "The Bob Hope Show" or "The Jimmy Durante Show," but BBC programmers evidently followed no set schedule.

V44.20, B50.39 "maybe *Lessie*?" That is, Lassie, the Academy Award–winning dog that made its screen debut in *Lassie Come Home* (1943), with Roddy MacDowell and Elsa Lanchester in the supporting roles.

V46.40–41, B53.33–34 Hospital of St. Veronica of the True Image St. Veronica met Jesus on the road to Calvary, lent him a handkerchief, and found afterward that it bore an image of his face. There was no such London hospital, in any event.

V47.3, B53.37 The Book Here and throughout *GR*, "The Book" is volume 2 of the *Lectures on Conditioned Reflexes* by Russian physiologist Ivan Petrovich Pavlov (1849–1936), which was published four years after Pavlov's death and which represented his effort to branch out of physiological studies and into psychology. One of Pavlov's American collaborators, Dr. Horsley Gantt, did the English translation (1941); thus there is no particular purpose to the secrecy of Pointsman, Spectro, and others who "rotate" their lone copy. A bit of melodrama from the narrator.

EPISODE 8

Yet another short episode. After 2:00 A.M., at the "Abreaction Ward" of St. Veronica's Hospital, doctors Kevin Spectro and Edward Pointsman talk shop (Pavlovian psychology) and in particular the puzzling case of Tyrone Slothrop. There are problems of causality: Slothrop experiences sexual excitation at the sites of *future* rocket strikes; moreover, when V-2 rockets did actually hit, observers first saw the blast, then heard the sound of the missile coming in. The symmetry of these reversals (further instances of *hysteron proteron*) gets Pointsman going, and other narrative threads introduced in his meditations will prove significant: Slothrop's link to a Dr. Jamf and Pointsman's conditioning of an octopus named Grigori.

V48.14, B55.16 Abreactions C. G. Jung's essay "The Therapeutic Value of Abreaction" (*Collected Works* 16:129–38) supplies a gloss. In 1928 Jung's concern was "the neuroses resulting from the Great War, with their essentially traumatic etiology" in otherwise healthy patients. Abreaction is a form of therapy for such traumas, hinging

on the "dramatic reversal of the traumatic moment, its emotional re-
capitulation" in the presence of a therapist. The therapist's role is
to guide the patient through a representation of the injury and to stand
as a point of transference for the patient's neurosis. Jung writes that
the transference is crucial and often takes much time: "It is imperative
that the doctor should get into the closest possible touch with the
patient's line of psychological development. One could say that as the
doctor assimilates the intimate psychic contents of the patient into
himself, he is in turn assimilated as a figure into the patient's psyche."
But there is the hitch. That transference must be "freely negotiated,"
not a "slavish and humanly degrading bondage."

In comparison, *GR* teems with instances of "slavish" abreaction.
Pointsman, for example, puts his commanding officer, Brigadier General
Pudding, through a nightmarish rehearsal of his Great War traumas
(in episode 4 of part 2). Slothrop's forced replay of his own neuroses dur-
ing the sodium amytal session of the next episode is yet another
example of Pointsman's manipulative "therapy." This is why Kevin
Spectro doubts the ethic of his technique: " 'I don't like it, Pointsman' "
(V48.16). The issue here and elsewhere in the novel is control.

**V48.29–31, B55.34–5   The reversal. . . . a few feet of film run back-
wards**   Focalized through Pointsman, this trope for the apparent reversal of cause and effect in the rocket's blast is another instance of
hysteron proteron.

V48.34, B55.39   "ideas of the opposite"   See V49.1–2n.

**V48.38–39, B56.2–4   into one of the transmarginal phases . . . past
"equivalent" and "paradoxical" phases**   Sends us into "The Book."
According to Pavlov, the intensity of a conditioned reflex depends obviously on the intensity of the stimulus used in its conditioning,
be it from a bell, a metronome, or any sensory apparatus. Yet the intensity depends just as importantly, though less obviously, on the mag-
nitude of such unconditioned factors as the subject's motivation
or emotional state. Let Pavlov's translator, Horsley Gantt, take it from
there (*Lectures* 2:13–14): "Beyond a certain maximal intensity, variations may lead to certain phases—the equivalent (in which strong and
weak stimuli produce the same effect), the paradoxical (in which
the weak stimuli give a greater response than the strong), the ultraparadoxical (in which the excitatory conditioned stimuli become
inhibitory, and vice-versa). Such . . . stimuli, too strong to give the
maximal conditioned reflex, Pavlov terms *transmarginal.*"

V49.1–2, B56.7–8   Pavlov writing to Janet   Sends readers once more
to "The Book," specifically to chapter 54, "Les Sentiments D'Emprise
and the Ultraparadoxical Phase." Originally the passage quoted here
was published in a French scholarly journal as an open letter from
Pavlov to Pierre Janet, the great French psychologist. Janet had recently

published a paper on feelings of persecution and paranoia in his patients (the *sentiments d'emprise*). He explained their feelings as stemming from the patients' weakened states (brought on by depression, disease, trauma, or terror), during which they are confused by "ideas of the opposite." Categories such as mine/theirs, giving/receiving, or master/slave become blurred. Soon, Janet theorized, the patient projects the pain of this conflict *outside*, objectifying the conflict by personifying it in others. In short, the patient becomes paranoid, feels persecuted. Janet called for a psychoanalytic therapy; but Pavlov, ever the physiologist, argued for chemical cures. Pavlov surmised that the "ideas of the opposite," which seemed irrefutably tied to the switchlike, on/off functions of cortical cells, would become confused in an addled, stressed, or terrified cortex. It therefore seemed a simple matter of the patient's having gone transmarginal, as defined above. Thus Pavlov (*Lectures* 2:148; the italics in *GR* are Pynchon's): "It is precisely the ultraparadoxical phase which is the base of the weakening of the idea of the opposite of [not Pynchon's "in"] our patients." Pavlov's remedy? He wrote (149): "In their turn, chemistry first, and then physics will be nearest these phenomena and their mechanism, approaching a final solution."

V49.13–14, B56.23–24 "M. K. Petrova was first to observe it" Petrova was a research associate at Pavlov's laboratory in the Russian village of Koltushy. His experiments with the hypnosis of dogs, one result of which Pynchon summarizes here, derive from volume 2 of the *Lectures*, chapter 47 ("Contributions to the Physiology of the Hypnotic State of the Dog"), especially pp. 75–77.

V49.31–50.1, B56.43–57.14 as once again the floor. . . . two o'clock dawn The abreaction of a St. Veronica's patient, who relives the V-2 striking a cinema in which he was seated, anticipating the novel's closing moments.

V50.22, B57.38–39 Realpolitik dreams Originally formulated in Ludwig von Rochau's *Grundsätze der Realpolitik* (1853), realpolitik had its greatest proponent in German chancellor Otto von Bismarck. Realpolitik elevates the strategic interests of the state—its relative security—over liberal domestic reform. Or, as Bismark once put it: "The great questions of our day cannot be solved by speeches and majority votes . . . but by blood and iron" (ODQ).

V50.25, B57.43 St. Veronica's Downtown Bus Station Fictional.

V51.6, B58.27 AWOL bags An AWOL bag was a small overnight bag, usually of canvas, so called because a serviceman might take it with him when "absent without leave."

V51.30, B59.15 a gigantic, horror-movie devilfish The Bantam misprints this as "develfish."

V51.31–32, B59.17 the Ick Regis jetty Unknown, if not fictional.

V52.23–24, B60.16–17   "the damned Rundstedt offensive . . . P.W.E. won't fund anything"   Pointsman frets over the constraints of foreign policy on funding. Gen. Karl Gerd von Rundstedt, whose stature in the German High Command was second only to that of Hitler's long-time associate and SS head Heinrich Himmler, directed the German counteroffensive in Holland, widely known as the Battle of the Bulge. It began on Sunday, December 16, 1944. P.W.E.: the Political Warfare Executive, an intelligence-gathering and propaganda wing of SHAEF.

V52.39, B60.35   "over Deptford"   London parish located four miles southeast of London Bridge, on the south bank of the Thames.

EPISODE 9

Early in the morning of December 20, Roger and Jessica lie sleeping in the abandoned house we learned of in episode 6. Like many of the episodes in *GR* this one has a circular movement. A rocket blast awakens Jessica, who leaves the bed to stand at a frosted window. Focalized through her, the narrative segues analeptically into Roger explaining statistical principles to Jessica, then into an omniscient analepsis in which Roger and Pointsman debate the efficacy of statistical versus deterministic views of the correspondence between rocket strikes and Slothrop's erections. The episode ends by returning us to Jessica at her frosted window and a discussion she and Roger once had about prewar England.

V53.6, B61.3   *their dollful and piteous cries*   Perhaps a misprint. "Doleful" fits the context, but so too would "doll-like," the grammatically correct form in context with the previous line: "smooth as dolls." Is "dollfull" one of Pynchon's portmanteau words?

V53.25–26, B61.27–28   frost gathering on the panes . . . out into the snow   The night of December 19–20 was, according to the *Times*, a cold one. Temperatures in London ranged down to 32–35 degrees Fahrenheit, with a "persistent fog" that turned to light snow in some areas. For a remarkably similar image framing episode 14, with Katje Borgesius watching "the long rain in silicon and freezing descent" upon her windows, see V93.34–35n.

V53.33, B61.37   AR-E forms   Probably, Air Raid Evacuation forms, Home Security's attempt to keep track of the one and a half million people evacuated from London during the German V-bomb blitz.

V54.25, B62.36   his Poisson equation   Named for the French mathematician Simeon Denis Poisson (1781–1840), the formula is useful in offering probabilistic statements about events that are exceedingly rare but possible. For example, the Poisson equation is commonly used in calculating the probability of radioactive emissions or in figuring the chances of actual death (as in a bridge collapse) for actuarial purposes. As Roger says, one can "look it up" (V54.40) in any handbook of mathematics; a working out of the formula appears at V140.6–10.

V55.11–12, B63.26–27   Roger's old Whittaker and Watson   A hand-held British view camera.

V55.22, B63.40   table-rapping   That is, séances (V29.31n).

V55.29–30, B64.5–7   "Summation," "transition," . . . "reciprocal induction"   A short catalog of Pavlovian "laws," most likely drawn from chapter 43 of volume 2 of the *Lectures*, "A Brief Outline of the Higher Nervous System" (esp. 48–50). According to Pavlov's "law of summation," the combination of "a number of weak conditioned stimuli" will result in "their exact mathematical sum" (48). The "law of transition" holds that if a conditioned positive stimulus continues unabated, it eventually "passes into a state of inhibition," a process Pavlov called "transition" (48). According to the "law of irradiation and concentration," the "processes of excitation and inhibition, originated at definite points of the cortex under the influence of corresponding stimuli, necessarily irradiate over a larger . . . area of the cortex, and then again concentrate in a limited space" (49). Finally, along with these processes a "reciprocal induction" may occur, that is, "intensification of one process by another taking place either in succession at the same point or simultaneously at two neighboring points" (50).

V55.36–37, B64.15   his Kyprinos Orients   Advertised in tiny, front-page notices in the *Times* of London as "a delightful, fragrant cigarette with a rich, satisfying flavour." Generally the British prefer cigarettes made from Virginia tobaccos, but like Ian Fleming's character James Bond, Pointsman prefers a Near Eastern blend, here from the island of Cyprus. There is more. "Kyprinos" derives from the Greek *Kypris*, recalling Cyprian Aphrodite, or Venus. According to Graves (*White Goddess* 140), "The cypress was sacred to Hercules . . . and the word cypress is derived from Cyprus, which was called after Cyprian Aphrodite, his mother" (140). So it is appropriate that Pointsman smokes this brand because, as we soon see, it was the "submontane Venus" (V88.10) of Pavlovian research that called him, as though he were Tannhäuser, out of traditional medicine and into the labyrinth of neurophysiology. Similarly, it is the same White Goddess of love-in-death that calls to the zany kamikaze pilots Tachezi and Ichizo when they gather luminiscent white "Cypridinae" from the Pacific surf (see V690.40n).

V56.8, B64.28   "That's the Monte Carlo Fallacy"   So called because, on a roulette wheel (for example), the fact that one number comes up does not mean that its chances of coming up again are lessened. Instead, statistical proofs show that with every new spin of the wheel the number has an equal chance against all others. With rockets, this means (as Roger says), "Everyone's equal. Same chances of getting hit. Equal in the eyes of the rocket" (V57.6–7).

V56.14, B64.35–36　no reflex arc, no Law of Negative Induction　Returns readers once more to Pavlov's *Lectures*. The concept of a reflex arc is a cornerstone in Pavlov's mechanistic theory. He represents the "arc" as a virtual "path" of cerebral causes and effects, from the time sensation is received until the body reacts to it. In volume 1 (117) he writes: "I represent the nervous path of the . . . reflex arc as a chain of three links—the *analyzer*, the *connection* or lock, and the *effector* or working part of the apparatus." The "Law of Negative Induction" appears later in Pavlovian theory, essentially as a version of the "Ultraparadoxical" phenomenon (see V48.38–39n). According to this law, a positive stimulus will, under certain conditions of trauma and stress, induce a negative response (*Lectures* 2: 176).

V56.24, B65.5–6　Reverend Dr. Paul de la Nuit　Paul "of the Night."

V57.8, B65.34　her Fay Wray look　In *King Kong* (1933), actress Fay Wray's "look"—wide eyes, tense neck muscles, lips puckered on the verge of a scream—is something she first practices for director Carl Denham aboard ship, in a highly erotic scene, then puts to unfeigned use on Skull Island, when she first sees Kong.

V57.31, B66.19–20　"another kind of Beveridge Proposal"　The 1944 report "Social Insurgence and Allied Services," by Lord William H. Beveridge (1876–1963), became a foundation piece in English policy toward the displaced persons of war-torn Europe. Beveridge argued that the last should be first, that those who suffered most should stand first in line for Allied aid. The "Bitterness Quotient" and "Evaluation Board" are Roger's exaggerations.

V58.38, B67.36–37　bleached by the Star's awful radiance　A Christmas tableau, with the Christ child in his manger; but "bleached" again calls up the image of Blicero (V30.12n).

V59.1–2, B67.42–68.1　staticky Frank Bridge Variations . . . over the BBC Home Service　Throughout the war two BBC "Programmes" were broadcast over separate radio bandwidths: the Home Service Programme and the General Forces Programme. The "Frank Bridge Variations" are unknown.

V59.3, B68.1–2　bottle of Montrachet　From the tiny, exclusive vineyard of Montrachet, in the Côte de Beaune district of France. A very expensive bottle of wine.

V59.16, B68.19–20　"Oh, Edward VIII abdicated. He fell in love with—"　With Mrs. Wallis Warfield Simpson, the American divorcée whom the king married in 1937, after abdicating the throne in 1936 amid a storm of protest (see also V177.28–29n).

V59.30, B68.36 "And one cried wee, wee, wee, all the way" From the old Mother Goose rhyme: "This little piggy went to market / This little piggy stayed home / This little piggy had roast beef / This little piggy had none / And this little piggy cried 'wee, wee, wee' all the way home." The pig/home motif will recur (see for example V114.12–13n).

EPISODE IO

The setting for this grotesquely surreal episode is St. Veronica's, the fictional hospital in London's East End where Tyrone Slothrop reports for his tour of duty as a testing subject. The time is unspecified, but probably December 18–20. Injected with sodium amytal, he lapses into an induced hypnotic vision, segments of which comprise the stream-of-consciousness "action" of this episode. In search of a fallen, lost harmonica, Slothrop journeys down a toilet in Boston's Roseland Ballroom, circa 1939. Then, in a western setting, a cowboy named Crutchfield the Westwardman prepares for a showdown with a bad figure named Toro Rojo. These visions introduce some of the most significant semantic contraries of *GR*: white/black, north/south, the word/shit. The prevalence of the color red is also noteworthy, and several motifs—the underground journey, westwarding progress, the lawless frontier—will reappear in the novel. In addition, like episodes 5 and 9 before it, this one seems to come full circle: it begins and ends with semantic play on an enigmatic phrase, "You never did the Kenosha Kid."

V60.5, B69.15 Bonechapel Gate, E1 A fictional London postal district, although the E1 designation would put this hospital around Whitechapel Road in the city's East End.

V60.8, B69.18 The Kenosha Kid One of the outstanding enigmas in *GR*. It may of course be Slothrop himself, who will recall sitting in a "white tile greasy-spoon" Kenosha restaurant (V696.10–11); or it may be the colonel "from Kenosha," whose apparently fatal haircut is played out to Slothrop's unwitting accompaniment on the recovered harmonica (see V643.11); then there is a "loony" Japanese radarman named Old Kenosho (V691.11). One of the many incompleted, nontotalized enigmas in *GR*.

V60.26–30, B70.2–7 the "Charleston" . . . all them dances, I did the "Castle walk," and . . . the "Lindy," too! The Charleston was a swing dance of the twenties and thirties, known for its "no-contact" positioning of the partners; the Big Apple was another swing dance, of the thirties, done to a fast six-beat count; the Castle walk was named for Vernon and Irene Castle, the dynamic duo of pre–Great War ballroom dance (he died during the war); and the lindy or lindy hop was a novelty dance, with exaggerated jumping and feet pendulously swinging, named for Charles Lindbergh's 1927 transatlantic flight.

V61.17, B70.26–27   10% Sodium Amytal   An intermediate-strength barbiturate, sodium amytal is the popular "truth serum" of countless Hollywood movies. Therapeutically, it can be used to induce a trancelike state. The drug comes in three dosage forms: intravenous (IV), intramuscular (IM), and blue capsules for oral induction. Its psychological effects range from profound states of hypnotic trance to mild sedation. Slothrop receives a strong intravenous jolt. Later he will recognize the drug's effects in another (see V512.1).

V61.24–62.2, B70.36–71.12   Snap to, Slothrop . . . Slothrop, snap to!   Sung to the tune of "Bye, Bye Blackbird," a song Eddie Cantor popularized in the late twenties. Compare the actual lyric (written by Mort Dixon):

> Pack up all my cares and woe,
> Here I go, singin' low,
> Bye-bye, blackbird.
>
> Where somebody waits for me,
> Sugar's sweet, and so is she,
> Bye-bye, blackbird.
>
> No one seems to care, or understand me,
> Oh what hard luck stories they all hand me.
> Make my bed, and light the light;
> I'll be home, late tonight,
> Blackbird, bye-bye.

V61.30, B71.6   Just give me my "ruptured duck"   When they were honorably discharged from the U.S. Army, soldiers were given a brass lapel button with a "screaming eagle" embossed on it. In popular slang these buttons were known as "ruptured ducks" (A. M. Taylor 172).

V61.34, B71.10   mike my brain   That is, measure it with a micrometer (technical argot).

V62.4, B71.15   the Negroes, in Roxbury   A suburb of Boston and a black ghetto since the twenties, Roxbury was founded in 1630 by William Pynchon (McIntyre 9).

V62.20, B71.31–32   "gage" smoke   In Afro-American slang from the thirties and forties, marijuana.

V62.22, B71.34   a process!   In Afro-American slang, the term signifies a tortuous method of straightening hair by applying a pomade (called "congolene") that contains lye (see V67.31n). Also known as "a conk." Malcolm X describes the terrors of his first one in *The Autobiography* (51–55).

V63.3, B72.18 men's room at the Roseland Ballroom The Roseland
State Ballroom, on Massachusetts Avenue in Roxbury. During the
summer of 1940, Malcolm X worked as a shoeshine boy in the Roseland
men's room. Pynchon has derived details about the Roseland from
chapters 3 ("Homeboy") and 4 ("Laura") of *The Autobiography*.

V63.5, B72.21 bottle of Moxie Trade name of an American soft drink
now marketed by the Monarch-Nugrape Company.

V63.6, B72.21 a Clark bar Brand name of an American candy bar,
chocolate coating around a brittle center.

V63.14, B72.31 his snow-white Arrow An American brand of men's
dress shirt.

V63.22, B72.41 Red, the Negro shoeshine boy This is Malcolm X,
whose nicknames included "Red" (because of his hair) and "Homeboy"
(because he'd come to Boston from the midwestern town of Lansing).
See chapter 3 of *The Autobiography*.

**V63.23–25, B73.1–3 "Cherokee" comes wailing up . . . moving rose
lights** The recollection derives from Malcolm X (47), who describes
hearing the gaiety from above, in the lavatory: "From down below,
the sound of the music had begun floating up . . . a few couples already
dancing under the rose-colored lights." Two pages further on he recalls
"Charlie Barnett's 'Cherokee,'" a song written by Ray Noble and
a late-thirties hit for several jazz bands. Pynchon refers to the lyric
as "one more lie about white crimes" (V63.27). Here are the words:

> Sweet indian maiden,
> Since I first met you,
> I can't forget you—
> Cherokee sweetheart.
>
> Child of the Prairie,
> Your love keeps calling,
> My heart enthralling—
> Cherokee.
>
> Dreams of summertime,
> Of lover-time gone by,
> Throng my memory—
>
> So tenderly, I sigh!
>
> My sweet indian maiden,
> One day I'll hold you,
> In my arms fold you—
> Cherokee! Cherokee!

**V63.32–37, B73.12–18 "Yardbird" Parker is finding out . . . Dan Wall's
Chili House** The details probably derive from Max Harrison's book

about saxophonist Charles ("Yardbird") Parker, who was nineteen when he played at Dan Wall's Chili House in Harlem. Parker began at that time to experiment with his playing, and he recalled the importance of those New York gigs in an interview Harrison quotes (8–9): "I remember one night I was jamming in a chili house on Seventh Avenue between 139th and 140th. It was December 1939. Now I'd been getting bored with the stereotyped changes that were being used all the time and I kept thinking there's bound to be something else. I could hear it sometimes but I couldn't play it. Well, that night I found that by using the higher intervals of a chord as a melody line and backing them with appropriately related changes I could play the thing I'd been hearing." Harrison explains how these "changes" or chord progressions involved thirty-second notes, or demisemiquavers, which Pynchon wants us to say in a midget "Munchkin voice," as if we were in *The Wizard of Oz*. Charlie Parker died on March 12, 1955, in the New York apartment of Baroness Königswater-Rothschild, of acute stomach ulcers and severe liver cirrhosis—both the result of his addictions to alcohol and heroin. It is the "dum-de-dumming" (V63.39) of his wasteful death that Pynchon wants us to hear as accompaniment to this historical digression. Note, however, that he has fudged the chronology: Slothrop's scene at the Roseland, like Charlie Parker's chili-house gig, occurred in December 1939; but Malcolm X did not begin shining shoes at the Roseland until June of 1940.

V64.13, B73.36   the cold Lysol air   After the Lysol brand of disinfectant cleanser.

V64.24, B74.8   those Sheiks   American brand of condom. Malcolm X (48) tells of dispensing prophylactics to wealthy white boys, buying condoms at the drugstore for a quarter and dealing them in the men's room for a dollar.

V64.28–29, B74.13–14   like topo lines up a river valley   That is, lines on a topographical map; anticipates the song (at V68.12–16).

V65.9, B74.40   Burma-Shave signs   In 1926, to advertise its brand of shaving cream, the Burma Shave Company launched an ingenious and highly successful campaign involving roadside jingles, one line per sign, as in "Don't take / That curve / At 60 per / We hate to lose / A customer."

V65.16, B75.7   Fu's Folly in Cambridge   Undoubtedly fictional (like Sidney's Great Yellow Grille, at V65.27), this Harvard-area restaurant was named after Ward's Fu-Manchu tales (see V277.34–38n).

V65.20, B75.11   here's Dumpster Villard   An apparent suicide who will reappear in another of Slothrop's dreams (V255.20).

V65.33, B75.28   Jack Kennedy, the ambassador's son   Reappears in "Mom Slothrop's Letter to Ambassador Kennedy" (V682–83). Joseph Kennedy, Sr. (1888–1969), was ambassador to England from 1937 until November 1940, when he stepped down to "keep America out of war" (Wheeler, *Founding Father* 293). John F. Kennedy had returned from England to Harvard University in 1939 to finish his senior thesis on prewar English diplomacy, a study that later became his first book, *While England Slept*.

V66.12, B76.9   MTA   Boston's Metropolitan Transit Authority.

V66.39, B77.1   the Capehart   American brand of radio receiver; "Your Private Window on the World," as the advertisements used to claim.

V67.8–9, 77.12   Decline and fall works silently   Echoing the title of Edward Gibbon's monumental history, *The Decline and Fall of the Roman Empire* (1788).

V67.31, B77.38   kid with the Red Devil lye in his hair   Here is the recipe for congolene according to Malcolm X (53): "can of Red Devil lye, two eggs, and two medium-sized potatoes."

V68.12, B78.21   RED RIVER VALLEY   Pynchon parodies the traditional lyric of western cowboys:

> From this valley they say you are going,
> We will miss your bright eyes and sweet smile;
> For they say you are taking the sunshine,
> That has brightened our pathways awhile.
>
> Come and sit by my side if you love me,
> Do not hasten to bid me adieu;
> Just remember the Red River Valley,
> And the cowboy who loved you so true.

V68.23, B78.33   little pard   The term "baffles" Fowler, but it's a common, friendly shortening of the western slang term "pardner"; it appears throughout Mark Twain's *Roughing It* (1872), for example.

V68.27, B78.38   San Berdoo   Slang for the town of San Bernadino, in the California desert.

V69.12, B79.23–24   in Eagle Pass from a faro dealer   Eagle Pass is a border town on the Rio Grande, about eighty miles upriver from Laredo, Texas. Faro is a card game; players wager on the top card of the dealer's deck.

V69.16, B79.28   "Rancho Peligroso"   The "Perilous Ranch."

V69.32, B80.7   "Toro Rojo"   "Red Bull."

V69.39, B80.16   Los Madres   "The Mothers," the Sierra Madres range of northern Mexico. But the article should be feminine—*Las* Madres.

V70.4, B80.24   platanos   Bananas, though in Spanish it should be accented: *plátanos*.

V70.29–30, B81.9–10   ten thousand stiffs humped under the snow in the Ardennes   Soldiers fallen in the Rundstedt offensive (V52.23–24n).

V70.32, B81.12–13 Newton Upper Falls Boston suburb.

V70.36, B81.18 segway Radio announcers' argot and musical terminology for a transition, a bridge between songs, an advertisement and a song, or parts of a musical composition. Here Pynchon deliberately misspells it.

V71.2, B81.27 Beacon Street Runs through Boston to Brookline and Newton.

EPISODE II

The time and setting of this episode are the same as for episode 9. By a bizarre method, Pirate decodes the message he received from that V-2 rocket of December 18. Later we learn that the note conveyed information about plucking Katje Borgesius out of Holland.

V71.11, B81.39 "Kryptosam" From the Greek *kryptos* (hidden). Here it is a form of "tyrosine" (an unknown and doubtless fictional substance; from the Latin *tyro*, "a young soldier"), and it is decrypted by the application of (here, Pirate's) seminal fluids.

V71.12, B81.40 IG Farben ... research contract with OKW The Interessen Gemeinschaft Farbenindustrie Aktiengesellschaft, or Dye Industry Community of Interests, Incorporated (IG Farben, for short), was Germany's largest industrial cartel during the thirties and, with the Krupp firm, a kingpin of the German rearmament program. Beginning in the nineteenth century as a patentee of the new coal-tar dyes, IG Farben metastasized into a multinational cartel concerned with drugs, synthetic fibers and rubber, films and dyes, and a variety of industrial chemicals. The firm plays a key role in *GR* from this moment on, and Pynchon's primary source for details about it is Richard Sasuly's book, *IG Farben* (1947); another minor source, as Hite points out (*Ideas* 165, n8), was Josiah Dubois's book, *Generals in Grey Suits* (1953). OKW was an acronym for the German Oberkommando des Wehrmachts, or Army High Command, with whom IG Farben maintained extensive research contracts.

V71.24, B82.12 Agfa, Berlin Agfa was a subsidiary of IG Farben specializing in the manufacture of photographic films and reagents. Its American cousin, Agfa-Ansco, became the American IG Company in 1929, then changed its name in 1939 to General Aniline and Film, or GAF, the name by which it still conducts business in the United States (Sasuly 27, 34, 182; Dubois 4, 24).

V71.26, B82.14 GEHEIME KOMMANDOSACHE "Secret Command-Matter," the designation stamped on top-secret documents in Germany (see the photostat of such a document in Irving 298).

V71.27, B82.15–16 after the style of von Bayros or Beardsley Aubrey Beardsley (1872–98) was a British graphic artist who had only begun to attract widespread attention when he died at age twenty-six. His grotesques, perhaps his drawings of Venus for an illustrated version of Richard Wagner's *Tannhäuser*, are the background here. Like Beardsley, the Marquis Franz von Bayros (1866–1924) was known as a graphic artist and an illustrator. His black-and-white drawings for turn-of-the-century German erotica by Hans Butsch and Max Somneraus won him a coterie following; his best-known work was a series of drawings for an edition of Dante's *Divine Comedy*.

V71.30, B82.20 a De Mille set The reference is to film director Cecil B. De Mille's *Cleopatra* (1934), with its immense sets and arrangements of diaphanous silk scrims behind which brown-skinned girls fan the empress (played by Claudette Colbert) in her milk bath. See also V559.16–17n.

V72.27–28, B83.18 like Wuotan and his mad army In Teutonic mythology Wuotan is "above all the arranger of wars and battles," and those who fall in battle will return to him. When ranging across the sky, he is accompanied by his "furious host," the *Wütende Heer*, or "Mad Army," of northern European legend (Grimm 132–35).

V72.29, B83.19 Pirate's own robot hands begin to search The Bantam misprints this, as "hands being to search."

EPISODE 12

Staff members at "The White Visitation" discuss their plans for Tyrone Slothrop. These include a "projective test" (with an octopus) that will lead off part 2. (In brief, a psychological projective test is designed to use a subject's responses to unstructured stimuli as measures of personality.) We also learn a good deal about the jealousies and internecine fights between these scientists and pseudoscientists. Internal references put the date as December 21, the onset of winter.

V72.32–34, B83.24–25 WAS TUST DU FÜR DIE FRONT . . . FÜR DEUTSCHLAND GETAN? A Nazi poster exhortation. A translation: "What are you doing for the front? For the war? What have you done for Germany today?"

V72.34, B83.26 the walls read ice This roughly coincides with the *Times* of London weather report for December 21.

V73.5, B83.35–36 taken at the manic whim of Henry VIII King Henry VIII plundered the Catholic monasteries after his 1536 break with Rome.

V73.23–27, B84.21–27 "I can hear the Lord of the Sea. . . . Bert" The

source of Reg Le Froyd's exclamations is Grimm's etymological somer-
saults in *Teutonic Mythology* (272–82). The goddess Bertha, along
with the masculine god Berchtold, or Bert, appears in the myths as (1)
"the promoter of navigation among men," and thus a "Lord of the
Sea"; (2) a *white* figure, for Grimm explains that "*behrt* or *brecht* signifies bright, light, white"; (3) a being whose host includes the souls of
children, and thus a reading that tallies with Pynchon's man-child
in this narrative digression; and (4) a figure whose festival occurs on
the winter solstice (December 21). The suicide leap of Reg Le Froyd
("Reginald the Cold") corresponds with later references to the Gadarene
swine and the rush of lemmings into the sea (V555.24–28).

V73.32, B84.33 Ick Regis See V51.31–32n.

V73.34, B84.35 Brighton England's most popular seaside resort town,
located fifty-three miles south of London on the English Channel.

V73.34, B84.36 Flotsam and Jetsam A comedy show on the BBC
Home Service Programme; according to the *Times* of London schedules
it was featured on Wednesday evenings, usually at 9:30.

V74.13–14, B85.18 the BBC's eloquent Myron Grunton A fictional
broadcaster. From *grunten*, Middle English for marine fishes of the
genus *Haemulon* that produce grunting sounds; and the Greek *muron*,
meaning "sweet" or "delightful." Thus a "Myron Grunton" is a "sweet
grunter."

V74.19, B85.25 P/W interrogations Like POW, an acronym for prisoner
of war.

V74.20, B85.26 the brothers Grimm Wilhelm (1786–1859) and Jacob
(1785– 1863), German philologists and folklorists, authors of the
world-famous collection of fairy tales. Jacob's magisterial study, *Teutonic Mythology*, is one of Pynchon's principal sources.

V74.21, B85.27 Dawes-era flashes In 1924 the American general
Dawes put forward a plan, according to which Germany would begin
making reparations payments to Allied governments involved in
World War I. Through the mediation of British prime minister Ramsey
MacDonald, the Dawes plan was accepted and the payments continued
for eight years, until Hitler's rise to power (A. J. P. Taylor 215–16).

V75.12, B86.26 "Schwarzkommando" Translated, the "Black Command" or "Black Detachment"; a (fictional) Nazi regiment of Hereros
transplanted from "Südwest," or South-West, Africa.

**V75.30–31, B87.5–6 worked with Pavlov himself at the Koltushy
institute** The source is Horsley Gantt's Introduction to volume 2
of Pavlov's *Lectures* (31–32). Koltushy was the village located outside
Leningrad where Pavlov established an experimental lab, the Institute of
Experimental Medicine. In 1929 the village was renamed Pavlovo
in his honor.

V76.2–6, 87.22–26 drops of saliva . . . castration A catalog of Pavlovian

experimental and surgical techniques for working with dogs:
measuring their saliva flow as a sign of the strength of any conditioned
response; conditioning their reflexes by using a metronome as a sound
stimulus; using bromides to give the dogs a calmer disposition;
cutting afferent nerves that send impulses from extremities to the
spinal cord and thus the brain; and surgically castrating them when
bromides failed (see, for example, Pavlov's discussion in chapter 2
of *Conditioned Reflexes*).

V76.6, B87.26–27   a colony *dégagé*   French for a "free colony," one
that is relaxed and unrestricted.

V76.12, B87.33–34   M.O. in Thunder Prodd's regiment   An M.O.
is a medical officer. The name of this fictional Great War commander
contains a pun: "Thunar" (also known as "Donar") was the Teutonic
god of storm and rain, a son of Wuotan; Thunar's bolts of lightning were
like "prods."

**V76.32–33, B88.15–16   the F.O. Political Intelligence Department
at Fitzmaurice House**   Source unknown. F.O.: the Foreign Office.

V76.34, B88.17–18   their OSS, OWI   Respectively, the U.S. Office
of Special Services (forerunner of the Central Intelligence Agency) and
the Office of War Information. A few lines further on, Pynchon also
mentions their political affiliations. The OSS was begun in June 1942
under the leadership of William J. ("Wild Bill") Donovan, who recruited
the likes of Allen Dulles and William H. Jackson, lawyers and (in
Jackson's case) venture capitalists whom the narrator (focalizing through
Pudding) rather accurately refers to as "eastern and moneyed Republi-
cans" (V77.3–4). After V-E Day, Dulles and Jackson both returned to the
agency, renamed the CIA, to lead it into the cold war. Whereas operations carried out at OSS were covert, the Office of War Information
handled overt activities associated with the media. Under Robert
Sherwood, an old New Dealer by 1942, there gathered a group of fairly
liberal newspapermen like Richard Hollander (of the *Washington
Daily News*) and Robert Bishop (of the *Chicago Sun-Times*).

V77.10–11, B88.38–39   filth of the Ypres salient   During World War
I the village of Ypres, in the low country of Flanders, was the site
of three battles. Its abominably muddy conditions come up again at
V79.36-41.

V77.22–23, B89.11–12   "Bereshith, as it were"   *Bereshith*—"In the
beginning"—is the first Hebrew word in the Book of Genesis.

V77.23, B89.12   "Ramsey MacDonald can die"   And so the former
prime minister did, in 1937. He had been the prime minister for two
terms, 1929–31 and 1931–35; and until the abdication of King Edward
VIII in early 1937 he kept his post as Lord President of the Privy
Council. When Edward stepped down MacDonald lost his power; he
died several months later.

V77.35–36, B89.27–28   Couéists . . . Dale Carnegie zealots   This
is a short catalog of some pop-psychology movements of the twenties
and thirties. Emile Coué (1857–1926), a self-proclaimed psychotherapist
from France, was best known for his proverbial formula "Every day
in every way I am getting better and better." His patients were coun-
seled to repeat it, mantra-like, to themselves. Couéism centered on this
type of autosuggestion as a means of subduing the will and thereby
"healing" mental and physical ailments. After the publication of
his book, *My Method* (1923), Coué attracted large audiences on a lecture
tour through England and the United States. On Ouspenskian beliefs,
see V30.37n. Pynchon's mention of the Skinnerites is an interesting one,
but not because it is (as Fowler claims) anachronistic. B. F. Skinner's
first book, *The Behavior of Organisms*, was published in 1938 as an expanded version of his Harvard dissertation, a development of his
thesis on "operant conditioning," which was widely known by 1940.
Still more interesting, during the war Skinner directed a University of
Minnesota project (under the acronym ORCON, for "Organic Control")
that involved animals (pigeons) as a possible "guidance system" for
rockets. The birds were shown film of a target and conditioned to guide
the missile toward it by pecking at a control panel. Skinner tells
the story of this secret research in "Pigeon in a Pelican," an essay included in *Cumulative Record: A Selection of Papers* (1972). There
are striking resemblances to the method he details there, and the operant conditioning of Octopus Grigori, in *GR*. Finally, then, there is
Dale Carnegie, best known for his 1937 book, *How to Win Friends and
Influence People*, with its Couéist enthusiasm for "positive thinking" as
a cure-all.

V78.6, B89.40–41   blindfolded subjects call Zener-deck guesses   That
is, in a test for extrasensory perception (see V40.18n).

V78.12–13, B90.6–7   like Cecil Beaton's photograph of Margot Asquith
Beaton was one of *Vogue* magazine's most famous photographers
of the twenties and thirties; Margot Asquith was the wife of British
prime minister Sir Herbert Asquith (1852–1928). Originally published
in *Vogue*, the photo shows Mrs. Asquith from behind, hair elegantly
styled atop her head, hooped earrings, shoulders bared above a striped
gown of some sheer fabric, gathered at the derriere in a kind of fan;
her left hand is poised at the arm of a chair, her right hand on her hip.
A copy of the picture, dated 1931 and signed by Beaton, appears as
the frontispiece to Margot Asquith's autobiography, *More or Less about
Myself* (1934).

**V78.32–33, B90.30–31   the traditional orange Pavlovian Cement of
rosin, iron oxide, and beeswax**   The source is a footnote in *Conditioned
Reflexes* (18), though Pavlov describes it there as "Mendeleéf's
Cement," after his chemistry professor at the University of St. Pe-

tersburg. The mixture was used to attach glass tubes to the surgically rerouted salivary ducts of dogs, tubes designed to drain (for measuring) through the cheek. The recipe: "Colophonium [resin], 50 grammes; ferric oxide, 40 grammes; yellow beeswax, 25 grammes."

V78.39, B90.39 he has moved into "equivalent" phase See V48.38–39n. Pynchon's fictional example of "equivalence" is textbook perfect.

V79.18, B91.21 Géza Rózsavölgyi In Hungarian his family name signifies an "evil valley."

V79.31–32, B91.37–39 what Haig . . . once said at mess about Lieutenant Sassoon's refusal to fight Sir Douglas Haig was field marshal of the British Expeditionary Force in the Great War. His secretary was Sir Philip Sassoon, cousin of Lt. Siegfried Sassoon, the poet, a soldier with the Royal Welsh Fusiliers. Siegfried's battalion-mates called him "Mad Jack" because of his reckless courage (he once attacked a trench full of Germans with only hand grenades and after routing them sat down among the dead to read a book of poems). When wounded in the neck he used his recuperation in England to compose a series of bleak and bloody poems about the war, beginning to argue that the struggle had changed from one of national defense and liberation to one of aggression and conquest. He claimed that the War Department was misrepresenting its aims to the British, and thereafter he was derogatorily labeled a pacifist. Presumably this would be the context of Haig's evidently apocryphal remark, as the fictional Pudding relates it.

V79.38, B92.3–4 duckboarded Soules (105) explains that "duckboards are what, in order not to walk in it, you lay across mud."

V79.41, B92.8 the whole Passchendaele horror Lloyd George, the British prime minister, called it "the battle of the mud" (A. J. P. Taylor 86). On July 31, 1917, Field Marshal Haig launched a third—and, it was hoped, decisive—attack near Ypres, in Flanders. It was called Passchendaele (literally, "Valley of the Passion") after the bloodiest of its wooded battle zones. The British historian A. J. P. Taylor (87) sums it up:

> Everything went wrong. The drainage system of Flanders broke down, as had been foretold. To make matters worse, it was the rainiest August for many years. Men struggled forward up to their waists in mud. The guns sank in the mud. The tanks could not be used. Haig had declared his intention to stop the offensive if the first attack failed. He did not do so. The futile struggle went on for three months. The British advanced, in all, four miles. This made their salient more precarious than before, and they evacuated without fighting when the Germans took the offensive in March 1918. Three British soldiers were killed for every two German. The British lost a third of a million men to casualties at Passchendaele.

V80.2–3, B92.10–11 cucurbitaceous improbabilities That is, using the pulp of one of the *Cucurbitaceae* family—including pumpkins, squashes, and cucumbers—for General Pudding's "Gourd Surprise."

V80.12, B92.23 a beet *risolé* This would be a triangular pastry canapé that has been deep fried to cook the "beet-mash" within.

V80.13, B92.24 some lovely pureed samphire Somewhat like the iceplant that grows along the Pacific shores of the United States, samphire has thick fleshy leaves and white flowers; it appears in great profusion along the coasts of Flanders and Dover.

V80.16, B92.28 any ordinary "Toad" The reference is to Pudding's surprise "Toad-in-the-Hole" recipe; but see also the electrified "Eisenkröte," or Toad-in-the-Urinal, the "ultimate test of manhood" (at V603.40–41).

V80.17–18, B92.29 Kings Road The main thoroughfare of Chelsea, home of Pirate Prentice, Osbie Feel, and the crew we met in episodes 1 and following.

V80.20–22, B92.33–34 eight bars, from "Would You Rather Be a Colonel with an Eagle on Your Shoulder, or a Private with a Chicken on Your Knee?" In U.S. Army slang, a "bird" or "chicken" colonel is a full colonel. A. M. Taylor supplies a helpful gloss: "A Colonel's eagles [his insignia] were called 'chickens' in World War I, as noted in a popular song of the day—'I'd Rather Be a Private with a Chicken on My Knee than a Colonel with a Chicken on my Shoulder.'" The narrator has got the phrasing backward.

V80.24, B92.37–38 the Electra House group Near Waterloo Bridge, Electra House is the London headquarters of British Cable and Wireless Ltd.; during the war it housed the British broadcasting and radio propaganda offices.

V81.2, B93.18–19 Maybe because this is 1945 Maybe someone fell asleep, for in the narrative *histoire* "this is" December of 1944.

V81.4, B93.20–21 the Führer-principle Literally, the "leader-principle"; the concept of charismatic leadership.

V81.8–9, B93.25–26 charisma . . . its rationalization should proceed In *The Theory of Social and Economic Organization*, German sociologist Max Weber analyzes three types of authority in society: the traditional or dynastic form in which power is handed along by right of birth; the rational or bureaucratic, with its abstract currencies and impersonal organization; and the charismatic, which is spontaneous and unstable and allied with ideals of love and brotherhood. Charismatic orders are in Weber's view (364) fleeting: "In its pure form charismatic authority may be said to exist only in the process of originating. It cannot remain stable, but becomes either traditionalized or rationalized, or a combination of both." Translations of Weber variously call this process of stabilizing the dynamic power of charisma its "routinization" or "rationalization," and Pynchon will use both terms throughout *GR*.

V81.22, B93.43   the MMPI was developed about 1943   Actually, the Minnesota Multiphasic Personality Inventory was developed in 1940 and made available to the military, which contracted for it, in 1943. See V90.8n for more detailed discussion.

V81.23–24, B94.1–3   Allport and Vernon's Study of Values, the Bernreuter Inventory as revised by Flanagan in '35   The Allport and Vernon Study was prepared by psychologists G. W. Allport, P. E. Vernon, and G. Lindzey in the early thirties. According to Anne Anastazi (487–90), whose undergraduate textbook was probably a main source for much of this detail, "this inventory was designed to measure the relative strengths of six basic interests, motives or evaluative attitudes": theoretical, economic, aesthetic, social, political, and religious. The Bernreuter Inventory was composed by R. G. Bernreuter for the Stanford University Press in 1931. The test measures self-sufficiency, introversion-extroversion, dominance-submission, and neurotic tendencies; it was especially targeted for young-adult populations and is answered with simple "yes-no-don't know" responses. J. C. Flanagan, who later became a major figure in psychological testing, noticed that the four Bernreuter categories of neurosis, introversion, submission, and low self-sufficiency were all statistically correlated, and to a very high degree of predictability. These discoveries led to a further refinement of the Bernreuter test, accurately pinpointed in *GR* as occurring in 1935.

V81.34–35, B94.13–15   "a so-*called*, 'projec-tive' test . . . the Rohrschach *ink*-blot"   Making allowances for Géza Roszavölgyi's halting, Hungarianized English, this summary of projective tests is substantially the same as that in Anastazi (493–94). The Rohrschach test was first described in 1921 and more formally developed by Swiss psychoanalyst Hermann Rohrschach in 1942. It consists of ten cards, each printed with a bilaterally symmetrical inkblot, which the subject is asked to interpret by telling what is "seen" in it. Implicit in the whole procedure, as Anastazi (495–99) points out, are the assumptions that test responses are typical of how a subject always perceives and that personality traits influence perception.

V82.31, B95.17–18   giant Gloucestershire Old Spots   In his biographical essay for *Playboy*, Jules Siegal recalls a late-sixties visit to Pynchon's apartment in Manhattan Beach, a Los Angeles suburb. His bookcase, Siegal (170) recalls, "had rows of piggy banks on each shelf and there was a collection of books and magazines about pigs." Reading these books, perhaps a book like Sillar's *The Symbolic Pig* (5), Pynchon may well have come across a description of Britain's native pig breeds: "Wessex Saddlebacks" (see also V5.27), "Large Black (and Little Black) Berkshires," "Dorset Gold Tips," and "Gloucester Old Spots."

V82.36–37, B95.24–25 The W.C.s contain frescoes of Clive and his elephants stomping the French at Plassy Fancy, patriotic toilet facilities (water closets). "Plassey," as most sources spell it, is a Bengal village on the river Bhagirathi, outside Calcutta. Not long after British colonial occupants of that city were massacred in the "Black Hole" atrocity, the British East India Company empowered Baron Clive (1725–74) to retake the city. He faced a native army of vastly superior numbers, and its nabob had also enlisted the help of French artillery troops. On June 23, 1757, Clive led his forces (assisted by elephant packtrains) against the French artillery, routing it in what proved the decisive battle of Clive's campaign. The victory was famous for solidifying the East India Company's hold over the region.

V82.37–38, B95.26 Salome with the head of John For the story of how young Salome danced for King Herod and won John the Baptist's head on a tray, see Matt. 14:1–12.

V83.9–10, B95.41–42 no two observers, no matter how close they stand, see quite the same building A visual example of indeterminacy resulting from parallax views. Also, another Bantam error: "not matter how."

EPISODE 13

Internal evidence shows that this episode occurs on December 22, at the Dover coast. The subject of the characters' discussion is once again Slothrop's enigmatic sexual member and what should be done to crack its "code." Interestingly, Brigadier General Pudding is the only one to raise the issue of Slothrop's welfare. Shaping the narration is a philosophical debate pitting the determinist view of Ned Pointsman against the statistical approach of Roger Mexico.

V83.25, B96.18 The Nayland Smith Press Named for Sir Dennis Nayland Smith of Scotland Yard, intrepid fictional hero of Arthur Sarsfield Ward's Fu-Manchu books. Note the date on this fictional catalog of insults: in 1933 Slothrop was fifteen years old, about thirteen years beyond the time of his "conditioning" at the hands of Dr. Laszlo Jamf.

V84.3–4, B96.33–35 if Watson and Rayner could successfully condition their "Infant Albert" John B. Watson and his wife Rosalie Rayner Watson were the parents of behavioral psychology. Their conditioning of eleven-month old "Infant Albert," in 1918, is summarized in *The*

Psychological Care of Infant and Child (1928). They first put into Albert's playpen a variety of furry animals and toys, which he displayed no natural predisposition to fear. Then an assistant began clanging "a carpenter's hammer" on a steel bar held just behind Albert's head. They repeated this procedure each time one of the animals was introduced and Albert reached for it. Terrified by the unseen noise, Albert quickly associated it with the animals and began registering his terror each time one was brought near him. His terror soon included *all* "furry objects," including his mother's feather boa, an item he'd previously associated with Mother's loving care. "You may think that such experiments are cruel," conceded Watson and Rayner (54), "but they are not cruel if they help us to understand the fear life of millions of people around us and give us practical help in bringing up our children."

V84.9–10, B97.5   Kekulé's own famous switch into chemistry from architecture   Friedrich August Kekulé von Stradonitz (1829–96) was the German chemist who laid the groundwork for the theory of structure in organic chemistry, beginning with his discovery of the cyclical, or "ring" structure of the benzene molecule. At the University of Geissen he was initially enrolled as an architect but switched to chemistry at the urging of his teacher, Justus von Liebig. On Kekulé's famous dream that anticipated the discovery of the benzene ring, see V410.34n.

V84.21, B97.19–20   the Larson-Keeler three-variable "lie detector"   John A. Larson was the author of *Lying and Its Detection* (1932), the first thorough analysis of lie-detection methods and machinery. His own device utilized a correlation of blood-pressure and respiration data, improving on the simple blood-pressure machine devised by William A. Marston in 1915 and already a part of American criminological folklore by the thirties. Leonarde Keeler was an associate of Larson's in the Berkeley, California, Police Department, but by the thirties he had moved on to Northwestern University and its newly founded Crime Detection Laboratory. There he devised a third variable, a card test designed to enhance a subject's faith in the machinery and to locate the so-called peak-tension moments when the subject was most likely to be concealing some guilty knowledge. In the film *Northside 777* it is Keeler himself who administers the lie-detector test to Richard Conte in his Joliet Prison cell, confirming what Jimmy Stewart has thought all along: that he is not guilty of the crime for which he's been sentenced.

V84.39–85.3, B97.41–98.5   as Ivan Petrovich himself said, "Not only must we speak of partial or of complete extinction . . . *beyond the zero*"   The quotation derives, verbatim, from chapter 4 ("Extinction") of Pavlov's *Conditioned Reflexes* (57; the emphasis is Pynchon's). In Pavlov's theory, the question of conditioned reflexes existing "beyond the zero" involves the way some will "spontaneously recover their full strength" after a long time-lapse. Occasionally, as in Slothrop's case, the recovery of that extinguished reflex may be "paradoxical" (see V48.38–39n).

V85.12–13, B98.16   Infant Tyrone   That is, "IT," in this elaborate game of tag?

V85.37, B99.2–3   The stars fall in a Poisson distribution   Poisson's equation (see V54.25n) describes the probabilistic distribution of rockets over London. The precise correlation of Slothrop's "stars" with rocket strikes would be a coincidence of extremely low probability, but not impossible.

86.11, B99.22   That points to the V-1   The Bantam edition misprints this as "The points to the V-1."

V86.15–16, B99.26–27   Slothrop instead only gets erections when this sequence happens *in reverse*   Note the *hysteron proteron* again.

V86.33, B100.5   Glastonburys   A flowering thorn said to bloom on Christmas Eve.

V86.39, B100.12–13   The very bottom of the year   That is, the winter solstice, on December 21–22. In 1944 it occurred on Friday, December 22. Next day the *Times* of London reported that the twenty-second had been "one of the coldest days" of the coming winter; temperatures ranged in the low thirties, with heavy frosts, just as Pynchon describes it here.

V87.17, B100.34   a flight of B-17s   The "Flying Fortress," built by the Boeing Company of America from 1934 until 1943. One writer (Angellucci 136) calls it "the most celebrated strategic aircraft of the war." Crewed by ten airmen, it was widely used in Allied bombing raids over Europe after 1942.

V87.23, B100.41   nacelle   In technical argot, a metal or plastic enclosure or windscreen, especially on an airplane.

V87.32–34, B101.10–13   Pavlov's open letter to Janet . . . and of Chapter LV, "An Attempt at a Physiological Interpretation of Obsessions and of Paranoia"   Pavlov's "open letter" is chapter 54, "Les Sentiments D'Emprise and the Ultraparadoxical Phase, in volume 1 of the *Lectures* (see V49.1–2n). It is followed by the chapter Pynchon mentions here.

V88.3, B101.25–26   Dr. Horsley Gantt's odd translation   That is, his translation of Pavlov's *Lectures*, volumes 1 and 2.

V88.9–10, B101.32–33   the first Forty-One Lectures . . . at age 28   Volume 1 of the *Lectures* was published in English translation in 1928, when Pointsman was "age 28."

V88.11, B101.34–35   to abandon Harley Street   Around the corner from the Royal Society of Medicine, on London's Harley Street, "the leading medical practitioners have their consulting rooms" (Baedeker's *London* 165).

V88.17, B101.42–102.1   Venus and Ariadne!   The Greek mythical hero Theseus sails to Crete intending to stand in for the seven young men and seven young women that King Minos demanded, as an annual tribute, from the Athenians. The fourteen were offered as sacrificial victims to the Minotaur, and Minos's bargain is that if Theseus slays the monster, his fellow citizens go free. Minos's daughter, Ariadne, falls in love with Theseus and seeks aid from Daedalus, who designed the Cretan labyrinth. Daedalus suggests that Theseus should carry with him a skein of thread to unroll and mark his pathway out. After killing the Minotaur, Theseus takes Ariadne with him but abandons her (some versions say) on Cyprus. The Cypriot cult of Venus, goddess of love, used to regard Venus and Ariadne as the same goddess.

V88.29–31, B102.15–18   "Pierre Janet. . . . 'The act of injuring and the act . . . joined in the . . . whole injury.'"   Pointsman is quoting from volume 2 of Pavlov's *Lectures* (147). Pavlov, in turn, was quoting from Janet's 1932 essay "Feelings in the Delusions of Persecution" for the *Journal de psychologie.*

V89.36, B103.35–36   "your P.R.S. categories"   Pointsman *means* to say "S.P.R.," acronym for the London-based Society for Psychical Research (see also V153.11).

V90.8, B104.9   "You've seen his MMPI.   His F Scale?"   The Minnesota Multiphasic Personality Inventory (see also V81.22n) includes four validity scales to help evaluate test results. The F Scale serves to indicate "undesirable behavior" during the test, for example, "deliberate malingering" or "gross eccentricity" or even "simple carelessness." The F Scale also tends to correlate with other indications of psychosis that may crop up in the main body of the test. Or it may indicate that the subject was trying to outwit the test, perhaps for reasons of paranoid psychosis (Anastazi 498–505).

V91.37–38, B106.12–13   cylindrical blocks to cripple the silent King Tigers   The King Tiger was Germany's largest battle tank, an awesome weapon that the Allies never matched. In preparation for a Nazi landing that Hitler never sent, Britain's south coasts were thronged with such things as barbed wire, bunkers, and (as an antitank obstacle) the cylindrical blocks described here.

V91.41, B106.17   improbable as a Zouave   In the nineteenth century, Zouave tribesmen were recruited into the French army out of Algeria, given colorful uniforms, and sent back to fight the enemies of colonialism. The dignified black skating here has just been used in the film made as a propaganda maneuver by Operation Black Wing. By V112.29 he is on his way back to his regiment in North Africa.

EPISODE 14

Like episodes 5, 9, and 10 before it, this one also takes a circular form. It begins on December 22 in the London maisonette belonging to Pirate Prentice. Katje Borgesius, just snatched out of Holland, stands before a camera filming the visual material to be used in the operant conditioning of Octopus Grigori. Then begins a narrative analepsis treating Katje, Blicero, and Gottfried with the V-2 battery in Holland. The narrative circles still farther inward and back in time as we get glimpses—focalized through Blicero—of South-West Africa from his tour of duty there during the twenties. The narrative returns momentarily to the second-order time (at the V-2 battery) in order to begin one more analepsis, this time focalized through one of Katje's seventeenth-century ancestors, Frans van der Groov ("Frank the Groove"). His enthusiasm for the annihilation of the dodo (*Didus ineptus*) on the island of Mauritius extends the theme of colonialization across nonhuman fields. Then the episode ends by cycling us back to the original base time, with Katje in London. The German folktale of Hansel and Gretel and the theme of colonial domination provide continuity over these narrative shifts.

V93.2–3, B107.23–24 *Amanita muscaria* . . . relative of the poisonous Destroying Angel *Amanita verna* is the poisonous mushroom popularly known as the Destroying Angel. Of its cousin, Robert Graves (*The White Goddess* 45) has written that "Dionysius's centaurs, satyrs and maenads, it seems, actually ate a spotted toadstool called 'flycap' (*Amanita muscaria*), which gave them enormous muscular strength, erotic power, delierious visions, and the gift of prophecy."

V93.25, B108.13–14 Huntley & Palmers biscuit tin Top-quality product, with His Majesty King George IV pictured on the tin lid; a frequent advertiser in the *Times* of London.

V93.26, B108.15 Rizla liquorice cigarette paper Like Slothrop's mouth harp (V63.1), another "jive accessory"; here, for rolling cigarettes of illegal substances.

V93.34–35, B108.25–26 the long rain in silicon and freezing descent The phrase concisely anticipates the details of a moment twenty pages later, when "invisible tattooing needles" of ice strike "the nerveless window glass" while Octopus Grigori watches the film of Katje (V113.30–33). See also V53.25–26n for discussion of a similar image framing the ninth episode.

V94.3–5, B108.37–40 the frock . . . from Harvey Nicholls, a sheer crepe . . . a rich cocoa shade Pynchon gives close attention to Katje's dresses throughout *GR*, and usually for a reason: here, because this frock will be the one she wears when Slothrop "saves" her from the octopus in part 2 (V186.3). Harvey Nicholls: a fashionable clothier located near Harrods, in Knightsbridge, and a frequent advertiser in the *Times*.

V94.17–18, B109.13 the *soignée* surface In this context, a "polished" surface.

V94.20, B109.15–16 to *Der Kinderofen* A reference to the German folktale "Hansel and Gretel," number seventy-two in *Grimm's Fairy Tales*. The term, however, does not appear in Grimm, where *der Backofen* (literally, a "bake oven") is used throughout. Pynchon's compound noun aptly conveys the cannibalistic idea of the story about an old crone who pushes children into her oven to bake them into breadstuffs.

V94.21–22, B109.18 yellow teeth of Captain Blicero See V30.12n for the etymology. "Blicero" is Captain Weissmann's adopted code name while stationed with the German rocket battery in Holland.

V94.26, B109.23 Gottfried At this point it will help to consider the origins of his name. It means "God's peace" (as Pynchon notes at V465.11), from the German *Gottes* and *Frieden*. Yet these etymological strands weave a still finer, broader net in *GR*. *Frieden* derives specifically from the ancient Teutonic god Frey, also known as Freyr and Frigg. Like his sister, Freya, he was a fertility god, a brother to the Greek god Priapus, deriving from the Indo-European root *prij* (love). Frey was at the same time a god of peace and sexual love, and our slangy sexual terms "fuck" and "prick" stem from these roots. Branston (134) reports that Frey's worship was celebrated with orgies. The god's disappearance underground is also related to the myths of Tammuz, Adonis, and Orpheus. Grimm (212–14) has also shown that the worship of Frey involved the sacrifice of pigs—a point that attests to the Tammuz/Adonis links—and that northern Europeans sacrificed a Yuletide boar in honor of Frey. This is striking because, as Branston comments, the word "Frey" often appears as a title of Christ: for example, in the Old English *Dream of the Rood*. Priapus, Orpheus, Adonis, Christ, Frey, peace, love, prick—the name Gottfried enmeshes all of these. Did Pynchon know sources like Branston and Grimm? Beyond a doubt: later in this episode he will quote a verse of Middle Dutch poetry from the very pages in Grimm's *Teutonic Mythology* where the origins of Frey/Freyr are set forward.

V94.35–37, B109.35–37 a mathematical function that will expand . . . a power series *with no general term* A power series is the sum of successively higher integral powers of a variable or sum of variables, each of which is multiplied by a "general term" or constant coefficient, perhaps out to infinity. The Poisson equation contains a power series. In the instance here, Blicero's cryptic phrases expand their referentiality like a power series; yet with no common coefficient, the possible referents might be unrelated or at least involve wild leaps, as below.

V94.38, B109.38–39   his phrase *Padre Ignacio* unfolding into Spanish inquisitor   *Padre Ignacio: or, A Song of Temptation* (1900) is a novella by Owen Wister. For kindly, wise Padre Ignacio of Wister's gold-rush California to "unfold" or regress to the punishing figure of a sixteenth-century Spanish Inquisitor is some leap backward—quite an instance of *hysteron proteron*—but that is just the idea. Wister's padre, incidentally, is "tempted" mainly by such worldly pleasures as opera, and the works of Rossini in particular. In the end he decides to stay with his Pacific Indians on the California shore. Meanwhile he receives word that the opera-loving "young scapegrace" who visited, and embodied his temptation, has died.

V94.41, B109.42   children out of old Märchen   Old fairy tales.

V95.3, B110.3   her NSB credentials   That is, as a member of the Dutch Nationalsocialistische Bewegung, or National Socialist movement (see V97.9–10n).

V95.6, B110.8   merkin of sable   *Random House Dictionary* partially identifies a merkin as "false hair for the female pudenda." But from its description here, it must be much more—a transsexual aid, for example.

V95.17, B110.21   expanses of polder, toward Wassenaar   Polder, drained land protected from the sea by dikes, is common in Holland. Wassenaar is a district at the north end of The Hague. Pynchon's source on Holland as a V-2 launching site is Kooy and Uytenbogaart (283–84), who write about a "Sonderkommando (Special Commando)" of rocket troops arriving in Wassenaar on September 7, 1944, and remaining until late March of 1945.

V95.33, B110.40   near Schußtelle 3   From Kooy and Uytenbogaart (284): "The Germans had marked all cars, apparatures and such-like 'Schuszstelle 1' and 'Schuszstelle 2' (sites 1 and 2)." They also report that "firing site 3" was located at "de Beukenhorst," near the Duindigt Race course. Pynchon has Germanicized the spelling.

V95.36–37, B111.3   the Captain's own "Hexeszüchtigung"   In German a *Hexe* is a witch; here, the reference is to a punishment meted out to suspected witches; literally, a "witch's whipping."

V96.18–22, B111.29–34   Late in October, not far from this estate, one fell back . . . killing 12 of the ground crew . . . fuel and oxidizer had gone off   The source again is Kooy and Uytenbogaart (284–85). Compare the closeness of the narrative in *GR* to theirs in *Ballistics of the Future*:

> On Friday the 27th of October at 2 P.M. the first great failure took place. A rocket launched from site no. 3 rose to a height of about 300 feet and then fellback [*sic*] on the site, which was destroyed. Twelve of the crew were killed.
>
> After this the site was abandoned and the launching was interrupted for about a week. The damage done to buildings in the neighborhood

was limited to roofs and window-panes. The latter were even broken at a distance of about 700 meters from the centre of the explosion. Immediately after the failure the Germans spread the rumour that the charge of this rocket had not exploded, but that the oxygen and ethyl alcohol alone had caused the damage. This was not true, the charge had also exploded.

V96.31–32, B112.3–4 Spitfires come roaring in low A British tactical fighter aircraft, the Spitfire was produced continuously from 1937 to 1945 in forty different models, over twenty thousand planes in all.

V97.9–10, B112.27 her record with Mussert's people Adrian Mussert headed up the Dutch Fascist party, or NSB (V95.3n), and collaborated without reservation in all operations the Nazis carried out in Holland, including the deportation of Jews to concentration camps and the deployment of V-weapons used against England. He was quickly tried and hanged after the Allies liberated Holland in 1945.

V97.11–12, B112.29–30 a Luftwaffe resort near Scheveningen To the immediate west of The Hague lies the coastal resort of Scheveningen, a town the German air force (the Luftwaffe) used for recreating and resting crews. It is also the site where Pirate Prentice picks up Katje for her trip to England.

V97.17–18, B112.36–37 "Want the Change," Rilke said, "O be inspired by the Flame!" From sonnet 12 in part 2 of Rainer Maria Rilke's *Sonnets to Orpheus* (1922). In the German this sonnet begins with the exhortation "Wolle die Wandlung. O sei für die Flamme begeistert." Pynchon uses the Leishman translation of 1957. The context of Blicero's thoughts just following this quotation makes it clear that he regards love from the standpoint of a decadent and very *literary* romanticism: "To laurel, to nightingale, to wind . . . ," he thinks, recalling subjects of the great romantic odes—Shelley's "Ode to the West Wind" and Keats's "Ode to a Nightingale," for instance.

V97.27, B113.7–8 her questing shoulders like wings On first glance the simile would seem to make of Katje a type of angel. Later, one will look back with the recollection that Leni Pökler has similarly winglike shoulders (see V162.37 and V218.31), and one of Vaslav Tchitcherine's lovers, Luba, is similarly endowed (see V339.35n). There is, in short, a striking homology among the various women, something deepened by subsequent images of the Angel of Death that "swooped in" on Walter Rathenau (V164.37) or of Rilke's "Tenth-Elegy angel coming, wingbeats already at the edges of waking" (V341.37–38). This angel, in sum, seems to presage a transition to the Other Side, to Death's other kingdom.

V97.34–35, B113.16 all Märchen und Sagen Respectively, the Germanic fairy tales and myths.

V98.1–2, B113.25–26 Und nicht einmal . . . this Tenth Elegy Pynchon

cribs his translation from Leishman and Spender's edition; see V98.7–8 for his rendering of the German. The reference throughout this paragraph is to the tenth of Rilke's *Duino Elegies*, especially lines 104–5:
Einsam steigt er dahin, in Die Berge des Urlieds,
Und nicht enmal sein Schritt aus dem tonlosen Los.
Leishman and Spender translate them as follows:
Alone he climbs to the mountains of Primal Pain,
And never once does his step resound from the soundless Fate.
Note how Pynchon diverges from this: he has "ring" instead of "resound," "not" for "never," "Destiny" instead of "Fate."

V98.7, B113.32–33   wildly alien constellations overhead Because Weissmann has journeyed to the Southern Hemisphere and doesn't know the constellations there. In Rilke's "Pain Land," the Angel teaches the traveler names for these "new" stars "up in the southern sky" (Elegy 10, 88–95). See also V99.35.

V98.24, B114.11–12   the Ufa-theatre on the Friedrichstrasse See Kracauer's description (48) of the "Ufa-Palast am Zoo," Berlin's "largest movie theatre" located on the Friedrichstrasse. "Ufa" stands for Universum Film A.G. During the Great War it was Germany's premier film studio, mainly because of backing from a War Department that wanted films made on nationalistic themes. Kracauer (36) writes that "the official mission of Ufa was to advertise Germany according to government directives. These asked not only for direct screen propaganda, but also for films characteristic of German culture and films serving the purpose of national education." After the war these controls were relinquished and Ufa became home to Germany's best-known, most creative directors, including Fritz Lang, Ernst Lubitsch, and Rudolf Pabst (see V112.33n).

V98.39, B114.30   royal moths the Flame has inspired That "Flame" is once more the fire of transformation in Rilke's sonnet 12 (see V97.17–18n). The royal moth is the *Saturnia pavonia* of Europe and Asia Minor, noted for its high-flying abilities when the moon is full.

V99.2, B114.35   a Wandervogel The term is best defined in a generic sense, as it applies to the remarkable proliferation of youth movements in Germany from 1900 to 1930. Ideologically varied, all the *Wandervogel* (wayward-bird) groups put the highest premium on organic wholeness, usually expressed as a pantheistic love of nature and mystical bonds to the fatherland. They romanticized medieval Germany as a refuge from petty commercialism and fragmented knowledge. Strong Oedipal forces were also behind the movement: Hans Bluhler (quoted in Bullock 38), its first "historian" (in 1913), explicitly claimed: "The period that produced the *Wandervogel* is characterized by a struggle of youth against age," in which Germany's alienated youth sought to form "a great confederation of friendship." In practice, this meant that a powerful air of homoeroticism was soon noticeable in many of the groups. The *Wandervogeln* often planned visits to venerable ruins, where they celebrated with plenty of folksinging around campfires, and during the twenties one group of *Wandervogel* songs was a ten-year best-seller in Germany. In literature, the groups preferred Stefan George and Rilke; in daily life, they were fastidious about their diet and health, usually forbidding the use of alcohol and tobacco, and often also meat. This, then, was the generation of Germans who marched enthusiastically toward the battlefields of World War I and, after the bitter truce, were ready to follow one of their own, Adolf Hitler.

V99.4–5, B114.38   nicht wahr?   Is it not?

V99.24–25, B115.19–21   to Südwest . . . the Kalahari   South-West Africa again, and its dominant geographical feature, the Kalahari Desert.

V99.34–35, B115.33   new stars of Pain-Land   The reference is to lines 88–90 of Rilke's Tenth Elegy:

And higher, the stars. New ones. Stars of the Land of Pain.
Slowly she [the Angel] names them.

V99.38, B115.37   to crush the great Herero Rising   South-West Africa became a German territory in 1884, under Chancellor Bismarck. Charitably described, the colonial plan amounted to little more than a protection scam. The Hereros, who had often been at war with neighboring tribes of Hottentots and Bondels, were offered "protection" in exchange for mineral rights to the precious diamond fields. The Herero chieftains soon saw through all this, however, and they rose up in rebellion against the German overlords in 1904. In August of that year the rebels were dealt a crushing defeat, and the surviving Hereros fled across the scorching Kalahari; those who made the trek had little more than their lives. What followed, for the Germans, was a mopping-up operation conducted for almost two years in a brutal, genocidal manner. Under the Vernichtungs Befehl (Extermination Order) posted by Gen. Lothar von Trotha, any Hereros refusing to submit voluntarily to life in the relocation camps could be summarily executed. By 1906 over two-thirds of the Herero population had perished. The "Rising" Pynchon refers to occurred later, in 1922, when the remaining Hereros banded together with their old enemies, the Bondels and Hottentots, to rise up against the white landowners. Pynchon has written a fictional account of those events in chapter 9 of *V.* German calvary units, supported by light artillery, put down the insurrection in two months.

V100.2–3, B116.2–3   We make Ndjambi Karunga now, omuhona   Luttig, Pynchon's principle source on the Herero, devotes the first chapter of his dissertation to Ndjambi Karunga, the divine creator of all Herero people, according to their myths. What is more interesting in this context of homosexual love, the god is also bisexual. Ndjambi

Karunga appears in Herero creation tales as the father of all being
and generally a benevolent deity. But while he is thus "the god of life,"
he is also "the master of death" (Luttig 8); and in that aspect he is,
in sum, the Herero version of Lord Death, *Blicero*. The god's bisexuality
is signified, Luttig explains (9), in the name itself: "Ndjambi reveals
more the characteristics of a [masculine] heavenly god and Karunga
those of a [feminine] god of the earth." He passes on these dual traits—
lord of the "other world" of the dead, as well as lord of *this* world—
to Mukuru, the mythical first man. And in his turn the *omuhona*,
Mukuru's embodiment in Herero society, also serves a dual role according to Luttig: not only "chief" but a "living Mukuru," and thus a
lineal descendent of the mythical creation tree, the *omumborumbanga*
(see V321.40–322.1n). As "one who has been proven" to be the inheritor
of these traits, the *omuhona* also embodies the bisexual principle
of his origin (Luttig 33–34). As one aspect of his lineal descent from
Ndjambi Karunga, the *omuhona* maintains a leather thong tied in
knots signifying each member of the tribe.

V100.25, B116.31 deep in the Harz The Harz Mountains of central
Germany, site of the Nordhausen underground rocket works.

V100.27, B116.32–33 auf Wiedersehen Good-bye.

**V100.34–38, B116.42–117.4 The Bodenplatte . . . red circle with a
thick black cross inside** Once more the source is Kooy and Uytenbogaart: for the compass bearing of 260 degrees (285) and, a few pages
further (287), for the detail about how trees were used in "determining
the direction of London with respect to the launching site. The trees
were always provided with marks for that purpose. The launching table
[that is, the *Bodenplatte*] was then placed in the triangle bounded
by those trees." The "red circle with a thick black cross" inside is from
the same text (467); comparing it to "a rude mandala" or a "swastika" is
Pynchon's touch.

**V101.1–2, B117.9–10 scratched in the bark . . . the words In hoc signo
vinces** A wonderful allusion. The Latin proclaims: "In this sign
you shall conquer." According to Edward Gibbon (chap. 20), whose
source was the Roman historian Eusebius, the emperor Constantine was
converted to Christianity when "the miraculous sign [of the cross]
was displayed in the heavens whilst he meditated for the Italian expedition." The phrase was inscribed horizontally on that airborne crucifix,
and its truth was affirmed when Constantine's troops were victorious.
Like his predecessor, Diocletian, Constantine was also called
Dominus. But readers may also want to examine the insignia on a
package of Pall Mall cigarettes, with its two lions rampant in the heral-
dic design and the same phrase inscribed below them. Still, the sure
source of this detail is Kooy and Uytenbogaart (467) again; they tell of
"a German who wrote in Duindigt Park at Wassenaar, under one of

the familiar red circles with the black cross with two nails in the middle
. . . *In hoc signo vinces.* He did not live to see his prophecy fulfilled."

**V101.7–9, B117.17–19   black India-rubber cables . . . the Dutch grid's
380 volts**   From Kooy and Uytenbogaart (284): "Some india-rubber cables were laid from the Rijksstraatweg via the Rus en Vrengdlan,
which established connection with the normal electrical network (volt-
age 380 volts/50 cycles)."

V101.9, B117.19   *Erwartung*   German for a sense of anticipation,
foreboding. *Erwartung* is also the title of a 1922 monodrama by composer Arnold Schönberg. His libretto presents a woman looking for
her lover in the midst of a pitch-black forest. Her estrangement, coupled
with the imagined horrors of the dark, soon overwhelms the woman
with feelings of *Erwartung* for the man's fate. When she finds him dead
she lapses into insanity. Theodor Adorno (42–43) wrote of the opera's
musical score that it "is polarized according to extremes: towards
gestures of shock resembling bodily convulsions on the one hand, and
on the other towards a crystalline standstill of a human being whom
anxiety causes to freeze in her tracks." *Erwartung*, he continues,
can be interpreted as the analytic case study, in music and verse, of
"fashionable alienation," even the enjoyment of psychic pain. Like
Rilke's depiction of "Pain-Land" in the *Duino Elegies* (1922, the year *Erwartung* was composed and the year Weissmann goes to South-West
Africa), Schönberg's opera is yet another reference point for the state of
Captain Weissmann's psyche, as shaped as by German expressionism.

V101.19–20, B117.33   a color-negative, yellow and blue   The most
useful discussion of color symbolism in *GR* appears in Hayles and Eiser,
who identify white, red, and black as "the basic triad"; within it,
red consistently symbolizes a burst of passion deflecting characters
from the routinized, mechanically achromatic opposition, white/black.
Yellow and blue are complements: yellow appears yellow because
it absorbs light in the blue range; the opposite holds for blue. Combining
blue and yellow wavelengths yields white; shining blue light on a
yellow background makes it appear black. As Hayles and Eiser (11) explain, this "complementarity is the physical basis for the code connecting Gottfried and Enzian, and explains how they can literally
be each other's shadow-images." Still more interesting, Gottfried and
Enzian will both be launched aloft in V-2 rockets: the white, Gottfried,
in the 00000 while clad in the black Imipolex shroud (see Greta
Erdmann's recollection, at V488.2); the black, Enzian, in the 00001,
while trying not only to repeat Gottfried's firing but also to coun-
terbalance his whiteness and thus to "recreate the coming together
of opposites that marked the center of the Herero village" (Hayles and
Eiser 12; but see also V321.3–4n). This always-insufficient approach
to the "Holy Center" is, as Hite argues ("'Holy Center-Approach-

ing'"), one of Pynchon's organizing metaphors for *GR*. Note, for example, that its accomplishment could only exist outside the novel, after the V-2 falls in the last episode of *GR*. Another instance of incompletion.

V101.23–26, B117.38–41   Bringt doch der Wanderer . . . gelben und blaun Enzian   These yellows and blues are from Rilke's Ninth Elegy, lines 29–31. Leishman and Spender translate them:

For the wanderer doesn't bring from the mountain slope
A handful of earth to the valley, untellable earth, but only
Some word he has won, a pure word, of yellow and blue gentian.

V102.14–15, B118.34–35   the archer and his son, and the shooting of the apple   In the story of Wilhelm Tell—for example, in the Rossini opera.

V102.29, B119.9   a Stuka pilot   The German-produced Junkers 87, or "Stuka," a two-man dive-bomber used throughout the war.

V103.5, B119.30   Mutti   German: mother.

V103.10–11, B119.37–38   *If you cannot sing Siegfried at least you can carry a spear*   In actor's argot, a spear-carrier is an extra.

V103.25–26, B120.14–15   the word *bitch* . . . will give him an erection   This turns into a bit of vital information. Not only does it remind one of Slothrop's seeming erection reflex; in part 3 we also discover that "the word bitch" works the same magic on Franz Pökler (V429.21–22n). So the reference links all three characters, as if in a rocket clan.

V104.18, B121.12–13   a precious TerBorch   Gerard Terborch (1617–81), a Dutch artist known for his portraits of commoners and depictions of everyday scenes.

V104.19, B121.13   Bombs fall to the west in the Haagsche Bosch.   According to Kooy and Uytenbogaart (286–87), "Schuszstelle 16" (their transliteration of the German *Schußtelle*) was located in this *Bosch*, or woods, but only "three or four" rockets were launched from there.

V104.25, B121.21   oude genever   Dutch: "old gin."

V104.30–31, B121.27–28   where the great airborne adventure lies bogged for the winter   English parachutists under the command of Field Marshall Montgomery were dropped behind German lines, at Arnhem, on September 17, 1944. Montgomery's adventuresome plan was to trap the German units stationed in Holland. It failed. Resistance proved to be stronger than he anticipated, and by December the English lines were still located south of The Hague, on the Scheldt River, where they remained through the winter.

V105.20, B122.21   flimsies   British secretarial argot for thin sheets of paper used to make carbon copies of documents.

V106.6, B123.13   a bulky, ancient Schwarzlose   An 11-millimeter, oil-cooled machine gun manufactured in Austria and used principally during the Great War.

V106.12, B123.20–21   the windmill known as "The Angel"   The Dutch windmills are often named. "The Angel," Katje's rendezvous point with Pirate, will be described in greater detail at V535.36–536.2. Then its wheel blossoms into a mandala-like image that *seems* to be reflected in Blicero's eyes on the day when Rocket 00000 is fired (V670.15–16n). Prior to this we have also noted London's Windmill Club in Picadilly (V39.1–2n).

V106.33–37, B124.4–9   Bela Lugosi . . . perhaps *Dumbo*   Osbie Feel's "All-Time List" of his favorite films takes no special order. *White Zombie* (1932) stars Bela Lugosi and Madge Bellamy in the story of an island sugar mill operated by zombies under the control of a megalomaniac (Lugosi). *Son of Frankenstein* (1939) stars Lugosi, Basil Rathbone, and Boris Karloff; in this version of the story, the famous doctor's son meets his father's monster. *Flying Down to Rio* (1933) stars Dolores del Rio and Gene Raymond, with appearances by Fred Astaire and Ginger Rogers; the plot is light comedy, with Raymond torn between flying airplanes and playing piano. *Freaks* (1932) will appear several more times in *GR*. Since its release, the film has slowly won recognition as a classic of horror. It initially brought storms of protest because of the midgets, Siamese twins, and other "freaks of nature" cast by director Tod Browning. At first it was banned in most European countries, England included; but underground showings were common enough so that, as Sadoul notes, it was acclaimed at Cannes in 1962. *Dumbo* (1941) is the Walt Disney animated film that almost disappeared, for a time, because of its racist depiction of the character Jim ("Hush Mah Beak") Crow. Here, Osbie hallucinates the face of Labor Minister Ernest Bevin in place of young Dumbo the elephant.

V107.23, B124.40   "the bloody Mendoza"   A lightweight machine gun developed in 1934 by Rafael Mendoza, for the Mexican army. The gun weighed 11 kilograms, over three times the 3.5 kilograms of the British Sten gun (V20.10n). Most of the Mendoza's features were traditional; the unique thing about it was the double-ended firing pin. In case of a broken pin—a common fault in light-action machine guns—one could quickly remove the firing bolt and reverse the pin; no need to rummage through one's kit bag for a replacement while an enemy advanced. This is the basis for Pirate's trade-off. The Mendoza was much heavier and used an odd-sized shell, but it was safer.

V107.26, B125.1   Portobello Road   A narrow winding street in London's North Kensington district, with shops and covered markets on one side, covered stalls on the other. Until 1948 it was home to the Caledonian Market, nicknamed "The Stones" because that is what its impoverished tradesmen slept on. Portobello has lost its rough edges and

its preterite, but Pynchon knows it through books—Baedeker's, no
doubt—where its reputation as a mean street would make it a likely
place to find a scarce size of ammunition ("7 mm Mexican Mauser") for
Pirate's Mendoza.

V107.34–35, B125.12   *façonné* velvet   Katje wears a stiff, formal gown
of red *molded* velvet.

V108.12–13, B125.32–33   ic heb u liever . . . goude ghewracht   The
Bantam edition misprints this Middle Dutch lyric as "ic heb u liever."
The source is Grimm (213), who translates:

I hold you dearer than a boar-swine
All were it of fine gold y-wrought.

Grimm notes that the lines derive from a Middle Dutch romance,
Lantslot ende Sandrin, verse 374, wherein the gentle knight makes
this tender declaration of love to his lady. As Grimm explains, the Norse
god Freyr (also Frey), a god of peace and love, often appeared with
a boar in attendance (see V94.26n). At Yuletide, "atonement boars"
were offered up to the god in anticipation of a year's peace and fruitful-
ness. Other "golden boars" in Norse and Teutonic myth attest to
Freyr's popularity, for the god embodied a wholly creative, generative
principle. He may even have been as powerful a god, in primitive
Teutonic culture, as Wuotan or Thunar.

V108.17–18, B125.40–41   off to Mauritius . . . toting his haakbus   The
Dutch twice tried to colonize the island of Mauritius, off the coast
of East Africa. In 1638 they tried to garrison a port where trading ships
could reprovision, but they abandoned the effort in 1658. Six years
later the Dutch East India Company, with whom Frans van der Groov
is associated, came to the island in force, attempting agricultural
development and the construction of permanent buildings. The company pulled out in 1700, leaving behind over a hundred black slaves. The
agricultural development had failed because of inclement weather,
rats, and shortages of manpower and tools. During this second attempt
the dodo bird (*Didus ineptus*) was brought to extinction, partly because
the Dutch hunted the clumsy creatures, but mostly because they
brought in foraging pigs that ate the dodoes' eggs, laid unprotected in
clumps of grass. Like Pirate Prentice, Frans also prefers to carry an
outmoded firearm. The *haakbus*, from the German for *hak-büsche*, was
a "hook-gun." Curved jaws held a piece of serpentine that was
threaded into the gun's touchhole, where (when lit) it ignited the powder
charge. The design was in wide use throughout Europe in the fifteenth
century, but by the late sixteenth most soldiers preferred the *snaphaan*,
a flintlock weapon. Its serrated metal wheel scraped against a flint,
sparking the powder charge. This was more expensive, more delicate,
and more prone to malfunction than the *haakbus*.

V109.30, B127.19   motionless as any Vermeer   The Dutch painter

Jan van der Meer, or Vermeer for short (1632–75), whose depictions of everday scenes often seemed to freeze motion in a kind of photographic stasis.

V110.6, B127.40 This furious host were losers Frans's Dutch cohorts as a parody, or preterite version, of the *Wütende Heer,* or "Mad Army" of Wuotan (V72.27–28n).

V110.22–23, B128.19 the island of Reunion A former French colony, 110 miles southwest of Mauritius.

V111.7–9, B129.8–11 *For as much as they are the creatures of God ... eternal life to be found* The source of this, evidently a prayer for new colonial subjects, is unknown.

V112.22, B130.37 Charing Cross station Near Whitehall and Trafalgar Square, where Katje departs for the vicinity of Dover and "The White Visitation."

V112.29, B131.4–5 The Zouave has gone back to his unit The Algerian tribesman (see V91.41n) has returned to fight for France ("the Cross of Lorraine").

V112.33, B131.9 Lang, Pabst, Lubitsch The Ufa directors, master craftsmen of German expressionist cinema (see V98.24n).

V112.39, B131.17 Flit American brand of over-the-counter pesticide, still marketed by the Exxon Corporation.

V113.1, B131.21 Meillerwagen A mobile trailer used to transport V-2 rockets to their launching sites; described and pictured in Kooy and Uytenbogaart (364–67).

V113.11, B131.33 rocket-firing site in the Rijkswijksche Bosch Wooded site of "Schuszstelle 19," according to Kooy and Uytenbogaart (287).

V113.36–37, B132.22–23 old, tarnished silver crown Brings readers back full circle to Katje's octopus-conditioning outfit, from the opening of this episode. In part 2 she appears in the same dress, with the same silver crown (see V186.3ff).

EPISODE 15

Internal references establish the date as December 23, 1944. Slothrop, just released after "these recent days" (V114.10) of confinement in St. Veronica's, returns to his cubicle off Grosvenor Square, meets one of his previous girls, and winds up with her in the East End flat of a Mrs. Quoad (Latin for "as much as"). Next, a "hopeless holocaust" (V118.12) of British wine jellies, followed by a vigorous intercourse.

V114.5, B132.29 a Section 8 A discharge for U.S. servicemen deemed unfit for further duty because they were "unable to adapt" to military life (A. M. Taylor). Usually a section eight was given for reasons of

mental instability, the sense at V182.9–10 when Slothrop uses the term
in the context of "raving maniacs." David Mesher (14) points out
that "Slothrop's allusion is to a remote but real hope of being
disqualified from further military service under Section Eight, Army
Regulation 615–360. But that regulation was in force only until July,
1944." Still, the term remained part of service slang for years after
the regulation was revised.

**V114.12–13, B132.37–133.1   on the order of the old woman's arrange-
ment for getting her pig home over the stile**   A reference to an old
folktale. The best version can be found in Clouston's *Popular Tales and
Fictions* (1:295–96). Stith Thompson's *Motif-Index* (5:546) also lists
a number of variants, scattered worldwide. Clouston calls it the story
of "The Old Woman and the Crooked Sixpence" and catalogues it
with types of cumulative stories, such as "The House That Jack Built."
Here, the old woman of the tale finds a crooked coin and buys a pig
with it, but the pig balks at her stile. She asks a dog to bite the pig, but
the dog refuses; so she asks a stick to hit the dog, and it refuses;
whereupon she turns to fire (to burn the stick), water (to douse the
fire), an ox (to lap up the water), a butcher (to slaughter the ox), a
rope (to hang the butcher), a rat (to gnaw the rope), and a cat (to eat
the rat). They all decline in their turn. Yet when the cat asks for a bowl
of milk from a nearby cow, and the cow gives milk after being given
hay, the old woman has milk for the cat, which eats the rat, which
chews the rope, and so on, until the dog bites the pig, which jumps
over the stile.

Clouston traces the tale to a sacred hymn in the Hebrew Talmud;
it also has ten intermediary steps, just as there are ten intermediaries
standing between the straw for the cow (a gift, a sustenance) and
the pig leaping over the stile (obedience, a residence). Note also that
the motif of ten, along with the *hysteron proteron* trope, recurs in
the launch countdown; and Pynchon will later link the motif to the
ten-stage order of Kabbala. Incidentally, there are also ten sounding
holes on Slothrop's Hohner harmonica; and there are ten generations of
Slothrops (and Pynchons). There are further references to Rilke's
Tenth Elegy (98.1–2), to an "aethereal Xth Programme" over the BBC
(V147.7), a ten-step children's game called "Himmel and Hölle"
(V567.25), Slothrop's ten thousand days of life (V624.18), and the ten-
card spread in the Celtic method of Tarot divination (V738.7)—among
many others. However, the main point in this context is Slothrop's
desire to return home and his being lost in a search for some formula,
some catalyst of a chain reaction that will bring him back.

V114.19, B133.8   Woolworth's   The F. W. Woolworth chain of department stores with branches in countless American cities. Here, probably
the store located in London's Marylebone district.

V114.20, B133.10 little-kid-size Enfields The British Arsenal is located at Enfield Lock, the place-name that has been used for decades as if it were the brand name for the various service rifles manufactured there.

V114.21–22, B133.11 his Humber See V24.13–14n.

V114.37–38, B133.30–31 hair flying in telltales, white wedgies clattering . . . an adorable tomato Of these slang terms, Partridge (*Forces' Slang*) tells us that "wedgies" are any women's "wedge-heeled shoes," and he dates the term from "circa 1945." A "tomato" was originally Australian service slang for "an attractive girl," but U.S. servicemen adopted it "circa 1943." "Telltales" are apparently undocumented by students of slang, but a friend explains that they are a way of dressing the hair in pigtails so that they dangle over the ears.

V115.3–4, B133.36–38 greensickness . . . a touch of scurvy These "antiquated diseases" will have turned Mrs. Quoad into nothing less than a rainbow-colored, toad-skinned old hag. Greensickness is an iron-deficiency anemia that turns the skin green. Tetter is an umbrella term for a variety of skin diseases—like worms, herpes, eczema, pimples, pustules, blisters, and milk-blotches. The third, kibes, is a reddish inflammation or chilblain of the feet. Purples are livid blotches, spots, or pustules; the term also sometimes refers to the bubo of the plague. Mrs. Quoad's fifth ailment, imposthumes, appears as open abscesses of the skin, and the next, almonds in the ears, describes the condition of swollen lymph glands. Seventh and last, scurvy is the subcutaneous bleeding, especially at the lips, that results from a vitamin C deficiency.

V115.16–17, B134.9–10 the dome of faraway St. Paul's Though several miles away, the dome of St. Paul's Cathedral, atop Ludgate Hill, would be visible from this East End room.

V115.19, B134.13 Primo Scala's Accordion Band Played over the BBC's General Forces Programme on Saturday, December 23, at 10:30 P.M., and at no other time during the month.

V115.32–33, B134.28–29 all the Compton Mackenzie novels on the shelf If we exclude the sixty or so nonfictional books he published during his long lifetime (1883–1972), even then Mrs. Quoad has a hefty shelf of books. Sir Anthony Edward Montagu Compton Mackenzie published as many novels as there are letters in his name: thirty-six in all. And they are *long* novels, written as if the aim was to crowd every page with detail.

V115.33, B134.29–30 glassy ambrotypes The phrase is somewhat redundant, the "glassy" being implicit in the "ambrotype" itself. In this nineteenth-century photographic process, the light tones are produced on glass by plating it with silver, while the darks are made with black paper backing.

V115.35, B134.31–32   Michaelmas daisies   They bloom for the Feast of St. Michael on September 29.

V115.36–37, B134.33–34   a Wardour Street shop   Located in London's Soho district: once, as Baedeker (*London* 153) explains, "synonymous with imitation-antique furniture"; now the center of London's film industry.

V116.21, B135.21   says Lafitte Rothschild   The two *t*'s in Lafitte are notable, for as Alex Lichine comments, only the very earliest nineteenth-century labels of Chateau Lafite Rothschild used that spelling. The wine is one of France's best, a rich and expensive red bordeaux.

V116.23, B135.24–25   "the Bernkastler Doktor"   Lichine (133) refers to it as "the most famous great Moselle wine," a white German vintage.

V116.24–25, B135.26   "slimy elm things, maple-tasting with a touch of sassafras   Mrs. Quoad means Slothrop's throat aids, Thayer's Slippery Elm Throat Lozenges (V18.8–38n). Billed as "Nature's Gentle Demulcent," since 1847 Thayer's has contained dextrose, elm bark, and vegetable stearate.

V116.35, B135.39   Gilbert & Sullivan   During their twenty-three year collaboration, British dramatist William S. Gilbert (1836–1911) wrote the librettos, and composer Arthur Sullivan (1842–1900) the scores, for such light operas as *The Pirates of Penzance* and *The Mikado*, operas in which Darlene here could be playing the "ingenue" role.

V117.8, B136.11   pure Nightingale compassion   After Florence Nightingale (1820–1910), pioneer of nursing and a founder of the Red Cross.

V117.15–16, B136.20–21   Hop Harrigan . . . Tank Tinker . . . playing his ocarina   Short-lived as a syndicated comic strip in 1941, "Hop Harrigan" did very well as an American radio serial. From 1942 until 1950, Hop ("America's Ace of the Airwaves") used to appear over ABC stations during the early evening hours. He was the pilot, and Tank Tinker his ocarina-playing mechanic of "Aircraft CX-4," which flew them through innumerable melodramatic adventures that made them, by 1945, "the best known juvenile heroes of the war" (Dunning 287). Why the ocarina? Because the U.S. Army issued these little yam-shaped instruments to servicemen headed overseas. Eastman Plastics manufactured ocarinas out of a revolutionary material, Tennite, also used in airplanes. And as a 1944 Eastman ad in *Time* explains: "Ocarinas made of Tennite have furnished the jive for many a jam-session held in foxholes, in canteens behind the lines, and on troop convoys." The army even issued "monthly hit kits," music sheets for popular songs.

V117.38–39, B137.7   a Mills-type hand grenade   The pin-and-lever, pineapple-shaped grenade developed for British troops in the Great War.

V118.1, B137.10   a .455 Webley cartridge   For decades after its introduction in 1868, the Webley was a standard "constabulary" revolver, especially popular in the colonies. Closely resembling the American Colt, it came in calibers of .445, .45, and .455.

V118.2, B137.11   a six-ton earthquake bomb   A twelve-thousand-pound bomb (the second-largest nonnuclear device dropped during the war), carried aloft in British "Lancaster" bombers on night raids. Some were used in the August 17, 1943, raid against Peenemünde (Irving 114–21).

V118.3, B137.12   a licorice bazooka   This is technically out of place in Mrs. Quoad's arsenal of "prewar" (V116.6) candies, because this anti-tank weapon was manufactured and named *during* the war. The name was in honor of American comedian Bob Burns (1896–1956), who played a crude wind instrument—somewhat resembling the weapon—he dubbed the "bazooka."

V118.31, B138.7   the Meggezone   British tradename for a throat lozenge, still registered for U.S. import.

V119.11, B138.30   Bond Street or waste Belgravia   Bond Street is located just two blocks from Slothrop's ACHTUNG "cubicle" (V18.3) off Grosvenor Square. Baedeker (*London* 96) calls Bond Street "the most fashionable shopping district in London for over a century." Similarly, Belgravia is "the most fashionable residential quarter of London" (ibid. 84), located just west of Buckingham palace. The adjective "waste" escapes me.

V119.15, B138.35   tourmalines in German gold   Tourmaline is a precious gem, a columnar silicoborate crystal that has a vitreous luster; it is mined in Ceylon and generally set in gold.

V119.16, B138.36   ebony finger-stalls   These provide protection for the digits during procedures "in some handicrafts, in dissection, or when the finger is diseased" (*OED*).

V119.30–31, B139.12–13   usurped the throne in 1878 during the intrigues over Bessarabia   During the summer of 1878 Europe's great diplomats—chief among them Bismarck of Germany and Beaconsfield of England—met in Berlin to settle the "Eastern Question." Russia's defeat of Turkey in the 1876 war, insurrections in several Balkan states (Serbia, Bosnia, Montenegro, Hercegovina), as well as the competing interests of Austria, Germany, and Russia—all these factors necessitated a "summit" conference. Each nation wanted a piece of the strategic action around the Dardanelles. Britain, for example, wanted to rein in the Russians and needed both access to and stability in the Dardanelles for the benefit of its Middle Eastern and African colonies. It was at the 1878 Berlin conference that Austria was allowed to garrison the sanjak of Novi Pazar (V14.34–36n); the nation-state of Bulgaria was created; Greece obtained Crete, Thessaly, and a portion of Macedonia; and Russia was given a strip of Bessarabia, while Romania lost a portion of it. Pynchon aptly calls the conference a business of "intrigues."

The Balkan states and Bessarabia had glimpsed a promise of independence when Russia defeated their Turkish overlords. Instead of independence, however, England and Germany maneuvered to install new overlords (the Austro-Hungarian Empire) in an effort to buttress the region against Russian expansion. England thus helped put into motion the sequence of events that led up to the Great War and, by extension, World War II. King Yrjo is wholly fictional, a carry-over from Pynchon's 1964 short story, "The Secret Integration." In this scene he is remembered touching Mrs. Quoad's throat, to cure her scrofula by the "miracle touch" associated with kings (see V119.33n, V119.37n).

V119.32, B139.14   golden galloons   From the French noun *galon*, a gold or silver braid or lace.

V119.33, B139.16   King's Evil   Scrofula, a condition affecting the tissues of young victims (like Mrs. Quoad, whose reminiscence harks back more than sixty years before 1944). Usually the affliction takes the form of lymphatic swelling, jaundice, respiratory infection, or tuberculosis. Those tracing the manifold references to pigs in *GR* note that *scrofa* is the Latin for "sow" and that scrofula got its name from the swelling in the "small sows" or lymphatic glands, which is why Mrs. Quoad must be touched in "the hollow of [her] throat" (V119.36–37). Scrofula was once known as "the King's Evil" in France and England, but the practice of royal cures was ended with the death of Queen Anne in 1714; five years later the office for this ceremony was removed from *The Book of Common Prayer*.

V119.37, B139.20   the miracle touch   Here, the cure for King's Evil. Yet the phrase also functions as a bridge into episode 16, which opens with the analeptic recall of "the very first touch" of Roger and Jessica. The idea of touching also forms an invitation at novel's end: "There is time, if you need the comfort, to touch the person next to you."

EPISODE 16

A chapter of chronologically unstructured analepses focalized through Roger and Jessica, which conclude by returning readers to the night of December 23. This date is established through several references to Christmas caroling, references taken from that day's *Times* of London stories. The Advent season and the carols establish a theme of anticipated redemption.

V120.29–30 B140.20–21   She came twice . . . important to both of them   Note that the reversal of cause and effect, of intercourse and orgasm or stimulus and response, is another instance of *hysteron* *proteron*. And the homology of these events with V-2 rocket strikes and other "trans-marginal" phenomena in *GR* might explain why this is "important to both of them." Their romance coincides, chronologically and virtually, with the rocket blitz.

V121.13–14, B141.8–9   at the Tivoli watching Maria Montez and Jon Hall   The Tivoli Theatre is located on the Strand in central London. A *Times* of London "Picture Theatres" guide reveals that from November 20 until December 10, *Gypsy Wildcat*, featuring Montez and Hall, was featured at the Tivoli.

V121.14–15, B141.9–10   peccaries in Regents Park Zoo   By 1940 the Zoological Gardens in Regents Park (in north-central London) housed the largest known collection of captive animals, nearly seven thousand species. Of them the American peccary would interest Pynchon because it's a wild boar.

V121.23, B141.21   the Bofors   A Swedish-made antiaircraft cannon.

V121.25, B141.23   The Mayfair Hotel   Should be "May Fair," for the hotel located on Berkeley Street in London's Mayfair district.

V121.29, B141.28   "Time enough for several assignations"   Roger riffs on T. S. Eliot's 1917 poem, "The Love Song of J. Alfred Prufrock":
And time yet for a hundred indecisions,
And for a hundred visions and revisions
Before the taking of a toast and tea. (ll. 32–34)

V121.35–36, B141.35–36   Roland Peachey and his Orchestra playing "There, I Said It Again"   The band is another (like Falkman and His Apache Band) that Pynchon derived from the *Times* of London BBC broadcasting schedules. The timing of this analepsis is indeterminate, as is the date of Peachey's performance. The song title is in error; it should be "There! I've Said It Again." The lyric, written in 1941 by Redd Evans and Dave Mann, was a million-seller for Boston bandleader Vaughn Monroe in 1944:
I love you, there's nothing to hide,
It's better than burning inside;
I love you, no use to pretend,
There! I've said it again.
And so on, in the same vein.

V122.24–25, B142.31–32   blue-petaled pergolas   Another parabolic archway. In ornate, high-ceilinged houses, a trellis-work pergola will have vines and flowering plants trained over it.

V122.28–29, B142.37–38   motoring up . . . near Lower Beeding   On the trunk road from "The White Visitation" (near Brighton) to London, Roger and Jessica would pass through the village of Lower Beeding, a few miles north of Tunbridge Wells.

V123.18, B143.29   ctenophile   Pynchon's portmanteau word, from the Greek *kten-* (comb) and *-philos* (loving); thus a "comb lover."

V124.12, B144.30   bit of the je ne sais quoi de sinistre   Bit of the "sinister something-or-other."

V124.24–25, B145.5–6   Turn off that faucet, Dorset   In the same spirit as "Girl in distress, Jess?" (V127.15) or "Got a fag, Mag?" (V127.18). A. M. Taylor compiled a list of rhymes like these, many of which became popular wartime songs, such as "A Fellow on a Furlough," and "Good Bye, Mama, I'm Off to Yokohama."

V125.19, B146.5   a Mersyside Labour branch   A British Labour party branch operating out of the industrial city of Liverpool, on the river Mersey.

V125.21, B146.7   on demob   In British wartime argot, on "demobilization," when released from military service.

V125.22, B146.8   the G-5-to-be   A. M. Taylor (88) explains that G-5 was designated as that "section of the Army set up to take over local government in lands occupied by invasion forces. Other sections are G-1 personnel, G-2 Intelligence, G-3 Training and Plans, G-4 Supply and Evacuation."

V125.25, B146.12–13   were-elves   These are unique in the annals of folklore.

V126.19, B147.12–13   this seventh Christmas of the War   A miscount: from the German invasion of Poland in September 1939 until V-J day in August 1945, this war encompassed six Christmas days. On the next page Pynchon gets it right: "six years of slander, ambition and hysteria" (V127.12–13).

V126.22, B147.16   stale Woodbines   A medium-priced brand of British cigarette, frequent *Times* of London advertiser.

V127.10, B148.8–9   Grafty Green, Kent   Unknown, if not fictional.

V127.16, B148.16   On the Tannoy   Registered trademark for a British radio, comparable to the American Capehart (V66.39n).

V127.19–20, B148.20–21   like a bloody Garbo film . . . nicotine starvation   In films like *Grand Hotel* and *Mata Hari*, actress Greta Garbo characteristically appears with a cigarette in hand.

V128.2–3, B149.6   the Star ready to be pasted up   The reference is to the traditional Advent calendar, marking off the days to Christmas.

V128.8, B149.12   but def   Slang abbreviation for "but definitely," an instance, also, of Zipf's "Principle of Least Effort."

V128.35, B150.3   High Holborn Street   Jamaicans grabbed, from London, the name for this downtown Kingston street.

V129.6–7, B150.18   a compline service   Held during the last of the seven canonical hours, just before retiring, and usually at 8 P.M.

V129.8–16, B150.20–29   Thomas Tallis, Henry Purcell, even a German macronic . . . attributed to Heinrich Suso . . . *Alpha es et O*   The word "macronic" (in the Viking; it is corrected in the Bantam) is a misprint; it should be "macaronic," a lyric composed in several different languages. The details for this interlude of caroling derive, directly and indirectly, from a story entitled "Macaronic Carols" in the *Times* of London (December 22, 1944, 6). The writer takes Suso's carol, "In dulci jubilo," as an example, commenting:

> No simpler or more persuasive demonstration of the unity of Christendom (even at the very time of the Reformation) and the universality of Latin could well be found than this example of macaronic verse, in which the vernacular and Latin are arranged so closely as to preserve the syntax of both tongues. There is argument over whether carols have a popular or clerical origin. The conclusion of the argument, according to Richard Leighton Greene in *The Early English Carols*, is that while the carol is not pure folk song, i.e. a product of communal growth and oral transmission, it is popular in its use of familiar phrases, and the Latin tags do not take it beyond the reach of the illiterate man who heard them constantly in church.

Suso was a German composer of the late fifteenth and early sixteenth centuries. The subject of this carol is Christ's nativity; the *Times* gives a translation:

> In sweet jubilation
> Let us our homage sing
> Our hearts' joy
> Reclines in the manger
> And shines like the sun
> In his mother's lap
> Alpha he is, and Omega.

The *Times* article does not mention the other two composers, but Greene's *Early English Carols*, to which Pynchon evidently turned next, gives the background. Thomas Tallis (1505–85) was organist at the Chapel Royal under Henry VIII and Queen Mary. Henry Purcell (1659–95) was also employed, like Tallis, at the Chapel Royal. He was a composer of devotional songs and, before his early death, wrote a number of songs for the Restoration stage. The *Times* also gives notice of caroling scheduled for the London area on Saturday, December 23, the time of Roger and Jessica's stop at this church.

V130.15, B151.35 from Harrow to Gravesend Harrow, twelve miles northwest of central London, is the home of Harrow School, where new Byrons and Churchills (two of its illustrious graduates) might be brushing their teeth before "quicksilver mirrors." Gravesend, twenty-four miles east of London on the mouth of the Thames, once was a popular resort. The two towns are also the rough boundaries within which the V-2 rockets fell, according to Irving's map (262).

V130.24, B152.4 Household Milk A packaged, price-controlled, dehydrated milk product sold to the British throughout the war under the auspices of the Ministry of Foods. Like the dried eggs at V252.16–17, it was frequently advertised in the *Times*, with recipes.

V131.1, B152.26   ein Volk ein Führer   Nazi propaganda slogan, "One people, one Leader!"

V131.11, B152.38–39   the Rundstedt offensive   See V52.23–24n.

V131.22–24, B153.10–13   Will he show up under the Star . . . Bring to the serai gifts of tungsten, cordite, high-octane?   A *serai* is the palace of an eastern sultan (*OED*). Here, it is imagined as inverting Christ's Nativity: the gifts of these "Magi" are brought to the sultan's palace, not to the savior's preterite birth site; and—instead of gold, frankincense, and myrrh—they are gifts of modern war materials (compare Matt. 2:10–11).

V132.3–4, B153.38–39   the prisoners are back from Indo-China   The source was a *Times* of London story entitled "Ordeal of War Prisoners" (December 20, 1944, 2). In September 1944 some twenty thousand British prisoners of war were rescued from labor camps in Siam (now Thailand). The Japanese had used sixty thousand prisoners of varying nationalities to build roads through the jungles. Of these, some twenty-five thousand died of malnutrition, disease, and brutal beatings. The *Times* story concerns the difficulty of their return to British society. Most had psychological problems, as signified by their "eyes from Burma, from Tonkin" (V132.14).

132.11, B154.5–6   Mr. Morrison   Herbert Morrison, minister of Home Security.

V132.16, B154.11–12   headaches no Alasils can cure   An American brand of aspirin pain-relieving tablets.

V132.20–21, B154.16–18   If these Eyeties sing . . . bet it's not "Giovinezza" but . . . *Rigoletto* or *La Bohème*   What the "Horst Wessel Lied" was to German Nazis, "Giovinezza" (Youth) was to the Italian Fascists under Benito Mussolini. After the Italian surrender, they would be careful to sing, instead, bits from light operas by (respectively) Verdi and Puccini.

V132.26, B154.24   Boxing Day   December 26, when the British give gifts, especially to servants and workers.

V132.31–32, B154.31–32   no *mano morto* for the Englishmen back from CBI   The former prisoners recently returned from the China-Burma-India theater of war are given no magical remedy. Folk superstition holds that a dead hand (the *mano morto*) has various powers as charm and miracle cure (see S. Thompson, 6:859–60). For an illicit, black-magic use of such a hand see V750.33n.

V132.37, 154.38   If the brave new world should also come about   Recalling Aldous Huxley's vision of a completely routinized society in his novel *Brave New World* (1932), the title of which was bagged from

Shakespeare's *Tempest* (V.i.183): "O brave new world, / That has such people in it!"

V133.3–4, B155.5–6 children have unfolded last year's toys and found reincarnated Spam tins Spam is a brand of canned meat product; the source for this otherwise curious detail is a *Times* of London story entitled "Toys from Spam Tins" (December 9, 1944, 2): "Months of painstaking, spare-time effort by men and women in barrage units and anti-aircraft batteries in Greater London have been largely responsible for the production of over 6,000 toys for Abbey District Entertainments, which intends to distribute the toys at children's parties and among hospitals, clinics, and day care nurseries in eight London boroughs at Christmas." The toy "railway engines, lorries, tanks, dolls, and animals, which are both attractive and durable," were made from the tins of Spam and canned fish by folks like Jessica and Jeremy, in their A-A batteries.

V133.14–15, B155.19 the Radio Doctor asking, What Are Piles? The "Radio Doctor" was a regular, weekly, five-minute program of the BBC Home Service Programme. At 6:25 P.M. on December 14, for example, he answered the question "What Are Boils?"

V133.29–30, B155.37 even Big Ben The clock tower at Westminster.

V134.24–25, B156.39–40 strange thousand-year sigh—*eia, wärn wir da!* Another line from Suso's "In dulci jubilo," the translation of which ("were we but there") Pynchon derives from the *Times* story (V129.8– 16n).

V134.40–135.1, B157.18–19 Mr. Noel Coward . . . packing them into the Duchess for the fourth year The play was Coward's *Blithe Spirit*, and the edition of the *Times* that discussed the macaronic carols also proclaimed the "Fourth Year" for the play at the city's Duchess Theatre, on Catharine Street. The action centers on a writer, Charles Condamine, who holds a séance; havoc breaks loose when his late wife materializes.

V135.2–3, B157.21–22 Walt Disney causing Dumbo the elephant to clutch to that feather See V106.33–37n.

V135.7, B157.27 the 88 fell An 88–millimeter canon shell.

V135.33, B158.18 SPQR Record-keeping The acronym stands for *Senatus Populusque Romanus* (The Senate and People of Rome), an official inscription on governmental documents of the Roman Empire. In financial circles, it also means "small profits and quick returns."

V135.38, B158.23–24 "Wendell Willkie . . . Churchill? . . . 'Arry Pollitt!" Respectively, they are Wendell Willkie, the surprise American presidential candidate of the 1940 election, whose book *One World* was a best-seller and whose death in October 1944 might mean that a chaplin's prayers would be for a safe passage heavenward; Winston

Churchill (1874–65), Britain's prime minister from 1940 to 1945; and
Harry Pollitt, leader of the British Communist party during the thirties.
V136.6–7, B158.35–36   O Jesu parvule, / Nach dir ist mir so weh   Two
more lines from Suso's carol, "In dulci jubilo." The *Times* translation
gives: "O little Jesus, / I am so sad for you." Sad? Exactly, because
he is born in such preterite surroundings and is fated to die on the Cross.

EPISODE 17

The time of this episode is indistinct, though from its placement it
would seem to occur on Sunday, December 24, 1944. By the time of
"this late English winter" day Slothrop already "ought to be on the Riviera"
(V143.24), the general location for part 2 of *GR*. The timing here is noteworthy: within a day of his release from St. Veronica's, Slothrop has been sent
to the south of France; moreover, we learn in this episode that a V-2 has
struck the ward in which Slothrop had his chemically induced excremental
fantasies. Pointsman sees this coincidence as confirming the determinist
interpretation of Slothrop's enigmatic sex organ, and he imagines himself
winning the Nobel Prize for finding the pathway through this mazy mystery. In fact, the story of Theseus's triumph over the Minotaur and the
Cretan labyrinth emerges in this episode as the mythic counterpart to
Pointsman's Pavlovian science of the brain.

V136.25, B159.18   Paradoxical phase   This is Pointsman diagnosing
the effects of his own exhaustion, much as (according to Horsley
Gantt) Pavlov used to diagnose the progressive effects of his own se-
nility. On the "paradoxical phase" see V48.38–39n.

V136.27, B159.20   Mosquitoes and Lancasters   The Mosquito was
the war's first radar-equipped night fighter, a light, fast, dual-engine
British airplane in service from 1942 on. The Lancaster was a four-en-
gine bomber plane in use from 1940 on.

V137.20, B160.16–17   You set out to the left   As Borges notes in his
story "The Garden of Forking Paths" (*Ficciones* 93), in a labyrinth
one turns to the left because "such was the common formula for finding
the central courtyard." The left is also the "sinister" side (see V138.3)
and that of the unconscious mind. Discussing mandala symbolism, Jung
(*Collected Works* 12:127) explains how "a leftward movement is
equivalent to movement in the direction of the unconscious, whereas
a movement to the right is 'correct' and aims at consciousness."
Elsewhere in his writings Jung connects rightward and leftward movement to, respectively, clockwise and counterclockwise cycles.
These motifs correspond with examples of mandalas that have laby-
rinthine patterns, where a leftward, counterclockwise pathway leads to

the center (see fig. 4 in *Collected Works*, vol. 9). By thus turning left-ward, counterclockwise, and into the unconscious, Pointsman in his dream becomes one of many characters in *GR* (like Slothrop and Enzian) who approach a "Holy Center" but never reach it. For an excellent discussion of this trope see Hite (*Ideas* 21–32).

V138.22, B161.27 Spectro$_E$ Subscript E because the late Kevin Spectro calls the word "Foxes" to Pointsman through Carroll Eventyr, whom we recall as the medium at the séance of episode 5.

V138.35–36, B162.2–3 helping fill out the threes prediction The Poisson equation can yield a prediction for the possibility of *three* rocket strikes per square of mapped territory. It is *very* low.

V139.36, B163.8–9 back to pigs Pigs are blocks of crude, impure cast iron. Notice also the *hysteron proteron* trope in this "Abreaction" (V139.34): from sheet metal back to raw earth.

V140.5–10, B163.21–26 this power series . . . number of wars per year The mathematical formula here is a working out of Poisson's equation. The variable terms—2!, 3!, and so on—correspond to the possibility of events that are extremely unlikely but that can occur since there are many opportunities. In "Fishy Poisson," Khachig Tölölyan has shown that Pynchon's likeliest source was George Udney Yule and M. G. Kendall's *Introduction to the Theory of Statistics*, a standard textbook in use for decades. In addition to deriving the formula (190), they also mention (193–94) exactly the examples Pynchon uses here. In addition, Yule and Kendall (194) discuss a 1948 study of flying-bomb (V-1) strikes over greater London. Statistician R. D. Clarke had divided the city into a grid of 144 squares and found that the 576 V-1s were distributed very much as Poisson's equation predicts. He concluded: "There appears no evidence that the bombs 'clustered' otherwise than by chance."

V141.2, B164.23 stayed in Harley Street See V88.11n.

V141.18, B164.42 sails and churchtops of Stockholm Pointsman dreams of traveling to Stockholm, Sweden, to receive his Nobel Prize, the "yellow telegram" of his fantasy having just brought the news. Pavlov was a Nobel recipient in 1904 for his work on the digestive system.

V141.21, B165.4 the Grand Hotel Travel handbooks list this castlelike hotel, with its 105 elegant rooms, as the finest in Sweden. It is located twenty minutes out of Stockholm, in the seaside area of Saltsjobaden.

V141.32–33, B165.16–17 Norrmalm . . . Old City Residential areas and districts of Stockholm.

V142.14, B166.1–2 a Minotaur waiting for him Like Theseus encountering the Minotaur of Greek myth.

V142.32–33, B166.23–25 Reichssieger von Thanatz Alpdrucken . . . champion Weimaraner for 1941 The dog's name will fragment, its parts

metamorphosing into *Alpdrücken* (Nightmare), a (fictional) film
by Gerhardt von Göll that links together many of the novel's characters
(see V387.36n); also into the character Miklos Thanatz (from the
Greek *thanatos,* "death"), who first appears in the narrative at V461.29.
A *Reichssieger* is a "soldier of the Reich."

V143.12, B167.8   the icy noctiluca   A noctiluca is a "night-light"
or atmospheric glow; Thermite is a brand of incendiary explosive.

V143.16, B167.13   Ariadne   She gave Theseus the thread with which
he tracked his way back out of the labyrinth.

V143.24, B167.23   Slothrop ought to be on the Riviera by now   The
first mention of Slothrop's hasty transfer to the south of France, this
anticipates the movement there in part 2. By V168.10, Pointsman
is getting "News from the Riviera."

V144.1–2, B168.3–4   *sentiments d'emprise,* old man   This is Pointsman,
warning himself against paranoia, Pierre Janet's "feelings of
persecution" (V49.1–2n).

**V144.13–14, B168.17–18   "irradiation," for example, and "reciprocal
induction"**   Pavlovian terminology. "Irradiation" is the spreading of
connections between cortical cells, so that a specific reflex begins
to generalize and to shape others in the organism (*Lectures* 2:49). "Reciprocal induction" is the process by which an excitatory stimulus
creates an inhibitory pattern of response; it is thus inversely symmetrical with the normal process of conditioning (ibid. 1:347).

V144.26, B168.34   in Whitehall   In this main district of central London
are located all the key government offices: for example, the War Office,
the Admiralty, the Treasury, the prime minister's residence.

EPISODE 18

O nce again the time of this episode is indistinct. It consists of analepses
to Berlin, circa 1930, and to Palm Sunday, in 1942, when a group of
British airmen experience a vision over the city of Lübeck. It was through
these historical moments that the medium, Carroll Eventyr, first gained
access to the Other Side, in particular to Peter Sachsa, the "control" Eventyr
uses in his séances. Sachsa was killed during a Berlin street riot in 1930.

V145.4, B169.11   the Embankment   North bank of the river Thames
in central London, from Charing Cross Bridge to Blackfriars Station.

V145.15–16, B169.25   the screever's wood box   A screever is an artist
who draws on sidewalks with colored chalks, as for example in the
1964 Walt Disney film *Mary Poppins,* where Bert (Dick Van Dyke) draws
such marvelous pictures that children walk into their imaginary
space.

V145.20, B169.31 to stand inside the central pentagon Waite, in
The Book of Black Magic and of Pacts (191–93), discusses the function
of this symbol. The pentagon itself appears in the center of a pentacle,
and in the process of occult divination they are often drawn with
"the blood of a black cock that has never engendered." In addition,
the figures are inscribed on "virgin parchment" and in accord with a
number of astrological and ritual prescriptions. To stand inside them
is thought to guarantee safety from whatever demonic spirits one
may intentionally or accidentally summon up.

V145.25–26, B169.37 called up the control During a séance, the
"control" is that deceased person who speaks through the medium;
in episode 5, it was Peter Sachsa.

V145.36–37, B170.12–13 under Rollo Groast's EEG Groast as in
"grossed"? The EEG is an electroencephalogram (see below).

**V146.1–7, B170.15–21 a stray 50–millivolt spike . . . slow delta-wave
shapes . . . "subdued petit-mal spike-and-wave alteration"** This enceph-
alographic record shows oscillating brainwaves, represented in milli-
volts, from different areas of the cortex. A "spike" is a sporadic, sharply
peaked wave that may indicate a brain lesion of some kind, perhaps
one that will cause a seizure. The "50–millivolt spike" would be strong
enough to suggest as much. Unlike the alpha waves of a resting brain
(oscillating at 8–12 cycles per second), or the beta waves of an active
brain (18–25 cps), the so-called delta waves (1–3 cps) arise from an
area of localized brain damage. This would be consistent with the spike.
However, delta waves are normal in infants and children, so this
one might indicate a deeply psychotic reversion to childhood states
of consciousness, a possibility consistent with the "petit-mal" indications. Complexes of spike-and-wave patterns that appear from both
sides of the brain, in regular rhythms of about three per second, are the
electroencephalographic sign of petit mal, the form of epilepsy occurring
mainly in children.

V146.16–17, B170.33 institute at Bristol Unknown or fictional.

V146.27, B171.4 during the Lübeck raid In 1942 Britain's Royal Air
Force bombed the city of Lübeck in northern Germany. The raid
occurred at night, on Palm Sunday, against a target with no strategic
value. Hitler was enraged. The fire-bombing brought his first threats of
Vergeltungswaffe, the "revenge-weapons" by which he meant to even
the score. Those weapons (buzz bombs and V-2s) were still more
than two years away from production, and he settled instead for
"Baedeker raids" on historic English towns of no strategic importance.
Here, the temporal symmetries are notable: Lübeck was bombed
on Palm Sunday, March 28, 1942, exactly three years before the last
V-2 was launched on London, during Easter week of 1945.

V147.1, B171.23 the winds of karma Here Pynchon uses the term

almost in substitution for "the winds of fate." But the Hindu-Buddhist
sense of karma reaches farther: it has to do with the cumulative effects
of one's actions during successive stages of being, in all one's incarna-
tions, as a determinant of one's destiny. In American sixties slang
the term "karma" was cheapened to simply mean "luck."

V147.7, B171.30–31   tuned in to the same aethereal Xth Programme   As
though the BBC had, beyond its General Forces and Home Service
programs, some Tenth Programme for the dead to enjoy.

V147.13, B171.37–38   What are we to make of Gavin Trefoil   He
appeared earlier at the séance, in secret conversation with Carroll Eventyr (V33.30). Here, the narrator explains the boy's so-called auto-
chromaticism, a (fictional) ability to willfully change his skin
pigmentation. This is what makes him a star in the film produced under
the aegis of Operation Black Wing—the plan to frighten Germans
with the prospect of Black Rocket Troops, a film fiction that becomes
(in the narrative) a reality. Later, Gavin's sexual promiscuity will
be another basis for Slothrop's recollection of the boy (at V215.30–
32). Thus we have been well prepared when the narrator gets around
to noting (at V276.30–31) that Gavin has a "face as blue as Krishna." A
trefoil is any of the lotoslike, three-petaled flowers common in Eurasia.
In Hinduism the divinity is symbolized as a threefold flower, the
Trimurti, composed of Brahma the Creator, Vishnu the Preserver, and
Shiva the Destroyer. But Brahma has nothing to do with material
being, leaving earth to the dialectical battle between love and hate,
white and black, salvation and destruction, Vishnu and Shiva. Note that
these are very much the contraries driving the novel. Still more, in
myths Vishnu is represented as appearing to man in ten different avatars, of which the bluish-black, sexually promiscuous boy, Krishna,
is the eighth. Following Krishna are the two last avatars: Buddha, who
is in Hinduism a red herring, a false deity masquerading as Vishnu;
then Kalki, the white avatar who signals a final transformation of material being back into its divine potentiality.

**V147.39–40, B172.28–29   tales of Jenny Greenteeth waiting out in
the fens to drown him**   One source may be Katharine Briggs's *Faeries
in English Tradition and Folklore* (46–47): "Lesser spirits with whom
the young were threatened a short time ago, were perhaps nursery
creations, invented by careful mothers to frighten their children away
from danger. One of these was Jenny Greenteeth, who lurked in stagnant
pools, grown over with weeds." And yet there is more. For instance,
Pynchon correctly identifies the locality of the Jenny Greenteeth tales
as Lancashire; the idea of Jenny's shapelessness is also quite accurate.
For like the deeply buried fears or bogeys haunting Rollo Groast's
psychological research, Jenny rarely shows herself and remains below
the surface. Roy Vickery of the Folklore Society (London) has sent

me more (unpublished) details: Pools of standing water in Lancashire are covered in summer with floating mats of duckweed (*Lemna minor*); if an unsuspecting child were to run out on them, he would be quickly swallowed up and possibly drowned. For many children, Vickery reports, Jenny Greenteeth was simply another name for the duckweed. Other children believed in Jenny as an actual bogey; one sixty-eight-year-old respondent told Vickery in 1980 that Jenny was sometimes thought to have "pale green skin, green teeth, very long green locks of hair, long green fingers with long nails, and . . . a pointed chin with very big eyes." Pynchon is remarkably concise about all this; *his* source for the details is unknown.

V148.4, B172.35–36 Mr Tyrone Guthrie's accustomed murk Guthrie (1900–1971) was director of the Old Vic Theatre in London from 1936 to 1948 and was known for his dark, chiaroscuro stage productions of *Richard III* and *Hamlet*.

V148.37–38, B173.36 Fragments of vessels broken at the Creation In Kabbalistic myth, the "vessels" of physical being were thought to have received the divine light at the moment of creation. They were meant to contain it, as instruments of divine being. Instead they shattered under its impact. This moment, "the breaking of the vessels," is the decisive crisis of all divine and created existence. As Gershom Scholem (*On the Kabbalah* 112–13) explains: "Nothing remains in its proper place. Everything is somewhere else. But a being that is not in its proper place is in exile . . . in need of being led back and redeemed. The breaking of the vessels continues into all the further stages of emanation and Creation; everything is in some way broken, everything has a flaw, everything is unfinished." On earth, the most abysmal of those shattered, lightless vessels are the Qlippoth, the "shells of the dead" that appear elsewhere in *GR*.

V149.7, B174.5 the faille gown Faille is a rubbed, woven cotton or silk.

V150.6, B175.11–12 Abdullas and Woodbines Two medium-priced cigarette brands regularly advertised in the *Times* of London.

V150.13, B175.20–21 a strange mac of most unstable plastic A raincoat, or "mackintosh." Anticipates the suit of Imipolex G worn by Gottfried for the launch of Rocket 00000.

V150.16–23, B175.24–33 Nora-so-heartless . . . the progress through his hands Ronald Cherrycoke's exploration of Nora's clothes and accoutrements calls to mind Graves's description of the White Goddess (72). Nora's clothes, the objects on her person, the palms and "Central Asian rugs," as well as the "rising snarls of incense" (V149.4–5) all tally with the description Graves provides from Apuleius. In part 2, Slothrop's erotic encounters with Katje Borgesius and her "Other Order of Being" (V222.17) are reminiscent of the moment here. In part

3, his encounters with Margherita Erdmann are another instance, and Frau Erdmann even thinks of herself as an avatar of the White Goddess—the *Shekinah* of Kabbalistic myth.

V151.23, B176.40–41   the fussy Norden device   In the twenties, engineer Carl L. Norden developed the bombsight that bore his name. The United States put it to use beginning in 1942, in all B-17 and B-24 bombers.˙The sight was linked to an autopilot. All one had to do was aim the aircraft over its target, and the Norden device made all required steering corrections. It even dropped the bombs, and Norden used to claim that with it he could put "a bomb in a pickle barrel" from twenty-five thousand feet. But the device was also very delicate. Rough weather and anti-aircraft fire too easily caused malfunctions.

V151.29–30, B177.5–6   his rainbowed Valkyrie over Peenemünde   In Norse mythology (for example in the *Verse Edda*) the Valkyries are Odin's handmaidens. Hovering over battlefields, they wait to conduct the souls of slain warriors up to Valhalla. Valkyries were sometimes depicted on horseback, and they always made their way back to Valhalla by way of the rainbow bridge called Bifröst. Behind that figural sense of airman Blowitt's vision, there is also the historical fact that in 1942 the German rocket engineers working at Peenemünde recorded their first successful launches of the V-2 rocket. The contrails from these test rockets were reported by pilots and became the first evidence available to British intelligence that the Nazis had a rocket program.

V151.31, B177.7   his Typhoon's wings   The Typhoon was a single-seat fighter aircraft produced in Britain from 1941 until the war's end.

V151.39, B177.17–18   a skyful of MEs   The German Messerschmitt aircraft works produced over thirty-five thousand fighter planes during the war; its ME-109 was the most abundant model.

V152.1–2, B177.21–22   problems with . . . Judgment, in the Tarot sense   The picture in Ouspensky's *Symbolism of the Tarot* is telling. There, card twenty, entitled Judgment, appears as an angel whose red wings are unfolding from a white cloud, with "an ice plain" below her (*Symbolism* 31). The image is suggestive of Basher St. Blaise's angelic visitation over Lübeck. Waite's interpretation (*Pictorial Key* 80–81) of the card is also helpful. He sees it as an image of the Last Judgment and as a messenger of the Empress, card three of the Major Arcana. The Empress signifies "desire and the wings thereof, as the woman clothed with the sun. She is above all things universal fecundity and the outer sense of the word." The Empress also represents an "entrance into the beyond . . . which is communicated to the elect." The Empress is very much the White Goddess in her materialistic, fecund aspect; Judgment is her "messenger" in a millennial, apocalyptic sense. Such are the "problems" the narrator seems to have in mind.

V152.6, B177.27   the Weimar decadence   That is, Germany in the

twenties. The Weimar Republic lasted from 1919 until 1933, when
Hitler took power.

V152.8, B177.29–30   in Neukölln   In Berlin's Innere Stadt, or central
city, the Neu-kölln am Wasser is a street running parallel to the south
side of the Spree River.

**V152.11–12, B177.34–35   More than any mere "Kreis" . . . full man-
dalas**   During these séances Eventyr experiences more than a mere
cross, appearing in the air and symbolizing physical dismemberment;
rather, whole mandalas appear, symbolizing a recuperated totality
of being.

V152.16, B177.40   "Taurus"   In astrology, Taurus is the Bull, second
house of the astrological year, from April 20 to May 20.

V152.17, B177.41   ""Hieropons"   A fictional drug; in the spirit of
Holopon and Nealpon (V345.8), Pynchon has created this one from
the Greek root *hieros*, that which is "holy," "of the gods," or
"supernatural."

V152.19, B178.1   Wimpe the IG-man   In the next episode we learn
more about this fictional agent, or *Verbindungsmann*, for the German
chemical cartel IG Farben (V166.18n).

V152.24, B178.7   high-albedo stockings   The Latin *albedo* means
"whiteness." In technical usage, albedo is the percentage of radiation
thrown back by any surface, such as the moon or silk-stockinged
calves.

V152.34, B178.17–18   good fill-light throw a yellow gel   In photographic
use "fill light" is radiation directed on a subject in order to eliminate
any shadows cast by one's main light source. A yellow gel is used to filter out shadowy blue from the opposite side of the color spectrum.
On the yellow/blue symbolism see also V101.19–20n.

**V152.39–40, B178.23–24   mba rara m'eroto ondyoze . . . mbe mu munine
m'oruroto ayo u n'omuinyo**   The first phrase was taken directly
out of Brincker (168), except that Pynchon has chosen to regularize
Brincker's transliteration of the Herero to make it consistent with
Kolbe, his English source on the language. Brincker gives the first
phrase as "mba rara me roto ondjoze" and translates it "Ich habe ein
Alptraum vertraumt" (I have dreamed a nightmare). Brincker uses
the phrase as an instance of the word *ondjoze*, the *Alptraum* or
Alpdrücken. The second phrase is also an example, this time out of
Kolbe: he translates it as "I saw him in my dream as if he were alive"
(36). Fowler doesn't identify these translations, but he does make
an important secondary observation: the Herero lexicon involves an
elaborate pattern of meanings organized around motions that are
animate (like a spider's) and inanimate (like the wind), or around things
in a state of rest (a stone). For instance, *ondjoze* (nightmare or
phantom) stems from the motion of a spider, and this spins us into

the "giant web" and the "twisting of yarns or cordage" in Pynchon's following lines.

V153.6, B178.33   the veld   An Afrikaans term for open grassland in South-West Africa.

V153.11, B178.39   the S.P.R.   The London-based Society for Psychical Research (V89.36n).

V153.12, B178.40   Altrincham   A suburb of Manchester, England, known for its villas built by industrial magnates.

V153.15, B179.1   chi-square fittings that refuse to jibe   See V40.18n.

V153.40, B179.31   the K.P.D.   The Kommunistische Partei Deutschlands, or German Communist party; outlawed by Hitler in 1934.

V154.7, B179.42   the rocket facility at Reinickendorf   Located five miles northwest of Berlin's Innere Stadt, Reinickendorf was a major industrial center in the thirties and home to the *Raketenflugplatz* (rocket launching site) established for the first testing of rockets. In 1932 the increasing involvement of Germany's Army Weapons Department brought about a move, first from Reinickendorf to a military proving ground at Kummersdorf, seventeen miles of Berlin (Dornberger 20–23); then, in 1937, to the site on the island of Peenemünde, on the North Sea.

EPISODE 19

A brilliant analepsis to pre-Hitler Berlin, circa 1929–30. The episode centers on Franz and Leni Pökler, especially her dissatisfaction with his idealistic devotion to Western science, depicted here as a dynastic succession. Pynchon's presentation of German geography (from Baedeker), economics (from Sasuly), cinema (from Kracauer), and rocketry (from Dornberger) is also closely interwoven with references to occult and astrological lore. Their combined effect reveals the historical background to the collective Germanic death wish, a Piscean striving for the Other Side.

V154.13–14, B180.8   second Reich   Germany's second empire or Reich lasted from 1871 until 1919, from the accession of Bismarck until the fall of Kaiser Wilhelm.

V154.19, B180.14–15   *Die Faust Hoch*   "The Raised Fist," a fictional leftist magazine (named, perhaps, for the raised-fist salute of American radicals—and especially dissident blacks—of the sixties). There is an echo here of "Die Fahne Hoch," the tune that became known in Nazi Germany as the Horst Wessel Song (V443.2n).

V154.24–25, B180.22   a woman born under the Crab, a mother   Leni was born under the astrological influence of Cancer (the Crab: June 21–

July 22). Like her husband, Franz, who is a Pisces (V154.35), Leni
is also a "water person." And it is a desire for all-inclusiveness symbolized in the water sign that stands behind her uncertainty over
the "nasty earth-sign belligerence" (V154.30) of her lover, Peter Sachsa,
for earth-sign persons are supposed to be known as "the most critical
or exacting" of the four types (Jones 58). Among the water signs, Cancer
differs from Pisces in being practically and not abstractly minded.
Cancers are supposed to have a strong sense of possession, and this is
why Leni's deserting Franz with just "one valise" seems out of character.
Cancer is also a very maternal sign—on the body, it rules the breast—
so it underscores Leni's concerns for her daughter.

**V154.35–36, B180.35 her Piscean husband . . . death-wish, rocket-
mysticism** A winter sign (February 19–March 20), Pisces or the Fishes
is a sign of death and endings, the twelfth and last house of the astrological year. Pisces individuals are thought to yearn for a dissolution of
self and a movement toward wholeness in the abstract. Jones notes
a special predilection for mysticism among Pisces types.

V155.3–4, B181.2 another Ufa masterpiece See V98.24n.

V155.5–6, B181.4–5 not even in the Kinos, no German *October* The
German cinema houses are called *Kinos*. Kracauer (172–75) reports
that in the twenties German production companies, and Ufa in particular, kept steadfastly away from depictions of Bolsheviks or leftist
revolutionaries of any kind. This is why German cinema would not
produce anything like *October*, the 1927 film by Russian director
Sergei Eisenstein, a film made especially to commemorate the tenth
anniversary of the Russian Revolution and subtitled "Ten Days That
Shook the World" in honor of John Reed's book.

V155.7–8, B181.7 Rosa Luxemburg Writer, activist, and Marxist
revolutionary, Rosa Luxemburg was a cofounder of the German Communist party, or KPD. Disparagingly known as "Red Rosa," she was
jailed for three years during the World War I. After her release she was
a leader of the Berlin uprisings of January 1919. Arrested during them,
she and KPD founder Karl Liebknecht (V621.40n) were taken to
Berlin's Eden Hotel, clubbed nearly to death, then shot in the head.
Luxemburg's body was thrown into an icy canal from the Lichtenstein
Bridge and not recovered until April 1919.

**V155.22–23, B181.26–27 "approaches . . . to that Absolute Com-
fort"** As with other approaches to Absolute Zeros, to various "Holy
Centers" in *GR*, this one is also depicted as unobtainable. Still more, in
this passage the "trope of the unavailable insight" (Hite, *Ideas* 26)
is referred to as a mass cultural tool, a means of socially conditioning
the *Volk*.

V156.18, B182.27 the Judenschnautze The term "-schnautze" has no meaning in German. No doubt Pynchon means "-schnauze," which can alternately mean "snout" or "jaw." The second meaning, as a "Jewish jaw," fits the context here.

V156.20, B182.29   not just with another woman   The Bantam misprints this as "women."

V156.40–41, B183.12   the Mausigstrasse   A fictional Mousey Street.

V157.22, B183.39   the gassen   German side streets or alleys.

V157.35, B184.12   Gymnasium friends   Friends from grammar school.

V158.8–10, B184.29–31   the President . . . asking the Bundestag . . . clogged and nasal voice   Paul von Hindenburg, Germany's president for the years until Hitler became dictator in 1934, was known (and satirized) for such a voice. His addressing the Bundestag, or lower house of the parliament, in this way is Leni's fantasy of a bloodless revolution.

V159.9, B185.36   Δt approaching zero   In calculus, the Δt stands for a time interval or change in time. When "approaching zero" (i.e., no change), it would define a point on the line of a graphed motion.

V159.19, B186.4   *Nibelungen*   Franz Pökler dozed off during the second part of Fritz Lang's 1924 epic. Entitled *Kreimhild's Revenge*, it shows the marriage of Attila to Kreimhild (whose first husband, Seigfried, has been killed). She encourages the Hun to sweep in on the Burgundians and massacre them, a scene Kracauer (93–94) describes as "an orgy of destruction," in which the violence unfolds as a carefully orchestrated sequence of "causes and effects" where "nothing is left to chance. An inherent necessity predetermines the disastrous sequence of love, hatred, jealousy, and thirst for revenge."

V159.33, B186.22   They saw *Die Frau im Mond*   Another Fritz Lang film for Ufa, this one from 1929. Here is Kracauer (151): "Lang imagined a rocket projectile carrying passengers to the moon. The cosmic enterprise was staged with surprising veracity of vision; the plot was pitiable for its emotional shortcomings."

V159.38–39, B186.28–29   the Jewish wolf Pflaumbaum   The name means "Plum-tree."

V160.11, B187.2–3   the T.H. Munich   That is, the Technische Hochschule, or Technical College, located in Munich.

V160.13, B187.5   Max Schlepzig   From the german verb *schleppen* (to drag or tug in a slow, tedious manner).

V160.15, B187.8   the tenement's Hinterhöfe   These are "back courts" within the *Höfe*, which Baedeker (*Berlin* 53) describes as "huge, many-storied buildings, often enclosing three or four interior courts."

V160.26, B187.21   Reinickendorf   See V154.7n.

V160.35–36, B187.33–35   to Schaffhausen . . . electric tram to the Rhine Falls   Baedeker's *Southern Germany* (65–66) characterizes this Bavarian village on the Rhine River as very picturesque, with a "fine view" of the Alps. Its main attraction is the Rhine Falls, two miles to the south. Baedeker describes it as "one of the grandest cascades in Europe . . . reached either by railway or electric tramway." The other details included here—stairway, pavilion, tour boats—are all derived from Baedeker. Note also that the waterfall as a form "of energy, abstractions" (V161.8–9) would be especially significant to the Piscean Franz.

V161.18, B188.20   the silver thing blew apart   The source is Dornberger's description (23–26) of a rocket engine that exploded on its test stand at Reinickendorf during the late twenties.

V161.22, B188.25–26   Kurt Mondaugen   The last name translates to "Moon-eyes."

V161.30, B188.35   drafty mansarde in the Liebigstrasse in Munich   A mansard is so called for its distinctive roof, with a lower vertical and an upper horizontal slant, designed by the seventeenth-century architect François Mansart. In Munich the Liebigstrasse is located about one kilometer from the Technische Hochschule; according to Baedeker, a statue of the German chemist Justus von Liebig (d. 1873) used to stand in a plaza just off the end of Franz's street (*Southern Germany* 289).

V161.34–35, B188.40–41   true succession, Liebig to . . . Jamf   Laszlo Jamf is fictional, the origin of his name seemingly linked to a pronominal form of "I" (see V287.1–4n). For a discussion of these patriarchs of modern chemistry see below (V166.1–9n).

V161.36, B189.1   Schnellbahnwagen   One of Munich's electric trolleys (Baedeker, *Southern Germany* 237).

V161.39, B189.5   some kind of radio research project   Mondaugen's South African project involved "sferics," atmospheric radio waves. Pynchon has described his southern sojourn in chapter 9 of *V.,* "Mondaugen's Story."

V162.12, B189.22   Wandervögel idiocy   The Viking and Bantam print the umlaut, which is unnecessary and inconsistent (see V99.2n).

V162.13–14, B189.23–24   the Society for Space Navigation   The Verein für Raumschiffart, or VfR, organized in the twenties as an amateur group; many early members (like Wernher von Braun) went on to Peenemünde and worked on the V-2. Pynchon's source is Dornberger (20).

V162.15–16, B189.25–26   in Lübeck . . . kleinbürger houses beside the Trave   The city of Lübeck is nearly encircled by the river Trave, which loops around it and leaves an opening to the north. Note that Leni's former residence there provides a thematic link to the prior episode, with its reference to the 1942 raid on Lübeck.

V162.20–21, B189.32   fussy Biedermeier strangulation   The Biedermeier style of furniture was a nineteenth-century German imitation of French Empire style (see V202.17–18n), but the German was plainer and less ostentatious. The emphasis was on *Gemütlichkeit* (comfort, coziness). The name was a portmanteau word, for Biedermann and Bummelmeier, comical characters in a Berlin journal who were meant to satirize bourgeois values.

V162.28, B189.42   Bürgerlichkeit   The "middle-class reflexes" of V163.14.

V162.38, B190.11   "oh, Leni, your wings"   See V97.27n.

V163.17–18, B190.34–36   Wines . . . the great '20s and '21s, Schloss Vollrads, Zeltinger, Piesporter   All are Moselle wines from the Rheingau region of Germany. Lichine (488) hails the wines from the Schloss Vollrad vineyard as "the best of the Rhine wines." The term "Zeltinger" designates any of the Moselles from the Zeltingen district, just as "Piesporter" wines come from the district of Piesport, both of which have prime south-facing lands on the Rhine River. The years 1920 and 1921 yielded very good vintages.

V163.19–23, B190.37–42   the late foreign minister . . . Die gottverdammte Judensau   A statesman, industrialist, and writer, Walter Rathenau was assassinated in 1922. His father, Emil, had purchased European patent rights to Edison's inventions, then amassed a fortune in the electrical power industry. Emil Rathenau founded the AEG (Allgemeine Elektrizitäts-Gesellschaft), and his son Walter inherited it. For thirteen months Walter Rathenau was also the Albert Speer of World War I; he organized a special board to oversee wartime production. Later he criticized the Armistice of 1918 because it seemed an unconditional surrender. His 1920 book, *Die Neue Wirtschaft* (The New Economy) argued for a fully rationalized system of industrial self-government, free of any treaty constraints. The book won him a post as a minister in Karl Joseph Wirth's reconstruction cabinet. However, fanatical nationalistic groups decried Rathenau's negotiations with the Allied governments over reparations. They saw him selling out to international big capitalism, and Rathenau's Jewish faith only added to their suspicions. On June 24, 1922, he was gunned down by a radical right group called the Organization Consul. Pynchon's source for the "anti-Semitic street refrain" is unknown, but it translates like this:

Blast the Jew Rathenau
The god-damned Jewish sow.

On Rathenau's contributions to the growth of the German cartel movement, see Sasuly (39–41).

V163.31–33, B191.9–12   IG Farben . . . unlucky subsidiary Spottbilligfilm AG . . . OKW   The ties between IG Farben and the Army High Command (OKW) are well documented in Sasuly; however, Spottbilligfilm AG (Dirt-cheap Films, Inc.) is a purely fictional subsidiary.

V163.37–38, B191.17–18   The Götterdämmerung mentality   Oblique reference to the fourth libretto of Wagner's *Ring, The Twilight of the Gods*.

V164.5, B191.24–25   Chemical Instrumentality for the Abnormal   One of several fictional avatars of the CIA in *GR*.

V164.10, B191.30–31   Generaldirektor Smaragd   In corporate circles the *Generaldirektor* is a managing director; *Smaragd* is German for "emerald."

V164.29, B192.10   Death as validator   In the Celtic Method of Tarot divination, the validator is the tenth and last card drawn from the deck; it summarizes all previous cards, indicating "what is to come" (Waite, *Pictorial Key* 299–305). Should it be the thirteen of the Major Arcana, Death, it would confirm an overall sense of "mystical death . . . and the passage into a state to which ordinary death is neither the path nor gate" (ibid. 123).

V165.21, B193.8   the Herrenklub   Literally, the "Men's Club." Sasuly (97) describes it as an elite inner circle of Berlin-based Junkers and financiers who used to meet regularly in the days before Hitler.

V165.26–29, B193.15–18   blinking under the bulb . . . a net of information   The light bulb in this scene is, presumably, Byron the Bulb of *GR*, who spent time in Berlin (V647.25).

V166.1–9, B193.35–194.2   "All right. Mauve . . . Herbert Gannister"   Here begins a dense, significant chain of references to the history of organic chemistry, specifically to the dye and pharmaceutical industries that burgeoned from it. Pynchon's main sources appear to be Sasuly and a book Sasuly mentions, *This Chemical Age*, by William Haynes. The English chemist William Perkins was the discoverer of mauve dye, synthesized from coal tar in 1856. Prior to that, coal tar had been a waste by-product of the steel industry. But Perkins, working with results formerly obtained by his teacher, August Wilhelm von Hofmann (1818–92), produced the first synthetic dye and revolutionized the dyestuffs industry. Hofmann, in fact, had been "imported" to England from the University of Munich, where he had studied under Justus von Liebig (1803–73), the founding patriarch of organic chemistry. Perkins had been attempting the synthesis of quinine from naphthalene, a coal-tar derivative. The process was messy, smelly, and very sticky; worse still, he failed. Yet in the process he derived aniline purple as a precipitate, called the substance "mauve," registered it as British Patent No. 1984, and gave rise to the "Mauve Decade" of Victorian England, for Queen Victoria wore a mauve dress to an exhibition at the Crystal Palace in 1862, establishing the fashion trend of her reign. Other dye colors quickly followed: tyrian purple, alizarin, and indigo were the most important. Some of them, such as gentian, also became known for their pharmaceutical properties, thus opening up still wider business opportunities. In England the fortunes of Imperial Chemicals, Inc., and in Germany the fortunes of IG Farben were raised on these discoveries. Herbert Gannister was one of the first re-

searchers to experiment with such pharmaceutical compounds. His
employer, the Bayer Company, had soon merged with IG Farben.

V166.10, B194.3 "Oneirine" Another fictional pharmaceutical; its
name stems from the Greek *oneiros*, "to dream." In chemical nomenclature, the "-ine" suffix signifies "from the family of."

V166.11, B194.4–5 "cyclized benzylisoquinilines" Presents a chemical
crux. If the speaker (Rathenau's ghost) means one of the isoquinoline
family, here with a benzyl radical attached, then he is talking rubbish,
for the isoquinolines are not drugs but large heterocyclic molecules
left behind from the refraction of coal tars and used industrially in coating the bricks of oxygen furnaces. Perhaps, then, the reference is
to quinidines, an alkaloid used as a cardiac depressant; or perhaps
to quinicine, another alkaloid. The present chemical literature does
not appear to acknowledge a "benzylisoquiniline."

V166.16–17, BN194.11 "von Maltzen . . . the Rapallo Treaty" In
1922 Baron Ago von Maltzen was head of the Eastern Department of
Germany's Foreign Office. Under Rathenau, in April, he negotiated the
Rapallo Treaty, normalizing relations with Soviet Russia and establishing the terms of reparations payments agreed to in the Treaty of Versailles that ended World War I. With the treaty came a lifting of trade
restrictions between Germany and the Soviet Union, and the Krupp
works immediately began shipments of steel and steel products—farm
equipment, for example—to the Ukraine. Von Maltzen went on to
become the German ambassador to the United States.

V166.18, B194.13 "the V-Mann" The acronym has nothing to do
with the V-2 rockets, which weren't conceived as "revenge-weapons"
anyway until 1942. In the parlance of the IG Farben cartel, Wimpe
is a *Verbindungsmann*, what we might call a "connection" or an
"agent." Sasuly (105) explains: "These men were generally well-estab-
lished sales representatives of the IG whose spy work could be carried
on under the cloak of business" (see also Dubois 58). V-men constituted
a highly placed network of industrial spies whose connections
provided a base of inestimable worth as World War II espionage became
more complex. Wimpe reappears in part 3 (V344.11); the name, mean-
ingless in the German, suggests the American slang "wimp"—a
weakling.

**V166.23–29, B194.19–27 "coal tar . . . Earth's excrement . . . Passed
over"** The mythology is certainly Pynchon's, yet listen to William
Haynes (44) describe attitudes toward coal-tar substances in Perkins's
time: "Few chemists knew anything at all about coal tar. Certainly
nobody suspected that it consisted of a mixture of more than two hundred different, definite substances, six of which would shortly become
the material for the manufacture of many thousands of new chemical

products. Inky black, evil smelling, oily, it is nasty to handle, and with the apparatus then available it was hard to work with." Thus for decades chemists had literally passed over coal tar; it was a preterite material and seemingly satanic, yet out of it emerged a virtual rainbow of colors.

V167.29–30, B195.35 Heinz Rippenstoss Translated from the German, "Heinz Kick-in-the-ribs."

EPISODE 20

A Christmas Eve party at "The White Visitation." Slothrop is safe on the Riviera. Here in the cold, white North, Pointsman troubles himself over Slothrop as a "miracle and human child" (V168.3)—another satiric inversion of the Christian Nativity story.

V167.36–168.1, B196.4–7 And the crowds they swarm in Knightsbridge, and . . . Pointsman's all alone. Note the ballad meter and rhyme. Crowds swarmed in the Knightsbridge area because shoppers were buying gifts from such exclusive London department stores as Harrod's and Harvey Nicholls.

V168.2, B196.8 any Spam-tin dog See V133.3–4n.

V168.10, B196.17–18 News from the Riviera In other words, Slothrop is in the south of France a day or so before Christmas.

V168.17–18, B196.27–28 the Latin _cortex_ translates into English as "bark" It does, and the etymological workings of this joke show how to solve the following riddle.

V168.21–22, B196.32–34 jokes . . . such as the extraordinary "What did the Cockney exclaim to the cowboy from San Antonio?" One way to solve this is to take as a model the etymological play of the _cortex_/bark/dogs/trees example above. The word "cockney" derives from the Middle English _cokeney_, or "cock's egg," archaic slang for a male homosexual. We recall Crutchfield, the "White Cocksman of the _terre mauvais_" (V69.1–2) in Slothrop's sodium amytal session. Just as the "White Cocksman" has his "little pards," so would the "cowboy from San Antonio" have his "Cockney," who might exclaim: "I'll be your Rose of San Antone," echoing the famous song (see V559.36–37n for the lyric). This is underscored when we recall the anal-erotic significance of the "rose" for Weissmann and _his_ "Cockney," Gottfried, at V104.7.

V168.24–25, B196.35–36 closet full of belladonna . . . thistle tubes Belladonna is the poisonous plant _Atropa_, also called "deadly nightshade." Its roots and leaves yield the drug atropine, used as an anesthetic (and to dilate the eyes). A "thistle tube" is a glass funnel with a flared, conical top, a large bulb below it, and then a spigot designed into the tube itself and used to separate immiscible liquids.

V168.29, B196.41 "gam" Thirties slang for a woman's leg, corrupted from the French *jambe.*

V168.41–169.1, B197.14–16 amphetamine sulphate, 5 mg q 6 h, last night amobarbital sodium 0.2 Gm. at bedtime In plain English, Pointsman has been medicating himself with stimulants and depressants. He took five milligrams of amphetamine sulfate, a powerful stimulant, every six hours during the day; before bed at night he took a fifth of a gram of amobarbital, a depressant, to encourage sleep. Incidentally, "amobarbital sodium" is another name for sodium amytal, the drug that induces Slothrop's hallucinations in episode 10. Pointsman takes the drug in capsule form, the least powerful dosage; according to the pharmacological handbooks his two-tenths of a gram would be appropriate to relieve anxiety and relax muscles.

V169.7–8, B197.23–24 some piece by Ernesto Lecuona, "Siboney" perhaps Lecuona was a composer and pianist, best known for his *Andalucia,* a suite that was pillaged for a number of popular forties songs. "Siboney" was a hit for him in 1929, when Grace Moore sang it in the film *When You're in Love.* It appears again in the music for a 1941 film, *Get Hep to Love.*

V169.31–33, B198.11–13 all the way to Stoke Poges ... from Luton Hoo, Bedfordshire This is pure whimsy. The airfields were located to the west of London, and Stoke Poges seven miles further west of the fields. (It was from the churchyard of Stoke Poges that Thomas Grey wrote his famous elegy.) The village of Luton, in Bedfordshire (due north of London) would be about fifty miles distant from Gwenhidwy's singing.

V169.34, B198.14–15 singing "Diadem" An eighteenth-century hymn by British composer Edward Perronet, it is also known by its first line:

> All hail! the power of Jesus' name,
>   Let angels prostrate fall;
> Bring forth the royal diadem,
>   And crown Him king of all.
>
> Crown him, ye martyrs of our God,
>   Who from His altar call;
> Extol the stem of Jesse's rod,
>   And crown Him lord of all.

It continues in this manner. The hymn has been translated into numerous languages and remains one of the ten most reprinted.

V169.36–37, B198.17–19 beef tea, grenadine ... lady's-slipper Gwenhidwy's mixture would gag an ox. Beef tea is brewed from the prolonged simmering of lean beef parts. Grenadine is a thick, sweet syrup prepared from red currants or pomegranates. "Blue scullcap" (in the Viking and the Bantam) is a misprint; it should be "skullcap," a plant with helmet-shaped flowers prescribed as a remedy for hydrophobia. Valerian root, the source for valerian (a liquid used in flavorings, perfumes, and pharmaceuticals), is known for its mildly sedative qualities. Motherwort gets its name from the fact that this purple-flowered weed was once used to ease uterine discomforts. Finally, the lady's slipper is an orchidaceous plant whose balsamic extracts were once widely used in cough syrups and ointments.

V169.39–40, B198.21–23   the Welshman in *Henry V* who ran around forcing people to eat his Leek   This is Fluellen, who wears a leek on St. David's Day (March 1) in honor of the Welsh patron saint. A nationalist, Fluellen takes offense when the English soldier Pistol disparages the custom. So he forces Pistol (pronounced "pizzle") to "eat, look you, this leek; because, look you, you do not love it, nor your affections and your appetites and your digestions doo's not agree with it, I would desire you to eat it" (V.i.25–28). This sexual punning becomes more blatant when Fluellen commands Pistol to eat, "Or I have another leek in my pocket, which you shall eat" (65–66). *Henry V* was also a very successful film starring Laurence Olivier. A certain nationalistic fervor lay behind this success: the drama celebrated the only other invasion of Europe that England had attempted before the Normandy Invasion of June 6, 1944.

V170.4–5, B198.28–30   Ashkenazic Jews . . . never heard in Harley Street   The Ashkenazic, or Central European, Jews occupied London's East End, so their accents would not be heard among the immensely successful doctors whose offices are on London's Harley Street (see V88.11n).

V170.10, B198.36   some BMRs   Acronym for a patient's basal metabolism rate, a measure of the amount of energy required to maintain vital functions in a state of rest.

V170.13, B198.40   Vincentesque invaders   That is, germs carrying the trench mouth infection. Vincent's disease is a form of gingivitis in the mouth, with symptoms of foul odor, pain, and pallid coloring around the inflicted gums (the ginges). It was named for French pathologist Jean Hyacinthe Vincent, who diagnosed it in the mouths of trench-bound soldiers of the Great War.

V170.24–25, B199.11–12   the Welsh once upon a time were Jewish too   See Robert Graves's *The White Goddess* (19): "The Cymry, whom we think of as the real Welsh, and from whom the proud court-bards were recruited, were a tribal aristocracy of Brythonic origin holding down a serf-class . . . they had invaded Wales from the north of

England in the fifth century A.D." The Cymry held fast to the belief
that they were descended from Japhet and had wandered north from Israel to Britain.

V171.7, B199.40–41   humming "Aberystwyth"   A protestant hymn
written (in 1740) by Charles Wesley and listed in Anglican hymnals as
number 415:

> Jesus, Lover of my Soul, Let me to Thy bosom fly;
> While the nearer waters roll, while the tempest still is high.
> Hide me, O my Savior hide, Till the storm of life be past;
> Safe into the haven guide, O receive my Soul at last.

> Other refuge have I none, Hangs my helpless Soul on Thee;
> Leave ah!, leave me not alone, Still support and comfort me!
> All my trust in Thee is stayed; All my help from Thee I bring;
> Cover my defenceless head with the shadow of Thy wing.

Aberystwyth is, in addition, a principal Welsh city and home of the
University College of Wales, site of the activities mentioned below.

V171.37, B200.36   Death's white Gymanfa Ganu   A Welsh singing
festival, organized by parts, with hundreds of (here, white-robed)
singers taking each part; it is held annually at Aberystwyth on St.
David's Day.

V173.29, B202.38   several enormous water bugs   The British would
likely call them cockroaches. The name "water bug" is American and
common mostly among Manhattanites. The cockroach population
of New York City exploded in the nineteenth century when the Croton
Aqueduct was completed; so Manhattanites often called the little
vermin Croton bugs or water bugs, as Pynchon (a sometime Manhat-
tanite) would have heard.

EPISODE 21

Part 1 of *GR* concludes on Boxing Day, December 26, 1944. The time
when the British exchange gifts in celebration of Christmas, Boxing Day
is in particular a day of rest for England's servant classes. The setting here is
the London flat of Jessica's sister. The German *märchen* of Hansel and
Gretel reappears in this episode, once more in connection with the V-2
rocket. The astrological sign of Pisces, the Fishes, broods over the day.

V174.11, B203.24   Penelope sits   The Bantam misprints this as "Penelope sit."

V174.19, B203.34   a golliwog   A grotesque black doll modeled on
illustrations in children's books by Florence K. Upton (d. 1922).

V174.21–22, B203.37–38 The pantomime . . . was *Hansel and Gretel*. Pantomimes are a part of British tradition on Boxing Day. For the Christmas of 1944, various groups were presenting shows for children, but the December 23 *Times* of London does not list *Hansel and Gretel*.

V176.14–15, B205.30 the Qlippoth, Shells of the Dead See also V148.37–38n. The Kabbalists held that the godhead, initially whole and androgynous, was at Adam's fall sundered not only into masculine and feminine aspects but also into a spray of "sparks" that mingle with material being. Material being is penetrated by this light, redeeming it from an otherwise hollow duration. The "shells" or Qlippoth are these hollow containers; they may assume demonic attributes, and it was thought that only a messiah could banish the Qlippoth and restore being to its whole state. Meanwhile, they are emissaries from the world of the dead who stalk the familiar world.

V176.38–39, B206.18 Quisling molecules have shifted A political personification of molecular events. Vidkun Quisling (1887–1945) was head of the Norwegian government from 1940 to 1945, and a Nazi puppet throughout that time. Traitorous, collaborationist molecules, in other words.

V177.11, B206.34–35 the rationalized power-ritual that will be the coming peace A further reference to Weber's theory of the "rationalization [or routinization] of charisma" (see V81.8–9).

V177.28–29, B207.13–15 Hark, the herald angels sing / Mrs. Simpson's pinched our King Edward Mendelson ("Gravity's Encyclopedia" 187) first pointed out the source of these lines: "This fractured carol is used by Iona and Peter Opie, near the opening of their classic book *The Lore and Language of Schoolchildren*, to illustrate the possibility of communication in a manner 'little short of miraculous.' The children's version of the carol, which could not have been broadcast or printed or repeated in music halls, managed to spread across all of England in the course of a few weeks, during school term, when there could have been little travelling to spread its transmission."

Part 2

*Un Perm'
au Casino
Hermann
Goering*

Part 2, whose French title means "A Furlough at the Hermann Goering Casino," opens around Christmas 1944 in Monaco. It ends five months later with Tyrone Slothrop departing from Nice for "the Zone" of Central Europe and, back in England, with Pointsman and Company at Dover for Whitsunday, May 20, 1945. Thus part 2 of *Gravity's Rainbow* is symbolically bounded by the birth of a savior and the proof of his resurrected glory, two key moments on the Christian liturgical calendar. The dominant astrological sign of part 2 is Aries, the Ram, a fire sign and an omen of spring but more especially a sign of strong personal identity. The irony here is that Slothrop *loses* his identity in episode 2, when Katje Borgesius literally makes "one American lieutenant disappear" (V198.13) under a red damask tablecloth, a ruse so that Slothrop's papers and clothing can be stolen. This leaves him without official identity papers until episode 7, when he assumes the role of "ace reporter" Ian Scuffling (V256.35–36).

In this part of the novel, Pynchon's principal sources treat the technology of the V-2 rocket, as well as the political backgrounds of its development in Germany and its detection in England. Pavlovian physiology continues to lend detail. Part 2 has eight episodes, a key number throughout the narrative. The epigraph derives from a *New York Times* feature of September 21, 1969, entitled "How Fay Met Kong; Or, the Scream that Shook the World" (sec. 2, 17). Fay Wray's story opens like this:

"You will have the tallest, darkest leading man in Hollywood."
Those were the first words I heard about *King Kong*. Although I knew the producer, Merian C. Cooper, was something of a practical joker, my thoughts rushed hopefully to the image of Clark Gable. Cooper, pacing up and down in his office, outlined the story to me . . . about an expedition to some remote island where a discovery of gigantic proportions would be made. My heart raced along, waiting for the revelation. I enjoyed his mysterious tone, the gleeful look in his eyes that seemed to say "Just wait until you hear who will be playing opposite you."
Cooper paused, picked up some pocket-sized sketches, then showed me my tall dark leading man. My heart stopped, then sank. An absolutely enormous gorilla was staring at me.

EPISODE I

The scene is the Riviera, shortly after Slothrop's arrival there just before Christmas, and this is one of the most stagy episodes in the narrative: Slothrop's British associates Bloat and Tantivy do a singing number; Slothrop "saves" Katje Borgesius from Octopus Grigori, whose conditioning was planned with this moment in mind. Slothrop quickly suspects the whole venture. Setting these contrived events at the (fictional) casino, named for Nazi air force chief Goering, establishes once more the conflict of causality and chance.

V181.1–2, B211.2   wood-soled civilian feet   When they defeated Western European nations, occupying Nazi forces quickly grabbed up available supplies of leather and rubber. Civilians were forced to wear wood-soled shoes during the war.

V181.4, B211.5   slow faro shuffle   See V69.12n. But the casino at Monte Carlo has never offered this Wild West card game to patrons.

V181.5–6, B211.7   along the esplanade   The beach-side promenade in Monte Carlo, according to Baedeker's *South-eastern France*.

V181.10, B211.12–13   along the *Cap*   Probably the Cap Martine, a spit of land located three miles eastward, across the bay from Monte Carlo.

V181.16, B211.20   electric fire   British term for an electric-coil heater.

V181.25, B211.31   Hispano-Suizas   The last word in prewar, luxury auto transportation for the wealthy. After 1914, Hispano-Suizas were assembled in Paris and shipped out of Spain. Until the factory closed in 1938, they were famous among Europe's rich and ruling elite as the most commodious, quiet, high-powered car in the world.

V182.4, B212.10   "I'm some kind of a Van Johnson"   With his good looks and gentlemanly ways, Johnson (b. 1916) was a favorite screen lover of the forties. Slothrop might well have in mind such films as *Two Girls and a Sailor* (1943), *Easy to Wed* (1944), and *Thirty Minutes over Tokyo* (1944).

V182.6, B212.13   green pack of Cravens   A medium-priced cigarette brand: "Craven Plain—This GOOD Cigarette, in GREEN packets," as the *Times* of London ads used to remind folks.

V182.10, B212.17–18   "a gang of those section 8s"   See V114.5n.

V182.17, B212.26–27   "you all turn into Valentinos"   Screen heartthrob Rudolpho Alfonzo Raffaele Piere Philibert Guglielmi changed his name to Rudolf Valentino in 1917. On screen from 1918 to 1926, when he died of appendicitis at the age of thirty-one.

V182.23, B212.34   Fox-trot   A dance song in 2/4 or 4/4 time, with alternating slow and fast sections.

V182.35, B213.4   a sort of e-rot-ic Clausewitz   Prussian military theorist Karl von Clausewitz (1780–1831) was the author of *Vom Kriege* (On War), a three-volume masterpiece of military strategy.

V183.8, B213.16   "Moi Tantivy, you know, Tantivy"   The girls might well be confused by an apparent pun: Tantivy's name sounds like the idiomatic French *tente ta vie*—literally, "chance your life," but in common usage, "take a chance."

V183.10, B213.19   "J'ai deux amis, aussi"   I have two friends, too.

V183.17, B213.27 **"où, you know, déjeuner"** Where, you know, [is] breakfast?

V183.24, B213.35 **"sur la plage"** On the beach.

V183.29, B213.41 **"an Impressionist. A Fauve. Full of light** The fauves were a loose association of Parisian turn-of-the-century painters, Henry Matisse chief among them, who extolled the beauty of pure colors, of tints displayed as if in unmediated light. They were greatly influenced by the late-impressionist works of, for example, Paul Cézanne. Like the impressionists, the fauves also strove for the immediate, uninterrupted rendering of experience.

V183.31, B214.2–3 **Berkshire Saturdays** When Slothrop used to get his hair cut, in the fictional town of Mingeborough, in the Berkshire Mountains of western Massachusetts.

V184.4, B214.16 **sporty Bing Crosby pompadour** Like the famous American crooner and film star (see V38.19n), Slothrop combs his hair in a well-oiled upsweep from his forehead.

V184.14–15, B214.28–29 **Norfolk jacket . . . Savile Row establishment** Tantivy offers Slothrop a woolen jacket, belted, pleated in the back, and purchased from one of the fashionable clothiers on Savile Row in London's Picadilly area.

V184.33, B215.8 **César Flebótomo** He takes his moniker from the Etruscan/Latin title for a dictator and the Greek *phlebotomeia* (bloodletting).

V184.39, B215.15–16 **Messerschmitt squadron** See V151.39n.

V185.8, B215.28–29 **drab singlet, Wehrmacht issue** Undershirts from the Wehrmacht, or German regular army, were green, as distinct from the black ones worn by the SS.

V185.12, B215.32–33 **lingua franca** From the Italian for any hybridized mixture of languages.

V185.19, B215.42 **Antibes** Cape of land seventeen miles west of Monte Carlo.

V185.21, B216.2 **the chines** Ridged intersections formed by the sides and bottom of a flat- or V-bottom boat.

V185.22, B216.3 **prewar Comets and Hamptons** Sailboats Slothrop recalls from earlier vacation days at Cape Cod: the Hampton (or Hampton Beach boat, after its point of origin in New Hampshire), a double-ended, open-hull day sailer, rigged with two spritsails and averaging twenty feet; and the Comet, a similar craft but single-masted.

V185.25, B216.7 **a *pédalo*** Pedal-driven paddleboat for hire to the tourists at Monaco.

V186.3, B216.32 **black bombazine frock** This is the cocoa-brown silken dress that Katje wore when Osbie Feel filmed her for the conditioning of Octopus Grigori (see V94.3–5n), a dress so dark brown it seems black, or "charcoal-saturated" (V94.11), against the light. Pynchon takes care over Katje's clothing, and the transitions come full circle: from brown-black, here, to a "long Medici gown of sea-green velvet" (V190.21), to a "white pelisse" (V194.27), to a "rainbow striped dirndl skirt of satin" (V208.8), then back into black (V224.23) before she breaks out of this cycle by appearing in "a red gown of heavy silk" (V225.38).

V186.5, B216.34   guiches   Little side-curls that frame the face, also known as "kiss-curls."

V186.40, B217.34   tetanus   Here, sharp muscular contractions brought on by a repeated stimulus.

V188.14–15, B219.21–22   Puritan reflex of seeking other orders behind the visible   Referring to the practice of hermeneutical interpretation among Puritan divines—a rigidly orthodox, deterministic mode of textual analysis. In a seventeenth-century treatise on the subject, William Whitaker (1687; quoted in Bercovitch 111) defined its rigid, a priori limitations: "When we proceed from the thing to the thing signified, we bring no new sense, but only bring to light what was before concealed in the sign."

V188.18, B219.26   no "found" crab   That is, not a randomly determined sign. In the "ready-mades" or "found objects" of modernist art, one enjoys the intellection of coincidental design in everyday things.

V188.37, B220.7   "nessay-pah?"   For *n'est ce pas?* (is it not?).

EPISODE 2

The episode opens on the evening of Slothrop's encounter with the "devilfish" (V192.19), Grigori, now safely back aboard ship with his keeper. Katje continues to play her role, setting up an assignation with Slothrop at midnight, "her hour" (V205.26), because it is the witching hour. Early next morning she contrives to make him "disappear" (V198.13). As they frolic beneath a red tablecloth, a cat burglar makes off with his clothes and papers of identity. Slothrop gives chase but is betrayed to gravity.

V189.20, B220.37   Grischa   Diminutive form of the Russian proper name Grigori.

V189.25, B221.4–5   the Bukharin conspiracy   Nikolai Bukharin (d. 1938) was a Trotskyite, revolutionary theorist, and writer. When the Stalinist regime brought him to trial in 1938, Bukharin "confessed" to a myriad of trumped-up "crimes," most of which involved ideological differences between the Trotskyite and Stalinite factions. He was executed in 1938, and the confessions tortured out of him sent more to death.

V190.8, B221.28   a warm pirozhok   A small Russian tart.

V190.23, B222.4   "RHIP," sings Tantivy, shuffling off sarcastic buffaloes   Serviceman's acronym for "Rank Hath Its Privileges." In the film *42nd Street* (1933), actor Dick Powell does a song-and-dance routine called "Shuffle Off to Buffalo."

V190.32, B222.14   "It's the Wormwood Scrubs School Tie."   See V33.31–32n.

V190.40, B222.24   bird Colonel   In the U.S. Army, a full colonel (see V80.20–22).

V191.2, B222.27   their sets   The burrow of a badger (*OED*).

V191.20, B223.6   White lightning   Illicit grain alcohol that's not been aged; instead, here it's been given a touch of the mythic: "mulled with the hammers of Hell" (V191.23) recalls the manner in which Thor cured liquour with his great hammer, named Mullicrusher.

V191.25, B223.11   the Uttermost Isle   Continuing the allusions to Teutonic mythology, Utgarth or "Outgard," is the uttermost island and home to Loki, mischief-maker among the gods (see also V709.39n).

V192.1, B223.25   Durban to Dover   A port city in eastern Africa and another in southern England.

V192.2, B223.26   four shaky sheets to the gale   Extrapolating from the slang metaphor describing one who is drunk as sailing "three sheets to the wind."

V192.4, B223.28   steeps of Zermatt   Alpine resort of Switzerland.

V192.5, B223.29   Plimsoll mark   On the hulls of ships, to indicate the amount of water "drawn" when loaded; named for Samuel Plimsoll (1824– 98), a member of the British Parliament who legislated the use of such marks.

V192.6, B223.30   He's been game to go off on a bat!   American thirties and forties slang for one who's been anxious to begin a drinking binge.

V192.8, B223.32   the high-sign   A discreet, usually secret gesture, to indicate it's time to depart.

V192.15–16, B224.4–6   humming "You Can Do a Lot of Things at the Sea-side That You Can't Do in Town"   Unknown song.

V192.38, B224.31   "He is with Supreme Headquarters"   SHAEF (see V17.7n).

V193.31–32, B225.26–27   "beyond Turl Street, past Cornmarket"   In Oxford, England, Turl and Cornmarket streets bracket Jesus College, originally established for Welsh students. Cornmarket is also home to the Union Society, a renowned debating and undergraduates' club, founded in 1823 and known for training some of the best orators in Parliament.

V194.6–7, B226.1–2   On to the Himmler-Spielsaal and chemin-de-fer till midnight.   A (fictional) Monte Carlo gaming room named for dreaded Nazi SS chief Heinrich Himmler. According to Baedeker, the gaming rooms close promptly at midnight; chemin de fer (Railroad) is a variant of baccarat.

V194.9, B226.5   rotogravure   Nineteenth-century process for mass-producing photographic images by transferring them to plates mounted on a rotary press.

V194.18, B226.17–18   red-dogging Choate boys   Choate is a boys' preparatory school of Wallingford, Connecticut (John F. Kennedy attended it when Slothrop would have been attending *his* school). In football, "red-dogging" is the (now archaic) term for an all-out defensive rush on the quarterback or backs, known in postwar argot as a "blitz."

V194.24, B226.25   malachite nymphs   Carved from a green and black mineral stone, a carbonate of copper, used for decorative and bas-relief statuary.

V194.26–27, B226.29   a white pelisse   From the Latin *pellis* (skin); a fur-lined robe. Note also the color shift, brown-black to white.

V195.13–14, B227.21–22   taffetas, lawn, and pongee . . . passementerie   Katje's handlers have carefully selected sheer, expensive fabrics for her wardrobe. Taffeta is a thin, woven, glossy fabric; lawn a thin linen; and pongee a loosely woven, knotted silk. Passementerie is trimming.

V195.23, B227.32   "got out by way of that Arnhem, then, right?"   In fact Pirate Prentice snatched Katje out of Holland by way of Scheveningen, as we know from V97.11–12; but Katje lets Slothrop think she escaped over the Scheldt River, near Arnhem, during the Rundstedt offensive.

V196.21, B228.30   Katje's skin is whiter   Her skin, the moonlight over this scene, the way parts of her darken with a "red animal reflection" (V196.29), and the various objects she wears like talismans— these details all suggest that Katje is another avatar of the White Goddess, like Nora Dodson-Truck of part 1 (see V150.16–23n).

V197.1, B229.12   a plastic shell   Recalls an earlier reference to the "shells of the dead," or Qlippoth (V176.14–15n). And it anticipates the black plastic shell of Imipolex G, designed for Gottfried's last ride in Rocket 00000. Note that Katje refuses to be "mounted by a plastic shell" of a man; but in part 3 Greta Erdmann will recall being dressed in the new plastic, Imipolex, and "mounted" by such a shell (see V488.2n).

V198.8–9, B230.28   a big red damask tablecloth   Yet another prop, and carefully selected. Recall the prevalence of the color red in Slothrop's sodium amytal session of episode 10, part 1. Clearly "They" have provided the tablecloth with such associations in mind. A reference to the red tablecloth, as a magician's prop, also appears later (V377.7).

V198.19, B230.40–41 "My little chickadee" This is W. C. Fields's line (as Cuthbert J. Twillie) to Mae West (Flower Belle Lee) in the film *My Little Chickadee* (1940). Miss Lee requires a consort for legal reasons and takes on Twillie, but through a series of hoaxes she frustrates his hope of a consummated marriage. In one scene she leaves a goat behind in her bed and, in the dark, Twillie makes florid declarations of passion to the blanketed animal, as Slothrop describes it here.

V198.33, B231.14–15 S'd against the S of himself Excepting the image of S-shaped spokes in a wheel (V4.19), this is the first of *GR*'s many "sigmoid" images: another sign of disease and disjunction.

V200.21, B233.16 "That blighter" In British slang, anyone whose presence blights; hence, a poor, downtrodden soul.

V200.28, B233.24–25 "*sauerkraut in the Strand!*" Along the north bank of the river Thames, the Strand is a major thoroughfare connecting the West and East Ends of London; here, used to figure forth the horror of sauerkraut-eating Nazis taking over Britain.

V200.39, B233.39 Kilgour or Curtis London tailors, located in Whitechapel.

V201.15, B234.18 "it's Lawrence of Arabia!" Thomas Edward Lawrence (1888–1935), who began his career as an Egyptologist, joined the British army when war broke out in 1914, commanded troops in the Mediterranean theater, and later wrote an account of his battle experiences in Egypt, Palestine, and Arabia. *Seven Pillars of Wisdom* made his literary fame in 1926.

V201.23–24, B234.29 Bristly Norfolk jacket See V184.14–15n.

V201.33, B234.39–40 Savile Row uniforms See V184.14–15n.

V201.35–36, B234.42–43 flimsies . . . a piece of Whitehall "Flimsies" are thin, multicolored papers used for making carbon copies (British argot). So neatly stacked, here, they are a synecdoche for the secretarial routinization of Britain, and specifically Whitehall, home of the War Office, Admiralty, and such.

V202.2, B235.9 "Didn't they teach you at Sandhurst to salute?" Home of the Officer's Cadet Training Unit (or OCTU), Sandhurst is a military college south of London.

V202.17–18, B235.27–28 Empire chairs A style of furniture imposed practically by an edict of Napoleon. The designs were based on the rectilinear forms of classical Greek and Roman architecture: massive and sumptuous, with laurel wreaths and torches adorning the design (in metal attached to wood).

V202.34–35, B236.4–5 golden, vaguely rootlike or manlike figure A mandrake root, a sign of secular crucifixion that will reappear in part 4, when Slothrop "becomes a cross himself, a crossroads" (V625.3–4).

V203.11, B236.22–23   the rainbow edges of what is almost on him   This
is Slothrop, feeling the anxieties of *Erwartung* (V101.9n). Later, when
he tries to explain his worries to Katje, she will remind him of his experience in this room, and she will connect it to one of her dresses,
a "rainbow-striped dirndl skirt," sign of a related anxiety (V208.8).

V203.34, B237.8   Bwa-deboolong   The Bois de Boulougne, the Paris
promenade well known as the turf of prostitutes. Maps and records tell
of no such street in Monaco, circa 1945.

**V204.1–4, B237.16–20   back to 1630 when Governor Winthrop came
... that *Arbella* and its whole fleet, sailing backward**   Aside from
the remarkable, extended use of *hysteron proteron* in this paragraph,
with its image of the fleet "sailing backward" to England, the historical
allusions are also significant. John Winthrop (1588–1649) was the
first governor of the Massachusetts Bay Colony, elected to that post
in 1629 before the Puritan fleet set sail from England, and reelected
seven times thereafter. Winthrop's flagship was the *Arbella*.
Thomas Pynchon's ancestor, William, was aboard the *Ambrose*, "rear
admiral" of the four-ship fleet. With others of the Puritan leaders,
William Pynchon came aboard the *Arbella* once during the journey,
about halfway across, when Winthrop invited the other patentees
to dine with him. According to Samuel Eliot Morison (73), they were
each rowed to the flagship during "a small gale." The heaving swells and
spilled pewter kettle of the scene in *GR* are doubtless Thomas
Pynchon's recreation of such a meal, with William Slothrop, as "mess
cook," in attendance.

**V204.33–35, B238.13–15   version of *L'Inutil Precauzione*... in *The
Barber of Seville***   In act II of Gioacchino Rossini's opera *The Barber
of Seville*, there occurs an opera-within-the-opera entitled "The Vain
Precaution." Rosina promises to sing the aria from this work to Doctor
Bartolo, her guardian but also—with strong hint of incestuous
desire—one of several men who are pressing Rosina for marriage. She
sings the aria because the mini-opera concisely parallels her own
situation: duty bound to Doctor Bartolo, but in love with the dashing
young Count Almaviva.

V204.39, B238.19–20   a lively Rossini tarantella   Dance music in
6/8 time, perhaps from *The Barber of Seville*.

V205.7–8, B238.31–32   *And if you need help, well, I'll help you*   Tantivy's words, from V194.3–4.

V205.13–14, B238.38–39   messieurs, mesdames, les jeux sont faits   Call
of the croupier at a roulettte table ("Ladies and gentlemen, the bets
are down") before he spins the wheel. In the film *Casablanca* (1943),
for instance, one hears the croupier, Ferrari, calling out these words in
dour, nasal tones to the patrons of Rick's bar.

EPISODE 3

His identity stripped, Slothrop begins his instruction in rocket dynamics. The time of this episode is indistinct; it seems to range over a period of some weeks, ending in "midwinter" (V224.25), or early February. The narration turns the reader's attention to language, its etymology, and how the lexicon of technology is suffused with an older, mythic lexicon. Another analepsis to pre-Hitler Berlin discloses how Peter Sachsa died. Katje leaves Slothrop for England, but not without first giving him a veiled warning.

V206.5, B239.30 "Oink, oink, oink," sez Slothrop Generations of Slothrops were swineherds (V555.5), and Slothrop himself will become a ceremonial pig (V567.34).

V206.14, B240.3 arrow-stable trajectories These involve the use of external fins to stabilize a projectile (Dornberger 122–24).

V206.15–16, B240.4–6 German circuit schematic whose resistors look like coils, and the coils like resistors See, for instance, the electrical schematics in Kooy and Uytenbogaart (356, 358). They follow the German system of designating a coil by means of a sawtooth line, which American technicians would understand as a resistor; conversely, their sawtooth line skewered with a straight line designates a resistor, whereas Americans use this indication for a coil.

V206.20, B240.10 Foreign Office P.I.D. Sir Stephen Dodson-Truck (whose moniker suggests the postwar brand of light truck, the Datsun, formerly produced by the Nissan Motor Works of Japan), works for the Political Information Division of the British Foreign Office.

V206.24–25, B240.16–17 "Old Norse rune for 'S,' sôl . . . German name for it is *sigil*" The source here is Grimm (620), whose etymological research discloses that "the sun was likened to a wheel of fire," represented by a circle with an axis point at its center: a mandala, in other words. Ancient Goths used this symbol, or rune, to represent the sun; later, "the Norse rune for S was named *sôl* sun," which is the Anglo-Saxon and Old High German *sigil* or *sugil*. This breakdown, from mandala to sigmoid line, seen here as a discontinuity in historical process, is not an imposition on Grimm's etymological details. Overall, his work documents the linguistic breakdown pursuant to the shattering of European tribal structures between A.D. 350 and 600.

V206.37, B240.31 a Plasticman comic Plasticman, or "Plas," was the creation of writer/artist Jack Cole, who took his own life in 1958. *Plasticman*, however, is still in print after forty years—a kind of immortality for comic book heroes. Plas made his debut appearance in a 1941 issue of *Police Comics*. His real name was Eel O'Brien, a petty crook who fell into a vat of acid while burglarizing the Crawford Chemical Works. Eel ran, awoke next day in a monastery, discovered that his entire body had become rubbery and pliable, and thereafter dedicated his life to stopping crime. By spring 1943 Cole had his own book for Plasticman, published by Quality Comics. It was a truly comical strip. Cole's plots hinged on slapstick humor, fast-paced and intelligent dialogue, and Plas's limitless ability to shape-shift and stretch. In fact, even a brief glimpse at the diction and rhythms of Cole's dialogue will suggest how much, and how often, the narrative voice in *GR* will slide into the rhetorical mode of *Plasticman*. One additional note on color: except for his outrageous white-frame glasses, Plas *always* appears in red.

V207.8, B241.6   "Telefunken radio control"   According to Dornberger (133–36), the Telefunken Radio Company worked on a centimetric guidance beam that would have delivered V-2 rockets over a distance of 150 miles and with "a dispersion of less than one thousand yards." If the system had gone operational, which it did not, the rockets would have become devastatingly accurate.

V207.12, B241.11–12   "it suggests *Haverie*"   Sir Stephen's etymological ramblings are accurate. The slang *abhauen* translates from the German as something like "Scram!" which is what the V-2 did on takeoff. *Hauen*, or "smashing someone with a hoe or a club" (V207.14–15), anticipates the analepsis to Peter Sachsa's murder (narrated in this episode, V220.31–39).

V208.8, B242.15   a rainbow-striped dirndl skirt   This is Katje's fourth principal change of clothes before once more donning her brown-black dress. On the rainbow significance of this one, see V225.2n.

V208.20, B242.30   before Arnhem   See V195.23n.

V208.21, B242.32   Palmolive and Camay   American bath soap brands.

V208.23, B242.34   Moxie-billboard   See 63.5n.

V209.20–21, B243.39–40   "I was in 's Gravenhage"   That is, in The Hague.

V209.25–26, B244.3–4   "the data on our side of the flight profile, the visible or trackable"   This corresponds with an idea presented in the novel's opening episode. That is, any naturally occurring rainbow wants to be a full circle, and if Earth did not intrude it would be (V6.33–35n). So there are two halves of the rainbow arch, just as there are two "sides" of "the flight profile." One side is visible; the other is not for it is betrayed to gravity (see also V726.19–20n).

V210.16–17, B245.1   sent away to that Johnson Smith   Based in Bradenton, Florida, the Johnson Smith Company distributes one of the most extensive lines of mail-order novelty goods in the United States.

V210.17–18, B245.2–3   from Fu Manchu to Groucho Marx   Fu-Manchu wore a long, wispy-thin moustache. Groucho Marx (1895–1977) wore a grease-paint moustache covering his entire upper lip, like an upside-down canoe.

V210.27, B245.14   "What about Wyatt Earp?"   The legendary lawman of Tombstone, Arizona. Slothrop's idea of Earp (1849–1929) derives from Stuart N. Lake's book, *Wyatt Earp, Frontier Marshall* (1931), the first biography to use extensive interviews with its subject, as well as interviews with those who recalled him from the Dodge City and Tombstone epoch. This was crucial, because Earp had previously been unwilling to discuss his past. Even more, Lake discovered a trove of documents hidden in Prescott, Arizona, that revealed Earp's questionable business dealings from the period. There had always been implications of greed and graft surrounding Earp, and the documents tended to support that view. Lake, however, chose to believe Earp's justifications; thus he presents (5) a "good" Wyatt, a man of "swift and decisive action," a leader "in the vanguard of those hardy, self-reliant pioneers who led the course of empire across the wilderness." This Wyatt met the rough-and-ready frontier on its own terms, willing to make shady deals for the good of all. Later historians, those "revisionists" (V210.30) the narrator refers to, have taken a much less generous view of the man.

V210.34, B245.22   "So did John Wilkes Booth's"   The subject is still moustaches. Booth (1838–65), Lincoln's assassin, had one whose ends were curved downward by gravity, as the encyclopedia daguerreotypes will show.

V211.10–12, B245.41–246.1   salvaged by the Polish underground . . . genuine SS shit and piss   The source for this detail was Irving (285). Allied intelligence made an important breakthrough when members of the Polish underground, along with several British scientists, followed the Russians into a V-2 test-firing site near Blizna, Poland, in September of 1944. The Russians had ravaged the site for anything technically significant, but one of the British scientists thought to check the latrines for discarded documents: "Sure enough," Irving writes, "in a pit which had been fouled by Russian militia no less than by German troops, he found a portion of a rocket test sheet." From this scrap, Allied intelligence determined that liquid oxygen and alcohol were the principal fuels for the V-2. The "genuine SS" excrement is Pynchon's flourish.

V211.15, B246.5   peroxide and permanganate lines   In the V-2, hydrogen peroxide and permanganate were combined to yield intense heat, to create superheated steam, to drive a turbine, to pump the rocket's supplies of liquid oxygen and alcohol, to drive the main engine. It was a chemically simple but mechanically complex system; see Kooy and Uytenbogaart (337–42).

V212.3, B246.38   clockwise around the table   Recall that clockwise is, according to Jung, the "correct" direction, the one involved with *conscious* process (V137.20n). This coincides with Slothrop's using the "Prince of Wales has lost his tails" game toward a well-reasoned end: he wants to loosen Sir Stephen's tongue, to find out "Their" designs.

V212.18–19, B247.16   "comprendez?"   Understand?

V212.27, B247.27–28   jeroboam of Veuve Clicquot Brut   A jeroboam of champagne holds four quarts; Veuve Clicquot is one of the prestige champagnes, produced in Reims; "Brut," a dry variety.

V212.33, B247.36   a Highlander in parade trews   A member of the Scots Guard wearing his ceremonial tartan plaid kilts.

V212.41, B248.4   dates of *degorgement*   The dates when bottles of champagne are opened to decant the deposits. Here, as those dates progress "into the war years," the champagnes become younger, less valuable.

V213.26, B248.36   Chateaubriand   A rich, seasoned, double cut of tenderloin steak.

V213.27, B248.37   ten-shilling panatelas   At exchange rates of the day, cigars costing about a dollar.

V213.35–36, B249.4   black Épernay grapes   In the Champagne district of France, Épernay is a town on the Marne River, whose fields produce some of the finest blancs de noirs (white champagnes from black grapes).

V213.36, B249.4–5   noble cuvées   The term derives from the French for a vat (*cuve*); a *cuvée* is thus a "vatting" or, in plainer terms, a batch.

V214.2, B249.9   sweet Taittinger   Because it's not produced from the Champagne district, a bottle from the Taittinger vineyard would be known among discriminating palates only as a "sparkling wine." Still worse, it is sweet. Another sign that vintage quality regresses as this game progresses.

V214.4–5, B249.12–13   playing "Lady of Spain"   The 1931 tune by Erell Reaves and Tolchard Evans:

> Lady of Spain, I adore you—
> Right from the night I first knew you,
> My heart has been yearning for you;
> What else can my heart do?
>
> Lady of Spain, I'm appealing—
> Why should my lips be concealing,
> All that my eyes are revealing;
> Lady of Spain I adore you.

V214.11, B249.20–21   a floating crown-and-anchor game   A favorite game of chance among sailors, who use three dice, the six faces of which will show either a crown, an anchor, or up to four "aces." The aim is to roll combinations of these. In underworld slang, a "floating" game is mobile, to elude the law.

V214.35, B250.7–8 of course Empire took its way westward Echoes Bishop Berkeley's famous paean to westward settlement in America, the "fourth act" of a historical drama before the revelation of Christ's millennial kingdom inaugurates the fifth and final act. The last stanza of his poem, "Verses on the Prospect of Planting Arts and Learning in America" (1752), declares:

Westward the Course of Empire takes its way;

The first four Acts already Past,

A fifth shall close the Drama with the Day;

Time's noblest Offspring is the last.

This was the ancient idea of the *translatio studii*, originally a classical concept about the westward progress of civilizations: Greece to Rome to Europe and then beyond.

V214.40–41, B250.14–15 the Angel that stood over Lübeck See V146.27n.

V215.5, B250.21 the night-going rake Lord Death That is, Dominus Blicero.

V215.18, B250.37 no milliards of francs A milliard is a thousand million; a franc, the French monetary unit.

V215.29, B251.7–8 "the *News of the World*" London news periodical.

V215.31, B251.10 "that kid who-who can *change his color*" Slothrop remembers how Nora Dodson-Truck was "caught" with Gavin Trefoil, whose "autochromatism" was the subject of earlier speculation (V147.13n).

V215.36–37, B251.17–18 "good chaps at Fitzmaurice House" See V76.32–33n.

V216.3–4, B251.27 "even a *touch* now and then" This is Sir Stephen, thinking about the needs of his wife, Nora; on the "miracle touch" see also V119.37n.

V217.14–16, B253.4–6 Carroll Eventyr . . . and his control Peter Sachsa Recalls the séance of episode 5, part 1 (see V29.31n).

V217.18, B253.8 Sammy Hilbert-Spaess The name suggests why he is the "most ubiquitous of double agents." In non-Euclidean geometry, Hilbert space (named for German mathematician David Hilbert, 1862–1943) is an abstract space. Whereas in ordinary space any point has three dimensional coordinates, any point in Hilbert space has a theoretically infinite number of coordinates; and any point in Euclidean space can be identified with an infinite-dimensional point in Hilbert space, so that the one is a "subspace" of the other. Sammy reappears in part 3 (V540.28).

V217.20, B253.10   scombroid face   The Scombroidei are a class of marine fishes that includes the mackerel.

V217.24, B253.16   Gallaho Mews   The mews of London are its stable alleys. This one is fictional, and the location of the novel's imaginary Twelfth House. Pynchon may well have derived the name from Chief Inspector Gallaho of Scotland Yard, a figure who appears in *The Trail of Fu-Manchu* (see V277.34–38).

V217.26–27, B253.18–19   They know . . . how to draw pentacles too   See V145.20n.

V218.10, B254.5–6   "a Zaxa"   The source once again is Jacob Grimm (203–5): a zax, from the Old High German *sax*, is a hatchetlike tool used to cut roofing slates. The point of this wordplay, when we recall Sir Stephen's etymological discourse on *sigil* and *hauen*, is to get at what happened, in 1930, to Peter Sachsa (his head was smashed in, as if in fulfillment of the name). There is more: Grimm mentions that the Saxons were so-called either because they wielded such an axlike weapon (the *saxum*) or because they worshiped a god by the name of Saxneat, a son of Wodin who wielded the weapon in battle. This god is Eventyr's "old Zaxa" of the next line.

V218.31–32, B254.31–32   She has swept with her wings another life   See Franz, to Leni, at V162.38.

V219.8, B255.12   the Hamburg Flyer   Express train from Berlin to Hamburg; the source may well have been Baedeker's *Berlin*.

V219.9, B255.13   industrial towers of the Mark   Short for the Märkisches Museum, a group of tall, plain buildings "dominated by a massive tower," as Baedeker (*Berlin* 257) notes. In "Old Berlin" the Mark was located several blocks from a railway station; thus Leni sees it as a (backward) reflection in the train window.

V220.31, B257.5–6   Schutzmann Jöche   Peter's killer is a *Schutzmann*, or constable; *Joche* (no umlaut) is the German plural for "yoke" (as for draught oxen). The origin of his name is otherwise unknown.

V221.13, B257.32   A rain-witch.   Another of the etymological puns derived from Grimm (1088), who notes that "in Germany witches were commonly called . . . *wetterhexe, wetterkatze*," that is, weather-witches or -cats. It was believed that they whimsically brought rain and storm; thus we have Katje, the *wetterkatze* often seen looking out on the rain.

V222.2, B258.26–27   I'm the Cagney of the French Riviera   In *The Public Enemy* (1931), actor James Cagney plays the role of a Prohibition gangster. In one scene he punches a grapefruit into the face of gun moll Mae Clark, the image Slothrop references here.

V222.32, B259.20   "the boundary-layer temperatures"   Kooy and Uytenbogaart (384–86) run through calculations for increases in the skin, or "boundary-layer," temperatures during the phases of the V-2's ascent and descent.

V222.37, B259.27–28 The bridge music A transitional device, like "segue" (V70.36n). The songs mentioned here are all pre–World War I tunes made famous by vaudevillians.

V223.8–10, B259.41–260.1 Nusselt heart-transfer coefficients . . . Reynolds numbers Both editions contain the same error; it should be "heat-transfer." The Nusselt number is a constant used in the calculation of forced convection, when a measure of total heat transfer is required. The Reynolds number, named for physicist Osborne Reynolds (d. 1917), is a quantity giving the amount of fluid moving through a tube, when velocity, diameter, viscosity, and liquid density are all known.

V223.13, B260.4 jet expansion angles From Kooy and Uytenbogaart again (310–12). They show how the expansion of jet nozzles, owing to heat, corresponds with Poisson's law for the increase in the pressure of flowing gases.

V223.19, B260.11 called the rocket *Der Pfau*. 'Pfau Zwei' This is Pynchon's fiction. None of the sources indicate that German rocket experts ever referred to the A4 rocket as *Der Pfau*, or "Peacock." The narrative logic of this invention? The peacock (or *Pavonia christatus*), with its rainbow tail, is a bird often linked symbolically with Christ.

V223.32, B260.27 draw-shots In the argot of pocket billiards, a shot that "draws" the cue ball off a cushion before striking its object ball.

V224.14–15, B261.8–10 Professors Schiller . . . Wagner . . . Pauer and Beck On Professor Beck, who designed "a circular slit injection nozzle" while at the Dresden College of Engineering, see Dornberger (132); on Professor Wagner of Darmstadt, co-inventor of the "integrating accelerometer" used in the V-2, see Dornberger (232). Professors Pauer and Schiller are unknown.

V224.25, B261.23 the midwinter sea If read literally, this fixes the date as February 3, 1945.

V225.2, B262.2 "the skirt I was wearing" This is Katje's "rainbow-striped dirndl skirt" (V208.8n). Note that she makes this comment to Slothrop with her (determinist) "mask of no luck, no future" (V225.5), dropped for a moment. And Slothrop will remember this clue: in part 3 (V285.18n) he examines documents showing the lifelong conspiracy against him, and his thoughts return, as Katje intended, to the moment in Monaco's Himmler-Spielsaal when she wore that rainbow-colored skirt which is the sign of a covenant he dreads.

V225.35–36, B262.41–42 Benny Goodman Jazz clarinetist Benjamin David Goodman (1909–87), leader after 1932 of his own band and, after 1937, of the first integrated jazz band to make the big time.

EPISODE 4

Back to England and "The White Visitation"; the time, late February, after Katje's return from Monte Carlo. Pointsman and colleagues discuss problems with funding and with keeping Brigadier Pudding in line. In the guise of a Teutonic witch, Domina Nocturna, Katje disciplines Pudding by means of an elaborately contrived, satirical inversion of the Kabbalistic ascent to the Merkabah, or divine throne.

V226.17–22, B263.26–33   "Ordinarily in our behavior . . . reactions in the given setting."   This quotation is from "The Book," Pavlov's *Lectures*, volume 2, lecture 52, "An Attempt to Understand the Symptoms of Hysteria Physiologically" (109). The paper was delivered before the Academy of Sciences of the USSR in 1932, when (as Pynchon notes) Pavlov was eighty-three.

V226.33, B264.7   an old *gorodki* stick   This reference occurs in a poem that is Pointsman's attempt at a dramatic monologue in the manner of T. S. Eliot, with Ivan P. Pavlov as the persona. As in Eliot, this poem takes the epigraphic quotation, above, as its point of departure. In the line referenced here, *gorodki* means "little towns" and designates a game. The source was Horsley Gantt's introduction to the second volume of Pavlov's *Lectures* (34):

> *Gorodki* is an ancient game popular among the peasants of Russia, played with the same informality and ubiquity as "horseshoes" in this country. Two squares about the size of a small room are marked out on the ground some 60 to 80 feet apart, and into these are placed a number of six inch blocks of wood. The members of the opposing teams attempt to get all the blocks out of the square by throwing from a distance of 50 to 60 feet sticks about the size of baseball bats but much heavier. As soon as all the blocks are out, another formation is arranged to be knocked out, until a series have been set up, representing castles, fortresses, etc. The side which removes the blocks in the fewest number of strokes is the winner. Pavlov was a champion player until the age of 80, outlasting and outplaying all his youthful companions.

Another possible source is Vladimir Nabokov's *Pnin* (105): "I still hear the *trakh!*, the crack when one hit the wooden pieces and they jumped in the air," Pnin recalls after telling his guests the rules of the game. The hurled stick is called a *bita*, and its parallel with the V-2 rocket is of course the obvious analogy at work here: both projectiles fall on their targets according to the statistical laws of distribution, which is why Russian peasants may wager on *gorodki*.

V227.31–32, B265.1   a Savile Row serenity   The serenity of high, conservative fashion (see V184.14–15n).

V228.1–2, B265.13   inquiries down from Duncan Sandys   A member
of Parliament since 1935, a disabled veteran after 1940, a parliamentary
secretary to the Ministry of Supply after 1941, and husband of Winston
Churchill's daughter, Diana, Duncan Sandys (1908–87) was named,
in 1943, to head Britain's intelligence-gathering work on the German
V-weapons program.

**V228.16–17, B265.29–30   "took an organic chemistry course or two
together back at Manchester . . . ICI"**   That is, at Victoria University
of Manchester; ICI is the acronym of Imperial Chemicals, Inc., whose
dealings are treated in greater detail at V250.36–39.

V228.18, B265.32–33   "working out of Malet Street"   Unknown, probably fictional; thus it seems that Pointsman is the one caught "lying,
or bluffing" (V228.23) here.

V228.37, B266.13–14   "this whole show can prang"   That is, crash
or blow up. Pynchon doubtless picked up this bit of British argot
from McGovern, who reports (31) that following the Allies' successful
1943 night raid against the German rocket facility at Peenemünde,
"Flight Lieutenant Mickey MacMichaelmore summed it up—'An excellent prang has been achieved.'"

**V229.8, B266.28–30   kidneys . . . vulnerable after a while to bromide
therapy**   Pavlov used injections of potassium bromide to aid the
inhibitory process, calming even the most excitable of his dogs. Nowhere that I know of does he mention kidney problems resulting
from bromide therapy; indeed, "The Book" (*Lectures* 2:95) claims that
"large doses of bromides given daily for many weeks or months have
proved in our hands to be free of any harm."

V229.14, B266.37   da screw   Underworld cant for "the jailer."

V229.34, B267.20   PAVLOVIA (BEGUINE)   A beguine is any slow dance
number, from the French *béguin* (flirtation). In 1930 the Russian
village of Koltushy, site of Pavlov's laboratories, was renamed Pavlova
in his honor (*Lectures* 2: 80).

V229.37, B267.23   Lysol   Registered American trademark of a liquid
disinfectant.

V230.21, B268.7   PWD   The Psychological Warfare Division (V76.36).

V230.21–22, B268.7–8   urges the Volksgrenadier: SETZT V-2 EIN!
Hitler's home guard, composed primarily of old men and boys
conscripted for the last-ditch defense of the fatherland, was called the
Volksgrenadier. The German verb *einsetzen* (to put in, insert; and,
when used with certain prepositions, to stand up or erect) gives a possible sexual pun here: "Erect V-2!"

V231.14, B269.2   the *Daily Herald*   London morning newspaper oriented
to Labour party interests.

V231.24–25, B269.15   "I am blessed Metatron."   Here begins a satirical
inversion of the Kabbalistic ascent to the Merkabah. In Kabbalistic

myths Metatron is foremost among the angelic host and is sometimes
depicted as standing beside or "keeping" Jahweh's throne, the Merkabah.
Pynchon's source here and in the following paragraphs is Scholem's
chapter on Merkabah Mysticism in *Major Trends in Jewish Mysticism*
(40–79). As he defines it, the visionary ascent to the throne takes
the initiate through seven antechambers, each confronting the aspirant
with a test. One of Scholem's sources puts it this way (78): "When
I ascended to the first palace I was devout (*hasid*), in the second palace
I was pure (*tahore*), in the third sincere (*yashar*), in the fourth I was
wholly with God (*tanim*), in the fifth I displayed holiness before God;
in the sixth I spoke the *kedushah* (the trishagion) before Him who
spoke and created, in order that the guardian angels might not harm
me; in the seventh palace I hid myself erect with all my might,
trembling in all limbs." The main theme of such visions, Scholem
argues, is the soul's ascent from earth and its return home through the
hostile antechambers and into God's fullness and light, all of it signifying redemptive process.

Note how Pynchon satirically inverts these representations. Brigadier
Pudding descends into a private hell, and into the darkness signified
by the muds of Passchendaele and symbolized in the Domina Nocturna
herself. And each of the seven anterooms through which Pudding
passes inverts the comparable motif in Kabbalistic lore. In the first,
a "hypodermic outfit" (V231.38) signifies not devotion but addiction.
The associations to "Severin" (V232.6) in the second (see below) point up
depravity instead of purity. In the third Pudding finds not sincerity
but scientific objectivity, and in the fourth an empty skull mocks the
idea of being "wholly with God." His trials go on like this until, instead
of standing erect before his God, Pudding kneels in abject servility
(but sexually erect) before an avatar of the *Shekinah*, the mother of material being and of dissolute death.

V232.6, B269.39–40   brand name is Savarin . . . it means to say "Severin"
The Savarin brand of coffee was frequently advertised in the *Times*
of London. Severin is the protagonist of Leopold von Sacher-
Masoch's novel *Venus in Furs* (1878). At Severin's insistence (and
later with no insistence at all), Wanda (Venus) takes him as her slave,
ordering Severin to stand in attendance while she bathes. Later they call
in a painter to "immortalize" on canvas their master/slave union—
she dressed in furs, whip in hand and posed with one foot on his back.

V232.15, B270.7–8   copy of Krafft-Ebing   The massive study of deviant
sexuality, *Psychopathia Sexualis* (1886), by Richard von Krafft-Ebing.

V232.16–17, B270.9   a Malacca cane   These canes are made from
the stems of rattan palms, from the Malaysian state of Malacca; characters in Ward's Fu-Manchu fictions often appear with them in hand,
symbols of constabulary discipline and autocratic power.

V232.20, B270.13–14   a tattered tommy up on White Sheet Ridge   A corpse of a British infantryman ("tommy") that Pudding recalls from a ridge in the Ypres Salient.

V232.21, B270.14   Maxim holes   Bullet holes from an air-cooled machine gun named for its designer, Hiram S. Maxim of the United States. During the Great War, Britain, Germany, Russia, and the United States all used versions of it.

V232.21–22, B270.15   eyes of Cléo de Mérode   She was a notorious dancer who became the mistress of King Leopold II of Belgium, on whose native soil were fought some of the nightmare battles Pudding recalls here.

V232.33, B270.30–31   a tall Adam chair   A neoclassical design, with great care for its proportionality and geometrical patternings; designed by eighteenth-century British architects Robert and James Adam.

V232.35, B270.33   "Domina Nocturna . . . shining mother and last love"   The source for Pudding's appellation is Grimm (1056), who discusses the diabolical "night-riding" that witches are famous for: "*Night-women* in the service of *Dame Holda* rove through the air on appointed nights, mounted on beasts; her they obey, to her they sacrifice. . . . These *night-women, shining mothers, dominae nocturnae* were originally demonic elvish beings, who appeared in women's shape and did men kindnesses." Like the Valkyries, the *dominae nocturnae* were thought to hover over battlefields to take off the souls of the dead. In this scene Katje appears to Pudding in the trappings of a White Goddess, the "shining mother" in her destructive aspect. On Dame Holda and her residence beneath Venusberg, see V364.22n and V374.39–375.2n.

V232.41, B270.40   recco photographs   From air reconnaissance; this bit of military argot occurs in Irving (passim).

V233.21, B271.23   Archies   In World War I slang, to "archie" meant to fire on an aircraft; thus "Archies" signify anti-aircraft guns.

V233.23, B271.26   a star shell   A phosphorous canon shell; it explodes in the air to illuminate a battlefield in white light.

V233.25–26, B271.28–29   she stood in No-man's Land   The ground between the trenches of opposing troops.

V234.7–8, B272.11–12   "At Badajoz . . . a bandera of Franco's Legion advanced"   The town of Badajoz, on the Portuguese frontier, site of one of the earliest and the most cold-blooded massacres of the Spanish civil war. After joining the struggle late, Franco won the assistance of both Hitler and Mussolini in flying his Army of Africa back to Spain over the Strait of Gibraltar. The Loyalist militiamen were quickly put into retreat and bottled up on August 16, 1936, in Badajoz, where the remaining two thousand of them were herded into the town's bullring and machine-gunned.

V234.28, B272.38   that Gourd Surprise   See V80.2–3.

V234.33, B273.2   gold-tasseled fourragère or his own Sam Browne   On the Sam Browne Belt see V9.40n. A *fourragère* is a braided cord worn around the left shoulder.

V235.38, B274.16–17   the smell of Passchendaele   See V79.41n.

V236.32, B275.17–18   effects of *E. coli*   Abbreviation for the bacteria *Escherichia coli*, a naturally occurring symbiont of the human lower intestine (or colon); toxic if orally ingested.

EPISODE 5

Back to Monte Carlo, where Slothrop's instruction continues, minus Katje; the time is March 20–21, 1945, the spring equinox. Slothrop uncovers perplexing evidence of collusion between businesses with interests in opposing sides of the war. He also inches closer to finding the links between his "conditioning" as an infant, the plastic called Imipolex G, and the rocket.

V236.36–37, B275.21–22   The great cusp . . . watersleep to firewaking   The spring equinox, separating the astrological house of Pisces (February 19 to March 20) from the house of Aries (March 21–April 19). Pisces, the Fishes, is the twelfth and last house of the astrological year, a water sign, and significant of dreaming, dissolution, and death. Aries, the Ram, is the first house of a new astrological year, a fire sign, and significant of identity, freedom, and rebirth. This transition is important in *GR*. Pisces dominated part 1, but Aries now takes over as the astrological sign under which events occur. As M. E. Jones (161) has put it, Aries symbolizes "the absolute freedom from social conditioning," and Slothrop will shortly slip free (or, at least think he's slipped free) of "Them." Jones also comments that the watchwords of the Aries type are "I AM," an idea the narrator will soon develop in playing on the name "Jamf," as well as in quoting from Rilke's *Sonnets to Orpheus*: "To the rushing water speak: I am" (V622.21). Finally, it is a notable moment because—if the calculations at V624.18n are correct—then Slothrop may have been born on this date, in 1918.

V237.1, B275.23–24   up in the Harz in Bleicheröde   The Harz Mountains are in central Germany. The town of Bleicheröde takes its name from *Bleich* (bleach, white), *Der Bleicher* ("Bleacher," a nickname for Death), and *öde* (a wasteland, or desert). Bleicheröde is near Nordhausen, where A4 rockets were manufactured underground, and the scene for early episodes in part 3. Note also the symmetry: von Braun in his "white waste" and Pointsman at his "chalk piece of seacoast" (V237.6) near Dover.

V237.1–2, B275.24—25 Wernher von Braun . . . his 33rd birthday Von
Braun broke his arm in an automobile accident on March 18, 1945.
In his memoir, *Peenemünde to Canaveral* (148), Dieter Huzel recalls
von Braun's thirty-third birthday celebration, on March 23. Looking
down from their perch in the Harz, the celebrants glimpsed signs
of advancing Russian divisions.

V237.4, B275.28 storks The Bantam misprints it as "stroks."

V237.9, B275.33 Lloyd George is dying. Former prime minister David
Lloyd George became gravely ill in early March; until his death on
March 26, the *Times* of London carried almost daily reports on his
condition.

**V237.12–13, B275.37–276.1 miles of secret piping . . . roast German
invaders** In 1940 the plan, should Germany have attempted a landing
on Britain's south coast, was to set the waters aflame with gasoline.
Gas pipes were laid in the tidal zone with that possibility in mind.

V237.14, B276.2 hypergolic ignition Occurs when a proper mixture
of fuel components spontaneously ignites, as with hydrogen peroxide
and sodium permanganate in the turbine drive of the V-2 (V211.15n).

V237.16–20, B276.4–8 Carl Orff's lively . . . Totus ardeo Orff (1895–
1978) was a German composer known especially for his interest in
reviving primitive rhythms and melodies. The lyric here is from his
musical arrangements for the *Carmina Burana* (1936). Originally
a thirteenth-century codex of song lyrics, it was made public in the
nineteenth century when the monastery from which it came was
secularized. Orff was taken by the irreligious qualities of the songs,
which Helen Waddell (208) also praised, in 1927, as "the last flowering
of the Latin tongue." Bavarian monks had used the goddess Fortuna,
with her wheel, as a frontispiece to their book; and the songs are all remarkable for their treatment of hedonistic motifs, followed through
the turning seasons of the year. Insofar as this episode occurs on "the
great cusp" (V236.36) of spring, the narrator appropriately selects
from the *Carmina Burana* a spring dance lyric, called "Tempus est
iocundum" (The Time Is Agreeable). To back the lyric, Orff arranged
a fast-paced combination of wind and percussion instruments. The
Latin translates to

    Oh, oh, oh,
    I bloom entirely!
    Now virginal love
    Burns me entirely . . .

V237.21, B276.9 Porstmouth to Dungeness That is, from the west
to the east end of Britain's coastal South Downs, with a lighthouse
marking each port city.

**V238.7–8, B276.38–40 has Roland been whispering from eight kilome-
ters . . . one of the Last Parabolas** The last V-2 of the London Blitz

was launched from Holland on March 28, 1945; it struck the village of Orpington, in Kent, at 7:45 P.M. on Ash Wednesday. Following that strike, a few final rockets were launched against advancing American positons in Europe, but apparently none were used after April 1, Easter Day. Here, Roland Feldspath occupies one of those final trajectories, but the "eight kilometers" is puzzling; the V-2 soared higher than *eighty* kilometers.

V238.22, B277.17–18   His cryptic utterances that night at Snoxall's   See V30.26–36, about the "control" being put *"inside"* the vehicle.

V238.25, B277.22   Schwärmerei   Idolization, fanaticism.

V238.30, B277.27–28   the Cybernetic Tradition   The reference is anachronistic. Cybernetics is the science of communication and control in and between animal and/or machine. But its father, Norbert Wiener, writes (12) that "the term cybernetics does not date further back than the summer of 1947."

V239.18–19, B278.22   demons—yes, including Maxwell's   British physicist James Clerk Maxwell (1831–79) introduced the idea of the "sorting demon" in his *Theory of Heat* (1871). His aim was to cast a playfully doubtful light on the second law of thermodynamics, which holds that producing "any inequality of temperature or of pressure" within a closed system is impossible without the expenditure of work, which expends energy, thus bringing the system back into equilibrium. Maxwell's "sorting demon" would however place himself in the passageway between two linked vessels. He would "see" individual molecules and select the faster ones for vessel A and the slower ones for vessel B: faster molecules, higher temperatures; and conversely so for the other vessel. Thus without an expenditure of work the demon would create an inequality of temperatures and pressures, contradicting the second law. There are many counterproofs. For instance, the demon needs light to "see" the molecules, but the introduction of light would *add* energy to the system, negating any effect the demon might have on it. For an excellent summary of this background, and the relations to cybernetic theory, see Mangel (87–89).

V239.24, B278.28–29   motion under the aspect of yaw control   The formula Pynchon quotes is from Kooy and Uytenbogaart (247).

V239.26–27, B278.31–32   Scylla and Charybdis . . . to Brennschluss   In the Strait of Messina, Scylla is a legendary rock standing opposite a whirlpool, called Charybdis. Homer personified the two seafaring hazards in book 12 of *The Odyssey*. On Brennschluss see V6.37n.

V240.5, B279.12   Plattdeutsch   That German dialect spoken in the low country of the northern provinces, Schleswig-Holstein and Niedersachsen, part of the British zone after May 8, 1945.

V240.5, B279.13   Thuringian   The central German province of Thuringia includes the Harz Mountains and what was then the main rocket works at Nordhausen. U.S. Army units reached there before the Russians, but in accordance with the Yalta agreements of February 1945, Nordhausen was transfered to Soviet hands in June.

V240.11–18, B279.20–29 seems that early in 1941, the British Ministry of Supply . . . first successful test in August of '42 The details here all derive from Irving (55). Compare the account in *GR* to that in *The Mare's Nest*:

> The remarkable story of Lubbock's petrol-oxygen rocket goes back to early 1941, when a £10,000 Ministry of Supply research contract was finally awarded to Shell International Petroleum Company to develop an assisted take-off rocket, using any fuel other than cordite, which was to be in short supply. In comparison with the millions of pounds spent by the Germans on rocket research, this sum was not impressive; and Shell had to pay all costs other than the cost of the actual materials and fuel.
>
> Isaac Lubbock decided to experiment with aviation fuel and oxygen, moderating the temperature with water. The Ministry of Supply placed at his disposal a part of the Petroleum Warfare Establishment at Langhurst, near Horsham. . . . a five-second trial was successfully carried out at Langhurst on 15th August 1942.

V240.19, B279.29–30 Lubbock was a double first at Cambridge The reference is to Lubbock's having scored two "firsts," or highest marks, on the tripos exams at Cambridge (V31.17n). The source, again, is Irving (154): "The Shell engineer had taken a Double First at Cambridge."

V240.21–22, B279.33 Mr. Geoffrey Gollin Isaac Lubbock's chief assistant at Shell, according to Irving (56). He helped find the excrement-stained documents mentioned earlier (V211.10–12n).

V240.23, B279.35 "an Esso man myself" In other words, before the war Slothrop used to gas up his Hudson Terraplane at a Shell Oil Company rival, the American Esso Company.

V240.25, B279.38 "whole bottle of that Bromo" Bromo Seltzer, an American brand of antacid, for mild, transient stomach disorders.

V240.35, B280.7–8 "That's Bataafsche Petroleum Maatschappij, N.V.?" Slothrop inquires about the Royal Dutch Shell Company. For details about the Nazi's use of Shell company headquarters on "the Josef Israelplein" (a city street) for siting a "radio guidance transmitter" (V241.3–4), see Kooy and Uytenbogaart (287).

V240.37, B280.10 a recco photograph See V232.41n.

V240.41, B280.15 like Cary Grant The American actor with the quasi-British accent; Slothrop parodies him at V294.11.

V242.6, B281.27–28 "Vorrichtung für die Isolierung" Literally, a "device for the insulation."

V242.9–15, B281.31–38 a DE rating . . . OKW . . . directs Slothrop

to a Document S G-1 ... "a state secret"   The source for these details
was a photocopy of the "Contract for 12,000 A4 Rockets" given as
an illustration in Irving (opposite 299). Documents pertaining to the
rocket were given a "DE 12" security rating—the "highest priority," as
Irving comments and Pynchon repeats. The OKW was the German
Oberkommando des Wehrmachts, or Army High Command. On
the photostat in Irving, the SS stamp and warning *Geheime Kommandosache* (Secret Command-matter) are clearly visible, along with
the (numerical) legal reference that Pynchon translates.

V242.38–39, B282.24   "specific impulse"   Slothrop uses the European
expression for "specific thrust," a measure of thrust usually given
in foot/pounds. The source here, and for the data quoted in the lines
to follow, is Kooy and Uytenbogaart (395–98).

V243.17, B283.2–3   Alkit uniforms   Unknown.

**V243.28—29, B283.16–17   a gold benzene ring with a formée cross
in the center**   See V249.24–25. It was Kekulé von Stradonitz who discovered the hexagonal benzene ring; a "formée" (that is, "styled")
design would resemble a Maltese cross.

V243.39, B283.30–31   George ("Poudre") de la Perlimpinpin   Derives
his name from the French *poudre* (powder) and the French slang *perlimpinpin* (a dash, a soupçon); but the meaning changes when they are
used together, as in *C'est de la poudre de perlimpinpin!* (That's a bunch
of baloney!).

V244.11, B284.2   in clear   That is, uncodified (military argot).

V244.18, B284.10–11   the trente-et-quarante table   Also known as
"red and black," trente-et-quarante is, with chemin de fer, one of the
principal card games played at the Monte Carlo casino. Six decks
of cards are shuffled together and dealt in two rows (one called "rouge,"
the other "noir"). Face cards and tens carry a value of ten; aces, one;
and the rest, their numerical values. The dealer lays out the rows until
they total thirty-one or more; the row most closely approaching thirty-
one wins. There are side bets on the color of the first card in each row.

EPISODE 6

D uring the spring of 1945, Slothrop attends a party thronged with underworld types. One of them, Blodgett Waxwing, confirms Slothrop's sus-
picion that the octopus incident was a manufactured event. Slothrop is now
ready to make his escape from Monaco, and Waxwing gives him the address
of a hideout in Nice.

V244.26, B284.20   hashish in the Hollandaise   The Bantam misprints
it as "Hallandaise."

V245.27, B285.24   Saxophony and Park Lane kind of tune   Park Lane forms the eastern boundary of London's Hyde Park and lies two blocks from Slothrop's former office near Grosvenor Square. Once a residential street for the wealthiest of Londoners, it had become, by 1945, a street of shops, offices, and hotels like the Dorchester and the Grosvenor House, with their facilities for ballroom dancing. In this context, "Saxophony" makes a kind of sense: as another of the narrator's etymological puns. In the nineteenth century Adolphe Sax invented the instrument that bears his name, but readers will also recall *saxo*, the etymological root from which the hatchet-wielding Saxons took their name (see V218.10n). In addition, Clarence Major's work on Afro-American slang records how, among jazz musicians of this period, an "ax" designated "any musical instrument but usually a saxophone." In these Park Lane ballrooms and at Perlimpinpin's party, then, what we have is "Saxophony"—imitations of the genuine article, faked attempts at the real jazz.

V245.29, B285.26–27   nodded out on a great pouf with Michele   Mr. Bounce naps on a hassock (the French *pouf*); but the term also signifies, in British slang, a male homosexual.

V245.36, B285.35–36   Tom Mix shirt . . . a Percheron horse   American cowboy-actor Thomas Hezekiah Mix (1880–1940) used to favor the old cavalry-style bibbed shirtfronts, with lots of piping and silver buttons. A Percheron horse is incongruous; the breed is a large French draught horse, usually dappled and with large hooves.

V246.1, B285.37   Bokhara rug   A Turkish style, with black and white octagons set on a background of red, sienna, and tan.

V246.4–5, B286.2–3   a white zoot suit with reet pleats   The origins of the zoot are obscure. Some attribute its elaborately pegged and pleated trousers—the "reat pleats" billowing out over one's thighs— to the style of trousers and long coats popular among American college boys of the twenties and thirties. An article in *Newsweek* (June 21, 1943) claims that the zoot also owes something to Clark Gable's costumes for *Gone with the Wind*. The zoot suit coat was double-breasted, with billowing arms, padded shoulders, and a knee-length cut ("the drape shape"). In March of 1942 the U.S. War Production Board virtually banned the zoot suit by severely restricting the amounts of material to be used in men's clothes. As a result, bootleg tailors sprang up in Harlem and East Los Angeles. In 1943 the War Frauds Division cracked down on this underworld commerce, forbidding sales of zoots at shops in New York, Chicago, and Los Angeles. The crackdown had racial overtones that were rather obvious: the main "zootsers" were Hispanics and blacks. After the Zoot-Suit Riots of June 1943, the Los Angeles City Council passed an ordinance making the wearing of the zoot a misdemeanor offense (see V249.4–5n).

V246.9, B286.8   a Shirley Temple   A glass of soda pop with a cherry on top; named for the child screen star (V466.4n).

V246.14–15, B286.16   Jean-Claude Gongue   Perhaps from the American underworld slang "gonga" or "gongue" (anus).

V246.21–22, B286.24   American Army yellow-seal scrip   Paper currency issued by the United States for use in the occupied zones of Europe. Because it was widely counterfeited and used in black-marketeering, it was withdrawn from circulation in May 1945 (see also V438.9).

V246.25, B286.28   a Groucho Marx voice   Because this sort of inane pun, on Tamara/tomorrow, is characteristic of those that Julius ("Groucho") Marx used to interject—for example, in movies like *A Day at the Races* (see V619.1–4n).

V246.35, B286.40   the Caserne Martier   This is mispelled in both editions; it should be "the Caserne Mortier." Pynchon's source was a feature article in *Life* magazine for March 26, 1945 (25–29), entitled "GIs Involved in Black Market Held in Caserne Mortier." There are lots of photos: the stockade, a grim, closely guarded brick structure; the inmates, all rugged, hardened-looking characters; and the guards, who look equally case-hardened. There isn't much of a written story. Most inmates, the *Life* correspondent notes, were charged with murder, rape, theft of military or civilian property, or black-marketeering. Escape, according to the jailers, was next to impossible.

V246.36, B286.41   the ETO   Acronym for European Theatre of Operations.

V246.37, B286.42   PX ration cards   Issued to ration a soldier's purchases (of cigarettes, for example) at the post exchange.

V246.37, B287.1   Soldbücher   The paybooks issued German soldiers.

V246.38–39, B287.2–3   AWOL . . . since the Battle of the Bulge   See V52.23–24n. Waxwing has been absent without leave since mid-December 1944.

V247.2, B287.7–8   deuce 'n' a half ruts   An army truck, load-rated at two and a half tons, with dual rear wheels that leave wide ruts.

V247.5, B287.12   hot-wire   In underworld slang, to reroute the ignition wires in order to steal a car. The inspiration for this detail is probably the *Life* article on Caserne Mortier once more; car thefts were a major problem for the Allied governments, and the writer even mentions how a soldier in possession of electrical gear for a jeep could be charged.

V247.6–7, B287.13–14   a good old Bob Steele or Johnny Mack Brown   After making his screen debut in *Near the Rainbow's End* (1929), Bob Steele went on to act in an average of seven cowboy pictures each year. Despite his small size, he became a matinee idol of the thirties and forties; his specialties: whirwind fighting and hot-dog riding. Johnny Mack Brown was a college football all-star who made his film debut in 1927 and had his first starring role with Wallace Beery

in King Vidor's version of *Billy the Kid* (1930). Like Bob Steele he
became a matinee idol: a handsome, dynamic, and above all young
cowboy, for it was Steele and Brown who supplanted the older generation of screen-cowpokes from the silent era.

V247.8–9, B287.15–16   thousands of snowdrops' brains   In U.S. service
slang, "snowdrops" are the military police, whose helmets, puttees,
gloves, and belts are all white.

V247.9, B287.16   he has seen *The Return of Jack Slade*   And, given
the time of the narrative *histoire*, it is a remarkable feat, because
the film wasn't made until a decade after these fictional events. Edward
Mendelson first pointed out the anachronism in his essay "Gravity's
Encyclopedia" (184). We might well ask why Pynchon makes the error,
and one answer would be that he meant to work out a certain parallel. In
Gravity's Rainbow, director Gerhardt von Göll plans a film version
of José Hernandez's two-part Argentinian epic poem, *Martín Fierro*. The
second part of the poem treats the "return" of that outlaw gaucho.
Similarly, *Jack Slade* (1953) and *The Return of Jack Slade* (1955) were
also based on a literary text, Mark Twain's *Roughing It*, chapters
9–11. As Twain tells the story, Slade was a decent but ruthless man,
a vigilante who was hanged in Virginia City for the "crime" of stamping
on a court order. On the gallows he broke down and wailed for his
wife. Taking its epigraph from Twain, *Jack Slade* attempted to show
the mitigating circumstances that turned a law-abiding cowboy into a
ruthless killer. The first film was something of a matinee hit, so
director Harold Schuster decided to go for the double play. *The Return
of Jack Slade* brings on the vigilante's son, who tries to restore his
father's tarnished reputation. The notable thing, here, is that the young
man "sells out"; he becomes a Pinkerton agent, and that is exactly
the sort of sell-out to "Them" that Pynchon also condemns in part 2
of *Martín Fierro*, the "return" section (see V387.12–13).

V247.11, B287.18–19   a typical WW II romantic intrigue   Perhaps
because the plot might be taken as a parody of some popular wartime
cinema thriller. Also, the Tamara-Italo-Waxwing-Theophile connection
makes yet another "progressive *knotting into*" (V3.25), or circling
into, that is complicated but not irrational, if one sorts out the vehicle
(an American-made Sherman tank), and the collateral ("front money"),
and the politics (Palestine was seething with intrigue as Zionists
attempted to carve an Israeli state out of the chaos Germany left behind), and the decadent motive (Turkish opium). We may also think of
it as a type, "another of them Tamara/Italo drills," as the narrator
soon notes (V261.39–40). They keep readers practiced at following and
interpreting plots; and this circular "drill" also keeps one in an open-
ended state of anticipation (or *Erwartung*), because nothing ever develops from it.

V247.30, B287.41   a face like Tenniel's Alice   British graphic illustrator John Tenniel (1820–1914) drew the original illustrations for Lewis Carroll's "Alice" books: *Alice in Wonderland* and *Through the Looking Glass.*

V247.35, B288.5–6   like the eyes of King Kong   In Merian C. Cooper's 1933 film, Kong's eyes have a way of "burning" when he first appears, crashing through the jungle to snatch away Fay Wray. Later, in New York, his eyes become pathetically lightless.

V248.2, B288.15   "One coup de foudre!"   From the French, "One bolt [of lightning] from the blue!" Also, an idiom for "love at first sight."

V248.7, B288.22   Jell-o   American brand of gelatin products.

V248.17–18, B288.35   swell enough looking twist   In American slang a "twist" is a chorus girl.

V248.28, B289.5–6   Tamara is escorted   The Bantam misprints it as "Tamar."

V248.32, B289.10   Errol Flynn   Known for his hard-living, swashbuckling style both on and off the screen, mustachioed Errol Flynn (1909–59) makes an ironic analogue here to girl-grappling Slothrop.

V248.41, B289.21   an address on Rue Rossini   See V253.33n.

V249.4–5, B289.26–27   the Zoot Suit Riots of 1943   The fighting broke out first of all in East Los Angeles. On June 1, 1943, two sailors stationed in Long Beach made unwelcome advances toward several *cholitas*, so-called slick chicks who traveled with gangs of Chicano zoot-suiters. The girls' boyfriends mauled the sailors and tensions rose. On the night of June 4, bands of sailors skirmished through East L.A., tearing the zoots off any *pachucos* (the gang members) who would not voluntarily disrobe. Next night, pachuco gangs retaliated in force and large-scale rioting broke out. Six nights of street fighting left about 120 injured; 18 sailors were treated for serious injuries. Arrests totaled 94 Chicanos and 20 servicemen. The usual bureaucratic gestures followed: Nelson Rockefeller, coordinator of Interamerican affairs for the Roosevelt administration, began a federal inquiry into the riots. Gov. Earl Warren of California impaneled a five-man board of inquiry. Meanwhile, in late June the Zoot-Suit Riots began to spread, with violence breaking out between whites and black "zootsers" in San Diego, Philadelphia, Detroit, and Toronto.

V249.5–6, B289.28   Anglo vigilantes from Whittier   Former California home of Richard Nixon and home also to Whittier College, his alma mater; San Gabriel (V249.11) is a nearby suburb of Los Angeles.

EPISODE 7

Next day, Slothrop learns the ostensible uses of Imipolex G in the rocket and learns also—while he scans an old *Times* of London—of Tantivy's death. This news pushes him over the edge; he departs for an address in Nice. Secret Service agents ("Apaches") still trail him. He becomes involved with a group of Argentine anarchists, runs errands for them between Zurich and Geneva, Switzerland—losing the U.S. agents as he goes—and when finished spends the night on an Alpine peak, at the grave of Laszlo Jamf. In payment for his anarchist legwork, a messenger brings Slothrop documents that confirm Jamf's role in his past, but readers do not learn of their contents until the opening of part 3. In this episode Slothrop assumes the identity of his next avatar: "He is now an English war correspondent named Ian Scuffling" (V256.35–36).

V249.21, B290.5 an aromatic heterocyclic polymer In organic chemistry, the aromatics are a class of compounds structurally related to, or based on, the six-carbon benzene ring. Looped together in still larger, heterocyclic chains, they form a polymer, a compound of very high molecular weight but based upon simple, yet infinitely repeatable, units. For example, the "polyethers" of V250.2 are formed from benzene rings with attached ether radicals, all strung into larger rings. As metaphor, note the idea of regression, of cycles within cycles, consistent with structural aspects of *GR* itself.

V249.28, B290.14 du Pont E. I. du Pont de Nemours and Company. In the twenties and thirties, the company's main research laboratories at Wilmington, Delaware, produced a score of new polymers, including nylon, neoprene rubber, and polyester fabrics.

V249.29–30, B290.16–17 Carothers . . . The Great Synthesist He is Wallace Hume Carothers (1896–1937). Du Pont hired him in 1928 for his research into linear polymers. During the next decade, his work led directly to a series of discoveries, most notably the discovery of nylon, at first called "Fiber #66." At du Pont, Ira Williams used Carothers's research to develop neoprene rubber; and the work of Carothers and his assistant Julian Hill also led to the production of polyester fabrics and plastics. Carothers was a melancholy genius who took his own life in 1937.

V250.2–3, B290.28–29 aromatic polyamides . . . polysulfanes The polyamides comprise the nylon family; polycarbonates are linear polyesters of carbonic acid, useful as injection-molded plastics; the polyethers are another family of plastics; the polysulfanes, a linear polyester of sulfuric compounds.

V250.17, B291.9 monomer Any of the molecular units—the amides, for example—that can be polymerized.

V250.23–24, B291.17–18 Psychochemie AG . . . Grössli Chemical Corporation The first company ("Psychochemistry, Inc.") is a Pynchon fiction; the second was an actual subsidiary of the IG Farben cartel (see V284.15–16n).

V250.25–27, B291.18–21   Sandoz . . . Ciba, and Geigy   Originally a Swiss dyestuffs manufacturer, the Sandoz company branched out into pharmaceuticals during this century. In 1943 Dr. Albert Hofmann of Sandoz was experimenting with a synthetic preparation of lysergic acid when he accidentally ingested a portion of it and experienced hallucinogenic effects. The acid, one of the two principal ingredients in the manufacture of LSD, is an indole compound. Ciba-Geigy Pharmaceutical, Ltd., is based in Basel, Switzerland.

V250.36, B291.33   ICI   This is the British firm Imperial Chemical Industries, of London, a cartel organized in 1926 to match the power of the German IG firm. By 1939 ICI was "second only to IG in Europe" and had reached agreements with the German firm concerning territories and trading rights (Sasuly 49).

V250.41, B291.38   the Schokoladestrasse, in that Zurich   A fictional Chocolate Street, for the fictional firm Psychochemie AG.

V251.10–12, B292.9–11   Mr. Duncan Sandys . . . the Ministry of Supply located . . . at Shell Mex *House*   All of this is historically accurate, though the inference of collusion with the Germans is entirely that of Pynchon's speaker. On Sandys, see V228.1–2n; on his offices at the Shell Mex House, Pynchon's source was Irving (70). The Shell Mex House is an office building on the Embankment, near Waterloo Bridge. The location of the German radar-guidance tower, atop the Royal Dutch Shell building in The Hague, appeared earlier (V240.35n).

V252.4, B293.10   "S-Gerät, 11/00000"   Pynchon's first extended discussion of the Schwarzgerät (black device) and the rocket number (the quintuple zero) it went into. All V-2 rockets were given five-digit serial numbers, as Huzel (87) explains: "For a reason I have never discovered, the first production missile number was 17,001. At war's end the assembly lines were turning out missiles in the 22,000 numbering block."

V252.14, B293.22   last Tuesday's London *Times*   Probably the *Times* of London for Tuesday, April 24, 1945. Slothrop's remark to himself two lines later—"Allies closing in east and west on Berlin"—correspond with the headlines and map on p. 2, the *Times*'s main news page. On April 17, the fighting was still some distance from Berlin; on Tuesday, May 1, the Russians had already entered the city. Slothrop also remarks on an advertisement from the Ministry of Foods on p. 5 of the April 24 edition. Entitled "Bacon and Eggs," it gave the (regulated) price of powdered eggs as "one and three," just as Slothrop comments to himself. The names he reads in the "Fallen Officers" column are all fictional. At the Empire Cinema throughout this period, however, was not *Meet Me in St. Louis* (1944), but another Judy Garland picture, *Under the Clock* (1945). If this "last Tuesday's London *Times*" is indeed that for April 24, then the date of this scene must be late April, perhaps around the thirtieth.

V253.10, B294.25–26 down the Corniche Leaving Monte Carlo, Slothrop drives west on the Moyenne Corniche, a twisting, switchbacking road initially built for Napoleon and linking the coastal cities of southern France.

V253.15, B294.32 a black Citroën During the prewar years, the Citroen Motor Works of France produced several models of powerful, comfortable, "saloon-type" automobiles.

V253.17, B294.33–34 a flopping Sydney Greenstreet Panama hat In the film *Casablanca* (1943), he played a panama-hatted merchant.

V253.19–20, B294.37 off Place Garibaldi Named for Italian anarchist Guiseppe Garibaldi (1807–82), whose so-called redshirts brought Europe its first inkling of the patriotic militarism in its future. Here as elsewhere, Pynchon's geographical references are fairly accurate. Coming into Nice, the Corniche would deliver Slothrop directly to the Place Garibaldi, near the center of town. He "ditches the car" there, walks south about a third of a mile toward the Mediterranean, then snacks in the Old Town district just east of the Port (called the Port Fausse, or False Port, because it was excavated). Next, he walks the three-fourths of a mile into the Quartier de la Croix of Nice, to the address on Rue Rossini.

V253.26, B295.2 April summertime Because the weather in Nice becomes so warm by April that the tourist season ends.

V253.33, B295.11 the Rue Rossini A street of residential flats and pensions in the Quartier de la Croix. Named for the Italian composer Gioacchino Rossini, and significant in light of the Beethoven/Rossini debate that will develop in part 3 of *GR*. Recall also the Rossini music playing at the Casino Hermann Goering (V204.33–39).

V254.5, B295.26 femme de chambre A chambermaid.

V254.33, B296.16 Apache sideburns Remember the Secret Service man decked out as "an Apache" (V244.23) and trailing Slothrop.

V254.33–34, B296.17 a braided leather sap In underworld argot, a socklike weapon packed with sand or stones.

V254.38, B296.22 Borsalini Pynchon's plural for the Borsalino, a black felt hat with its narrow brim turned up in front, down in back.

V255.20, B297.7–8 "it's Dumpster, Dumpster Villard" See V65.20.

V256.2–5, B297.36–39 "Jenny, I heard your block was hit . . . the day after New Year's . . . took me to that Casino" She was one of Slothrop's former "stars" from London and appears now from the Other Side because her block was rocketed (one must suppose). His dream thoughts also confirm the earlier chronology: that he arrived on the Riviera around Christmas.

V256.11–12, B298.4–5   bend . . . like notes on a harmonica   The player's ability to "bend" notes is an important but difficult harmonica skill. Slothrop has mastered it by part 4 (V622.14n).

V257.8, B299.5   like Katje on her wheel, off on a ratchet   The image is of a roulette wheel, knocking Katje like a ball "from one room to the next, a sequence of numbered rooms . . . till inertia brings her to the last" (V209.6–7). Slothrop saw it that way during the revelatory moment in the Himmler-Spielsaal, when Katje wore her "rainbow-striped dirndl skirt." Now, if Slothrop were on top of his game he would realize that, like Katje's, his moves are still under "Their" control and that (as Clive Mossmoon later puts it), he is being sent out into the Zone " 'to destroy the blacks' " (V615.36). He doesn't, and this is another case of a missed message.

V257.35–36, B299.40–41   Hotel Nimbus . . . in the Niederdorf or cabaret section   The Nimbus appears to be a fictional hotel; the Niederdorf district lies in the central part of Zurich, on the west bank of the Limmat Canal, which divides the city in two.

V257.39, B300.2   the Limmatquai   Main arterial running parallel to the canal, through Niederdorf.

V258.3, B300.6   lieder   Songs.

V258.4, B300.6–7   gentian brandy   French and Swiss liqueur distilled from the roots of gentian plants; also called Enzian, "one of the most aristocratic forms of schnapps" (Lichine 250).

V258.9, B300.13   Moxie   See V63.5n.

V258.26–27, B300.35   Ultra, Lichtspiel, and Sträggeli   Fictional nightclubs. Grimm (934) notes that at "some places in Switzerland the *Sträggeli* goes about on the Ember Night, Wednesday before Christmas, afflicting girls that have not finished their day's spinning." The word means "specter," a "play of light" (or *Lichtspiel*); in the same context, "Ultra" refers to the very high frequency light waves in any spectrum of illumination.

V258.32, B301.1   rösti   German-style fried potatoes.

V258.37, B301.6   séracs   Glacial ice pinnacles in the Swiss Alps.

V260.30, B303.4, "interested in some L.S.D.?"   The source, here, of a monetary pun ("pounds, shillings, and pence"); it is the Sandoz hallucinogenic indole compound again.

V261.4, B303.20–21   indole people   Those who focus their research on compounds of indole, a white, powdered coal-tar derivative with various pharmacological uses—for instance, in the preparation of LSD. Note that in all respects the drug LSD is linked in *GR* with the North, the color white (symbolic of death), the IG Farben, and an "elect" of researchers and business tycoons who are imagined "at the end of a long European dialectic" (V261.9) of progress toward Death's "other kingdom."

V261.17, B303.36 the Uetilberg Southeast of Zurich, an hour away by tram, the Uetilberg is a peak rising to an altitude of 874 meters (2,841 feet).

V261.29, B304.5 the Gemüse-Brücke Literally, the "Vegetable Bridge." But of the thirteen Zurich bridges across the Limmat Canal, Baedeker and other maps record none by this name.

V262.5–6, B304.27–28 William Tell Overture From Rossini's opera by that name; also popularly known as the theme music to the "Lone Ranger" program on American radio and television.

V262.11, B304.34 the Luisenstrasse Street in northwest industrial quarter of Zurich.

V262.35, B305.19 the Odeon James Joyce, Vladimir Ilyich Lenin, Leon Trotsky, Albert Einstein, and Tristan Tzara (the Dadaist) all lived in Zurich, circa 1916, and all used to frequent the Odeon Café, in the Niederdorf district. The fact is fairly well known: Richard Ellman mentions it in his biography of Joyce, and Tom Stoppard's 1975 play, *Travesties*, brings Joyce, Lenin, and Tzara together there.

V263.18, B306.5 Argentine poet Leopoldo Lugones During the early decades of this century Lugones (1874–1938) became Argentina's leading literary figure. A liberal in politics, he always demonstrated sympathies with Argentina's disenfranchised people.

V263.20, B306.8 the Uriburu revolution Occurred September 6, 1930, when army general José F. Uriburu, nephew of a former Argentine president, seized power after the Radical party failed to resolve the havoc that worldwide depression was wrecking in the country. Uriburu stepped in because the military elite had decided that only its forceful guidance could save the nation from what was seen as a divisive party politics of bickering intellectuals (like Lugones).

V263.24–26, B306.13–15 Graciela Imago Portales, hijacked . . . U-boat in Mar de Plata Her name means Graciela "Window Image," and she has hijacked the German submarine at the Argentine port city of Mar del Plata, misspelled in the Viking and corrected in the Bantam.

V263.33, B306.24 Rivadavia At 46 degrees southern latitude, a port city that is the southernmost of Argentina's populous cities.

V263.34, B306.25–26 "with Perón on his way" Juan Domingo Perón (1895–1974) was among a group of army officers who seized power in June of 1943. Appointed to head the Argentine Department of Labor and Social Welfare, Perón swiftly established himself as champion of Argentina's lower classes. This reputation won him the vice-presidency in the 1944 elections. And it won him the distrust of President Ramirez, who packed Perón off for two years of imprisonment on the island of Martín Garcia, where he remained until October 1945. Here, in April 1945, Squalidozzi's remark is therefore at best only hopeful; at worst, it's anachronistic.

V263.34–35, B306.26 "our last hope was Acción Argentina" A militant Catholic organization, outlawed in 1945.

V263.39, B306.31 "He already has the *descamisados*" This is anachronistic by half a year. On October 17, 1945, several days after his release from prison and exile, Perón addressed a mass demonstration of workers in the Plaza de Mayo of Buenos Aires. The crowd drew many of the nation's most impoverished people. The rich, meanwhile, coined the term *descamisados*, or "shirtless ones," in derogation of the crowd cheering Perón that day. But he turned the tables on the wealthy and in the following months used the term as a rallying cry for social reform.

V264.4, B306.38 *"Pero ché, no sós argentino"* "Why not, it's not Argentine."

V264.6–7, B306.41–42 Bob Eberle's seen toasts to Tangerine raised in ev-ry bar The allusion is to the third stanza of "Tangerine," the song written by Johnny Mercer that was a hit for Bob Eberle in 1941. On screen he sang it in the 1942 musical *The Fleet's In*. The lyric:

Tangerine! She is all they claim,
With her eyes of night,
And her lips bright as flame.

Tangerine! When she dances by
Señoritas stare
And caballeros sigh.

And I've seen toasts to Tangerine
Raised in every bar
Across the Argentine.

V264.8, B307.1–2 *Europe's groaning, clouded alembic* In alchemical terminology, an alembic is the sealed vessel in which the adept seeks to achieve a conjunction of all opposites to produce gold. Here, the European counterpart of the American "melting pot."

V264.16, B307.10 In the Kronenhalle A restaurant in the Kronenhof Hotel, just off the Limmatquai; guidebooks such as the Michelin list it as a so-so eatery.

V264.26–27, B307.24 "Look at Borges" Squalidozzi refers to the dichotomy of openness as opposed to rationalized space, the "labyrinth" that is a common symbol in the work of Argentine poet and fictionist Jorge Luis Borges.

V264.27, B307.24–25 "The tyrant Rosas" Juan Manuel de Rosas, a cruel and repressive dictator, ruled Argentina from 1829 to 1851. His relentless persecution of the Indians, and his practice of dragooning the gauchos into military service to kill Indians, forms the historical backdrop to José Hernandez's epic poem, *Martín Fierro*.

V265.37, B308.42   a battered DC-3   Pynchon uses the aircraft's designation as a twin-engine commercial transport; but to the military, for whom the Douglas Aircraft Corporation produced over ten thousand after 1940, it was known by Americans as the C-47 "Skytrain," and by Britishers as the "Dakota."

V266.7, B309.14   Spencer Tracy   American actor Tracy was in Africa for the shooting of *Stanley and Livingstone* (1939), in which he played Welsh explorer Henry Norton Stanley (see also V587.36).

V266.11, B309.18   Richard Halliburton   An adventurer and popular writer: *The Royal Road to Romance* (1925), *The Glorious Adventurer* (1932), and *Seven League Boots* (1935) were his most famous works. He died in March 1939, when the ship on which he was traveling went down in heavy North Pacific seas.

V266.23–24, B309.33–34   Lowell Thomas, Rover and Motor Boys . . . National Geographics   Thomas (1892–1975) was a popular American adventurer, radio and television commentator, and writer: *With Lawrence in Arabia* (1924) made him famous. The Rover Boys were the creation of Arthur M. Winfield (1862–1930), author of more than sixty books "For Young Men and Boys," mostly on themes of adventure, heroism, and patriotic history. Under the pseudonym Edward Stratemeyer he published nine Rover Boys books from 1900 to 1922. The Motor Boys were the creation of Clarence Young, who published their motorized adventures (boat, plane, car) in twelve books between 1902 and 1916. The *National Geographic* is of course the well-known magazine of the National Geographic Society, in continuous publication since 1888.

V266.31, B310.2   Cointrin   A *commune* (township) three miles northwest of Geneva and the site of its airport.

V266.34, B310.4–5   Mont Blanc . . . lake sez howdy   At an altitude of 4,856 meters (15,782 feet), the peak of this "White Mountain" (south of Geneva) is the highest of the Alpine chain; the lake is Lake Geneva.

V266.38, B310.9   Café l'Éclipse   Unknown or fictional.

V267.10, B310.25   *Como no, señor?*   Why not, mister?

V267.15–16, B310.32   He gets off at Schlieren   A suburb of Zurich. Slothrop disembarks the Geneva-Zurich train here, instead of riding it into the main depot (or *Bahnhof*). Thus he gives his followers the slip.

V267.17–18, B310.34   St. Peterhofstatt   Hitching a ride from Schlieren, Slothrop arrives here, at a street in central Zurich some three or four blocks from his room at the Hotel Nimbus in Niederdorf. And his precautions appear to have been effective; in the next episode we learn through Pointsman that "military intelligence lost him in Zürich" (V270.5).

V267.19–20, B310.36–37   connects to Ivy League quadrangles   For example, at Harvard University, Slothrop's alma mater and site of his conditioning by Laszlo Jamf.

V267.26, B311.3   Fatimas   American cigarette brand.

V267.36, B311.15   Zwingli's town   Theologian Huldreich Zwingli (1484–1531), the leader of the Swiss Reformation, is fourth from the end in the Chicago Edition of the *Encyclopaedia Britannica*, as the narrator remarks.

V268.1, B311.22   *Vanitas*, Emptiness   From the Latin: *vanus*, "empty."

V268.2, B311.24   Allen Dulles   Brother to John Foster Dulles, who became Dwight Eisenhower's secretary of state, Allen Dulles (1893–1969) was the wartime master spy of the OSS. From 1942 to 1945 he was posted in Switzerland and assigned to gather information about anti-Nazi Germans inside the Reich. His 1947 book, *Germany's Underground*, discusses some of these operations. When the OSS was renamed the CIA, in 1947, he returned to lead it into the fifties.

V268.6, B311.29   *oss*, the late, corrupt, Dark-age Latin   The classical Latin for "bone" was *os*, from the Greek *osteon*; but in medieval Latin the spelling was corrupted to *oss*, from the stem *oss-* (as in *ossuarius*, "of bones"). The OSS was founded in 1942 with William ("Wild Bill") Donovan as its head.

V268.17, B311.42   when Shays fought   A reference to Shays' Rebellion of 1786–87, the result of five years' dissatisfaction among the farmers of Massachusetts. High taxes and declining farm income contributed, but the decisive factor was the repeal of legal-tender status for paper currency. This meant that debts had to be repaid in scrip, which carried a 6 percent surcharge. Daniel Shays was a former officer in the revolutionary army; he led the insurrectionists as they descended on Springfield, Massachusetts, where they attempted to seize the federal arsenal. Tyrone Slothrop may have a "bland ignorance" (V268.24) on the topic but Thomas Pynchon does not, for his ancestor William Pynchon founded Springfield in the seventeenth century, and that ancestor's great-great-great-grandson, Major William Pynchon (1740–1808), served among the federal troops that ended Shays's revolt.

V268.18–19, B312.2–3   sprigs of hemlock in their hats   As a counterpart to the white-papered federals, this is an ambiguous reference. Pynchon seems to mean only the green leaves, but hemlock with its "white-flowered, mousey-smelling" blossoms supplied the poison used to execute Socrates (Graves, *The White Goddess* 12). Graves reports that hemlock was sacred to the White Goddess and was often prescribed in witches' "flying ointments" (ibid. 201).

V269.9–10, B312.39   Atlantis, of the Suggenthal   Atlantis is the mythical kingdom that Plato discusses in his *Timmaeus* and in his unfinished work, *Critias*. British Masonic philosopher Francis Bacon used that background while developing the idea of his utopian society in *The New*

Atlantis (1625). Pynchon's source on the "Suggenthal," or sunken city of Teutonic mythology, was Grimm (982–84), who notes that in some versions of the Nibelung saga, this city houses the Nibelungen gold hoard.

V269.13, B313.2 Lucky Strike   An American cigarette brand.

EPISODE 8

Part 2 of *Gravity's Rainbow*, which opened on Christmas, now closes on Whitsunday, May 20, 1945, with Pointsman, Roger, Jessica, and Katje at a seaside resort, probably Brighton. This feast day occasions some light parody. On Whitsunday, or Pentecost, Christians celebrate the descent of the Holy Ghost on Christ's disciples; in this scene Pointsman, a kind of disciple to the mock-hero Slothrop, hears voices. They intimate the same delusions of power that have dogged Pointsman all along. Pynchon also takes the opportunity to sum up their relationship now that peace has descended.

V269.26, B313.17 Whitsun   The feast of Pentecost, which falls on the seventh Sunday, or fifty days, after Easter. Easter having been celebrated on April 1 in 1945, Pentecost fell on May 20. In England Whitsun, or "White Sunday," derives its name from the medieval practice of clothing the newly baptized Christians in white robes on this day.

V269.30, B313.22 parkinsonism   Not the muscular tremor of Parkinson's disease (these people are "frozen"), but the stooping posture and facial distortions of it.

V269.32, B313.24 Trafalgar Square on V-E Night   During the noon hour on May 8, over sixty thousand Londoners listened to the king's victory broadcast over loudspeakers; that night, the *Times* of London reported, more than a hundred thousand celebrated around Nelson's brightly lit column, skyrockets and firecrackers bursting around them.

V269.33–35, B313.26–28 the Blavatskian wing . . . White Lotos Day pilgrimage to 19 Avenue Road, St. John's Wood   Elena Petrovna Blavatsky (1831– 91) was the founder of the Theosophical Society. Its three aims: to promote the unity of mankind; to promote the comparative study of religion, philosophy, and science; and to explore human psychic faculties. Theosophists adopted the Hindu white lotos, a symbol of the *Trimurti*, or threefold godhead, as a sign of these unified aims. To them, the lotos also symbolized the unity of world religions: in Hinduism it is *padma*, birthplace of the gods, and in Buddhism it is the Buddha's throne, just as in Egyptian religions the lotos was Horus's seat. It came to Christianity as the multifoliate rose. Blavatsky died on the Buddha's birthday, May 8, 1891, at the address Pynchon gives on Avenue Road, just north of Regents Park. Thus,

fifty-four years later, on V-E Day, the day both Harry Truman and
Thomas Pynchon celebrated their birthdays (the one was sixty-one, the
other eight), these fictional Blavatskians from "The White
Visitation" make their "pilgrimage" in her honor.

**V270.4–5, B313.33–34   no word of Slothrop for nearly a month . . .
lost him in Zürich**   Readers previously saw (at V267.17–18n) that
Slothrop's evasive maneuvers in Zurich might have easily given his pursuers the slip (or at least those pursuers sent by Pointsman, for
others—such as Clive Mossmoon—seem to think that Slothrop, out
in the Zone, is still under their watchful eyes). These lines underscore
that reading and also confirm the chronology: Slothrop slipped free
in late April, "nearly a month" before this remark.

V270.6, B313.35   browned-off   British service-slang from World War
I meaning bored, disgusted with, or embittered (Partridge, *Forces'
Slang* 28).

**V270.14–15, B314.8–9   the Tennysonian comfort of saying "someone"
has blundered**   An allusion to stanza 2 of Tennyson's famous poem
"The Charge of the Light Brigade" (1854):
"Forward, the Light Brigade!"
Was there a man dismay'd?
Not though the soldier knew
   Someone had blunder'd.
Theirs not to make reply,
Theirs not to reason why,
Theirs but to do or die;
Into the valley of Death,
   Rode the six hundred.

**V270.19–20, B314.14–15   Munchkins . . . into the erotic Poisson. Don
Giovanni's map**   Munchkins are the midget beings of *The Wizard
of Oz*; in the film, they help start Dorothy along the Yellow Brick Road.
Here, they are imagined skipping off into the Poisson distribution
of Slothrop's erotic adventures, like the mapped conquests of the legendary Don Juan. In Mozart's opera *Don Giovanni*, act I includes a remarkably long list of the Don's conquests, organized by nation (in
Leporello's "Madamina" aria).

V270.23, B314.19   mindless pleasures   Once the working title of
GR.

V272.19, B316.28–29   young Sigmund Freud   This is the initial reference
to Freud (1856–1939) and his research into deviant sexuality, circa
1905; he comes up in a similar context at V737.6.

**V272.32–34, B317.2–5   Special Projectiles Operations Group . . . Opera-
tion Backfire . . . Cuxhaven**   Dennis Joint is a fictional "representative"
but these bureaucracies are not. SPOG was a subsidiary organization

of CIOS, for Combined Intelligence Objectives Subcommittee, created by "British-American Combined Chiefs of Staff in the Summer of 1944 to plan and administer an orderly exploitation of German scientific targets" (McGovern 102). The British name for the recovery and testing of V-2 rockets was Operation Backfire; in October 1945 this program did succeed in launching three rockets northward from Cuxhaven (Huzel 200–204). The comparable American effort, code-named Project Hermes, involved the transfer of one hundred partially completed V-2 rockets to White Sands, New Mexico, for test-firings.

V272.37, B317.8   a l'état c'est moi frame of mind   It was Louis XIV who announced, in 1651, before the assembled parliament of France, "I am the state."

V273.3, B317.16   They took Peenemünde in the spring   The Russian army advanced into the Rugen Peninsula, and the island of Peenemünde, in mid-April 1945.

V273.3–5, B317.17–18   they will be given . . . Nordhausen . . . dealings at Yalta   In accordance with the boundary lines drawn at the Yalta Conference of February 4–11, 1945, Roosevelt, Churchill, and Stalin agreed that the Russian zone of occupation would extend through Thuringia, including the Harz Mountain town of Nordhausen, where, unbeknownst to any of the allies, Germany was producing V-2 rockets at an underground factory. The Americans overran Nordhausen in April; under the Yalta accords it was ceded to Soviet control in July.

V273.5, B317.19   VIAM, TsAGI, and NISO   The source here is McGovern (126): "A special council under the Council of People's Commissars, headed by Malenkov, had . . . been formed in 1944. Representatives of VIAM, the All-Union Institute of Aviation Materials; TsAGI, the Central Aerodynamics and Hydrodynamics Institute; NISO, the Scientific Research Institute for Airplane Equipment; and engineers from various other commissariats had been given special powers and a mission." They were charged with gathering scientific intelligence on the V-weapons, especially the rocket.

V273.10–11, B317.25–26   von Braun and 500 others . . . at Garmisch   Huzel's account is the best, and most likely it was Pynchon's source. Through his brother, Magnus, Wernher von Braun arranged for his own surrender and that of his entire technical staff on Wednesday, May 2, 1945. They gave themselves up to the Americans, who decided to detain five hundred of them at the Bavarian town of Garmisch-Partenkirchen, where all remained for several months of interrogation, until the Allied governments had decided they would not be tried for war crimes.

V273.24, B318.12–23   the Dodgem cars   This and other details suggest that the seaside resort is Brighton, with its promenade of amusements that Baedeker describes (*Great Britain* 108). The cars are electrically propelled (hence the "smell of ozone") and are known in the United States as "bumper cars."

V273.30, B318.8 Eton hats Little flat-top hats with narrow, flat brims; so-called for the students who wear them at England's exclusive Eton School.

V273.37–41, B318.17–18 Rossini's overture to *La Gazza Ladra* . . . without snaredrums or the sonority of brasses Rossini's overture to *The Thieving Magpie* opens with a long snare-drum roll and, at its end, the brasses laying down a sonorous melody line for the violins. These motifs recur in the overture. Without them, then, the piece would be severely diminished.

V274.18, B319.2 "Twelfth House" Probably because Pisces is the twelfth house in astrology and a sign of dissolution and death.

V274.25, B319.11–12 like Rita Hayworth Her 1939 film *Only Angels Have Wings* was the first big film role for American actress Rita Hayworth, and *Cover Girl* (1944) capitalized on her popularity among U.S. servicemen.

V275.1, B319.27–28 a Wheel of Fortune A carnival game, like an upright roulette wheel.

V275.11, B319.40 her Fay Wray number The second time Jessica has deployed it (see V57.8n).

V275.13, B320.1 the Fist of the Ape Referring to the big scene in *King Kong*, when the ape picks up Ann Denham (Wray) outside the huge wall dividing Skull Island.

V275.25–26, B320.16–17 Murphy's Law . . . restatement of Gödel's Theorem A humorous axiom of engineers everywhere, Murphy's law (origin unknown) holds that "when nothing can go wrong, something will" (or, in another version, "if anything can go wrong, it will"). Gödel's theorem is named for German mathematician Kurt Gödel (b. 1906), whose famous paper of 1931 addresses the long-standing problem of "axiomatic consistency." When Gödel wrote, the consistency of all axioms had evidently been established within the system of arithmetic by Alred North Whitehead and Bertrand Russell's *Principia Mathematica* (1910). They employed a method of "mapping," or translating, arithmetical expressions onto sentences of formal logic. These sentences could then be verified and tested for consistency as purely logical statements. But the results would also be applicable, by reversing the mapping, to the system of arithmetical axioms: for example, the axioms governing multiplication. *Principia Mathematica* ran to three cumbersome volumes. Gödel's relatively succinct paper, "On Formally Undecidable Propositions in *Principia Mathematica* and Related Systems" (1931), overturned the work of Russell and Whitehead in just over thirty pages. Using the same methods of "mapping" as appear in *Principia*, Gödel was able to produce a sentence that demonstrated that Russell and Whitehead's work, "or any related system," was inherently incomplete. There would always exist, within the rules of the system, the possibility of a sentence or proposition the validity of which could not be decided by the rules themselves.

Half a century later, Gödel's theorem now stands with Einstein's relativity theory and Heisenberg's undecidability principle as one of the cornerstones of modernist science. In *GR*, Gödel's incompleteness theorem is a hopeful sign. When it crops up again (V320.19), it is in the context of an infinite postponement of suicide, because something might be missing from one's catalog of worldly disgusts and denials. In formal logic and metamathematics, the incompleteness theorem establishes that formal closure, completeness, and the internal consistency of any complex, logical system may all be pipe dreams. As such, it makes a telling background to Pynchon's representations of closed versus open fields, of being "shut in by words" (V339.36–37) as opposed to breaking free by means of them. Some twenty pages back Slothrop thought to himself: "Free? What's free?" (V256.33). As metaphor, Gödel's theorem—in its vernacular version, Murphy's law—begins to answer that question.

V275.34–35, B320.26–27 legend of the black scapeape . . . tallest erection in the world The reference is to King Kong, machine-gunned from New York's Empire State Building in the closing scenes of Marian Cooper's film.

V276.21, B321.16 the Tavistock Institute Founded in 1920 by Dr. Hugh Crichton-Miller, a specialist in shell shock and similar war-related neuroses, the Tavistock Institute of England brought psychoanalytical techniques, both Freudian and Jungian, to England. In 1946 the group was reconstituted as the Tavistock Institute of Human Relations, administered through the newly established National Health Service.

V276.30–31, B321.28 Gavin Trefoil, face as blue as Krishna On Gavin Trefoil, his role in the Operation Black Wing films, and his resemblance to Krishna, see V147.13n.

V277.14, B322.16 gemütlich German for "genial," or "cozy."

V277.24, B322.27–28 like Lord Acton always sez The reference is to Acton's famous comment in an 1887 letter to Bishop Creighton: "Power tends to corrupt; absolute power corrupts absolutely."

V277.34–38, B322.40–323.3 the eloquent words of Sir Denis Nayland Smith to young Alan Sterling . . ."the best ointment for the burns" The quotation is from *The Trail of Fu-Manchu*, Arthur Sarsfield Ward's 1934 sequel to *The Bride of Fu-Manchu* (1933). The earlier book had left its romantic hero, a young American named Alan Sterling, engaged to Fleurette Petrie, daughter of a friend of Nayland Smith, intrepid detective of Scotland Yard. In *The Trail of Fu-Manchu*, the "insidious yellow doctor" kidnaps Fleurette, and the words quoted here are Nayland-Smith's advice to Sterling. Not many libraries still carry the book (New York: Doubleday, Doran, 1934), but readers can find a serialization of the narrative in *Collier's* magazine; the quotation here is from the edition of May 5, 1934 (15).

V277.38–39, B323.4   what Nayland Smith represents   Mostly he represents a single-minded, puritanical devotion to work and a chivalric devotion to battling the dragons of evil.

V278.16, B323.27   "Yang and Yin"   In the dualistic philosophy of Chinese Buddhism, Yang is the active, masculine principle of being, which always exists complementarily with the passive, feminine principle known as Yin. Yang is the sun and enlightened consciousness; Yin is the moon, and shadowed unconsciousness. Together they form a circular whole, a mandala.

Part 3 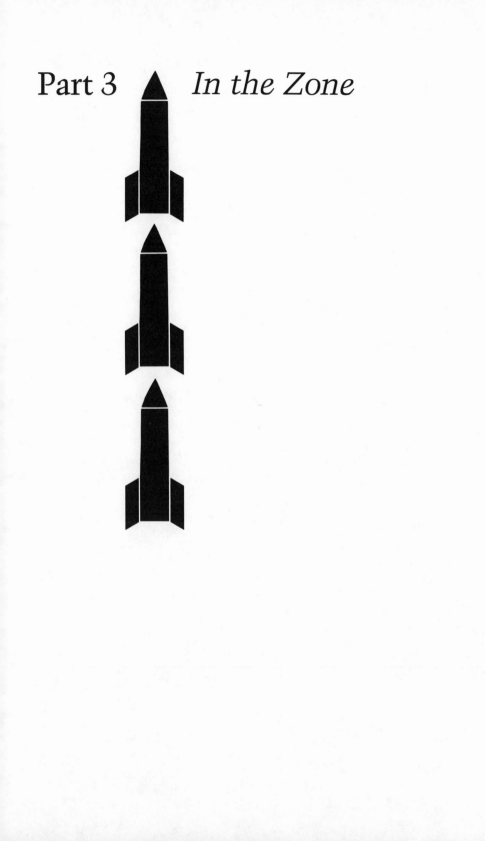 *In the Zone*

REE? What's free?" Slothrop wondered during his first day in Nice. Part 3 of *Gravity's Rainbow* begins to answer that question. Set in the occupied zone of Central Europe during the summer of 1945, its dominant astrological sign is Leo, a fire sign and, as M. E. Jones (263) has phrased it, a time when "the bringing of facts into a simple conformity to the ideals held for them is a necessity." Here, the possibilities for Slothrop's freedom are put to the test. The action begins around May 18, several days before the end of part 2, on Whitsunday. Part 3 will end just before dawn on August 6, 1945, the Feast of the Transfiguration, when Christianity celebrates the radiance of Jesus' divinity revealed to his disciples on a mountaintop. In the novel Slothrop will experience a parody of that sacred revelation as part 4 begins, but part 3 will draw to a close on the morning of August 6, when the *Enola Gay* and the atomic bomb it cradles are approaching the city of Hiroshima.

The epigraph, "Toto, I have a feeling we're not in Kansas any more," derives from the film *The Wizard of Oz*. In Dorothy's trauma-induced dream, her house has just fallen to the ground of Oz, killing the Wicked Witch of the East. This is her first comment on stepping through the door into a brilliantly colored world, the drab black-and-white of Kansas now behind her.

Part 3 of the novel includes thirty-two episodes, perhaps because the gravitational pull on matter is a constant thirty-two feet per second and perhaps because the number is significant in Kabbalistic mythology, where it is associated with the acquisition of wisdom. Specifically, Jahweh is thought to have inscribed his being in thirty-two paths of knowledge, comprising the ten numbers of the *Sephiroth* and the twenty-two letters of the Hebrew alphabet. C. G. Jung (*Collected Works* 12:205–6) quotes one Kabbalistic text in which the number thirty-two represents "the differentiation which appears in the organic world; not creative generation, but rather the plan and arrangement of the various forms of created things which the creator has modelled." In the open field of "the Zone," a geographical slate momentarily wiped clean, Tyrone Slothrop thus begins his quest for wisdom. Along the way he will change his outward self four more times: as part 3 begins he is still Ian Scuffling, war correspondent; but soon he becomes Rocketman, then Max Schlepzig (a Russian soldier), and finally Plechazunga (a pig hero). As Plechazunga he narrowly escapes castration at the hands of Edward Pointsman's agents from the now-declining "White Visitation."

EPISODE I

Internal references place the date of this episode as around May 16–18, 1945. Slothrop has traveled from Zurich to the Harz Mountains of central Germany. He arrives in Nordhausen pursuing information about the rocket, while simultaneously pursuing details of his own childhood. Reading over documents handed to him in episode 7 of part 2, he is stunned to learn the welter of ties binding him to Laszlo Jamf, Imipolex G, and the V-2 rocket.

V281.1–2, B327.1–2   the Eis-Heiligen—St. Pancratius, St. Servatius, St. Bonifacius, die kalte Sophie   These "Ice Saints" are, in order: Pancratius and Servatius, whose feast days occur on May 12 and 13, respectively; Boniface of Ferentino, a pope (608–15), whose feast day is May 14; and "Sophia the Cold," a baffling reference. Christian hagiographies speak of just one Sophie or Sophia: the second-century martyr of Rome whose three children (Faith, Hope, and Charity) all suffered martrydom under Hadrian. But her feast day is September 30. Sources on Germanic folk tradition and legend are equally mum about "die kalte Sophie."

V281.11–12, B327.14   dragon's teeth, fallen Stukas   In the Hellenic myth of Cadmus, the hero kills a dragon guarding the pond where he means to establish the city of Thebes. Cadmus is unaware that the creature is sacred to Ares, the god of war. Athena appears and orders Cadmus to make reparation by sowing half the dragon's teeth; he no sooner does so than an army sprouts up and begins squabbling. Five "Sparti" (or "sown men") remain from that fighting, and they form the nucleus of Theban culture. Cadmus, meanwhile, is also forced to give eight years' service to Ares. Stukas: German dive-bombers (V102.29n).

V281.14–15, B327.17–18   The vintage . . . will be fine   Vintage calendars note that 1945 was indeed a fine year for German white wines.

V281.20, B327.24–25   some DP   Acronym for displaced person.

V281.23–24, B327.27–29   red tulip . . . reminder of Katje   Because tulips are virtually the national symbol of Holland and perhaps also because Katje made Slothrop "disappear" under a red tablecloth (V198.8–9n).

V281.25, B327.30   the Zone   Slothrop stands in what is at the moment the American zone of occupied Germany. In July it is to be ceded to the Soviets.

V281.33, B328.2   Herero beliefs about ancestors   The Herero believe that their dead ancestors dwell in the North (V327.11–17n), a myth that gathers resonance as Slothrop arrives in Nordhausen ("North-houses"). Also, the Herero believe that cattle are gifts from dead ancestors (V316.28–29n), an idea present, here, in the image of "God clamoring" to black-coated Puritans in "every turn of a leaf or cow" (V281.35–36).

V282.6, B328.14–15   Major-General Kammler's rocket units   An SS general, Hans Kammler was appointed deputy special commissioner for A4 matters by Hitler in 1943 at the request of the SS head, Heinrich

Himmler. Thereafter, Kammler proceeded to wrest control of the
rocket program from the regular army, a power play Dornberger (196–
99) describes with some bitterness. Five battalions of rocket troops
operated under Kammler in 1944–45.

V283.5, B329.21–22   the lovely little Queen of Transylvania   This
is the last line of the "Vulgar Song" from the Casino Hermann Goering
in part 2 (V213.21–32).

**V284.15–16, B330.34–36   on the board of directors of the Grössli Chemi-
cal Corporation as late as 1924**   Here and in the following paragraphs
Pynchon weaves the fabric of Laszlo Jamf's life from Sasuly's disclosures
(especially 180–90). A manufacturer of dyestuffs, Grössli (or
Grasseli—Sasuly uses the Americanized spelling of the umlauted "o")
was acquired by IG Farben, in stepwise fashion, beginning in 1925.
This is why Jamf's tie-in, until "as late as 1924," assumes significance.
DuPont purchased Grössli's chemical operations in 1928, and IG
Farben took over the company's dyestuffs production. Then, in 1929,
IG Farben formed the American IG Company, a hodgepodge of interests
that included Agfa-Ansco (producers of photographic materials), as
well as a firm with the fine Puritan name of Winthrop Chemicals. All
of these American companies under the IG umbrella maintained
close ties with DuPont, which had clearly been compensated for IG
Farben's American push by the acquisition of Grössli back in 1928. This,
at least, was Sasuly's contention. If the calculations at V624.18n
are fairly close, then Slothrop is six years old in 1924, and this is how
his file, with all its data on his conditioning, passes into the institutional labyrinth of these corporate cartels.

V284.23, B331.7   the Hugo Stinnes operation in Germany   Once more
the details are adapted from Sasuly (42–44). Compare, for example,
Pynchon's "Based out of the Ruhr, where his family had been coal barons for generations" (V284.24–25), with Sasuly's "His family had
been prominent in the coal industry of the Ruhr for generations" (42).
Pynchon's narration of how Stinnes put together a "super-cartel"
(V284.31) of electric and coal/iron industries derives, in similar fashion,
from these pages in Sasuly.

V284.37, B331.24–25   he was blamed for the Inflation   Stinnes engi-
neered the inflation of 1921–25 as a means of negating the stiff reparations payments levied against Germany by the Treaty of Versailles.
The details on Stinnes's arrangements with the German financiers
Krupp and Thyssen derive from Sasuly (45–47).

**V285.9, B331.39   another of Hjalmar Schacht's many bookkeeping
dodges**   Horace Greeley Hjalmar Schacht headed the Reichsbank during
the carefully orchestrated inflation of the twenties. Like Stinnes's,
his strategy was to drive down the value of German marks so as to make
reparations payments in devalued currency. At the same time he

supplied German manufacturers with another, secret currency, the
Notgeld, for transactions among themselves. In the thirties, with
Krupp von Bohlen and steel magnate Albert Vogler, he arranged massive
donations of cash that sealed Nazi party victories in the crucial elections of 1933. Known worldwide as "Hitler's Banker," Schacht was acquitted of war crimes at the Nuremberg Tribunal, then acquitted
of being a Nazi functionary at the Lüneberg trials. He died in 1970 at
age ninety-three.

V285.18, B332.9   these eight ink marks   That is, in the name "Slothrop."
Yet the number eight has widespread signficance throughout *GR*:
there were eight episodes in part 2; Slothrop assumes eight different
identities in the narrative; V-E Day, White Lotos Day, and Pynchon's
birthday all fell on May 8; the text references Krishna, eighth avatar of
Vishnu (V147.13n); and in Judaeo-Christianity eight is the number
of letters in the Tetragrammaton, the symbolic Eightfold City of Light
in which the divine word dwells. This is why the Hanukkah candlestick
has eight candles, the last of which is lit on the twenty-fifth day of
Kislev, the winter solstice; thus eight is not only Krishna's number but
also Christ's, for on December 25 the divine word was made flesh.

V285.37, B332.33   Jim Fisk style   In 1869 "Jubilee Jim" Fisk (d. 1872)
and his partner Jay Gould attempted to hoard gold and ruin the stock
market. Fisk was a principal owner of the Erie Railroad, which operated
a line through western Massachusetts, and his stock market gambit
was intended to destroy competitors so that the Erie would ultimately
emerge triumphant. His rambunctious career is well documented
in Henry and Charles Adams's *Chapters of Erie* (1871) and in chapter
3 of Mathew Josephson's *The Robber-Barons* (1934). Fisk reappears
at V378.16, and V438.15–17.

V286.5, B333.1   Schwarzknabe   That is, "Black-child."

V286.6, B333.3   Schwindel   Means "swindler," an apt code name
for a double-dealer like Stinnes.

**V287.1–4, B334.4–7   dictionary of technical German . . . JAMF . . .
definition would read: I**   A paranoid Slothropian fantasy.

V287.23, B334.30   hitched a lift on a P-47   This would have been
difficult, or at the least very cramped, since the American-built P-47
"Thunderbolt" fighter plane was designed as a single-seat attack aircraft.
But Marvy could have "hitched a lift" on a C-47 transport plane (see
V265.37n), an aircraft much more likely to be plying the skies during
peace time between two medium-sized cities like Kassel and
Heiligenstadt, in Thuringia.

V287.25–26, B334.33–34   Project Hermes people from General Electric
Under the code name Hermes, GE and U.S. Army Ordnance worked
to sneak one hundred dismantled A4 rockets out of Germany to White

Sands, New Mexico, for extensive testing. Pynchon's source on these details is McGovern (101–2).

V287.36, B335.4   Old Blood 'n' Guts   Nickname of U.S. Army general George S. Patton (1885–1945), whose armored divisions defeated the German general Rommel in the North African deserts.

V288.2, B335.13   P/Ws   Another acronym, like POWs, for prisoners of war; more common in British usage.

V288.4, B335.15   "Russkys, frogs, limeys"   Slang for Russians, Frenchmen, and Englishmen.

V288.25, B335.41–42   A crescent moon has risen   A waxing crescent moon appeared in the night sky from May 16 until May 18, 1945.

V289.12, B336.31   Quit kvetchin', Gretchen!   From *kvetch*, Yiddish verb meaning "to complain."

V289.18–19, B336.39   makeshift PXs   U.S. Army acronym for the post exchange.

V289.28, B337.10   the Dora camp   The Nazi SS operated this concentration camp next to the Nordhausen Mittelwerke, and its inmates assembled the A4 rockets and V-1 buzz bombs (McGovern 79, 121–22).

V289.29, B337.11   175 badges   Designating them as prisoners interned for violating Paragraph 175 of the German Penal Code, "which exacted punishment for certain abnormal sex practices" (Kracauer 45).

V290.7, B337.29   Under the rose   From *sub rosa*, the Latin phrase indicating that which is secret, spoken in confidence. Also the title of a short story Pynchon published in *Noble Savage* (1961), later rewritten as chapter 3 of *V.*, subtitled "In which Stencil, a quick-change artist, does eight impersonations" (so will Tyrone Slothrop, in *GR*).

V290.16, B337.38–39   a Soviet intelligence officer named Tchitcherine   Qazi calls attention to Theodore von Kármán's book as a source (Von Kármán 276). There we read: "Frank Tchitcherine was of Russian origin, and in fact had been related to the first Minister of Education in the Kerensky government. This Tchitcherine helped convince the Germans to disclose their hiding place for literally tons of research documents pertaining to the rocket and supersonic flight." David Seed ("Pynchon's Two Tchitcherines") adds that Pynchon may have also meant to reference the Georgi Tchitcherine who negotiated the Rapallo Treaty of 1920; but Pynchon writes that his "Vaslav" is "no relation" to him (V238.3–4).

V290.21, B338.5–6   Nordhäuser Schattensaft   A fictional wine. A *Schattensaft* would be a "shadow-juice"; and in any case Nordhausen is not a wine-producing region.

V290.39, B338.27   G-5   See V125.22n.

V291.32, B339.23   a Baby Ruth   An American brand of candy bar.

V292.25, B340.20 "like that Ernest Hemingway" The subject once more is moustaches. Future novelist Ernest Hemingway was still a cub reporter for the Kansas City *Star* in 1917; later, while recovering from his war wound, he worked as a correspondent for the Toronto *Daily Star*, and by that time had grown a moustache.

V292.41, B340.39–40 best Cary Grant imitation See also V294.11n.

V293.10–11, B341.8–9 "if the *Guardian* will even be interested" Slothrop fakes an employer, probably the Manchester *Guardian*, an English weekly newspaper.

V293.14–15, B341.14–15, "I was voted the Sweetheart of 3/Art. Abt. (mot) 485" The German troop designation Geli mentions here is fictional, but the numbering system derives from Collier (108). It would be the Third Motorized Squadron of the 485th Artillery Division. Collier shows the organizational chart for General Kammler's rocket squadrons, which were divided into Northern and Southern Groups. The 485th was Gruppe Nord, operating out of The Hague; it was divided into First and Second Squadrons. There was no third.

V293.17, B341.17–18, "been up to the Brocken yet?" Jutting peaks of the Harz Mountains, site of the Walpurgisnacht, or eve of May Day, celebrations. In part 1 of Goethe's *Faust*, on the night of April 30, Mephistopheles conducts Faust to the Brocken, an area known for its strangely beautiful light, the so-called *Brocken-Gespenst*, or Brocken specter. Goethe (*Goethe's Color Theory* 89) experienced it in December 1777:

> During the day, owing to the yellowish hue of the snow, shadows tending towards violet had already been observable; these might now be pronounced as decidedly blue, as the illuminated parts exhibited a yellow deepening to orange. But as the sun last was about to set, its rays greatly mitigated by the thicker vapors began to diffuse a most beautiful red color over the whole scene around me, the shadow-color changed to a green, in beauty to the green of an emerald. The appearance [*Gespenst*] became more and more vivid: one might have imagined oneself in a fairy world, for every object had clothed itself in the two vivid and so beautifully harmonizing colors.

Goethe had witnessed the phenomenon of complementarity across the rainbow spectrum of colors. The moment would spark his use of Germanic legend for situating his demonic festivities in *Faust* atop the Brocken; it also inspired his scientific researches into "the color wheel"—a way of representing the color complements in a circular, mandala form. For a description of the Brocken itself, and a note on Pynchon's source for its modern amenities, see V330.9–11n.

V293.26, B341.29–30 a Nagant blazing In 1895 the Russian army adopted as its service revolver this six-shot pistol designed by the Nagant brothers of France. Russian officers used it through the forties.

V293.28, B341.32 a Stalin tank   The main-line Russian battle tank, first commissioned for service in 1943.

V293.38, B341.43 "In clear"   That is, an uncoded message.

V294.5, B342.9 "Blodgett Waxwing"   Slothrop guesses wrong here. The man waiting for him will be "Der Springer," Gerhardt von Göll. A waxwing can be any of several species of birds belonging to the genus *Bombycilla*, with red-tipped wings.

V294.11, B342.16 "Cary Grant. Ge-li, Ge-li, Ge-li"   Slothrop mimics the exclamations of pilot Geoff Carter (Cary Grant) to "Ju-dy, Ju-dy, Ju-dy" (Rita Hayworth) in the Howard Hawks film *Only Angels Have Wings* (1939). Notice also the onomastic pun: the German-sounding name Geli Tripping and the English "gaily tripping," no doubt also in the sixties slang sense of "tripping," as in a drug-induced fantasy.

EPISODE 2

Next day, Slothrop arrives at the Nordhausen Mittelwerke, and here several strands of myth are woven together. First, the episode is scattered with items from the lexicon of Teutonic myth, signified in references to ancient runes, and the Tannhäuser legend. Second, there are references to ancient Herero myth and custom. Finally these two strands—northern and southern, the white and the black—converge in a contemporary, technological mythology of rocketry. Slothrop's journey into the Nordhausen works, altered slightly for this convergence, provides a locale for the main action—a Hollywood-style chase scene, with Maj. Duane Marvy hot on Slothrop's trail.

V295.13, B343.23 This rail   Here and throughout *GR*, slang for a lieutenant in the U.S. Army, after the brass bar insignia, or "rail."

V295.15, B343.25 English SPOG   See V272.32–34n.

V295.27–28, B344.2–3 Nick De Profundis, the company lounge lizard   From the Latin *de profundus*, "of the deep" or "of the profound." In American slang, a "lounge lizard" is one who spends most of his waking hours basking in the alcoholic glow of cocktail lounges; usually a sponger, perhaps also a gigolo.

V295.34, B344.11   the Telefunken units   Radio-guidance machinery built for the rockets by Telefunken AG, a German electronics firm.

V295.36, B344.14   the Stollen   That is, the tunnels (of the underground rocket works).

V296.14–16, B344.31–32 "When the Americans liberated Dora . . . a rampage after the material"   In early May 1945 American troops liberated the German concentration camp at Nordhausen, called Dora, and shortly afterward a full-scale riot broke out among the former internees. McGovern (156) describes their "rampage," which included looting (see also V299.29–30n).

V296.21, B344.39   the elegant Raumwaffe   Literally, "Space-armor"; or, as the narrator says here, a "spacesuit."

V297.12–13, B345.38   The milk calabashes   Pynchon's source was Luttig (33– 36), who explains that milk from the sacred cattle was stored in the gourds of calabashes. Only women milked the cattle, and the liquid was stored in the center of the Herero's mandala-shaped village.

V297.20, B346.5–6   "The Promise of Space Travel"   From the brief comments, Pynchon probably has in mind the 1924 treatise by German rocket pioneer Hermann Oberth, *Wege zur Raumschiffart* (The Way to Space Travel).

V297.29, B346.17   this salt underground   The Nordhausen Mittelwerke was constructed in a former salt mine; hence the blazing white walls of this scene.

V297.38, B346.28–29   the bristlecone pines outracing Death   The *Pinus aristata* or bristlecone pine is a small species (fourteen to forty feet) that grows only in the western United States. One stand of trees near Wheeler Peak, Nevada, includes a four-thousand-year-old specimen, earth's oldest living organism.

V297.40, B346.31   *polymerized* indoles   See V249.21n.

V298.15, B347.6–7   the young tanker   Army argot for anyone associated with tanks, like this eighteen-year-old. However, to old navy hands the term also signifies those shipmates whose filthy work it is to maintain the fuel-oil tanks. In American underworld slang, it also signifies anyone who spends his nights in the city drunk tank. This is the sense Pynchon has in mind in "The Secret Integration" (*Slow Learner* 180) when he has McAfee, the drunken black bass player, recalling "tanks he had known."

V298.19–20, B347.12   The Albert Speer Touch   Trained as an architect, Speer had ambitions that led him to become Hitler's designer for civil works projects in Berlin and eventually minister of Armaments and War Production. Though he had nothing directly to do with designing the Nordhausen works, Speer did inspect the factory in December 1943, when the SS was readying it for full production. In his memoir (366–71), Speer recalls the visit and the scene: "In enormous long halls prisoners [from the Dora Camp] were busy setting up machinery and shifting plumbing. Expressionlessly, they looked right through me, mechanically removing their prisoners' caps of blue twill until our group had passed them." Appalled at their mistreatment ("sanitary conditions were inadequate, disease rampant"), Speer futilely urged SS general Kammler to make improvements. To his credit, Speer is the only memoirist to acknowledge forthrightly the brutal slavery used to construct the V-weapons. Huzel and Dornberger and von Braun, who became American citizens while Speer was imprisoned at Spandau for war crimes, entirely sidestep the moral issue to concentrate on the romance of rocketry. Here, the detail about parabolas is a Thomas Pynchon touch. Speer was no more enamored of the parabola than any other form. In any case, Pynchon may have in mind Speer's well-known design for the Berlin Arch of Triumph that Hitler wanted built. It never was.

V298.24, B347.17–18 a Speer disciple named Etzel Ölsch A fictional character, whose first name stems (we're told a few lines further on) from Attila (the Hun); thus "Etzel" signifies a little Attila. The last name is from the German *öl*, "oil."

V298.25, B347.19 u.s.w. The German abbreviation for *und so weiter* (and so forth), the equivalent of "etc."

V298.36–37, B347.31–32 the colonel heading up the American "Special Mission V-2" He was Col. Holger Toftoy, who became the prime mover behind American efforts to ship one hundred dismantled V-2 rockets secretly out of Europe (McGovern 112).

V298.37–38, B347.33–34 B Company, 47th Armored Infantry, 5th Armored Division According to McGovern (156), these troops were responsible for "cordoning off" the Mittelwerke during May and June 1945, when the Project Hermes people removed their hundred rockets.

V299.10, B348.5–6 how long you sfacim-a dis country From the Italian noun *sfacimento* (a wreck, or ruin). Thus, "How long you been wreckin' dis country?" Note also the pun on *Dis*, Dante's underground hell.

V299.13–14, B348.10 Tannhäuserism The tragic error of Tannhäuser— for example, in Richard Wagner's operatic version of the myth— was to postpone his quest in order to linger for one year of sensual, "mindless pleasure" with the goddess Venus under her mountain called Venusberg. Grimm (934–35) , Pynchon's source, has shown that in German folk tradition Frau Holda, a White Goddess who leads (like Wuotan) a "furious host," is virtually equivalent to Venus, and it was her delights the hero descended to savor in medieval versions of the myth.

V299.20, B348.18 a Minnesinger A troubadour, a singer of folk tunes like Henry Tannhäuser in the Teutonic myth. Denis de Rougement has shown that the German *Minnesänger* was nurtured on twelfth-century Catharist heresies and symbolism, a source of references as *GR* closes (see V732.22–24n).

V299.29–30, B348.30–31 When the Dora prisoners went on their rampage Again, see McGovern (156). He notes that when liberated, former prisoners joined citizens of Nordhausen to scavenge the factory works, "stealing such items as light bulbs."

V299.38, B348.40–41 Picture the letters SS each stretched lengthwise Descriptions of the underground Mittelwerke can be found in every

one of Pynchon's sources: in Dornberger (241–42), Huzel (86), Irving
(144–45), and McGovern (78). There are photos available in Irving
and McGovern. All agree: instead of Pynchon's forty-four cross-tunnels
(*Stollen*) linked to two main tunnels in ladderlike fashion, there were
forty-seven rather irregularly spaced tunnels. The double-S configuration
is also Pynchon's fiction, a sigmoid fraud that becomes suggestive
in its links to related images.

V300.4, B349.5–6   Apprentice Hupla   Or "hoopla"; from the French
houp-là (confusing or botched speech).

**V300.38–39, B350.4–6   a double integral . . . Summe, Summe, as Leibniz
said**   In the seventeenth century Baron Gottfried Wilhelm von
Leibniz demonstrated methods of double integration used in describing
the trajectories of moving objects. *Summe* is the German for "integration" or "an adding up." More extensive treatments of the calculus
can be found in Slade (218–19) and Ozier ("Calculus" 193–99).

V301.13, B350.26   pulling gs   Engineers' argot for a body under the
influence of gravitational pull. One "g-force" equals a pull that would
equal thirty-two feet per second square.

V301.26, B350.41–42   "A life of its own," she said   For Katje's remark
see V209.23.

V301.31, B351.5–6   a Wheatstone bridge   This is used, in electronics,
to measure resistance or to balance automatically any difference
thereof.

V301.33, B351.8   this so-called "IG" guidance   Because in German
it was called an *Integrationsgerät* (integration device). Willy Ley
(*Rockets* 224) refers to it as "one of the most important inventions
that went into the A4." Once more, though, Pynchon has stretched the
historical facts to suit his sigmoid fraud. All versions of the A4 were
fitted with a double-integrating device that controlled the steering vanes
(Dornberger 45). But the device controlling *Brennschluss* was more
complex. Dornberger explains that all operational models of the A4
rocket were fitted with the ground-control device manufactured by Telefunken. When the rocket reached a set velocity, as recorded by ground-
controlled telemetering equipment, a radio command was beamed to the
rocket, ending the burn. This method had inherent disadvantages:
for instance, it was "susceptible to interference by suitable counter-
measures," wrote Dornberger (231). The solution was an "integrating accelerometer," built by Kreiselgeräte GmbH according to designs
developed at the Technical College of Darmstadt. However, this
"IG" was trouble-ridden, and while rockets fitted with it were tested
over the fields of Poland in 1944, the revised design never went into production (Dornberger 232). Pynchon may have been following Kooy
and Uytenbogaart (351), who leave the mistaken impression that some
IG accelerometers were used in combat.

V302.2–3, B351.20–21   the ancient rune that stands for the yew tree, or Death   Not so. According to Graves (*White Goddess* 194–95, 245–46), the yew (or *Taxus*) was represented by the rune "I," and its day on the calendar was the last of the year, corresponding to the pagan Saturnalia and to the Judaeo-Christian Kislev, or Christmas. The rune "SS" signified the blackthorn (*Bellicum*), a tree symbolizing "strife" and appearing on the calendar at April 15.

V302.20–21, B352.1–2   a 13th sign of the Zodiac   Not as offbeat as it initially seems. Some astrologers hold that there always was a thirteenth sign or house of the zodiacal calendar and that this house is Christ's. In astrology, writes Fern Wheeler (15–20), each of the twelve houses is characterized by an offsetting, countervailing force: Aries, for instance, is a house of love the ruling planet of which is Mars, symbolic of war. But the thirteenth house has no opposites because it integrates all such polarities in the body of Christ. He was the thirteenth person at the Last Supper, claimed to unite within himself the twelve tribes of Israel, and was certainly—as the narrator would put it—an "interface" between "one order of things and another." In short, we may take this as a further sign of messianic hope in *GR*.

V302.39, B352.25   The Penis He Thought Was His Own   Sir Stephen Dodson-Truck's vulgar song of V216.38–217.11.

V303.19–20, B353.9   the legendary ship *Marie-Celeste*   Under the command of Benjamin Briggs, the *Marie-Celeste* left New York on November 5, 1872. Aboard were Briggs, his wife, his daughter, and a crew of seven. Three weeks later the two-masted ship was discovered virtually abandoned, yet still under partial sail. Everyone aboard vanished without a trace or clue, and a board of inquiry failed to resolve the enigma.

V304.10–11, B354.5   "Ah, so reizend ist! . . . Hübsch, was?"   "Ah, it's so enticing! . . . Pretty, eh what?"

V304.31, B354.32–33   expansion nozzles   Details of size and shape probably stem from drawings appended to the back of Kooy and Uytenbogaart.

V304.36, B354.38–39   Lally columns   The track for an overhead hoist.

V305.6–7, B355.11–12   a red von Hindenburg mustache   Paul von Hindenburg was president of Germany from 1925 until 1934, when Hitler assumed full powers. His very large moustache drooped broadly down and across his cheeks.

V306.2, B356.5   A fat cracker   According to the *Dictionary of American Regional English*, "cracker" is a slang term generically designating any white, southern backwoodsman; specifically the term often designates one from Georgia.

V306.4, B356.8   "the WPA"   President Roosevelt's depression-era

job-relief and civil works corps, the Works Progress Administration
(1934–40).

V306.34, B357.3   "i-it's *Tarzan* or something!"   On film, the talkie
Tarzans began with Johnny Weissmuller in the starring role for *Tarzan
the Ape Man* (1932). Buster Crabbe got the part in 1933, with *Tarzan
the Fearless*; but it was Weissmuller's again in 1934, for what became
a series of seven more Tarzan films before 1945, the time of this
episode.

V307.32, B358.5   "here to see that GE"   See V287.25–26n.

V308.36, B359.16   "Gruss Gott!"   "Great God!"

V309.7, B359.29–30   Monel bars   Bars of nickel-alloy steel.

**V309.11–12, B359.35–36   Glimpf, Professor . . . of the Technische
Hochschule, Darmstadt**   The professor's name derives from the Ger-
man adjective meaning "lenient" or "mild." Faculty at the Technical
College of Darmstadt developed the integrating accelerometer
(V301.33n).

V310.6, B360.33   sharp "Himmel"   Another exclamation, short for
"Gott im Himmel!" (God in Heaven!).

V310.27, B361.15   Shouts go dopplering   Pynchon's verb derives from
the Doppler effect, where the frequency of sound or light waves appears
to vary because the source emitting the waves and the observer re-
ceiving them are in rapid motion relative to one another, usually in opposite directions.

V311.32, B362.24–25   the Icy Noctiluca   An "Icy Night-light," caused
here by the explosion of the white phosphorous flare in the white
salt tunnel. Symbolically, it's the night-light of the frozen North.

V312.17, B363.7   white Stetson . . . two .45 automatics   Wearing his
prestigious Stetson brand of cowboy hat, and with his modern
automatic service pistols, Marvy is a mix of cowboy and modern
marine.

V312.21, B363.12   the Amatol   Each V-2 warhead carried a ton of
this explosive.

V313.11, B364.9   Thunderbolts   The American P-47 fighter plane.

V313.14, B364.13   deuce-and-a-half   Again, U.S. service slang for
the two-and-one-half ton truck.

V313.27, B364.28   "Zwitter"   In German the man's name signifies
a hermaphrodite.

V313.32, B364.34   from the T.H. in Munich   Franz Pökler's alma
mater (V160.11n).

V313.40, B364.43–365.1   GEHEIME KOMMANDOSACHE   See V242.9–
15n.

V314.2, B365.5   Frederick the Great hairdos   That is, in tight waves
encircling the head in layers from the ears up, like a beehive.

EPISODE 3

The time of this episode is indistinct. It provides, as background for Pynchon's fictional Schwarzkommando, an extended introduction to Herero folkways and mythology. Motifs introduced here—the mandala symbolism, a culture's intercourse with the dead—correspond with signifiers the narrator finds in other, European cultures.

V314.30, B365.34 Bleicheröde See V237.1n.

V315.8, B366.8 Steve Edelman He will reappear in the closing moments of *GR*, as a "Kabbalist spokesman" (V753.9), and as a blues-harpist (V755.21). The etymology of his name: *Edelman*, from the German for a nobleman and from the Greek *stephein*, "to encircle."

V315.15, B366.17 Jaeger underwear A kind of wool union suit with a drop-seat, introduced for German men and women by Dr. Gustave Jaeger in the 1880s (*Fairchild's* 297).

V315.17–18, B366.19–20 the great Herero rising of 1904–1906 See V317.2n.

V315.21–22, B366.25 Germany's plan for the Maghreb The Maghreb region of North Africa includes what are now Libya, Tunisia, and Algeria. During World War II, Germany's plan, had Rommel been successful in holding North Africa, was to use garrisons there as bases from which to reclaim former South-West African colonies.

V315.27–31, B366.32–37 Among the Ovatjimba . . . in the open Compare this passage to its source paragraph in Luttig (53, my emphasis): "The Ovatjimba may at present be *considered as a group of outcasts*, as *they do not possess the requisite number of cattle* necessary for social significance. This explains the fact that *they do not live in villages* as do the rest of the tribe. *They live a scattered existence in the veld.* Possessing small herds of cattle, in sufficient [*sic*] for subsistence, they are forced to *dig their food from the ground.*" Luttig follows this discussion with a derivation of the name: *Ova-* is the Herero prefix signifying "people," while *-tjimba* signifies the "ant-bear"— the aardvark, or *Erdschwein*. Hence they are the "ant-bear-people"; and they do not eat the animal because of their spiritual, totemic association with it.

V315.38–316.13, B367.4–21 who was the woman alone in the earth . . . The holy aardvark has dug her bed. The source again is Luttig (53, my translation), who notes that the aardvark's power as a totem among the Ovatjimba is suggested by one tribal myth that relates of a woman all of whose children were stillborn, and who was cured after having been placed in an ant-bear hole: "Als sie wieder schwanger war, sagte man, man solle sie in eine Erdschweinhöhle stecken, um sie su entzaubern, dann würden ihre Kinder am Leben bleiben. So geschah es, sie wurde in eine Erdschweinhöhle gesteckt und bekam lebensfähige Kinder" (that is, "As she was pregnant again, it was said that she should be planted in an aardvark hole, to disenchant her, then her children would be able to survive [birth]. It so happened, that she was planted in the aardvark hole and she bore viable children).

Pynchon's fictional rendering of this legend is addressed to a second-person narratee, a hypothetical old South-West African hand who (in a passage that well represents the embedding of narrative perspectives in *GR*) is called upon for remarkable powers of empathy in the face of such strange practices.

V316.6–7, B367.13–14 the village calabashes See V297.12–13n.

V316.16–19, B367.25–29 Inside the Schwarzkommando there are forces, at present, who have opted for sterility and death . . . it is political struggle Luttig (107) clarifies why, for the Hereros, a plan involving "tribal suicide" might be construed as an act of "political struggle." The reason is that for them suicide could also be an act of "blood vengeance." He explains: "A person who commits suicide under these circumstances is also actuated by the thought that the dead are capable of bringing about evil and death more effectively than the living." If so, imagine the whole tribe going into an avenging battle from the Other Side.

V316.22–23, B367.32–33 Otyikondo, the Half-breed The name derives from Kolbe, who lists the Herero noun for "mulatto" as *otyi-kondo*.

V316.28–29, B367.40–41 Eanda and oruzo have lost their force Herero society was organized around a system of double descent, a combination of matrilineal and patrilineal clans that could vary for each individual. In the *eanda*, all trace their descent to a single matriarch; in the *oruzo*, to a single patriarch. These clan designations used to play a key role in the distribution of cattle, but in the twentieth century these organizations, like much else in Herero society, disintegrated (Luttig 68–70).

V316.31, B368.1–2 the Rhenish Missionary Society See V317.2n.

V316.31–35, B368.2–7 as noon flared . . . the omuhona took from his sacred bag, soul after converted soul, the leather cord . . . and untied the birth-knot The source here, again, is Luttig (72): after a child's birth the "funicle, when it has fallen off, is handed over to the priest-chief (or *omuhona*) to be preserved in a sacred skin bag. In this bag leather straps with knots are kept, and each knot relates to a particular member of the oruzo. These knots are untied if the child should die or go over into Christianity." The untying of such knots "as noon flared" is Pynchon's touch, consistent with similar moments of judgment in *GR*.

V316.38, B368.11 Otukungurua Kolbe (177) gives *kungurua* as a plural noun for "emptied" containers—for example, the Herero milk calabashes. The substitution of the inanimate prefix *otu-* for the animate *omu-* shows that the empty ones already consider themselves among the dead, perhaps like the Kabbalistic "shells of the dead," or Qlippoth.

V317.2, B368.17–18 after the 1904 rebellion failed A brief sketch of Herero history will help. After the Rhenish Missionary Society (based in Bremen, Germany) sent representatives to the settlement of Windhoek, during Christmas of 1842, the region was slowly settled and assessments made of its mineral wealth. In 1884 Bismarck declared the *Südwest* a German territory, and five years later he placed it under military rule in order to safeguard the diamond mines. During the next two decades German military commanders sought to consolidate their power by backing the rise of a single Herero *omuhona*, a centralizing move that was strange to the previously scattered tribes. Samuel Maherero, picked as that new ruler, realized all along that he was being played as a puppet. He turned against the German overlords in 1904, leading his newly united tribes in revolt. The war itself was brief. Under Gen. Lothar von Trotha, the Germans embarked on a plan of extermination. Von Trotha's infamous Vernichtungs Befehl (Extermination Order) stipulated that German soldiers could with impunity take the life of any Herero found outside the settlements. Samuel Maherero escaped to neighboring Bechuanaland, whose chieftain, King Khama, had provided the fleeing Hereros assistance in making the grueling trek across the Kalahari Desert (see below, V323.10–11). Pynchon could have pieced together the account in *GR* from early chapters in many of his Herero sources, for example, Goldblatt, Vedder, and Hardinge.

V317.7, B368.24 rinderpest A deadly cattle plague that renders the animal's flesh poisonous to humans.

V317.21, B368.41–42 the poppy, and cannabis and coca Respectively, the opium poppy, the marijuana plant, and the plant source of cocaine.

V317.22, B369.1 ergot and agaric Ergot is the fungal source material for LSD; agaric, the white mushroom formerly used as a cathartic and as a coagulent in medicine and as a fixing agent in the dye processing of fabrics.

V317.30–33, B369.10–13 rational men of medicine attributed the Herero birth decline to a deficiency of Vitamin E . . . long and narrow uterus of the Herero female The source is Steenkamp (22). He discusses the hypothesis of others who had connected infertility to diets deficient in vitamin E and notes as well that after the European incursions a typical Herero diet, formerly consisting of milk products and beans rich in E vitamins, began revolving around vitamin-deficient white rice. Steenkamp himself is one who advanced the "narrow sex-organ" hypothesis, although Pynchon misstates several of its suppositions. Here is Steenkamp (my emphasis): "The Herero woman is tall and slender. Her legs are very long and so are her fingers and arms . . . . This brought me on the idea that all the other organs in the body must be proportionately longer. I thereupon began to examine the *length of the cervix* with Herero [women] . . . and found to my surprise that this was the case. . . . In one instance I even found a cervix so long that it was impossible with a digital examination to feel the body of the womb (*corpus uteri*). This much longer cervix must thus logically and virtually form a much longer incubation bed *for the development of the gonococcus.*" Note that in Steenkamp's view it was the long Herero cervix (not the uterus) that was the condition, and gonorrhea (not Pynchon's "poor chances of fertilization") that was the supposed mechanism of female infertility. Steenkamp's theories are the source of still more detail at V519.14.

V318.18, B370.5–6   they are spieling   That is, "gaming," in the (German) sense of gambling.

V319.7, B371.1   Josef Ombindi   His name derives from the Herero *ombinda*, noun for a "wild pig" (Kolbe 369).

V320.8, B372.8   Der Bingle   Nickname of Bing Crosby (V184.4n).

V320.12, B372.12   Mothers who used to be baby vamps   In *This Side of Paradise* (1920), F. Scott Fitzgerald (65) defines the jazz age as a time when "the flirt had become the 'baby vamp.'" The sense here is the same: a sexual tease who affects a childish manner.

V320.14, B372.14   the Cards or Browns   Baseball's St. Louis Cardinals, of the National League, and the St. Louis Browns, formerly of the American league. The World Series of 1944 pitted these two neighboring teams against each other in what became known as the "Streetcar Series" (the Cards won, four games to two).

V320.19, B372.19–20   by Gödel's Theorem   See V275.25–26n.

V321.3–4, B373.8–9   the village built like a mandala   Luttig (32–34) and Vedder ("The Herero" 168–69) both describe the traditional Herero village as circular, with the cattle pens (the *kraals* in Afrikaans) located in the center and the villagers disposed around the circumference according to certain rules: concubines to the north, unmarried boys to the south, the senior wife of the *omuhona* to the east, and everyone else (including the *omuhona*) to the west. As in a mandala, the arrangement consists of opposite signifiers held in equipoise. However, by the time of Gibson's observations in the early fifties, this order had degenerated to an arch or bow shape, placed only with the aim of protecting the village from prevailing winds.

V321.6–7, B373.12   the Siege Perilous   The Castle Perilous of chivalric romances.

V321.19–20, B373.28–29   before the continents drifted apart   Geologist

Alfred Wegener first put forward the theory of "continental drift"
in 1914 in his book *The Origins of Continents and Oceans*. For decades
the majority of geologists laughed at his theory. Then in the sixties
they dusted it off, transforming it into the new dogma, now called plate
tectonics. Interestingly, former Peenemünde rocketman Willy Ley
also produced a book on the topic, called *The Drifting Continents* (1969),
giving a lay (Ley?) explanation of plate tectonics and locating the
origins of the new theory in Wegener's work.

**V321.40–322.1, B374.13–15   the south pole of his Adam's apple . . .
pole . . . axis . . . axle-tree . . . Tree . . . Omumborombanga . . . Mukuru
. . . first ancestor**   The ellipses are Pynchon's; the source is Luttig.
In Herero creation myth the Omumborombanga is "a great fig-tree
which is thought of as a seat of all ancestors" and thus a "tree of
life, from which all life emanates; its location is in the North" (25).
Mukuru is regarded as the "first ancestor" (21), like the Judaeo-Christian
Adam; as a god, Mukuru was thought to have sprung from the great
tree. His color is red, and he is "intimately associated" with the holy fire
and the sacred cattle (30). Mukuru's name means, simply, "the old
one" (18). The Herero think of Mukuru as one who will be "present in
the grave" with them (21), just as he is present during everyday life
by his extension (symbolized in the "birth-knots") through the
patrilineal clans.

V322.6, B374.21   each sunset is a battle   All details in the surrounding
passage, including the killing of the sun, whence it passes into the
North (land of the dead), thus to rise newly born each morning, are in
Luttig (12–13).

**V322.21–22, B374.40–42   in mythical times, when the sly hare who
nests in the Moon brought death . . . instead of the Moon's true message**   Luttig (15) explains that the moon is referred to as a "hare's
nest" (*ein Nest des Hasen*), and he relates the story: "The hare func-
tioned as the messenger of the moon, and was responsible for the
appearance of death among mankind by the wrong interpretation and
delivery of a message from the moon to humanity. For this the hare
was punished by the moon." Furthermore, the moon is associated
in Herero mythology with the netherworld, abode of Ndjambi Karunga,
a deity who is, as Pynchon notes a few lines further, "both the bringer of
evil and its avenger." Finally, this is why "the Herero sang of the
Germans: 'Sie kommen daher wo der Mond ist,' i.e. out of the Netherworld . . . [for when] European ships emerged from the horizon, West
Coast tribes thought they were coming up out of the spirit land
and were confirmed in their opinion by the pale skins of the
mariners. . . . So was Hahn, the first [Rhenish] missionary among
the Herero, addressed as Karunga, the god of the netherworld" (Luttig
15). The story of the hare and the moon will reappear at V730.4–6.

V322.29–30, B375.9–10   "Blicker," the nickname the early Germans gave to Death On this Teutonic myth see V30.12n.

V322.41, B375.23   the Kakau Veld Dry range lands bordering on the Kalahari Desert and home to the Herero bushmen or *Ovatjimba*.

V323.4, B375.27–28   had the child out of wedlock For more details on Enzian's birth and lineage, see V349.37–352.7. Note, however, that in being born "out of wedlock," as in being "passed over" by a Herod-like figure, his birth and infancy parallel Christ's.

V323.10–11, B375.35–36   Samuel Maherero's great trek across the Kalahari See V317.2n.

V323.41–324.1, B376.31–32   the move from Peenemünde down here to the Mittlewerke The move occurred in February-March of 1945, as Russian troops advanced across Poland toward the Rugen peninsula, forcing all staff still involved in research to move south to Nordhausen, where A4 rockets were already in full production.

V324.10, B377.2   Bürgerlichkeit played to Wagner A bourgeois drama acted out to the strains of a Richard Wagner operatic score.

V325.3, B377.42   the Autobahns German national highway system.

V325.4–6, B378.2–4   the women . . . having their breasts milked into pails An amusing error in the Bantam: "their beasts."

V325.29–30, B378.31   "a 'routinization of charisma'" See V81.8–9n.

V325.31, B378.32   Outase Brincker (229) defines this Herero word as "Frischer, weicher Kuhmist" (fresh, soft cow dung); Kolbe (170), as "the dung of large cattle, if fresh."

V325.36, B378.38   the Rocket's Hawaii II guidance See V207.8n.

V326.4, B379.6   the second dog watch In U.S. naval argot, the twenty-four-hour day is divided up into six "watches." Also, the watch between 4:00 and 8:00 P.M. is further "dogged," or halved, in order for sailors to eat their supper; the "second dog watch" thus runs from 6:00 to 8:00 P.M.

V326.17, B379.22–23   Celle, Enschede, Hachenburg These are all towns on the road from Hanover to Lüneberg, through which Blicero would have passed while retreating from The Hague in late March of 1945. There is, however, a misprint in both editions: "Enschede" should be "Eschede."

V327.5, B380.16   flummeries Of Welsh origin, and initially signifying a coagulation of oatmeal, the word now signifies someone's empty triflings and gestures.

V327.11–17, B380.24–32   a symphony of the North, of an Arctic voyage . . . it is a return The reason why a northward journey would be both "a return" and a trek into Death's kingdom is made clear in Luttig (13): "When mention is made among the Herero of the 'land over the sea' or the 'region of the north' reference is made to the underworld.

It is to this world that the dead depart, for they are buried facing that region." The north is not only a "place of annihilation, but is also a place where new life is created," for the North is where the first ancestor appeared from the Omumborombanga tree; and it is the place to which all Hereros hope to return after death.

V327.34, B381.11 SCHWARZE BESATZUNG AM RHEIN! Black Garrison on the Rhein!

V328.7, B381.17 Onguruve His name is synonymous with the *Ombinda*, or "wild pig," of V319.7.

V328.25, B382.6 Pervitins Proprietary name of a methamphetamine hydrochloride compound, popularly known in America as "speed" because of its effects as a stimulant. Enzian keeps plentiful supplies on hand (see V522.6).

V328.29–30, B382.12–13 okanumaihi, the little drinker of sweet milk Kolbe (187) identifies it as "the evening star" (the planet Venus), which appears at milking time; thus "the little sweet milk drinker."

EPISODE 4

Internal references place the time of this episode as May 28, 1945. The location: Slothrop and Geli stand atop the Brocken, site of the Walpurgisnacht celebrations on the night of April 30. Slothrop makes a madcap escape to Berlin in a hot-air balloon.

V329.13–14, B383.4–6 May Day Eve's come and gone . . . nearly a month later May Day Eve (*Walpurgisnacht*) was April 30.

V329.15, B383.7 Kriegsbier That is, "war beer"; reference otherwise unknown.

V329.19, B383.11 "the devil's kiss" According to Grimm (1065, 1070, 1077), newly admitted witches were "marked by the prick of a needle, the while they cursed their maker, and signified their faith and homage to the Evil one, as to worldly rulers, by a kiss." This "blood mark," which was often stained with inks, was thought to be without feeling ever afterward.

V329.23, B383.16 the suss. per coll. crowd From the Latin *suspendatur per collum* (hanged by the neck), an entry common in legal registers next to the names of those convicted and executed for capital crimes. In his Introduction to the Pynchon Court Records from seventeenth-century Springfield, Massachusetts, Joseph H. Smith (24–25) notes that in June 1645 (exactly three centuries before these fictional events), William Pynchon sat on the General Court at which Margaret Jones, a Bay Colonist, was indicted, found guilty, and executed—*suspendatur*

per collum—in the first American case of capital punishment for
witchcraft. In Springfield William Pynchon also tried and convicted
the second such person, Mary Parsons, brought up on a witchcraft
charge but guilty by her own acknowledgment of murdering her child.
Mary Parsons was also sentenced to hang but appears to have died
in prison in 1657. These two cases preceded by forty years the more
widely known witchcraft trials in Salem.

V329.25, B383.18–19   Amy Sprue . . . turned Antinomian   She is
fictional ("sprue" is an archaic term for a type of throat infection).
The name "Antinomian" was given to those radical, charismatic Puritans who held that faith alone was sufficient for the attainment
of salvation.

V329.26–27, B383.20   Crazy Sue Dunham   In his 1964 short story
"The Secret Integration" (*Slow Learner* 151), Pynchon identifies this
apparently fictional character as "that legendary and beautiful drifter
who last century had roamed all this hilltop country [of western
Massachusetts] exchanging babies and setting fires."

V329.28, B383.22   Snodd's Mountain   Fictional locality named for
Grover Snodd, a character in "The Secret Integration" (*Slow Learner*
142) and a resident (like Tyrone and Hogan Slothrop) of the fictional
Berkshire hill town of Mingeborough, Massachusetts.

V329.30–31, B383.25   young skipping Dorothy's antagonist   In the
film *The Wizard of Oz* there are two "wicked" witches: the Wicked
Witch of the East, killed when Dorothy's house crash-lands on her; and
the Wicked Witch of the West, who tries to incinerate Dorothy's
friend the Scarecrow and who melts away when Dorothy splashes water
about in rescuing her straw-headed friend.

V329.32, B383.27   headed for Rhode Island   Because that was home
to Separatist and Antinomian leaders Anne Hutchinson (1591–1643),
who was banished there in 1637, and Roger Williams (1603–83), who established the colony in 1636.

**V330.9–11, B384.1–4   six toes on each foot . . . Nazi transmitter tower
up on the Brocken**   The descriptive details of this scene derive from a
May 28, 1945, story in *Life* magazine (122–24). Pictures show the
Brocken with a hotel and radio tower perched atop it. Inside the trans-
mitting tower are the murals, photos of which show the women riding
black rams; the *Life* caption reads: "GI who is inspecting mural found
one witch with six toes." The accompanying, brief story goes on, in the
alliterative style of *Time/Life*, Inc.:

On the eve of May 1, according to German legend, weird witches
whip wildly through space, riding broomsticks and goats, with
long-tailed monkeys under their arms. On their mad way they bring
blight, drain cattle dry, spread havoc. They gather at the *Teufelskanzel*
(Devil's Pulpit) on Brocken and hark to the exhortations of their

master, the devil. Then, after devouring a great dinner of toads and mice, they dance and revel until dawn around the bonfire lit before the pulpit.

In 1933 the celebration of this pagan ritual called Walpurgisnacht (Walpurgis was a medieval saint) was adopted as a ceremonial of the Hitler Youth. Until this year they gathered from all over Germany on Brocken, which is the highest peak of the Harz mountains southeast of Hanover, and listened to the demoniacal diatribes of their leaders. This year there was again a fire burning on Brocken before the Devil's Pulpit. It was lit by a cold and bored American sentry who saw no witches.

This story and its accompanying photographs were the source for details of this scene.

V330.13, B384.7 von Bayros See V71.27n.

V330.21–22, B384.16–18 past Clausthal-Zelterfeld . . . toward Weser Cities that lie in a west-northwesterly direction from the Brocken, opposite the rising sun.

V331.2, B384.42 Atlantis See V269.9–10n.

V331.3, B385.1 Brockengespenstphänomen Literally, the "Brocken-specter phenomenon." See V293.17n.

V331.12, B385.10 *warum* Why?

V331.32–33, B385.35 down in Bad Harzburg, Halberstadt Resort towns on the lower northern slopes of the Harz Mountains, an hour or so by car from the Brocken.

V332.4, B386.8–9 those Rolls Roycers who were after him in Zürich That is, the "Apache" Secret Service men to whom Slothrop gave the slip in part 2 (see V267.17–18n).

V332.5–6, B386.10 GE, that's Morgan money Backed with capital from financier John Pierpont Morgan, Charles Coffin founded the General Electric company in 1892.

V332.15, B386.21 K-rations An abbreviation for the German *Kämpfen-Zuteilengen,* or "combat-rations."

V332.16, B386.23 the Goldene Aue Baedeker's *Northern Germany* describes it as a fertile valley located nineteen miles east of Nordhausen in the Harz Mountains. The town of Eisleben, home of Protestantism's father, Martin Luther, lies on its edge.

V332.19, B386.26 "Liebchen" German for "sweetheart," or "lover."

V333.14–15, B387.29–30 Nordhausen: Cathedral, Rathaus, Church of St. Blasius This is Slothrop's view, as he peers down from the balloon. But Pynchon was looking down at his Baedeker (*Northern Germany* 370): "The cathedral is a fine late-Gothic edifice . . . the Church of St. Blasius contains two pictures by Cranach, an Ecce Homo, and the Raising of Lazarus . . . near the Rathaus rises a Roland's Column."

V334.3, B388.21   "Kot!"   Here and throughout *GR*, the German exclamation "Shit!"

V335.11, B389.33   the vane servomotor   Inside the A4's thrust chamber were four graphite vanes for guidance, controlled by servomotors.

V335.24, B390.9   a LOX generator   To pump liquid oxygen, one of the A4's principal fuels.

V336.12, B390.39–40   "the Ur-Markt"   The "primeval market" (German).

V336.18–19, B391.6–7   "At this latitude the earth's shadow *races across Germany* at 650 miles an hour"   Schnorp (or Pynchon) is roughly correct. Relative to an equinoctial sun, a point on the earth's equator spins at roughly 1,100 miles per hour. But here, at 51.5 degrees of northern latitude, and with the sun nearly at its northernmost solstitial latitude, the shadow would be moving at approximately 640 miles per hour. Similarly, over the French area of Carcassonne, at 43.2 degrees, the shadow would be speeding along at roughly 770 mph, 32 more than the speed of sound. Still, a "shadow" never breaks the sound barrier (V336.26–32).

EPISODE 5

The time is now "full summer" (V336.33), or around June 21, 1945. This episode brings the first extensive treatment of Vaslav Tchitcherine, Slothrop's Soviet antagonist. As with Pynchon's Hereros, an elaborate research stands behind this analepsis to the Soviet province of Kirghizistan, represented during a time of linguistic and cultural upheaval in the twenties and thirties.

V337.17, B392.13   *stvyehs* and *znyis*   T. S. Soules (106) explains: "These are suffixes. (*Sdravstuyeh* means hello, for example; *nebreznieh* means careless.) Just catch these typical word endings on the wind and you know you're hearing Russian."

V337.31, B392.31   TsAGI   See V273.5n.

V338.3–5, B393.5–7   no relation at all to the Tchitcherine who dealt the Rapallo Treaty with Walter Rathenau   On Walter Rathenau, see V163.19–23n; on the Rapallo Treaty, V166.16–17n. David Seed has noted that a Georgi Tchitcherine helped Rathenau negotiate the Rapallo Treaty in 1922, settling the questions of reparations payments to the Soviets. The same Tchitcherine also participated in the Lausanne Treaty that brought formal peace with Turkey in 1923. At that time, Georgi Tchitcherine met young reporter Ernest Hemingway, who wrote him up in the Toronto *Daily Star*. Georgi was, as Pynchon notes, "a long-term operator, a Menshevik turned Bolshevik" who was forced to flee Russia and take exile in Germany, where he evidently found it easy to cooperate with a capitalist like Rathenau. Vaslav, on the other hand, remains true to his "anarchist" beliefs.

V338.21–22, B393.29–30   a remote "bear's corner" (*medvezhy ugolok*), out in Seven Rivers country   The source for this bit of detail is a 1916 travelogue by Stephen Graham, a British adventurer who passed through Kirghizistan in 1914–15. His book is entitled *Through Russian Central Asia,* and in treating one of the smaller towns in Semi-retchenskaya Oblast, or "Seven Rivers Land," he comments (192) that it "is what the Russians call a *medvezhy ugolok* (a bear's corner), a place where in winter the wolves roam the main streets as though they did not distinguish it from their peculiar haunts."

V338.25, B393.33   played *preference*   According to Hoyle, this Russian card game is a variant of vint, a contract game that hybridizes hearts and bridge. Preference, or Russian preference, is played with a deck of thirty-two cards (7 through ace). The counting suit is hearts (preference); three active players (plus an inactive dealer) bid, declare trumps, and attempt to make their contracts.

V338.26, B393.35   the Moisin   This is misspelled in both editions. It should be "Mosin," for the Russian bolt-action rifle that uses the 7.62-millimeter ammunition of V340.3. The gun was the standard Russian infantryman's rifle from 1891 until 1945.

V338.28–30, B393.37–40   because of the earthquakes . . . false fronts   The source again is Stephen Graham. Here (156) he describes Verney, capital city of Semiretchie: "It is so subject to earthquakes that it is difficult to see in it a permanent capital. No houses of two stories can with safety be built, so it is more suited to remain a military center and fortress than to be a great city. In order to look imposing, shops and stores have fixed up sham upper stories; that is, they have window-fronts up above, but no rooms behind the fronts."

V338.33–34, B394.2–3   the local Likbez center . . . the "red džurts"   These derive from Thomas G. Winner's *Oral Art and Literature of the Kazakhs of Russian Central Asia* (142). He describes the Soviet campaign against illiteracy: "Individuals were hurriedly trained in the essentials of reading and writing in order to instruct the population. 'Red caravans' and 'Red džurts' on the model of the Russian 'red clubs' became the centers for the anti-illiteracy campaign, or, as it was officially called, 'liquidation of illiteracy' (*Likbez*)." A *yurt,* or *džurt,* is the "tent-like conical felt structure in which the nomadic Turks of Central Asia live." (ibid. 14n).

V339.1, B394.11   the NTA   In his 1952 essay on alphabetic reform in central Asia, Winner describes how, in the twenties and thirties, Soviet-trained teachers attempted to substitute a Latinate alphabet for the Arabic script used by the nomadic Turks. The new letters were dubbed the "New Turkic Alphabet."

V339.11, B394.23–24 dessiatinas of grasses A Russian land measure; 1 *dessiatina* equals 2.7 acres.

V339.35, B395.11 the verst-long dive Another Russian measure: three versts equal two miles (a verst is just slightly longer than a kilometer). Note the motif of winged flight and the dive, recalling the "wings" of Katje Borgesius (V97.27) and of Leni Pökler (V162.37), as well as the death-dealing angel swooping in on Walter Rathenau (V164.37).

V340.1, B395.19 Džaqyp Qulan His first name means "Jacob"; *qulan* is the Kirghiz word for a wild horse (Winner, *Oral Art* 63n).

V340.1–3, B395.20–22 black theodolites . . . 7.62 mm rounds . . . chunks of lepeshka A theodolite is a commonly used surveying instrument; the 7.62 bullets would be for the Mosin rifle; and the lepeshka are flat, hard loaves of bread. A photograph in Stephen Graham (opposite 84) shows a stack of such loaves, like stones, for sale in an open-air market.

V340.7–8, B395.27–28 the 1916 rising . . . Kuropatkin's troops When compulsory military service was imposed on all Russians in 1916, the Kazakhs rebelled against the crown, and a detachment of cavalry under Colonel Kuropatkin was sent to suppress the revolt. The czar had been moving settlers into Kirghizistan for some decades, and many of these Russians used the revolt as a pretext for seizing land and ousting dissident Kazakhs, sometimes murdering them at random (Winner, *Oral Art* 133–34).

V340.27, B396.10–11 The Georgian has come to power Joseph Stalin, or Iosif Vissarionovich Dzhugashvili, was a young Communist from the Georgian Soviet Socialist Republic; he came to power in 1922, then became premier in 1941.

V340.33–34, B396.19 among the auls Soules (106) mistakenly identifies these "auls" as the "tents of the nomads" (the *džurts* are the tents). *Auls* are subclans, composed of several nomadic families traveling together (Winner, *Oral Art* 5–6).

V341.18–19, B397.8–9 O, wie spurlos zerträte ein Engel den Trostmarkt Line 20 of Rilke's Tenth Duino Elegy. Leishman and Spender translate: "How an Angel would tread beyond trace their market of comfort." Pynchon's rendering, "to trample spoorless the white marketplace" (V341.38), neatly preserves the excremental sense of *spurlos*, which is apt for a street trod by horses. "White" is a curious reading for *Trost* (comfort); perhaps it is meant to distinguish between a black market and a white (or legitimate) one.

V342.11, B398.7–8 an Appaloosa from the United States named Snake We're later informed (see V482.34n) that this is the horse ridden by

Greta Erdmann in her film *Weisse Sandwüste von Neumexiko;* and evidently also it is the one ridden by Crutchfield the Westwardman of Slothrop's sodium amytal fantasy of episode 10, part 1.

V343.15–16, B399.22   the winged rider, red Sagittarius   Sagittarius is the Archer, ninth house of the astrological year, from November 22 to December 21. The winged red horse was also a symbol adopted by the Red Army during the 1917 Revolution.

V343.19–20, B399.26–27   some whistling sweep of quills across her spine   Here, the direct reference is to the Red Army symbol of the winged horse (above). Behind that, one hears an allusion to the myth of Leda, forcibly taken by Zeus, who adopted the shape of a swan. Pynchon may also, finally, have had in mind the Kazakh legend of Tulpar the Winged Horse, though Winner (*Oral Art* 239–40) mentions it only in passing, and without any details matching the context here.

V343.28, B399.37   Horse-fucking Catherine   The reference is to Catherine II, empress of Russia from 1762–1796, about whose sexual appetites this folklore (for evidently it was mainly lore) quickly grew.

V343.30, B399.40   neo-Potemkins   Prince Grigori Potemkin (1739–91), a Russian army officer and Catherine the Great's favorite paramour (see also V388.27–28n).

V344.4, B400.17–18   Ostarzneikunde GmbH   Eastern Pharmaceuticals, Inc., one of Pynchon's fictions.

V344.7, B400.21   "NW7"   The code number for IG Farben's top-secret intelligence-gathering office, based out of the cartel's Berlin office building (Sasuly 97–101).

V344.31, B401.9   Schwärmerei   Fanaticism, or idolatry.

V345.1–2, B401.23   cyclized benzylisoquinolines   On the problems with the chemical nomenclature here, see V166.11n. The significant thing is that a (fictional) compound mentioned by the spirit of Walter Rathenau in a séance, circa 1930, has attained reality in Wimpe's office.

V345.6–10, B401.29–35   "Eumecon ... Eucodal"   All the drugs listed in this catalogue are opium alkaloids, but only Pantopon (a proprietary name) appears to have been available in the United States as an injection for pain (Gilman 509).

V345.17, B402.1 Valerian   Dried roots of *Valerian officinalis* were formerly used as a mild sedative.

V345.35–36, B402.23–24   It's magnificent, but it's not war   General Bosquet's exclamation once again (see V10.28n).

V346.2–3, B402.33–34   deadly ogive of their Parabellum rounds   In architecture, an ogive curve is a gothic-style arch; in statistical applications it is the graphic representation of a frequency distribution. "Parabellum" was originally the telegraphic address of the Deutsche Waffen und Munitionsfabrik (DWM, the German Weapons and Munitions

Factory) of Berlin. DWM manufactured the famed Luger pistol, chambered for a uniquely bottle-nosed cartridge of 7.65-millimeter caliber, known from 1900 on as a "Parabellum round."

V346.4, B402.35–36   Napoleon's *on s'engage, et puis, on voit* Advice to generals: "One joins [the battle], and later, one looks!" Source unknown.

V347.6–7, B404.5–7   everything from Mille-Feuilles . . . La Surprise de Vésuve That is, everything from Brain Fondue to Vesuvius Surprise.

V347.32, B404.37   an old *Enbekši Qazaq* A newspaper, "The Kazakh Toiler," founded in 1920 as the official Communist journal (Winner, *Oral Art* 176).

V348.8, B405.16   the ACS Journal The *American Chemical Society Journal*, official publication of that professional society.

V348.12, B405.22   Carothers of du Pont See V249.29–30n.

V348.21, B405.32–33   the Heisenberg situation Physicist Werner Heisenberg formulated the indeterminacy principle in 1927. It states the impossibility of determining simultaneously both the position and the velocity of a nuclear particle: the more exactness used in specifying one, the more indeterminacy results in stating the other quantity.

V348.31, B406.2   Weltschmerz German for a sense of world-weariness.

V349.28, B407.7   Chemnyco of New York See Sasuly (101) and Dubois (25). Sasuly explains that "the United States was so important in German plans that IG [Farben] found it necessary to set up a special organization—called Chemnyco, Inc., of New York—to siphon out technical data of military importance." Chemnyco was established in 1931, and most of its secret information was sent to Germany through the NW7 office (V344.7n).

V349.38, B407.18   the Krasnyy Arkhiv The Red Archive of Moscow, a trove of documentary materials. From 1922 until 1941 the archivists also edited a sociohistorical journal, eventually published six times annually, for a total of 106 issues. Its main focus: articles and archival materials on the Bolshevik party, the October Revolution, the civil war of 1918–20, and outstanding figures of the Communist party. Tchitcherine's research involves prerevolutionary materials, which may explain some of his fears about how "They" will use the information.

V349.39, B407.19–20   the epical, doomed voyage of Admiral Rozhdestvenski The Russo-Japanese War began in the spring of 1904, and following months of siege the main Russian garrison at Port Arthur fell just after Christmas of 1904. However, in October the Russian Baltic Fleet had been dispatched under the command of Admiral Rozhdestvenski with orders to relieve the beleaguered garrison. The fleet had rounded the Horn of Africa by late December, and the admiral was informed of the Russian defeat at Port Arthur when he arrived at Madagascar in January 1905. There was some discussion of turning back, but Rozhdestvenski took his fleet into the South China Sea, then into the Strait of Tshushima, off what is now Korea. The Japanese, under Admiral Togo, managed to bottle up the Russians on May 27; that day the *Suvarov*, Rozhdestvenski's flagship, was sunk, and later that night Togo's torpedo boats cut up the remainder of his fleet, most of which sank.

V350.2–3, B407.25–26   a touch of Dante . . . Simple talion   In Dante's *Inferno* the damned are carefully classified and situated in one of the circular "bulges" or levels, each according to his or her sin. The term "talion" derives from the Latin *lex talionis*, retributive justice.

V351.6, B408.37–38   the Jablochkov candles   Unknown.

V351.17–18, B409.9–11   kari . . . means "the drink of death"   This stems from Steenkamp (23): "They [the Hereros] brew a potent beer called Kari, which translated into English means 'The Drink of Death. It is brewed from potatoes, peas, sugar, and yeast. It makes them, in Captain Bowker's words, 'fighting mad.'"

V351.35, B409.32   a few bars of *Madame Butterfly*   This music would be especially appropriate here, because Giacomo Puccini's opera was introduced in 1904, when Tchitcherine's father was en route to Port Arthur, and because its plot concerns a woman left pregnant by a sailor.

V352.10–11, B410.10   the era of Feodora Alexandrevna, she of the kidskin underwear   Feodorovna Alexandra (1872–1918) was the granddaughter of Queen Victoria of England and was the empress of Russia following her 1894 marriage to Czar Nicholas II. She was a woman of endless scandal because of her relations with the mystic Grigori Rasputin, a favorite of the royal family. Her highly refined tastes in clothes (the "kidskin underwear," here, whose specific source is unknown) only added to that reputation.

V352.15–16, B410.15–17   how his own namesake and the murdered Jew . . . at Rapallo   On Georgi Tchitcherine's role in working out the Rapallo Treaty for Walter Rathenau, see V338.3–5n.

V352.23, B410.25   apparatchik   A Soviet party functionary, a bureaucrat.

V352.26–27, B410.29–30   first plenary session of the VTsK NTA   From Winner's "Problems" (139). The abbreviation stands for the All-Union Central Committee on the New Turkic Alphabet. The group first met in plenary session in Baku, during 1927, to establish a headquarters for the literacy movement in central Asia.

V352.30, B410.33   a kind of G, a voiced uvular plosive   The New Turkish letter was *tenth* in the alphabet (Winner, "Problems" 140).

V353.24, B411.35   zapekanka   A pudding.

V354.15, B412.31–32   on the model of one ratified at Bukhara in 1923   In a footnote, Winner reports in "Problems" (135n) that an Arabic script was "ratified in Bukhara in 1923 . . . but did not take hold."

V354.21, B412.39   the Night of Power   In Islamic myth, the night when Allah gave to Mohammed the alphabet in which he was to write the Koran.

V355.37–39, B414.24–26   Tiflis . . . Samarkand . . . Tashkent   Tiflis (formerly Tbilisi) is the capital of the Georgian SSR; Pishpek (formerly Frunze) is the capital of Kirghizistan; Samarkand is the former capital of Uzbekistan, and Tashkent its present capital city.

V356.10, B415.1   an ajtys—a singing-duel   In *Oral Art* (29–30), Winner describes this social convention as "a singing competition between two individuals, professional bards or amateurs, or two groups. In such duels the words were generally improvised and the most successful improvisor was declared the winner. The content of the songs was usually drawn from everyday life. Each party might recite as many simple tales as could be recalled or the competition might be carried on in the form of a witty debate, or a mock love duel in words and song."

V356.13, B415.5   qobyz and dombra   The source again is Winner, *Oral Art* (46): "Generally, legends and tales were recited and were accompanied by the music of the *dombra* (a plucked instrument similar to the *balalaika*) or the *quobyz* (a 2–stringed instrument with a round body, open at the top)."

V356.25, B415.20   qumys   An intoxicating drink made from mare's milk.

V356.33, B415.29   aqyn   Kazakh name for a professional bard (Winner, *Oral Art* 26n).

V357.1, B415.35   lepeshka   See V340.1–3n.

V357.29, B416.27   Džambul   Winner (*Oral Art* 158) reports that by the twenties Džambul Džabajev (1846–1945) had become "the most significant Soviet *aqyn*, celebrated not only in Kazakhstan but throughout the entire Soviet Union."

V357.33, B416.31   older than Qorqyt   In Kazakh legend, Qorqyt is the patriarch of song. Legend has it that, "unable to accept the idea of death, Quoqyt flees from the people to eternal nature. But nature in the shape of trees, mountains, steppes, and forests tells him that even she does not have the power of immortality. Qorqyt then fashions from the wood of the tree *Sryghaj*, the first *qobyz*, and plays on it the first Kazakh song" (Winner, *Oral Art* 47).

V357.37, B416.35   the Kirghiz Light   Pynchon's fiction.

EPISODE 6

We left Slothrop high over the Harz Mountains in Schnorp's hot-air balloon. He has now been in occupied Berlin for several weeks, and by the time this episode concludes he will be on his way to Neubabelsberg and the midst of the Potsdam Conference of July 17 through August 2, 1945.

The writing in this episode brims with local color gleaned from journalistic accounts of Berlin after V-E Day. Slothrop assumes his next disguise: Raketemensch, or Rocketman.

V359.24, B418.27 the Tiergarten six hundred acres of paths, ponds, statuary, and forest situated to the immediate west of central Berlin.

V359.27–28, B418.30–31 the center of the bulb is deadly poison The genus *Tulipa*, like many members of the lily family, stores in its bulbs a yellowish alkaloid gum, colchicin, which can cause gastroenteritis, coma, and death.

V360.25, B419.34 in Basic American service slang for the basic training given new recruits and inductees into the armed forces.

V361.5, B420.19 insigne Latin spelling for a sign or mark.

V361.10, B420.25 wide-awake hat A soft felt hat, wide-brimmed, one side pinned up to the forehead or temple.

V361.12–13, B420.27–28 Klar, Entlüftung, Zündung, Vorstufe, Hauptstufe This five-position switch plate, from the launch vehicle, derives from the *A-4 Fibel*, where it is depicted. After being filled with propellants and preheated at key places, the A4 rocket was attached by wires to an armored "firing car" or *Feurlitwagen*. In it sat a "firing officer" and his two assistants. They controlled the launch according to the following five-stage declarations: *Klar*, or "clear," indicated that all hoses and cables had been disconnected from the rocket and that the area was clear of people; *Entlüftung*, or "ventilation," meant that the first flow of alcohol and liquid oxygen had been released into the combustion chamber; *Zündung*, or "ignition," was their call when the mixture was ignited by a torch; *Vorstufe*, or "first stage," meant that the flow of auxiliary fuels (hydroperoxide and calcium permanganate) had begun driving the turbopumps to increase the flows of alcohol and oxygen; and *Hauptstufe*, or "main stage," meant that those primary fuels had begun to lift the A4. Kooy and Uytenbogaart (375–76) give an overview of the launch sequence as does Dornberger (6–8). Pynchon's best source was certainly the *A-4 Fibel*; however, if he used the English version (virtually the only publicly available one), he also chose to use the German terms.

V361.18–19, B420.35–36 *Der Meistersinger* The Bantam edition corrects a pronoun error in the Viking: the "Der" should be "Die," as in *Die Meistersänger von Nürnberg* (The Master-Singers from Nuremberg), Richard Wagner's 1863 opera. Its plot centers on a lover's pursuit that is fulfilled (with the aid of a cobbler, Hans Sachs) on Midsummer's Day, by means of a singing contest.

V361.22, B420.39–421.1 Wernher von Braun's birthday See V237.1–2n; it comes up again in connection with African adventurer Dr. Livingstone (V588.1–2n).

V361.23–25, B421.2–4 rolled flower-boats through the towns . . . young Spring and deathwhite old Winter Such equinoctial celebrations on March 21 were many and varied throughout Europe. Grimm (763–65) discusses some Teutonic variants, including the flower-laden carts accompanying the person of Spring, who drives out the personified figure of aging Winter.

V362.12–13, B421.36 Search-and-destroy missions A phrase widely used by U.S. military strategists and personnel during the Vietnam War. It meant, simply, to send out patrols ready for any contact with an enemy.

V362.14, B421.38 butcher named von Trotha See V317.2n.

V362.17, B421.41 "mba-kayere" From the Herero first-person prefix, *mba-*; and from *-kayere*, a verb signifying any overhead motion, as of birds. Thus, "I am passed over" (Kolbe 361).

V362.38, B422.25, "Was ist los, meinen Sumpfmenschen?" "What's up, my swamp-men?"

V363.13, B422.43–423.1 "der Fünffachnullpunkt" The "quintuple zero." On the five-digit numbering of the rockets, see V252.4n.

V364.22, B424.15 Tannhäuser, the Singing Nincompoop Here and in what follows Pynchon alludes to the Teutonic legend of Tannhäuser, the troubadour who succumbs to the temptations of sensual pleasure and spends one year underground with Venus (Dame Hulda or Frau Holda in some versions). Boredom and jaded appetites eventually get the better of him, and he leaves for home again. There he boasts of his dalliance during a competition of minnesingers, shocking his beloved Lisaura, the girl who had awaited his return. That is his first stupid error: kissing and telling, as it were. Judged guilty of violating the conventions of courtly love, Henry Tannhäuser makes a pilgrimage to Rome. The pope denies him absolution, declaring (in Richard Wagner's operatic version):

Thou art forever accurs'd!
And as this staff I hold
Ne'er will put forth a flower or leaf,
Thus shall thou never more behold
Salvation or thy sin's relief!

Hearing this, Lisaura wastes away and dies of grief, and Henry is doubly overcome by his preterition. But then the compounding irony: word comes that the pope's staff has miraculously bloomed. Medieval versions (related in Grimm) used to end here; Wagner, however, adds a romanticist coda: Lisaura's sacrifice is shown winning Tannhäuser an eternal love in heaven.

V364.25–26, B424.19–20 William Slothrop . . . that *Arbella* See V204.1–4n.

V364.36, B424.32 Along the Havel in Neubabelsberg The community of Neubabelsberg (situated on an arm of the river Havel about fifteen miles southwest of central Berlin) became the center of the German film industry after World War I.

V364.39, B424.36 a magenta gel Magenta is a blood-red coal-tar dye (discovered in 1859 and named for the bloody Battle of Magenta of that year). Impregnated in a photographic gelatin, it serves as a filter. But thrown over a "key light," it would make Greta Erdmann appear red, the color opposite to green—the dominant color pair in these episodes (see Hayles and Eiser 18–19).

V365.3, B424.42 Chanel suits Designer-made clothes from the famous Paris salon of Madame Coco Chanel.

V365.10, B425.8–9 mangel-wurzel A yellowish beet.

V365.13, B425.13–14 near the Grosser Stern Translated, "Great Star"; a street running east–west through Berlin's Tiergarten.

V365.17, B425.18–19 a REEFER! Underground slang for a marijuana cigarette. Some say it derives from the verb "reef," to roll up a sail; more likely it originated from a phonetic spelling of Er Rif, the Moroccan hills known for their production of marijuana. Thus Pynchon's comment on "the Rif's slant fields" in the next lines.

V365.23, B425.26 "Säure" German for "acid" (as in vinegar). Thus Emil is an "acid bummer," American sixties slang for an unpleasant experience while under the influence of LSD.

V366.3, B426.7–8 "the Tauschzentrale" German for the Central Exchange; a troop depot with its commercial post exchange.

V366.12, B426.21 Tonto On the "Lone Ranger" programs for American radio and television, Tonto was the masked man's "faithful Indian companion." He saved the life of Texas Ranger Dan Reid, and after Reid became the Lone Ranger, Tonto rode along, doing good deeds and helping to search for the outlaws who dry-gulched Reid and his fellow Rangers.

V366.14, B426.22 "Raketemensch!" Rocketman was originally the creation of Ajax Comics in the early forties. In 1952 Ajax/Farrell Comics published a single *Rocketman* issue (all devoted to his adventures), now a rarity. Recently, Pacific Comics revived the character under a slightly different moniker, *Rocketeer*, doubtless a ploy to avoid copyright trouble. Rocketman, originally a stunt pilot named Cliff Secord, comes into the accidental possession of a rocket pack coveted by both Allied and Nazi forces, which operates by hand controls. He uses it for heroic and patriotic deeds. The rest of his get-up: a finned helmet that covers his face, except for eye and mouth vents; a brown cavalry waistcoat; tight riding breeches; and knee-high boots—much like Slothrop's attire here.

V366.28, B426.39 "any armies?" Servicemen's slang for army-issue cigarettes.

V367.19, B427.35   "Listen, Kerl"   The term is conversational German for a guy or fella.

V367.27–28, B428.4–5   Like the ballroom in St. Patrick's . . . none in these trousers here   An old locker-room pun. In New York City, St. Patrick's Cathedral is located on Fifth Avenue.

V368.9, B428.32   pisscutter   Partridge (*Forces' Slang*) claims that the word means "top-notch" and traces it to Canadian naval slang from World War II. In popular usage, it meant anything cordially, fraternally approved.

V368.13, B428.37   Reichstag building   The Reichstag, located at the southeast corner of Berlin's Tiergarten, was the parliamentary seat of German government prior to Hitler's takeover. The July 16, 1945, issue of *Time* magazine includes a photo, one of the first taken after the Allies were allowed into the Russian-occupied sector of the city. Here is how the correspondent described the scene (28–29): "In the rubble-heaped city, now opened to Anglo-U.S. forces for the first time since its capture ten weeks ago, two things at once impressed the Americans: the mark of Death, and the mark of the Russians. Death stared from the cadavers of mighty buildings; the smashed, charred bones of the Reichstag . . . the stench of death rose too from corpses still rotting under debris, from the corpse-clogged . . . canal, from the hasty shallow graves dug in every park and platz." As to the "mark of the Russians," see below.

V368.17, B428.41–429.1   a big chromo of Stalin   This is the "mark of the Russians" on devastated Berlin. The *Time* story (above) has just such a picture of Stalin's face staring down on passing Berliners from a huge chromolithograph. *Time*'s correspondent noted (29) that after taking Berlin the Russians "placarded the ruins with portraits of Stalin."

V368.28, B429.14   GI fartsack   Normally, in U.S. service slang, a sleeping bag; but here used metaphorically as a body bag.

V368.37, B429.24   M.O.s   That is, medical officers.

V368.41, B429.30   John Dillinger   Photos of the legendary outlaw of the thirties would be appropriate decor for this (evidently fictional) bar, because Dillinger was gunned down outside Chicago's Biograph Theater (see V741.6–26).

V369.18, B430.7   mountain of hash!   Hashish.

V369.20, B430.9   the Romilar River   Romilar is the registered trademark of an American cough syrup, a mildly opiated sedative.

V369.28, B430.17   Panama Red   More underworld slang from the sixties; here, for the reddish-green variety of Panamanian marijuana.

V369.34, B430.23   a narco man   A narcotics agent.

V370.5–6, B430.34–35   "Potsdam . . . the Wilhelmplatz"   Potsdam is located across the Havel from Neubabelsberg and was the site for the

Potsdam Conference of late July and early August 1945. The Wilhelmplatz is a large square located in the center of town.

V370.25, B431.13   "the CBI"   The China-Burma-India theater of wartime operations.

EPISODE 7

In full Rocketman regalia, Slothrop makes a raid on the "Berlin White House" occupied by President Harry Truman. The approximate date is July 18, 1945. Slothrop recovers a kilogram of hashish buried below Truman's window, makes his way back to Berlin, is intercepted by Tchitcherine, and as the episode ends, is sliding once more into a sodium amytal—induced hallucination.

V371.32–33, B432.26   villa at 2 Kaiserstrasse, in Neubabelsberg   President Truman's address for the Potsdam Conference. Journalistic accounts of the house, located on the south shore of the Greibnitz See, agree that it was an ugly, squat building and not white but yellow.

V371.34–35, B432.28   the Avus Autobahn   This highway runs southwest out of Berlin through the middle-class suburb of Zehlendorf, through Neubabelsberg, then over the river Havel to Potsdam.

V372.10, B433.2   "Plunging fire"   U.S. Army handbooks define it as gunfire from high emplacements, striking earth at an oblique angle.

V372.12, B433.5   an AGO card   Issued through the Adjutant General's Office of the U.S. Army to military personnel who are awaiting, or in the midst of, either a reassignment or some special assignment.

V372.23, B433.18   "to Cuxhaven"   The North Sea town where, by this time, English rocket experts were beginning to study and test the A4 rocket for Operation Backfire.

V372.29–30, B433.25–26   Mare's-tails . . . the Berliner Luft   White cirrus clouds. Ancient Europeans regarded them as hairs from the White Goddess, Rhiannon or Demeter. They were signs therefore of *Albina* (the White Goddess) and of the *Alpdrücken*, or "nightmare." The "Berliner Luft" is the Berlin sky.

V373.19, B434.21   the Winterhilfe one-course   The Winterhilfswerk (Winter Relief Project) was a 1933 brainchild of Nazi propaganda chief Joseph Goebbels. It began as a campaign to raise funds for social relief, originally for items of food but later for clothing and other articles. Donors to the program were given WHW lapel buttons and stickers for their door announcing: "We gave." The WHW also established one Sunday each month as a "one-course Sunday," when a simple meal of pickled meat was to be substituted for the usual multicourse spread. The return of goods to the needy took the form of mass feedings, free clothes, and the like (Heiber 185–86).

V373.26–27, B434.30–31   giant photographs are posted out in the Friedrichstrasse   And indeed they were. Truman, Stalin, and Churchill were all in a row at the intersection of Under den Linden and the Friedrichstrasse (see the photograph in *Time*, July 23, 1945, 21).

V373.32, B434.38–39   "Roosevelt died back in the spring"   Specifically, during the afternoon of April 12, 1945, while Slothrop was "jiving on the Riviera" (V374.10).

V373.39–40, B435.4–6   Slothrop was going into high school when FDR was starting out in the White House   Roosevelt took office on March 4, 1933. If Slothrop was born in March 1918 (see V624.18n), he would have been about fifteen and a high school freshman.

V374.22–23, B435.34   posing in the black cape at Yalta   In February 1945 Roosevelt, Churchill, and Stalin met in the Crimean city of Yalta to discuss plans for the occupation of Germany and Europe. The picture of Roosevelt in the black cape, flanked by the other two allies, was widely published. He died two months later.

V374.39–375.2, B436.11–16   the Evil Hour, when the white woman . . . comes out of her mountain . . . offering the Wonderflower . . . with long teeth   A reference to Dame Holda (V364.22n), from Grimm's *Teutonic Mythology*. The goddess appeared under two aspects: as a kind and helpful maid, white and often associated with the glittering snow; and as an ugly old woman, in Grimm's description (269) "an old witch with long teeth" who has a dark and dreadful disposition. The "Wonderflower" or *Wunderblumen* is a folk talisman, a key to open Dame Holda's mountain with its miraculous treasure. Usually the Wonderflower is a forget-me-not, and white, and associated with Dame Holda in her helpful aspect. In many of these stories the hero has been banished to the mountains; in order to redeem his freedom, he must recover this enchanted treasure, "and the white woman, the snake woman, or simply snake and dragon, are they that guard it (ibid. 970). In this context, Grimm also notes that Christ was frequently interpreted as a "treasure" who went down to harrow hell. The "Evil Hour" thus explains itself: Christ was crucified at noon, and the noon hour gathers significance as *GR* unfolds: see also V439.37, V500.40, V625.5, V667.3–4, and V674.19–20.

V375.4, B436.18   P-38s   Lockheed Aircraft produced nearly ten thousand of these twin-engine fighter planes, nicknamed "Lightning." The models built for the army air force were green and black; those for the navy, silver and blue.

V375.7, B436.21–22   a "stick" of "tea"   Here, self-conscious underworld slang for a cigarette of marijuana.

V375.16, B436.33–34   "It was our Captain Midnight"   "Captain Midnight" was a radio program that got its start over the Mutual Network, out of Chicago, in 1940. By 1943 it was carried nationwide, every weekday evening. Captain Midnight was an agent whose wartime job was so secret that his identity, beyond the code number SS-1, was unknown even to his superiors. Ovaltine sponsored the show, and for a dime plus the label from one jar, a kid could buy membership in the Captain's "Secret Squadron," including a "decoder badge" to decipher messages broadcast at program's end.

V375.21, B436.39–40 "Something in that rocket needed potassium permanganate" In the A4 rocket, permanganate of *calcium* was used in the autocatalytic ignition of hydrogen peroxide to power the turbines. In underworld use, as Pynchon describes it here, permanganate of *potassium* can indeed be used to separate cocaine. In aqueous solution, as permanganic acid, it is a purple liquid (the "Purpurstoff"); hence the "purple target" (V376.6) on blotting paper. Notice also the reversal or *hysteron proteron*: in this case, the target unfolds from the outside in, the outermost rings being the most valuable.

V375.31–32, B437.8–9 "over Berlin a gigantic Laurel and Hardy film, silent" Stan Laurel (1890–1965) and Oliver Hardy (1892–1957) made their first film together in 1917, a silent short called *Lucky Dog*. Ten years later they had formalized their partnership with director Hal Roach; there followed a series of shorts and features, nearly all of them with sound.

V376.26, B438.7–8 "der Springer" German name given to the knight in chess. Also, Ludwig "Der Springer" was an eleventh-century Thuringian king remembered in Baedeker's *Northern Germany* (369) for erecting churches in the vicinity of Nordhausen.

V376.27–28, B438.9–10 "to spend my last several decades as the Sublime Rossini did" Italian composer Gioacchino Rossini retired from the public eye in his thirties. For three decades thereafter he continued to write songs and instrumental pieces but lived mainly for pleasure's sake.

V376.36, B438.20 "Zorro? The Green Hornet?" Two more American heroes. From 1936 until 1952 "The Green Hornet" was a regular feature of the Mutual Radio network. He hunted down "the biggest of all game, public enemies that even the G-men cannot reach!" as the announcer used to exclaim in the show's opening moments. The Hornet was Britt Reid, son of Dan Reid (The Lone Ranger). With "his faithful valet, Kato," he matched wits with the underworld, always won, and like his famous dad forswore the use of deadly force. In 1932 actor Douglas Fairbanks played the sword-dazzling lead in the film *The Mark of Zorro*.

V376.41, B438.26 "Glück" That is, "Luck," as in "Good luck."

V377.2–4, B438.28–31 the mountain has closed . . . that White Woman Dame Holda once again (V374.39–375.2n).

V377.7, B438.35   Katje, her damask tablecloth   Slothrop recalls how
Katje made him "disappear" beneath it at V198.8–13.

V377.11, B438.39–40   Suomis or Degtyarovs   The Degtyarev (not
-ov) is a Russian submachine gun with a forty-seven-shot magazine,
an infantry standard during World War II. The Suomi submachine
gun looks very much the same, except that its "drum magazine" is located below the barrel (see also V513.15n).

V377.25–26, B439.16   "Stiefeln, bitte"   "Boots, please."

V377.30, B439.21   the Funkturm   The radio tower.

V377.35, B439.28   A SNAFU FOR ROCKETMAN   From the popular servicemen's acronym for "Situation Normal, All Fucked Up."

V378.7, B439.42   "Stimmt, Herr Schlepzig"   Or, "[It's] in order, Mr.
Schlepzig."

V378.12, B440.6–7   what the Book of Changes calls Youthful Folly   See
V13.1n. The image from the *I Ching*, or "Book of Changes," is of
a mountain with a lake or spring pond below it. So too is the setting
here: the waters of the Greibnitz See at Slothrop's feet and above
him the "White House"—looming like a mountain, from beneath which
he must snatch a treasure.

V378.16, B440.11   Jubilee Jim   The second reference to James ("Jubilee
Jim") Fisk, the notorious robber baron and womanizer. With Jay Gould
he masterminded a takeover of the Erie Railroad, which was at the
time (1868) laying track through the Berkshire hills of western
Massachusetts (see also V285.37n and V438.15–17n).

**V379.25–26, B441.26–27   back on Midsummer Eve . . . fern seed fell
in his shoes**   Midsummer's Eve is the solstice (June 22). On the fern
seed Pynchon's source was Grimm (1210): "Fern seed makes one
invisible, but it is difficult to get at: it ripens only between 12 and
1 on Midsummer Night, and then falls off directly, and is gone. A man,
who on that night happened to be looking for a lost foal, passed through
a field where fern seed was ripening, and some fell in his shoes. Next
morning he was invisible."

V380.6, B442.10   Amateur Fritz von Opels   Opel was a member of
the German family that began producing automobiles in 1898, but he
distinguished himself for daring feats of speed. In 1927, for example, he
called on Society for Space Travel expert Max Valier, who designed
him a rocket-propelled automobile. On Berlin's Avus Autobahn, Opel
pushed the car to speeds of over 125 miles per hour, setting a new
land-speed mark.

V380.11, B442.16   Garbo fedoras   Perhaps a hat like the fedora that
actress Garbo wore in *Anna Christie* (1930).

V380.14, B442.20–21   a lean gray Porsche   The Porsche trademark
did not exist on automobiles until 1948. Before the war, however, Ferdi-
nand Porsche did design automobiles for Steyr, Mercedes, and Volks-

wagen. In VW's Stuttgart plant, he also built three streamlined sports cars for the Rome-to-Berlin road race of 1939. But when the war intervened these designs were never raced; they sat in storage through the war and were hauled out as prototypes for the first Porsche production cars built in 1948. If this "lean gray Porsche" was one of those three, then Slothrop has had what auto enthusiasts would call a religious experience.

V380.25–26, B442.34–35 Hey! Leaps broad highways in a single bound! The narrator riffs on the radio announcer's introduction of "Superman," who "leaps tall buildings in a single bound!"

V380.37, B443.7 BMW limousines Like the Porsche reference, above, a puzzling one. The Bayerische Motoren Werke of Eisenach and Munich was known, from the time it began in production in 1928 until well after the war, as a manufacturer of sports cars and "drop-head" (convertible) coupes. A production-line "BMW limousine" is undocumented and probably a Pynchon fiction.

V381.6, B443.18–19 Some think he is Don Ameche, others Oliver Hardy Perhaps these servicemen are blind, or else Slothrop really is next to invisible. Ameche (b. 1910, in Kenosha, Wisconsin) was the thin, boyish star who made his screen debut in 1936 and for years was best known for his role as the great inventor in *The Story of Alexander Graham Bell* (1939), or for his role in former Ufa director Ernst Lubitsch's comedy *Heaven Can Wait* (1943). Oliver ("Ollie") Hardy (see also V375.31–32n) was, of course, the fat, moustachioed member of the Laurel and Hardy duo.

V381.10–14, B443.24–29 Miss Rheingold 1946 . . . Dorothy Hart . . . Helen Riickert Every summer the Liebmann Breweries, Inc., of Brooklyn, sponsored a contest to find the new poster girl for their Rheingold Beer, with patrons casting their votes "at Rheingold Stores and Taverns everywhere," as the ads used to note. Hart, Rickert, and Darnley were—with Jean Welch and Maggie Long—the losers in balloting that closed on August 31, 1945. The winner, blonde Rita Daigle, received three thousand dollars and a modeling contract that would lead to her picture being displayed in ads and on billboards throughout the greater New York City area. Dorothy Hart went on to roles in a few B-grade movies of the late forties.

V382.3–4, B444.25–26 "Don't Sit Under the Apple Tree" . . . Andrews Sisters The song (by Brown-Tobias-Stept) was a 1942 hit for the Glenn Miller Orchestra and a hit once again in 1944 for the Andrews Sisters. The lyric is in parts. First the male voices sing:

Don't sit under the apple tree
With anyone else but me [repeat twice, then the whole stanza]
Till I come marching home.

Don't go walking down lover's lane
With anyone else but me [repeat as before]
Till I come marchin' home.

Well I just got word, from a guy who heard
From the guy next door to me;
The girl he met just loves to pet,
And she fits you to a tee—

But don't sit under the apple tree
With anyone else but me [repeat as before]

Then the female voices come in:

Don't give out with those lips of yours
To anyone else but me [repeat as before]
Till you come marchin' home.

So watch the girls on those foreign shores,
They'll have to report to me [repeat as before]
When you come marchin' home.

You're on your own, where there is no phone,
And I can't keep tab on you;
Be fair to me, and I'll guarantee,
There's one thing I won't do—

I won't sit under the apple tree
With anyone else but you [repeat, all together now].

V382.15–16, B444.40–41   Mickey Rooney . . . Judge Hardy's freckled madcap son   From 1936 to 1958 actor Mickey Rooney made fourteen Andy Hardy films. During his early years, the films also featured Andy's father, played by Lionel Barrymore, a judge who always fought for the rights of little people. In *Judge Hardy's Children* (1938), he battles an electric cartel and its Washington lobbyists.

V382.22, B445.7   Minsky's   Famous New York striptease club of the twenties.

V383.1–2, B445.34   hair combed lionlike . . . glimmering steel teeth   This is Tchitcherine, whose "steel teeth wink as he talks" (V337.22–23).

V383.2, B445.35   eyes black and soft as that Carmen Miranda's   The singer, dancer, and actress famous for her fruit-filled hats, but also for her dark Brazilian eyes.

EPISODE 8

A board a hijacked German submarine named *Der Aal* (The Eel), off the coast of northern Germany, the Argentine anarchists lazily plan a film version of José Hernandez's epic poem of the Argentine pampas, *Martín Fierro*. They propose to shoot this film on the Lüneberg Heath, the place (as it happens) where the quintuple-zero rocket was fired. The time of this episode is unspecified, but probably mid-July.

V383.10, B446.2 Leopoldo Lugones See V263.18n.

V383.11, B446.4 the chug of the "billy-goat" The sound of the submarine's bilge pump. Its below-decks compartment, in naval slang, is called "the goat hole" (used again at V594.38).

V383.12–13, B446.5–6 El Ñato He derives his moniker from a character in canto 22 of Hernandez's *Return of Martín Fierro*. It means "pug-nose."

V383.13–14, B446.7 tristes and milongas Respectively, Spanish for "laments" (or any sad songs) and "dances."

V383.18, B446.12 Cipriano Reyes Next to Juan Perón, Reyes was once one of Argentina's most charismatic political figures. During the summer and fall of 1945 he parlayed his leadership of the Packinghouse Workers Union into leadership of the entire Partido Laborista, the Labor party. Reyes was an anarchist and also a Perónist in 1944–45. However, by the spring of 1946 he had broken with Perón over the role of the military, and by 1948 he was accused of plotting with U.S. diplomat John Griffiths to assassinate Perón. Reyes never recovered from that charge, which appears to have been trumped up anyway (Alexander 54– 60). Note also his first name: "Cipriano" means "of Kyprian Venus"; compare, for example, "Kyprinos" at V55.36 and "Cypridinae" at V690.40.

V383.19, B446.13 Acción Argentina See V263.34–35n.

V383.20–22, B446.15–17 Borges . . . ("El laberinto . . . la disquietante luna") Here is a curious puzzle. The quotation does not appear in the *Obras Poeticas* (Poetical Works) of Jorge Luis Borges, nor does it crop up in the course of his fictional works. It *is* neatly consistent with the rhythms and motifs in Borges's poems, and if the lines are not his then Pynchon has worked up a decent imitation—a neat trick, given the way Borges's fictions reinvent literary history. The lines translate: "The labyrinth of your uncertainty / detains me with the anxious moon."

V383.25–26, B446.20–22 "pitos . . . puchos . . . mamao" El Ñato (like Pynchon) is showing off his facility with tough-guy, gaucho slang. The glossary appended to Walter Owen's translation of *Martín Fierro* provides most of the terms: a *pito* is a kind of knife blade; *puchos* derives from the gaucho exclamation "la pucha!" (the whore!); *caña* is a drink high in alcohol content and distilled from the juices of various fruits; *la tacaura* is the gaucho term for a stout bamboo lance that the pampas Indians once used as a weapon. The term *mamao*, for "drunk," is of unknown origin.

V383.29, B446.26   Beláustegui   The name is of unknown origin.

V383.30, B446.27   from Entre Ríos   An inland province of Argentina, located northwest of Buenos Aires.

V383.36–37, B446.35   Lugones's "Pavos Reales"   On Leopoldo Lugones see V263.18n. The "Pavos Reales," or "Peacocks," are six short lyrical poems (for those tracing the references to the number eight in *GR*, the poems are *octets*). Published in his 1922 book, *Las Horas Doradas* (Golden Hours), the six poems are arranged in a cyclical order, treating a theme of redemption. The Peacock (or *Pavos christatus*) provides a symbolic center for that theme, for it is the traditional symbol of messianic hope. In order the six poems are "La Pompa" (The Display), "La Rueda" (The Spread), "El Orgullo" (Arrogance), "La Aurora" (Dawn), "La Tarde" (Evening), and "La Noche" (Night). Finally, note that like many works and events referred to earlier—the *Duino Elegies*, to *Erwartung*, Stalin's coming to power, the Herero uprising, German expressionist cinema . . . and many more (Joyce's *Ulysses*?),—the Lugones book appeared in 1922, one of the *anni mirabili* in *GR*.

V383.37, B446.36   off Matosinhos   A Portuguese coastal city.

V384.28, B447.30–31   pero ché, no sós argentino   See V264.4n.

V384.31, B447.34   green Perspex   Perspex is the registered trademark for a transparent polymerized methyl methacrylate plastic, very lightweight and capable of "piping" light around bends (see V487.24n).

V384.34, B447.38–39   a harmonica factory   Given their worldwide monopoly on the market, this can only be the Matteus Hohner Company in Trossingen, Germany, just over the Swiss border from Zurich.

V385.1, B448.6   the Caligari gloves   With their "deep violet" color laid over "bone white," these are the gloves pictured in the still photo from *Das Kabinet des Doktor Caligari* and tinted violet (by the Princeton University Press) for the cover of Siegfried Kracauer's scholarly book *From Caligari to Hitler*. The film itself is black-and-white.

V385.8, B448.14–15   the smell of freshly brewed maté   A slight misreading on Pynchon's part. In *Martín Fierro*, the gauchos suck herb tea, or *yerba*, through metal straws projecting from a *maté*, a gourd that holds the steaming tea (Hernandez 309).

V385.20, B448.29   a Bob Steele   See V247.6–7n.

V385.32, B448.42   his *nom de pègre*   His gangster name.

V385.39–40, B449.9   Edouard Sanktwolke   Edward Saint-Cloud.

V386.6, B449.17   "¿verdad?"   "True?"

V386.16, B449.29   *I Promessi Sposi*   "The Betrothed," Alessandro Manzoni's nineteenth-century novel, a melodramatic story of two peasants who fall in love and struggle against all socially determined odds—tyranny, poverty, disease, prejudice—to do the right Christian thing and marry.

V386.21–22, B449.36–37   "the Gaucho Bakunin. . . . a Gaucho

Marx"   Respectively, Squalidozzi is an Argentine version of the nineteenth-century Russian anarchist Mikhail Bakunin (d. 1876); and,
in a (lively, Marx Brothers' style) pun, he is a gaucho version of either
film comedian Groucho Marx (1895–1977) or political philosopher
Karl Marx (1818–83).

**V386.37–387.2, B450.12–17   Aquí me pongo a cantar / . . . con el cantar
se consuela**   This is the opening stanza of *Martín Fierro*. Giving
himself wide latitude with the translation, in order to preserve the
prosody, Owen translates:

I sit me here to sing my song,
To the beat of my old guitar;
For the man whose life is a bitter cup,
With a song may yet his heart lift up,
As the lonely bird in the leafless tree,
That sings 'neath the gloaming star.

V387.4, B450.19   the estancia   The ranch.

V387.5–6, B450.21   General Roca's campaign   It lasted six years, from
1880 to 1886, during which time Roca pursued a ruthless strategy
against the Indians of South America. In this he shared the genocidal
passion of the German general Lothar von Trotha in Southwest Africa.
Roca pursued his ends by dragooning other natives, the gauchos,
into his army. The gaucho could ride and fight, he was also a
dispossessed person, and (as we see in *Martín Fierro*) he could do little
to resist, except desert and become an outlaw with a bounty on his
head.

V387.14, B450.33   Gesellschaft   A socioeconomic partnership, or
company.

V387.29, B451.8   Punta del Este   Point of land on the northern Argentine
coast.

V387.29–30, B451.9–10   Anilinas Alemanas . . . Spottbilligfilm   The
first was German Aniline, a subsidiary of IG Farben based out of
Buenos Aires (Sasuly 167–68). On fictional Spottbilligfilm see V163.31–
33.

V387.36, B451.17   *Alpdrücken*   The dog in Edward Pointsman's dream,
Reichseiger von Thanatz Alpdrücken, has fragmented and the parts
of his name now begin to metamorphose. Here, *Alpdrücken* (Nightmare)
is an imaginary film tying together any number of characters and
events in *GR*. Margherita Erdmann acted in it; her daughter was conceived during the shooting of a scene from it; Franz Pökler watched that
scene and was emboldened to go home and conceive his daughter,
Ilse; and Slothrop, in the guise of "Der Springer," will be sexually linked
to both Margherita and Bianca. Tchitcherine will be linked to Margherita through a horse named Snake, his mount in central Asia; Snake
was the first horse Greta ever rode (while filming *Weisse Sandwüste*

von Neumexiko in America); and it's the horse of Crutchfield the
Westwardman in Slothrop's sodium amytal nightmare. The term
alpdrücken derives from an old folk belief that the devil rode men
as if they were horses, so that by morning their "mane" (hair) would
be tangled and their bodies dripping with perspiration (Grimm 1246–47).
Graves (*The White Goddess* 67) also discusses the etymology: "*Alpdrucken*, the nightmare or incubus, is connected with the Greek words
alphos, meaning 'dull-white leprosy' (Latin *albus*) . . . and *Alphito*,
the 'White Goddess.' "

**V387.38, B451.20–21   singing-duel between the white gaucho and
the dark El Moreno**   In cantos 29 and 30 of *The Return of Martín Fierro*,
the gaucho contests with a Negro, El Moreno, in a singing duel. A
fight nearly breaks out at the end, but Martín and his sons ride peace-
ably into the west, to freedom.

V388.1, B451.24   wipe   A transitional device in film making, where
the new scene "wipes" vertically, horizontally, or diagonally across the
frame.

**V388.13–15, B451.39–40   "I can take down your fences . . . lead you
back to the Garden"**   Another of the novel's potential "returns."
Also, another instance of *hysteron proteron*.

V388.21, B452.7   "Back to Gondwanaland . . . *Luderitzbucht*"   Still
more *hysteron proteron*. In theory, Gondwanaland was a Mesozoic continent that once included South America, Africa, India, and Australia.
They split and drifted apart (see also V321.19–20n). Lüderitzbucht
is a port city of South-West Africa.

V388.27–28, B452.15–16   Prince Potemkin's fake villages   During
the winter and spring of 1787, Empress Catherine of Russia journeyed
to the southern provinces ruled by her lover and adviser, Prince Grigori
Potemkin (1739–91). He had wrought enormous changes in the south:
ports had been constructed, a system of roads built, and imperial
administration spread to even the smaller towns. Catherine made a
float trip down the Dnieper River in May and saw for herself its scores
of thriving villages and well-dressed people. In St. Petersburg, however,
Potemkin's detractors insisted that it was all a show, that those
people were slaves dressed up for the occasion and leap-frogged along
the riverbank for Catherine's benefit. Even the villages were fake,
they charged. No proof was ever, or has ever, been introduced to prove
this charge. Still, in German the phrase *Potemkinsche Dörfer* became
synonymous with such fakery.

V389.3–4, B452.36–37   Spyros ("Spider") Telangiecstasis   In medical
terminology, "telangiecstasia" is a chronic vascular disorder in which
groups of capillaries dilate, causing transient red blotches, like
birthmarks, on the skin. The Greek *spyros* designates a coil.

V389.23–24, B453.18 writes Shetzline American novelist David
Shetzline (b. 1937) was at Cornell University with Thomas Pynchon
and Richard Fariña (to whose memory *GR* is dedicated). Shetzline
is the author of two novels: *Deford* (1968) and *Heckletooth 3* (1969).
He is also married to novelist and short story writer Mary F. Beal,
one of whose fictions ("Gold") is the subject of an allusion at V612.33.
The quotation here does not appear in Shetzline's published writings, its
reference doubtless private.

V390.1, B453.40–41 the Dreyfuss Affair After the French general
Alfred Dreyfuss (1859–1935) was convicted of treason in 1895, following
a long trial rife with anti-Semitic bias, the French Zionists rose united
in his defense. Dreyfuss was retried, acquitted, and released in 1906.

V390.4, B454.1–2 Will you go to the Heath? An important question,
to whomever it is addressed. The Lüneberg Heath is the setting for
Weissmann's last stand, during Easter/April Fool's of 1945, in the concluding episode of *GR*.

EPISODE 9

An exceptionally short episode, set sometime in mid-July, outside Berlin. Tchitcherine, having taken half of the Potsdam hashish, puzzles
over the results of Slothrop's latest sodium amytal session.

V390.7, B454.5 Džabajev The fictional namesake of Džambul Džabajev,
celebrated Kirghiz *aqyn* (see V357.29n).

V390.8–9, B454.7–8 combs his hair like . . . Frank Sinatra That
is, in a slick pompadour, in the style of the American singer and actor
(b. 1915).

V391.19, B455.24–25 SPOG, CIOS, BAFO, TI On SPOG and CIOS,
see V272.32–34n; TI is British Technical Intelligence, concerned
with intercepting and interpreting data about enemy manufacturing
and supply; BAFO is baffling, unrecognized in the source literature.

**V391.22, B455.28–29 from the Hook of Holland all across Lower Sax-
ony** Retreating from their positions in Holland, German V-2 units were
forced to exit The Hague northward along the Zuider Zee, skirt around
Montgomery's divisions located just to the south, then turn east
toward Hanover and the Lüneberg Heath. The units left on Thursday,
March 28, 1945, and were in the Hanover area by Easter Sunday,
April 1. Various sources (the *Times* of London, Irving, Huzel) agree
that from there, around Easter, the last rockets of the war were fired
on advancing Allied troops.

V391.33–34, B456.1 Malenkov's special committee During the war

Georgi M. Malenkov directed Russian heavy industry. In particular, he oversaw the production of planes and tanks. So when the Soviet army overran German rocket facilities at Peenemünde, in March–April of 1945, the gathering of information and the removal of equipment fell under his administrative purview.

V391.35, B456.2　TsAGI　See V273.5n.

EPISODE 10

A nother short episode, which occurs later the same day as episode 9, now identified as occurring in a whitewashed room above a disused Neubabelsberg movie studio. Slothrop awakens from his sodium amytal session to encounter "his Lisaura," Margherita Erdmann. Her yellow-and-purple iris assumes, in this satirically inverted context, the power of a *Wunderblumen* (V374.39–375.2n), a talisman associated with Venus and capable of unlocking secret treasures.

V393.11–12, B457.31–32　phony-gemütlich love nests . . . Wagnerian battlements　That is, phony-comfortable love nests, and battlements of the sort that Fritz Lang constructed for *Nibelungen*, his two-part screen epic described (and illustrated) in Kracauer (93–94, ills. 10, 11).

V393.32, B458.15　his helpless Lisaura　Alluding to the Tannhäuser myth (see V364.22n).

V393.37, B458.21　worked as a movie actress, at Templehof and Staaken　Kracauer (17) reports that after World War I the German film companies were first established at Neubabelsberg and Templehof, both Berlin suburbs. Later, in the early thirties, the great director Fritz Lang moved his studio to Staaken, another Berlin suburb (ibid. 219).

V393.41–394.1, B458.26–27　no Dietrich, nor vamp à la Brigitte Helm　Marlene Dietrich (b. 1901) was the German actress best known for her role as Lola Lola in the film *Der Blaue Engel* (1930); Brigitte Helm, another actress, played a series of "vamp" roles: as a prostitute (in *Unholy Love*, 1928), as a bourgeoise who loses herself in debaucheries (*Crisis*, also in 1928), and as the lead in both *Anna Karenina* (1929) and *The Countess of Monte Christo* (1932). Kracauer (passim) was probably the source here.

V394.23, B459.13　Ludwig II　Hitler's favorite kaiser was Frederick the Great. Ludwig II was a nineteenth-century king of Bavaria; before he went insane, in 1886, he was known as a supporter of Wagner and as a patron of the arts. When his mind snapped, he murdered one

of his attendants, then drowned himself. This is why von Göll's selection of Ludwig would probably get the fictional director "blacklisted"
by the Nazi regime.

V394.32–33, B459.25 *Das Wütend Reich* Literally, "The Mad Empire."

V394.36, B459.29 "Königreich" "Royal Empire."

V396.28, B461.35 *singularities* In mathematics, a point at which
the rate of change approaches infinity. Lance Ozier's 1975 essay identified as the background mathematician Alexander Friedmann's
calculation (in 1922, one of the *anni mirabili* in *GR*) for the phenomenon of red-shifting. The theory described how light waves from stars
in rapid motion away from the point of observation "shift" to infrared
color spectra; his theorem made way for the currently accepted Big
Bang theory in cosmology, as well as the concept of "black holes"—singularities in which the density of matter approaches infinity, a state
known as "gravitational collapse."

Singularities are points in a function of calculus where the rate
of change, or derivative, is discontinuous; indeed, as Hayles (190–91)
has stated, the behavior of the function "ceases to be mathematically ex-
pressible, except in a purely formal way." The function has only an
abstract reality; it escapes into a zone of the unknown. Hayles quite aptly sees the concept of a black hole as "a powerful metaphor of the
absolute annihilation of no Return" figured throughout *GR*, but errs
is seeking to establish a textual link between astronomer Karl
Schwarzschild, whose name has been given to the "event horizon" of
a black hole (a zone beyond which there's no return), and Tyrone
Slothrop. In *GR*, "Schwarzchild" is not "the code name for the infant
Slothrop" (Hayles 194); his code name is *Schwarzknabe* (see V286.5).
The connection is tenuous: wholly reliant upon the reader's (not
Pynchon's) translation.

V396.31, B461.39 scenic Berchtesgaden The Bavarian site of Hitler's
mountain redoubt, "Wolf's Lair." As a place-name, it invokes a familiar
mythic code: named for the Teutonic goddess Berchte, who is closely
related to Dame Holda, it is derived (according to Grimm 272–74) from
the etymological roots meaning "bright, luminous, glorious," and
from an evil version of the White Goddess noted among children as
a terror who slits open the bellies of disobedient boys and girls.

V396.33, B461.41–42 the Russian mathematician Friedmann See
V396.28n. He noted that light from stars moving *away* from the observation point, at speeds approaching that of light, will show illumination
mainly in the longer, or infrared, spectrum: again, the phenomenon
of red-shifting.

V396.41, B462.10 under the rose Once more pointing to that which is uttered in secret (sub rosa); and to the title of Pynchon's short story (see V290.7n).

EPISODE 11

N ote how this episode is linked to the one preceding it: that one ends with Slothrop whipping Margherita Erdmann into a passion at the Neubabelsberg movie studio where *Alpdrücken* was filmed, and Bianca Erdmann conceived; this begins with Franz Pökler remembering that film and how he went home from it to conceive his daughter, Ilse. For a similar linking device, see the transition between episodes 15 and 16 in part 1, where the word "touch" provides a bridge. Here it consists of the words "Bianca" and "bitch." Several triads of characters overlap at this moment: there are Franz, Leni, and Ilse Pökler; Max Schlepzig, Margherita, and Bianca Erdmann; Slothrop (on paper, an avatar of Schlepzig), Margherita, and Bianca; also Weissmann, Katje, and Gottfried, for it was "the word bitch" that similarly brought Gottfried to arousal (see V429.21–22n). A theme of repetition and incest runs throughout. This episode is also the longest in the novel and is placed very much at its center. The nominal time is July 9, 1945, or shortly thereafter; but the narration ranges back over sixteen years, its analepsis beginning in the late twenties, in Berlin, where the German rocket program began as an apparently innocent club, the Society for Space Travel. Franz Pökler's recollections of these and subsequent events, up to the present moment, stem largely from Walter Dornberger's memoir of the German rocket program, entitled *V-2*. As the episode ends, readers also learn some crucial bits of information about the time when Rocket 00000 was fired.

V397.28–29, B463.7   the Ufa theatre on the Friedrichstrasse   See V98.24n.

V398.3–4, B463.21–22   the onion-topped Nikolaikirche   Countless German towns and cities have their Nikolaikirche, or St. Nicholas Church, as a glance through Baedeker's *Northern Germany* will show. So it is impossible to pinpoint the locale of Pynchon's fictional place Zwölfkinder (Twelve Children). The name, as well as the idea (a kind of German Disneyland?), is also of unknown origin. We can only note that it sits somewhere north ("up," at V398.32) from Lübeck and that from it one sees Denmark across the Baltic Sea (V398.36).

V398.4–5, B463.23   the great Wheel   A Ferris-wheel.

V398.8–9, B463.28   a moon newly calved   The new crescent moon appeared in the nighttime sky on July 9, 1945.

V398.19, B463.41   Frieda the pig   Named for Freya, sister of Frey,

the etymology of whose name gives us *fried* (peace: see V94.26n). Frieda
is an apt name for Pökler's pig because the Teutonic goddess Freya
often appears riding a sow or boar, sometimes one with gold bristles
(Grimm 214–16, 299–303).

V399.19, B465.8 strands of steel cable Another Bantam error: "steels."

**V399.38–39, B465.32–33 tracing patiently the xs and ys, P (atü) . . .
moving always** The origin of this formula is unknown.

V400.25, B466.25 "Kadavergehorsamkeit" The German for "corpse-
obedience"; a kind of zombie state.

V400.30, B466.32 Verein für Raumschiffahrt The Society for Space
Travel (V162.13–14n).

V401.6, B467.9 Major Weissmann Note his rank. Sometime between
the early thirties and 1944, when we meet him in Holland, Weissmann
has evidently been "busted" from major back to captain (his rank
at V94.22).

V401.25, B467.32–33 a weapon to . . . leap like a chess knight The
V-2 rocket as *Der Springer*.

V402.5–6, B468.18 the Spree The shipping canal that runs through
Berlin.

V402.11, B468.25 to Kummersdorf Seventeen miles south of Berlin,
where the German army established Experimental Station West to
begin its initial experiments in rocketry (Dornberger 23).

**V402.29–32, B469.3–4 a model no more than 4 or 5 centimeters . . .
manometers outside** The *Halbmodelle* (half-model) "solution" derives
from Dornberger (118), who describes wind-tunnel testing: "The
models, 1.5 to 2.0 inches wide and 12 to 16 inches long, were . . . halved
along their longitudinal axis and mounted on plates. The pressure
changes were then simultaneously measured at as many as one hundred
and ten separate points over the body." In the same context, he
reports that they used a "manometer" to measure pressure changes
on the models. Evidently Pynchon translated the linear measurements
back into metric equivalents.

V403.5, B469.25–26 then, in '34 . . . Dr. Wahmke A description of
his death, along with two others, when a rocket engine exploded
on its test bed in March 1934, appears in Dornberger (29).

**V403.11, B469.32–33 reading Hesse, Stefan George, and Richard
Wilhelm** Hermann Hesse (1877–1962) was a German poet and novelist, winner of the 1946 Nobel Prize for literature. His fictions often
involve the theme of paired opposites, the possible reference here. Stefan
George (1868–1933) was a German poet whose freedom with diction
was counterbalanced by his adherence to the strictest of structural and
prosodic rules. Richard Wilhelm was known chiefly as a translator
of Eastern texts, for example, *The Book of Changes* in 1923.

V403.23, B470.5 **"Folgsamkeitfaktor"**   Literally, an "obedience factor" or "willingness to follow"; in ballistics, German researchers applied the term to problems of arrow-stable trajectories.

V403.35, B470.19–20 **uprising by the Bondelswaartz in 1922**   Here Pynchon summarizes events he treated in chapter 9 of *V.*, "Mondaugen's Story."

V404.16, B471.5–6 **the Versuchsanstalt**   The Research Institute at Kummersdorf.

V404.38–405.3, B471.33–41 **They used an ancient ferryboat . . . the late sun**   These details are from Dornberger (42–43), who describes the move to Peenemünde in a more matter-of-fact way:

> That Spring the tranquility of the inlet had been interrupted. One day a number of small motor launches filled with building personnel and surveyors had arrived in the little harbor. Next came a large vessel of unusual appearance, such as had never been seen before on the Baltic. She carried building materials and equipment. Halliger had recollected that he had come across that antediluvian craft once before, in Stralsund. She had been a car and passenger ferry then. A typical example of mid-nineteenth century shipbuilding, she possessed large cabins with decrepit furniture upholstered in red plush, a quantity of gleaming brass fittings and mountings, towering upper works, and high funnel."

V405.10, B472.7 **Lot's wife.**   An allusion to Gen. 19:26.

V405.26, B472.26 **good company at Herr Halliger's inn**   Dornberger again (42): "Herr Halliger, owner of the island . . . attended with inexhaustible good humour to our bodily needs and to the warmth of the inner and outer man, a matter of dire necessity at this cold season of the year."

V405.34, B472.36–37 **ephedrine pre-dawns . . . ja, ja, stimmt**   Ephedrine is a mild stimulant, taken here to ward off sleep while solving engineer's problems and nodding "yes, yes, correct."

V406.11–12, B473.17 **Stodda's treatise on steam turbines**   Unknown.

V406.13–16, B473.19–23 **the propulsion group were testing . . . exhaust velocities of 1800 meters per second**   The data are from Dornberger (46).

V406.37–38, B474.7–8 **the A3, christened . . . with flasks of liquid oxygen**   More detail from Dornberger (44): "We baptized our rockets with liquid oxygen." The A3 measured 21 feet high and 2½ feet in diameter, less than half the size of an A4.

V407.1, B474.13–14 **the camera photographed the needles swinging on the gauges**   See Dornberger (45), who recalls fitting test rockets with crude instruments: "A barograph, a thermograph, and a small motion picture camera for photographing these two instruments in flight."

V407.3–4, B474.16–17 **Heinkels were also dropping iron models of the Rocket from 20,000 feet**   The Heinkel was a German bomber plane.

Dornberger (57) explains its use in researching the flight of supersonic projectiles: "We built several iron models about 8 inches in diameter and 5 feet in length. . . . In September 1938 we began to drop these missiles from a Heinkel HE-111 at 20,000 feet. The trajectory was recorded by photo-theodolites and cinetheodolites."

V407.19, B474.36 in Peenemünde-West Home of a testing station for the German Luftwaffe (Air Force). The Messerschmitt-262, the world's first jet plane, was tested from this airfield.

V408.15, B475.39 from a place in the mountains Ilse has arrived from the Dora camp, next to Nordhausen in the Harz Mountains.

V410.11, B478.6–7 crater in the Sea of Tranquillity, called Maskelyne B In July 1969 the Apollo 11 astronauts landed, as Ilse dreams, "right on the rim" of this crater, and astronaut Neil Armstrong became the first man to walk on the moon. The rocket that took Apollo 11 there was built under the direction of Wernher von Braun, second in command at Peenemünde under Dornberger.

V410.34, B478.34–35 Friedrich August Kekulé von Stradonitz, his dream of 1865 This is the second reference to the famous chemist (see V84.9–10n). Kekulé dreamed of the "cosmic serpent," Ourobouros, which devours its own tail. From this he intuited the cyclical, six-sided structure of the benzene molecule, opening the study of "aromatic" compounds in organic chemistry.

V410.38, B478.39 nice of Jung to give us the idea of an ancestral pool Swiss psychoanalyst Carl Gustav Jung (1875–1961) and his theory of "the collective unconscious," a sort of ancestral-semiotic background from which are taken the elemental structures (here, a "mandala archetype") of dreams.

V411.16, B479.21 Atlantes Plural form of Atlas, Greek god who supports all heaven on his shoulders.

V411.19, B479.24–25 Once again it was the influence of Liebig See V166.1– 9n.

V411.25–26, B479.32–33 sorting-demon such as . . . Clerk Maxwell once proposed See V239.18–19n.

V411.34–35, B480.1–3 *Mrs.* Clerk Maxwell's notorious "It is time to go home . . . you are beginning to enjoy yourself" Her remark is probably apocryphal. Mrs. Maxwell was Katherine Mary Dewar, whom he married in 1858. The Maxwells were a deeply pious couple who used to write each other meditations on Scripture whenever they were forced to be apart. But Maxwell himself was known as a conversationalist and sometime practical joker. So his wife's remonstration seems plausible, even though undocumented (for example, it is not noted in Campbell and Garnett's biography).

V411.38, B480.6–7 the double-integrating circuit in the guidance See V301.33n.

V412.35, B481.10–11   "the old refrain, 'I lost my heart in Heidel-berg'"   Riffing on the title of crooner Tony Bennet's 1955 hit song "I *Left* My Heart in San Francisco."

V413.15–16, B481.37–38   a quote from Rilke: "Once, only once..."   From Rilke's Ninth Duino Elegy. The poem poses the contradictoriness of human destiny, which is both beyond yet also reliant on those transitional forms that lie around us. That which is absolute and eternal is transformed, Rilke argues, from that which is ever-changing around us. After asking the question, why long for this this destiny? Rilke answers:

Not because happiness really
Exists, that premature profit of imminent loss.
Not out of curiosity, not just to practice the heart
that could still be there in laurel . . .
But because being here amounts to so much, because all
this Here and Now, so fleeting, seems to require us and strangely
concerns us. Us the most fleeting of all. Just once,
everything, only for once. Once and no more, And we, too,
once. And never again. But this
having been once, though only once,
having been once on Earth—can it ever be cancelled?

This is the Leishman and Spender translation of the *Duino Elegies*; note that Pynchon works his own rendering of "Einmal / jedes einmal."

V413.22–23, B482.4–5   a gold hexagon with the German formée cross   The same kind that bounces above Hilary Bounce's navel (V243.28–29n).

V414.35–415.3, B483.27–34   Nur ... ein ... Op-fer! ... Wer zum Teufel die Freiheit, braucht?   The narrator here riffs on the 1931 hit song for Louis Prima, from whom Bing Crosby snatched it, whence it appeared in several films. The song is "Just a Gigolo," a translation of a 1929 German hit, "Schöner Gigolo," music by Leonello Casucci and lyrics by Irvin Caesar, who also did the English translation:

Just a gigolo, everywhere I go,
People know what part I'm playing;
Paid for every dance,
Selling romance,
Ev'rynight some heart betraying.

There will come a day,
Youth will pass away,
Then, what will they say about me?
When the end comes, I know they will say
Just a gigolo—

As life goes on without me,
Life goes on without me.

Reworking this lyric, Pynchon makes a mordantly masochistic mac-
aronic, which translates:
Just a victim
In a vacuum

.   .   .

Won't someone even take advantage of me?
Just a slave without a master . . .
Who the devil needs freedom?

V415.29–30, B484.23 "The new planet Pluto" In 1930 astronomer
William Tombaugh confirmed the previous calculations of Percival
Lowell, who had predicted, on the basis of gravity-related oscillations in
the orbits of neighboring planets, the presence of a planet-size mass.
The "new" body was called Pluto in 1930; here, the significance of that
name involves the way Nazi party leaders were blaming Germany's
economic woes on Jewish "plutocrats" like Walter Rathenau.

V415.31, B484.24–25 long Asta Nielsen upper lip Swedish-born
film star Asta Nielson (1883–1972) gained her reputation as the "Duse
of the Screen" because of her facial features: large passionate eyes,
expressive upper lip, strong cheekbones. After moving her career to Germany in 1910, she became Europe's pin-up girl of World War I.
Kracauer (ill. 29) includes a still photo from Georg Pabst's *The Joyless
Street* (1925), in which the expanse of upper lip is well displayed.

V415.36, B484.31 Brunhübner and that crowd Unknown, or fictional.

V416.8, B485.3 *Schicksal* Destiny.

V416.10, B485.5–6 an uncontrolled series of A5s These launchings
occurred in 1938. The A5 rocket used the same motor as the A3 but was
somewhat larger in diameter. The details in this passage stem from
Dornberger (56–58).

V416.13–14, B485.9–10 vanes made of graphite . . . down to five degrees
Once more, Dornberger (57) is the source: "The oscillations we had
seen in no case exceeded 5 degrees."

V416.23, B485.21–22 Poehlmann's work Ernst Pöhlmann (Pynchon
uses the unaccented spelling) devised a method for irrigating "the
inner wall of the chamber with alcohol" (Dornberger 53; but see also
Klee and Merk 24).

V419.2, B488.20–21 nearly the end of peacetime Germany invaded
Poland at dawn on September 1, 1939.

V419.32, B489.15 Hugo Wolf An Austrian composer and disciple
of Richard Wagner, Wolf (1860–1903) wrote some two hundred songs
and a number of instrumental works.

V420.4, B489.32   sastrugi   Wind-plowed grooves in the snow; plural from the Russian *sastruga* (groove).

V421.32, B491.34–35   Juch-heierasas-sa! o tempo-tempo-ra!   An idiomatic German exclamation of unknown origin: "Hip-hip-hooray for Time!"

V422.2, B492.6–7   General von Trotha's brave men   See V99.38n.

V422.26–28, B492.34–37   the great sphere, 40 feet high . . . 20 seconds of supersonic flow   The description of this wind-tunnel compressor stems from Dornberger (114–15).

V423.5–6, B493.17–18   In '43 . . . Pökler missed the British air raid on Peenemünde   At midnight on August 17, 1943, the German V-weapon facility was attacked by over six hundred British bombers, collectively carrying over fifteen hundred tons of high explosives and several hundred tons of incendiary bombs. Among the research staff at Peenemünde, the most serious loss was the life of Doctor Thiel, as the narrator mentions here. But by far the most tragic loss occurred (as Pynchon notes) at the nearby slave labor camp at Trassenheide, where 650 died. Research at Peenemünde was not seriously impeded. On the raid see Dornberger (154–68), Huzel (54–58), Irving (100–115), Klee and Merk (43–44), and McGovern (16–31).

V423.21, B493.36–37   the gradient was to run east to west   It happened just so, and this dispersal of bombs over the island explains why the Trassenheide camp was so severely damaged. Irving (106–12) explains how such a tragic error happened. Note, also, that this bomb pattern recalls how the devastation of V-2 rockets was greatest over London's East End, home of that city's poor (V15.12–13n), and how the devastation of Berlin was greatest in that city's poorer, eastern sector (V433.17n).

V423.23, B493.39   "foreign workers," a euphemism   Dornberger (168) waves off the whole issue of concentration camp labor at Trassenheide by calling the camp a site for "foreign construction workers." Huzel tries the same moral sleight-of-hand, and in his writings von Braun never even mentions the workers. Out of sight, out of mind, as it were.

V424.14, B494.32   the test series at Blizna   In November 1943 field tests of the A4 began at Blizna in western Poland. They continued until the spring of 1944 (Dornberger 213–24).

V424.17–18, B494.36–37   Maj.-Gen. Kammler's empire-building   Dornberger describes the appointment of S S general Kammler as special commissioner for A4 matters in chapter 22 (208–11).

V424.18–23, B494.38–495.2   an airburst problem . . . perhaps the insulation on the alcohol tank was at fault   From Dornberger (218): "Von Braun declared that the alcohol tank and its ventilation were the culprit. I was more inclined to blame the oxygen tank."

V424.32–33, B495.12–14   Green rye and low hills all around: Pökler

was by a small trench . . . pointing his binoculars south Compare the
narrator's account to this one, from Dornberger (220) : "We were
in a small observation trench at the foot of a long, low hill. . . . We
were at exactly the spot marked on the map as the current target
area. That morning the first rocket had come down successfully 150
yards away . . . lumps of clay, almost as big as a man, lay scattered
far and wide in the fields of green rye round the crater. We had never
yet been able to catch with our binoculars the white cloud heralding an
explosion."

V424.34, B495.15 Erwartung See V101.9n.

V424.38, B495.19–20 dark eels of rivers catching the sun From Dornberger's recollection (220) that "winding curves of a clear little stream
sparkled in the sunshine."

**V425.25–29, B496.13–17 Chances are astronomically against a perfect
hit . . . the Ellipse of Uncertainty.** The historical details again derive
from Dornberger (220–21). But note how this event constitutes a
ballistic instance of what Hite (*Ideas* 26) calls "the trope of the unavailable insight." Here, the rocket approaches "the very center . . . the
holy X" (V424.39); yet statistical probabilities are massively against
a direct hit, which is why it seems the reasonable place to sit. Another
case, therefore, of what the narrator of *GR* will soon call "Holy-Center-
Approaching" (V508.35).

V426.5, B496.38 the penetralia From the Latin *penetralium*, the
deepest, innermost chamber of a temple.

V427.3, B498.1–2 The bulb was explaining the plot to him This
anticipates the story of Byron the Bulb (V647–55).

V427.29–30, B498.34 "a 'flying laboratory,' as Dr. Thiel said" See
Dornberger (215): "Could Dr. Thiel and the senior staff at Peenemünde
have been right after all? Was our flying laboratory too much for
soldiers to handle?"

V428.28–29, B499.36–37 the gift of Daedalus To Theseus, who slew
the Cretan Minotaur, the gift of this artificer was a roll of thread.
Daedalus explained that it was to help the young warrior find his way
out of the labyrinth. To Icarus, Daedalus gave the fatal gift of flight.

V429.15, B500.28 the Volkssturm A creation of Martin Bormann,
Joseph Goebbels, and Heinrich Himmler for the last-ditch defense of
Germany, these "People's Brigades" were christened on October 13,
1944, and filled with the Reich's young boys and aging men.

**V429.21–22, B500.37–38 who was the slender boy . . . so blond, so
white** It was Gottfried. The blond hair and white skin partly identify
him. His link to the von Göll film, *Alpdrücken*, underscores the
link. Here Ilse is Gottfried's female doppelgänger just as Katje was
in part 1. And the Blicero-Katje-Gottfried triad now slides into place
with the others, for Gottfried has experienced a curiously Pavlovian re-

flex erection whenever "the word bitch" is spoken (V103.25), just
as the word formed a bridge into this episode (V397.18). A side point
here: Gottfried was at Zwölfkinder in August 1944.

V429.27, B501.1–2   Gnostic symbolism in the lighting   Because it
involves a precise distinction between polar opposites: evil and good,
Cain and Abel. That bipolarity was a major trait of Gnostic Christianity
and (evidently) significant to the fictional director von Göll: see
V394.18–20 on his use of light "from above and below."

V431.21, B503.7   in the spring, he did see Weissmann again   When
Pökler assists with the Imipolex *Schwarzgerät*. The timing is crucial:
spring arrived on March 21, the equinox; the last V-2 rockets were
fired during Easter week, from March 25 to April 1, 1945.

V431.29, B503.18   SD   Acronym for Sicherheits Dienst (Security Service), the most feared of all the Nazi SS units. SD men wore black,
with a silver or white death's-head insignia.

V431.36, B503.25   one rocket, only one   Echoing the line from Rilke,
at V413.15–16.

V432.6, B503.38–39   "Vorrichtung für die Isolierung"   The "insulation
device" of V242.6n.

V432.9, B503.42   The first week in April   Once more the timing is
crucial. Weissmann disappears with his Imipolex shroud in the "Spring"
(that is, after March 21), leaving Frans to his own devices during "The
first week in April," that is, *after* April 1.

V432.13, B504.5   "Gaudeamus igitur"   May very well be the oldest
extant student song. Some sources claim that this lyric, an expression
of the loose and lively student life, dates from the thirteenth century
and the University of Paris. It was *the* most popular student song
in the German universities of the eighteenth century, where it became
known by the first line: *Gaudeamus igitur, juvenes dum sumus*
(Therefore rejoice, so long as we have youth!).

V432.27, B504.23   The Obersturmbannführer   The camp commander—
for example, at a concentration camp.

EPISODE 12

B ack to Berlin, in the city's Russian (eastern) sector. Slothrop delivers the
Potsdam hashish, less Tchitcherine's expropriation, to "Der Springer."
A musical debate ensues. Slothrop and Margherita resume their sadomas-
ochistic pas de deux. The time: still the later half of July.

V433.17, B505.18   the Russian sector   This area included all the industrial and working-class neighborhoods of east Berlin, neighborhoods
that were the most devastated—as the narrator notes—because fighting

there had progressed house-to-house before the advancing Russian divisions in April.

V433.17, B505.19 Königstiger tank The largest German battle tank, with its "monster" 88–millimeter canon.

V433.32, B505.37 DER FEIND HÖRT ZU "The Listening Enemy."

V434.26–27, B506.38 Biedermeier chair See V162.20–21n.

V434.29–30, B506.42 *Tägliche Rundschau* A Berlin newspaper nearly as old as the *Times* of London, whose title translates as "The Daily Review."

V434.30–31, B506.42–507.1 chalcedony doorknob . . . ferrocyanide A doorknob made from this milky-gray quartz with its ferrocyanide compounds could, under the right circumstances, react with sodium or potassium salts to replace the ferrous radical and produce a deadly white powder, sodium or potassium cyanide ($NaCN$ or KCN).

V434.31–33, B507.2–4 B . . . or H . . . the rejected Locrian mode In German musical notation the "hard" or "square" "B" is written as an H, and only the "soft" or "rounded" "B" (the flat) is designated by the "B" itself. This detail plays a key role in Thomas Mann's *Doktor Faustus*, which may be on Pynchon's mind here. In *Faustus* the "H" allows composer Adrian Leverkuhn to devise a "note-cipher," his "haetera esmeralda," in honor of his beloved, the woman who is also the source of his disease. Yet this bit of musical nomenclature has no essential relation to the "Locrian" or "Hyperphrygian" mode of music handed down from Hellenic culture. In that mode, which has only a theoretical existence, the interval between the first and the fifth is a diminished rather than a true fifth.

V435.8, B507.24 George Raft suits American actor George Raft (b. 1903) was on screen from 1929 until 1961, almost always in underworld roles that put him into a succession of high-grade gangster suits: neatly cut, padded shoulders, in black or gray sharkskin, handkerchief neatly folded in the breast pocket. See, for example, *Scarface* (1932), *The Glass Key* (1935), or Fritz Lang's *You and Me* (1938).

V435.10, B507.27 Gunsels Partridge (*Macmillan Dictionary*) lists it as a variant spelling of "gonsel" or "gonzel," designating "a boy, a youth, with implications of sexual perversion; a passive male homosexual." Thus one of them "licks his lips and stares at Slothrop." A second meaning common to American detective novel cant is "hired gun." Both meanings apply.

V435.20, B507.39–40 "Fickt nicht mit der Raketemensch!" "Fuck not with Rocketman!"

V435.21, B507.40–41 a hiyo Silver here Slothrop imitates the call of ABC Radio's Lone Ranger (Bruce Beemer) to his horse, Silver.

V435.29, B508.9 *Saturday Evening Post* faces Edited by the Curtis Publishing Company of Philadelphia, the weekly *Post* was famous by

the forties for covers that presented images of a folksy, cracker-jack
America and its cute, or at least sweetly grotesque, faces in the crowd,
all drawn by the likes of Stevan Dohanos, Mead Schaeffer, Albert
Straehle, and Norman Rockwell. So taken was Rockwell by the desire
to depict such scenes realistically that he would use dozens of photographs for a single picture. But these images, while they come to
Slothrop on this fictional "Saturday Evening," are delivered by
messengers from a sort of margin, "in from out of the long pikes";
the junkyard messages are available entirely on their "surface," perhaps
like the empty Qlippoth.

V436.16–17, B508.42–43   "As B/4" . . . Dillinger's old signoff   Details
about outlaw Dillinger (1903–34), who also used to sign his letters
to the FBI with "Bye-Bye" and "Johnie," probably stem from Toland's
Dillinger Days. See also V516.3n and V741.6–7n.

V436.24, B509.9–10   the Chariot gleaming like coal   A reference
to the copper sculpture atop the Brandenburg Gate in Berlin, at the
west end of the Tiergarten. Since 1962 this has been the principal gate-
way through the Berlin Wall separating East and West Berlin. Baedeker
(*Berlin* 55) describes its former glory: "The structure (85 ft. in height,
including the figure, and 205 ft. in width) is surmounted by a Quadriga
(Four Horse Chariot) of Victory, in copper."

V436.32, B509.19   Hinterhöfe   Once again, the back courts of tenement
buildings; here they are "nested" inside the building, and Slothrop
passes through each one below a numbered parabolic arch: first ("Ers-
ter"), second ("Zweiter"), and so on.

V437.18, B510.9   kif   Hemp (marijuana) from the Maghreb region.

V437.21, B510.12–13   Bosendorfer Imperial concert grand piano   Pynchon
has omitted the umlaut. This Austrian firm of piano makers was
founded by Ignaz Bösendorfer in 1828 and made famous by Franz Lizst,
who discovered theirs to be the only grand piano capable of with-
standing his playing. Their "Imperial" concert grand has an extended
compass in the bass register.

V437.28, B510.21   the racetrack at Karlshorst   In southeast Berlin,
a steeplechase track that, according to Baedeker, operated in spring,
summer, and fall.

V438.9–10, B511.6–7   American yellow-seal scrip . . . discontinued   See
V246.21–22n.

**V438.15–17, B511.15–17   what Jubilee Jim Fisk told the Congressional
Committee . . . in 1869**   Specifically, in October 1869, while answering
charges that he had conspired to corner the gold market in September.
When a congressman asked what happened to the fortune in railroad
money Fisk had sunk into his scheme, he answered: "It has gone where
the woodbine twineth." Asked what *that* meant, Fisk replied: "Up
the spout" (Adams, *Chapters* 128).

V440.4, B513.11–12   who is better, Beethoven or Rossini   Here begins the Beethoven-Rossini debate, anticipated in *GR* for some time. Recall, for example, the "Rossini tarantella" heard at Monte Carlo (V204.39), or Slothrop's first night of freedom on "the Rue Rossini" of Nice (V253.33). The narrator dresses out this debate in plenty of satiric passementerie, elaborating on what is really an old contrast—as old, indeed, as the uncomfortable 1822 meeting between the two composers. Säure's arguments have been anticipated by Stendahl's 1824 biography of Gioacchino Rossini, the mainspring of which is the perceived difference between the German (northern) music and the (southern) Italian style preferred by Stendahl. In fact, when his distinctions between the two are cross-listed, they look strikingly like the binary differences Pynchon weaves into his narrative:

Italian	German
warm, southern	cold, northern
simple, unsophisticated	complex, erudite
irrational	rational
organic	mechanical
emphasis on melody	emphasis on harmony
comedy (*opera buffa*)	tragedy (*opera seria*)
Scarlatti & Rossini	Bach & Beethoven

Stendahl (132) derogates the German emphasis on harmonic complexity as "a scientific discipline of doubt and analysis applied to something one loves." Later (306), he describes harmony as "mechanical technique," an impersonal force "moving rapidly towards a state of perfection" that will make all the notes "equal," just as "ciphers" are equal. Beethoven's mania for harmony he therefore paints (128) as "a black night" that diminishes simple compassion in favor of "scientific knowledge." By comparison, he argues, Rossini's music expresses a simpler folk wisdom, a pure passion for song.

As for Gustav in this scene, his position is probably indebted to Schauffler's biography, *Beethoven: The Man Who Freed Music* (1933). This Beethoven "unshackled music" from "concreteness," from its referential and representational bonds, and brought it instead toward "imaginative liberty," to a dependence on instrumentation alone (69). To Schauffler, this music expresses a pure idealism, an "overarching transcendence" characterized, for instance, in a familiar signature that recurs in Beethoven's work, the so-called Mannheim rocket, an arpeggio rising sequentially through the scales (69). But Schauffler's Beethoven was also "eccentric, lonely, unattractive, in urgent need of a woman's loving companionship" (273). Worse still, he was paranoically locked inside himself. Like Pynchon's character Stencil, in *V.*, Beethoven used to address himself in the third person; he once scribbled a note to himself, lamenting that "there is no happi-

ness from without, thou must create it all from within thyself, only
in the ideal world findest thou friends" (273). Carved on the obelisk over
Beethoven's grave is a striking symbol of this Germanic idealism:
the worm Ouroboros devouring its own tail, and inside that a butterfly.

Slothrop overhears but does not recognize in this debate the strains
of a much larger ethical struggle between, on the one hand, empathy and
the responsibilities of friendship and, on the other, an idealistic alienation made culturally fashionable. Slothrop has been prepared for this
moment by various pieces of music and even street names, but the
debate goes on, with musical compositions hurled back and forth like
missiles—Rossini's *La Gazza Ladra* and *Tancredi* thrown against
Beethoven's "Ode to Joy" and the *Ninth Symphony*—and through it
all Slothrop is mute. As the debate ends, he will "paranoiacally" escape
(V442.40).

**V440.26–27, B513.38–39   "Italian girl is in Algiers, the Barber's in
the crockery, the magpie's stealing everything in sight!"**   In order, these
reference the title characters of three Rossini operas: *L'Italiana in
Algeri* (1813), *Il Barbieri di Siviglia* (1816), *La Gazza Ladra* (1817).

V440.31, B514.2   Anton Webern is dead   An anachronistic allusion.
The time of this fictional episode is late July, but Webern was shot on
the evening of September 15, 1945, in the Austrian village of Mittersill.
He was sixty-two. Pynchon has all the other details correct. Webern's
brother was under investigation for dealing in illegal substances.
That night, a contingent of Allied soldiers approached the house in
Mittersill; at the same moment Webern stepped out on his brother's
patio to light a cigar. A jumpy American boy from North Carolina
was startled by the light and shot Webern once with a .45 caliber pistol
(Wildgans 112–17).

V440.39, B514.11   going on since Bach   Implies an extension of the
patriarchal line Stendahl discusses: Bach to Beethoven to Wagner
to Schönberg to Webern.

V440.39, B514.12   music's polymorphous perversity   The term is
derived from Norman O. Brown's *Life Against Death*. Brown (291)
hypothesizes a man "freed from all sexual organizations—a body freed
from unconscious oral, anal, and genital fantasies or return to the
maternal womb. Such a man would be rid of the nightmares which
Freud showed to be haunting civilization; but freedom from those fantasies would also mean freedom from that disorder of the human
body which Freud pitilessly exposed. In such a man would be fulfilled
the mystic hope of Christianity, the resurrection of the body, in a
form, as Luther said, free from death and filth." To be "polymorphously
perverse" in this way is to delight in the full life of the body rather
than in its separate, rationalized "sexual organizations" or "erogenous
zones."

This is the one direct allusion in *GR* to Brown's psychoanalytical theory of history, although, as Wolfley has shown, its presence is strong throughout the text. To Brown, the metaphysics of human history is defined by repression—the repression of physical desire, which is compensated by man's sublimating, "civilizing," activity. "The dynamic of history," Brown argues (230), "is the slow return of the repressed" in ever more complex forms of violent technology. This much of the theory was orthodox Freudianism. Yet Brown foresaw two possible outcomes. First, the disappearance of man: the products of his sublimating activity (weapons, for instance) would lead to self-extinction. Second, the disappearance of history: this would mean, simply, the disappearance of repression, the rebirth of a "polymorphously perverse" erotic being that stands beyond guilt and even consciousness; it is the childish, "mindless pleasures" Pynchon represents in *GR*. Yet the psychosocial barriers to the second alternative are so great, and man is so inured to the first, that man has both feared and desired his death. Through this paradoxical law, Wolfley argues, repression gives form and "plot" to history just as gravity plots, or imparts form to, the earth. In *GR*, then, gravity is "the ultimate metaphor" of the "human repression that is its theme" (Wolfley 104). And it is their own "gravity," their dream of annihilation, that characters both seek and seek to escape.

V441.2, B514.15 **"Another Götterdammerung"** The *Twilight of the Gods*, fourth and last opera in the *Ring* cycle of Richard Wagner.

V441.11, B514.25–26 **"do we have to start da capo with Carl Orff?"** Taking it "from the top" with German composer Carl Orff might mean two things. First, Orff is well known for his programs of musical instruction designed for children. Second, his principal works (the *Carmina Burana* among them) avoid harmony in favor of an archaic diatonic scale. Orff once said of his music that its purpose was "to achieve a unification of spiritual attitudes, which will lead to a binding and universally valid sense of community" (Leiss 82). To progress toward this apparently millennial end, he regressed toward ancient patterns of rhythm and tonality.

V442.8, B515.30 **"Fabelhaft, was?"** "Marvelous, isn't it?"

V442.14–27, B515.37–516.11 **"Hübsch . . . A trifle *stahlig* . . . more *zart* than that"** Säure and Gustav disagree over the taste of their marijuana, and in virtually the same pattern of binary differences as shapes their taste in music. Gustav opens the debate when he "allows" that the reefer is nice (*Hübsch*), though rather metallic or steely (*stahlig*), perhaps even tasting of dirt (*Bodengeschmack*) behind its body (*Körper*), tasty (*süffig*) as that is. But instead of the metallic or dirty taste Säure finds the smoke to have a certain dampness or sprightliness (*spritzig*), even an aromatic (*bukettreich*) quality. Gustav counters: as an "herbage" grown in the High Atlas regions of Morocco, it has its manners (*Art*). He claims that it is nutty (*kernig*) and, like the clean (*sauber*) marijuana from the Oued Nfis region of Morocco's northern slopes, piquant (*pikant*). Again Säure disagrees. He tastes, instead of these northern characteristics, a southern liveliness, as from Jebel Sarho (just above the Sahara); and for proof he cites the play (*Spiel*) of this smoke, which is smooth (*glatt*) and fragrant (*blumig*), having a suggestion of fullness (*Fülle*) in its seasoned (*würzig*) audacity.

V442.36, B516.23   Zig-Zags   A package of a French brand of cigarette papers, with a bearded Moroccan depicted on the cover.

V442.39–40, B516.28   an Irving Berlin *medley*   In his long career, tunesmith Irving Berlin (1888–1975) wrote some nine hundred songs ("Alexander's Ragtime Band," "Cheek to Cheek," and so on). Thus there are plenty select to from in making this medley.

V443.2, B516.31–32   Horst Wessel Song   The original title of this song was "Die Fahne Hoch" (Banners Up). A student of Joseph Goebbels, Horst Wessel was a young copywriter and *Sturmführer* of Berlin's most notoriously violent faction of the SA (Sturmabteilung). In 1929 he was living with an ex-prostitute in a house belonging to a Frau Salm. Salm wanted Wessel and the woman out, they refused, and she invited some comrades from the Red Veterans' Organization, a rival Communist storm troop, to eject the pair. When the Reds showed up, one of them shot Wessel in the presence of his lover. This was on January 14, 1930. But Wessel did Goebbels and the Nazis a great favor: he didn't die for six weeks, until February 23, by which time he had been transformed into a Nazi Galahad. "Die Fahne Hoch" had made its debut in 1929, and nobody cared much about the tune then (indeed, it was widely acknowledged that Wessel stole the melody from a Communist songbook). But Goebbels transformed Wessel's little opus, with its petty chauvinism ("The banners flutter / The drums roll, / The fifes rejoice, and from millions resounds the hymn / Of the German Revolution!") into a national anthem. See also V653.14n.

V443.5–7, B516.34–37   A parabola . . . tonic to dominant . . . to tonic   Aside from the pun ("to tonic"/Teutonic), here again is the symbol of the parabolic arch, this time as a symphonic structure. Beethoven, for example, is widely noted for his three- and four-part structures in the major symphonies. His so-called *per aspera ad astra* (from struggle to victory) motif works like this: (1) outer struggle, (2) comfort and reassurance, (3) internal struggle, and (4) victory. Beethoven's Fifth Symphony perfectly exemplifies this parabolic movement.

V443.10, B516.40   the Mark   The Markische Schweiz, a damp, low-lying district about thirty miles northeast of central Berlin.

V443.11, B516.41–42   the Kurfürstendamm   In West Berlin's Charlottenburg district, a main arterial running southwest from the center city and past the Tierpark, or Zoo.

V444.19, B518.15   the Mungahannock   A fictional river, in fictional Mingeborough.

V444.22, B518.19   "the president died"   On April 12 (V373.32n).

V445.14, B519.18   yellow loach   A bewhiskered European freshwater fish.

V446.14, B520.25   the Alexanderplatz   Just east of the Spree, this plaza in what is now East Berlin used to be the home of the Berlin Police Headquarters.

V446.16, B520.27   snowdrop   Once more, an American MP, or military policeman.

V446.16–17, B520.28   the Titaniapalast   Unknown Berlin theater.

V446.18, B520.29–30   at Wannsee   Arm of the river Havel running north from Berlin.

V446.21, B520.34   *Hauptstufe*   See V361.12–13n.

EPISODE 13

The time is still late July. Enzian and the Hereros interrogate Horst Achtfaden (the last name means "Eight-thread"), an aerodynamics engineer formerly of Peenemünde. As with Slothrop's scatological fantasies during his sodium amytal interrogation of part 1, so this "Toiletship" is evidently a hallucination of Achtfaden's. His fantasy recodifies, in terms of excremental process, the science of aerodynamics.

V448.3–4, B522.24–25   the *Rücksichtslos* here lists . . . angle of 23° 27'   The angle at which the axis of the earth inclines, relative to the plane of the celestial equator. The sun reaches a northern latitude of the same angle on June 21–22, the summer solstice. The ship's name, in English, is the *Reckless*.

V448.23–24, B523.10–11   like the American cowboy actor Henry Fonda   Early in his career, and before his role as Tom Joad in *Grapes of Wrath* (1940), Henry Fonda (1905–82) acted almost entirely in cowboy films like *The Trail of the Lonesome Pine* (1936) and *Jesse James* (1939).

V448.25, B523.13   RHIP   See V190.23n.

V448.28, B523.17   a whole Geschwader   German for a squadron.

V448.30–31, B523.20   Degenkolb was heading up the Rocket Committee by then   In 1943 the German general Gerhard Degenkolb was brought into the A4 project. In chapters 7–9 of his memoir, Walter Dornberger describes the struggles he and von Braun had with Degenkolb and his powerful Special A4 Committee.

V449.7, B523.36   a gofer   Workplace slang for a lackey, one who "goes for" things.

V450.24–25, B525.18   BDM volunteers   Acronym for the Bund Deutscher Mädchens (League of German Girls), a support group comparable to Britain's Auxilliary Territorial Services.

V450.31, B525.26   Wagner and Hugo Wolf   See V419.32n.

V450.34, B525.29–30   from Swinemünde to Helgoland   That is, from the Baltic Sea bay forming the mouth of the Swine River, just east of Peenemünde, westward to the small North Sea island on the coast of Schleswig-Holstein.

V451.35, B526.40   the Kiel Canal   North of Hamburg, the Kiel Canal links the city of Kiel on the Baltic Sea with the North Sea estuary of the Elbe River.

V452.1–6, B527.6–12   1904 was when Admiral Rozhdestvenski sailed his fleet . . . the year the American Food and Drug people took the cocaine out of Coca-Cola   On Admiral Rozhdestvenski's doomed voyage of 1904, see V349.39n. But with Coca-Cola and the FDA, there is an apparent anachronism. Coke historian E. J. Kahn writes (99, my emphasis): "Two words that irritate the Coca-Cola company are 'cocaine' and 'caffeine.' In its formative days, the drink did contain a minute quantity of cocaine, since this drug was not removed from the coca leaves that constituted a tiny fraction of its makeup, but *even before the passage of the Pure Food and Drug Act in 1906, the last trace of cocaine had gone.*" The FDA did not exist before the 1906 congressional action, and the Coke people evidently took out the cocaine entirely of their own volition.

V452.8, B527.15   Ludwig Prandtl proposed the boundary layer   As Theodore von Kármán (61) explains it, Prandtl "ingeniously assumed that the total effect of friction on any part of the airplaine can be estimated by the trick of restricting the investigation of the forces to a thin sheet of air close to the surface, which he called 'the boundary layer.'" As the narrator claims, this was in 1904 (another of the novel's *anni mirabili*), and it put the science of aerodynamics into business.

V452.21, B527.31–32   Hermann and Weiselsberger's tiny window   Dr. Rudolf Hermann was head of the supersonic wind tunnel at Peenemünde, where he came from a similar facility at Aachen, bringing along his assistant Weiselsberger (Dornberger 49, 114).

V452.26–27, B527.37–39   Professor Wagner . . . air would liquefy   Aside from his mistaken theory about supersonic airflow, Professor Rudolf Wagner of the Darmstadt Technische Hochschule is also remembered for developing the accelerometer used in the later A4s (Dornberger 232).

V452.30–31, B527.42–528.2   "Bingen pencils" we would call the helical

contrails. . . . The Schlieren shadows danced From Dornberger (120):
"The Schlieren equipment had been built by Zeiss of Jena after pro-
tracted experiments undertaken in the wind tunnel. . . . All differences
in air density caused by pressure or heat showed up on the screen
as bright or dark lines." The "helical contrails" are Pynchon's flourish.

V452.38–39, B528.11 Cranz's *Lehrbuch der Ballistik* According
to which "it was impossible for bodies with arrow stability to accomplish perfect flight at supersonic speeds" (Dornberger 34).

**V452.39–40, B528.12–13 memorized Ackeret, Busemann, von Kármán
and Moore, some Volta Congress papers** The Fifth Volta Congress
of High Speed Flight convened in Rome in 1935. All the researchers
mentioned by the narrator were in attendance and, as von Kármán
recalls in his autobiography (216), the talk was "seriously hinting of
rockets to the moon and of speeds of thousands of miles per hour." Jakob
Ackeret of Zurich was a friend of von Kármán and an early student
of supersonic flight; he subsequently worked for NASA. Norton Moore
studied for his Ph.D. under von Kármán in the early thirties at Cal
Tech. Adolf Busemann developed the swept-wing design that made it
feasible for jet planes to break the sound barrier. On all these men
see von Kármán (216–20).

V453.3, B528.18 the Gomerians That is, inhabitants of Gomera,
one of the Canary Islands off the North African coast, where Columbus
stopped on his way to the New World.

V453.6, B528.21 the KdF ship Stood for *Kraft durch Freude* (Strength
through Joy), one of many euphemistic slogans by Nazi propagandists.
This one labeled a plan to increase industrial output. For example,
the Volkswagen was originally called a "KdF-wagen"; and at
Peenemünde there was a so-called KdF Plant that produced rocket
components. Here, one from a line of KdF cargo ships.

V453.9, B528.25 mountains around Chipuda Unknown.

V453.20–21, B528.39–40 Reynolds, Prandtl, Péclet, Nusselt, Mach The
Reynolds and Nusselt numbers have appeared earlier (V223.8–10n).
Prandtl numbers are named for pioneer aerodynamicist Ludwig Prandtl
and measure "drag" (von Kármán 60–61). Mach numbers, named
for Ernst Mach, are the familiar numbers corresponding to multiples
of the speed of sound. The Péclet number is unknown.

V453.35, B529.15 Weichensteller, ask Flaum, and Fibel All are fictional
Peenemündans. A *Weichensteller*, in German railroading nomenclature, is a pointsman or switchman. *Flaum* is fluff or fuzz. A *Fibel*
is an introductory handbook or primer; one of Pynchon's sources
was the *A-4 Fibel* handed out to German rocket troops and translated
into English at the Redstone Arsenal of Alabama.

V454.6, B529.29 mad Fahringer Another fictional Peenemündan, but the pheasants are not. Dornberger (45) recalls hunting them with the troops and the sudden popularity of pheasant feathers in everyone's hats.

V454.13–14, B529.38–39 *Chinesische Blätter für Wissenschaft und Kunst*   A fictional "Chinese Journal for Science and Art."

V454.34–35, B530.19–20   —What is it that flies? —Los!   In a figurative sense, the German *Los* is "fate"; in a contrary and literal sense it means "free." As represented in *GR*, the V-2 flight profile embodies both. Hite (*Ideas of Order* 164, n4) also points out Soviet poet Andrei Voznesensky's "Ballad of the Parabola" as a possible context. It begins:
> Fate flies
>   like a rocket, on a parabolic curve—
> Mostly in darkness, but sometimes—
>   it's a rainbow.

V454.36, B530.21–22   the Wasserkuppe, rivers Ullster and Haune   The Wasserkuppe (Water-cup) is a volcanic cone in central Germany, just east of the Thuringian town of Fulda. The Ullster and Haune rivers flow around it.

V455.7, B530.35   the madness of Donar   Donar is "Thunderer," Old Saxon for Thor, the god who rules over clouds and rain. His signs are the flash of lightning and the roll of thunder.

V455.24–25, B531.12–13   Gessner's section . . . Prof.-Dr. Kurzweg's shop   From Dornberger (116): "I was met by Dr. Kurzweg, in charge of [wind-tunnel] research, and Chief Engineer Gessner, constructor of the wind tunnel."

V455.35, B531.24–25   "'Spörri' and 'Hawasch' . . . I was called 'Wenk'"   The first two names are of unknown origin. But Achtfaden's nickname, "Wenk," stems from State Prosecutor von Wenk, who pursues the mad Dr. Mabuse in Fritz Lang's 1922 film *Doktor Mabuse der Spieler* (Kracauer 81–82).

V455.37–38, B531.28   "CG for a device of a given weight"   The acronym is for center of gravity.

V455.39, B531.29   "something kilos. 45? 46?"   Or, 99 to 102 pounds, the approximate mass of a small human body, for example, the boy Gottfried.

V456.37, B532.31   "M'okamanga"   From Kolbe (361), who translates the Herero *mokamanga* as "instantly."

EPISODE 14

Slothrop and Margherita depart Berlin on a barge, journey to a fictional resort town called Bad Karma, link up with the *Anubis*, and head northward to Peenemünde. Margherita is reunited with her daughter, Bianca ("White"). Slothrop meets Miklos Thanatz, who was with Blicero before the launch of Rocket 00000.

V457.1, B532.36   the Spree-Oder Canal   This canal will carry Slothrop and Margherita eastward out of Berlin to the Oder River, on which they journey northward to Stettin and Swinemünde, on the Baltic Sea.

V457.2, B532.37–38   Geli Tripping's clew   In Greek mythology, Theseus's "clew," or ball of thread, helped him wind his way back out of the Cretan labyrinth.

V457.4, B533.2   the Lublin regime   See V34.28–30n.

V457.26, B533.27   "the Polish invasion"   Germany invaded Poland at dawn on September 1, 1939.

V457.30, B533.32   Bad Karma   A bad pun. The place is fictional, though patterned after such German resort towns as Bad Sachsa, in the Harz Mountains, or Bad Freienwalde, just off the Oder River north of Berlin. *Karma* is the Hindu term for the whole of a person's deeds, seen as determining his fate in future reincarnations. During the sixties, "bad karma" was popular countercultural slang for "bad luck."

V458.14, B534.13–14   The Sprudelhof   A courtyard built around the curative mineral springs.

V458.36, B534.41   the Kurhaus   Literally, a "cure-house"; here, a pavilion housing the mineral baths at a spa.

V459.10, B535.16   the *Anubis*   This boatload of degenerates is named for the jackel-headed god of Egyptian mythology who conducted the dead to judgment. In Gerhardt von Göll's film *Alpdrücken*, the "jackal men" ravish Margherita Erdmann (see V461.15).

V459.14, B535.21   spaetzle   German-style noodles.

V460.12, B536.25   *Świnoujście*   Polish spelling for the bay called Swinemünde by Germans.

V461.18, B537.39   Goebbels   Josef Goebbels, the Nazi propaganda chief.

V461.20, B537.41   at Bydgoszcz   The German name for it was Bromberg; a Polish industrial city 150 miles northwest of Warsaw.

V461.32, B538.15   "Miklos Thanatz"   Derives his name from the Greek god Thanatos (Death). Grimm (840–41) describes him as "a genius, with hand on cheek in deep thought, or setting his foot on the psyche (soul) as if taking possession of her. . . . At times he appears *black* . . . or black winged." Grimm also connects Thanatos with the German Valkyries, who gather Wuotan's elect from the battlefields when they fall. "Thanatz" also closes the circle of references generated around the name of E. W. A. Pointsman's imaginary dog, Reichssieger von Thanatz Alpdrucken (see V142.32–33n).

V462.28, B539.19   Marie-Celestial   See V303.19–20n.

V462.38, B539.29   the *Titanic*   The passenger liner that went down on April 14, 1912, in the midst of the maiden voyage from Southampton to New York.

V463.2, B539.31   very Walpurgisnacht   See V330.9–11n.

V463.11–12, B540.1–2   Baron de Mallakastra . . . Mme. Sztup   The baron's moniker is of unknown origin; that the powder he "sifts" into the drink is "white" infers its proneness to systems of death. As to Mme. Sztup, her name is from the Yiddish verb *sztup* or *shtup*, meaning "to push" or, by vulgar extension, "to fornicate with."

V463.26, B540.20   a bitt   A vertical, phallus-like post for securing cables on board a ship.

V464.30, B541.29–30   "a Max Weber charisma"   See V81.8–9n.

V465.11, B542.14–15   "His name was Gottfried. God's peace"   On the etymology, see V94.26n.

V465.14, B542.18   "that terrible week"   Easter week of 1945, March 25 to April 1, when Weissmann's battalion fled eastward across Niedersachsen, the state in northern Germany.

V465.18, B542.23   "the captain in *Wozzeck*"   German composer Alban Berg's 1921 opera, the story of a helpless soldier (Captan Wozzeck) caught in a vastly unjust machine, shares a great deal with Schoenberg's opera *Erwartung*, especially in its technical presentation of anxiety. Wozzeck's atonal shrieking was widely criticized at the time, but it was, like the expressionist cinema of the period, a powerful statement of the German spirit after the Great War.

V465.22–23, B542.28   "that ungodly coloratura"   The trills and high-register runs in Wozzeck's vocal score.

V465.30, B542.37–38   "the Urstoff wakes, and sings"   An *Urstoff* is any primal substance. The allusion here is to Isa. 26:19 (translation from *Oxford* edition):

> The dead shall live, their bodies shall rise;
> O dwellers in the dust, awake and sing for joy!
> For thy dew is the dew of light,
> And on the land of the shades thou wilt let it fall.

V466.4, B543.12   "On the Good Ship Lollipop"   A Sidney Clare and Richard Whiting song for Shirley Temple, in a starring role for the 1934 film *Bright Eyes*. The lyric:

> On the goo-o-ood ship, Lolli-pop,
> It's a swee-e-eet trip, to a candy shop,
> Where bon-bons play,
> On the sunny beach of Peppermint Bay.
>
> Lemona-a-ade stands, every-where,
> Crackerja-a-ack stands, fill the air,

And there you are—
Happy landing on a chocolate bar.

See the sugar bowl do the Tootsie Roll,
With the big bad devil's food cake;
If ya' eat too much— oooh, oooooh!
You'll awake with a tummy ache!

On the goo-o-ood ship, Lolli-pop,
It's a ni-i-ight trip, into bed you hop,
And dream away—
On the good ship Lolli-pop!

V466.16, B543.26–27 "'Animal Crackers in My Soup'" Another
song written for Shirley Temple, this one by Ray Henderson for her
1935 film *Curly Top*:

Animal crackers in my soup,
Monkeys and rabbits loop-the-loop;
Gosh oh gee!, but I have fun,
Swallowin' animals one by one!

I make 'em jump right through a hoop,
Those animal crackers in my soup.
When I get ahold of the Big Bad Wolf,
I just push him under to drown,
Then I bite him in a million bits,
And I gobble him right down.

[Repeat the chorus]

Stuff my tummy like a "goop,"
With animal crackers in my soup.

**V467.8–29, B544.24–545.8 Everyone is kind of aroused. . . . back down
the Oder River a ways** Notice the circularity of this orgiastic groping,
which begins and ends with the "juicy blonde."
V468.5, B545.30 "Chattanooga Choo Choo" A Mack Gordon and
Harry Warren song for the 1941 film *Sun Valley Serenade* and a monumental wartime hit for the Glenn Miller Orchestra:

Pardon me boys, is that the Chattanooga Choo Choo?
Yes, yes!
Track twenty-nine!
Boy you can give me a shine.

Can you afford to board the Chattanooga Choo Choo?
I got my fare,
And just a little to spare.

You leave the Pennsylvania Station 'bout a quarter to four,
Read a magazine and then you're in Baltimore . . .

And so on.

V468.10, B545.36   her chignon   The bun in the woman's hair.

EPISODE 15

S till aboard the *Anubis*, and the time is still late July. Bianca and Slothrop
couple violently, and doing so plugs Slothrop into the erotic fantasies of
a host of others: Franz Pökler, Max Schlepzig, Miklos Thanatz, Gerhardt
von Göll, even Tchitcherine.

V468.19, B546.6   Llandudno   A resort town in northern Wales, on
the Irish Sea. Slothrop dreams of Lewis Carroll because, like the Oxford
mathematician, photographer, and writer whose lifelong passion
was little girls, Slothrop's passion of the moment is "11 or 12"
(V463.18)-year-old Bianca Erdmann ("White Earth-man"). The presence
of that White Rabbit statue in the square of Llandudno is unattested,
so far.

V469.17, B547.12   Alençon lace   Fine-quality lace and brocaded fabric
from the French mill town of Alençon.

V470.10–11, B548.13–14   this exploding *emprise*   The French *emprise*
signifies "mastery." Here it echoes the *sentiments d'emprise*, or paranoid delusions, over which Pavlov had debated Pierre Janet (V49.1–2n).

V470.11–12, B548.14–15   sense of *waiting to rise*   The sense once
again of *Erwartung* (V101.9n).

V470.18, B548.22–23   out the eye at tower's summit   A curious image,
whose intratextual reference must be not only to Slothrop's penis
but to Rocket 00000, with Gottfried's little window cut into the top
of it. Intertextually, it also recalls the mystical symbol of God's eye atop
a pyramid or tower, as for example on the back side of an American
dollar bill. In Masonic or Kabbalistic interpretations, such an eye represents the transcendent vision of an adept after his seven- or ten-stage
climb toward the divine throne (see also V484.33).

**V470.37–38, B549.3–4   The Pope's staff is always going to remain
barren**   Alluding once more to the Tannhäuser myth (V364.22n).

V471.10, B549.21   a Pullman   The American railroading term seems
misplaced in this German context; Bianca would imagine herself
riding in a *Schlaffwagen*, a railroad sleeping car.

V471.24, B549.38   tin Moxie signs   Slothrop imagines advertisements
for this American brand of soft drink (see V63.5n).

V471.28, B550.1–2 Murphy's Law V275.25–26n.

V471.30, B550.3 drowned Becket Following his disagreements with King Henry II over the taxation of the church, Archbishop of Canterbury Thomas à Becket was murdered on December 29, 1170.

V472.20–21, B550.43 this Eurydice-obsession In Greek myth, Orpheus was allowed to bring his wife, Eurydice, out of Hades, provided he did not look back. He did. So will Slothrop.

V472.35–36, B551.17–18 never threatened along any rookwise row or diagonal In this chessboard analogy, applied to a grid of theater seats, all the moves are accounted for except those of the knight (*Der Springer*).

EPISODE 16

S till aboard the *Anubis*. The subepisode entitled "Ensign Morituri's Story" reveals Margherita Erdmann as a destructive avatar of the *Shekinah*, a Kabbalistic version of the White Goddess. Greta's homicidal mania for children bodes ill for Bianca, her daughter.

V473.3–4, B551.27 Ensign Morituri An ex-kamikaze trainee who derives his name from the greeting of Roman gladiators to their caesar: *Morituri te salutant* (We who are about to die salute you). Perhaps, as a spy or agent, he also owes something to W. J. Lueddecke's spy thriller entitled *Morituri* (1964), made into a 1965 movie starring Marlon Brando and Yul Brynner. The plot: a German merchant ship carrying secret cargo sets sail for Japan, amid plentiful intrigue, during the middle of the Battle of the Pacific.

V475.11, B554.5 curanderos In his notes for Hernandez's *Martín Fierro* (332), translator Walter Owen defines the *curandero* of South America as a quack doctor, "expert in remedies which were a strange medley of nature lore, superstition, mother-wit, and pretension."

V476.7, B555.8 an aquatic corso From the Italian signifying the "course" or main channel of a river.

V476.11, B555.13 Garbo hats Such as the "Garbo fedora" referenced at V380.11.

V476.21, B555.25 the Sprudelstrasse Street leading to the Sprudelhof, the courtyard with its mineral springs.

V476.39–40, B556.5 the Trinkhalle Literally, the "drink-hall"; a pump room at a spa for taking the waters.

V477.1–2, B556.9 the Kursaal A main pavilion or hall at the spa, where the *Kur-Orchestra* would play the songs noted below.

V477.5, B556.13–14 *The Merry Widow* and *Secrets of Suzanne* Franz

218 In the Zone

Lehar's opera, *The Merry Widow*, with its famous waltz, premiered in 1906. *Il Segreto di Susanna*, by Ermanno Wolf-Ferrari, premiered in 1909. (Her secret was smoking.)

V477.24, B556.37 the Brodelbrunnen A bubbling, gurgling mud spring.

V478.14–17, B557.35–38 "I wander all the Diaspora . . . you fragment of smashed vessel" The Kabbalists regarded Israel not only as a historical community but as an esoteric symbol, a container or "vessel" of the *Shekinah*. Members of the community are parts of it; and thus, with Jews scattered throughout the European Diaspora, all are considered "fragments of a smashed vessel," as Pynchon notes. The *Shekinah* is the earthly presence of Jahweh, usually the last of his ten emanations, or *Sephiroth*, and it is a feminine presence, "seen at once as mother, as wife, and as daughter" (Scholem, *On the Kabbalah* 105). After man's fall the *Shekinah* always wears black garments, like Greta's in this scene, for black is the token of mourning. The "righteous man" or Messiah would strip off these somber robes to reveal her rainbow radiance (ibid. 67). The proper home of the *Shekinah* is with the sun, symbol of Jahweh's masculine light. But she also has a dark side, appearing as the moon, a lightless receiver of light. As such, she is especially susceptible to domination from demonic powers from the Other Side, when she appears as the tree of death, symbol of punishment and retribution. Thus, in her black garments and through her connection with the preterite mud (Erdmann, again, signifying an "Earth-man"), Greta appears to the boy as exactly this demonic emissary from the other side. She is the *Shekinah* as destroyer, not as the rainbow symbol of Jahweh's covenant. Note, in addition, the presence of another *hysteron proteron* trope: the boy is a "fragment" of a "smashed vessel" seeking to reconstitute itself.

V478.27, B558.8 d'Annunzio's adventure at Fiume After the Treaty of Versailles was signed in 1919, the Italian poet Gabriele D'Annunzio attempted to forestall the cession of Fiume, a valuable port city, to Austria. For two years he held it as self-appointed *duce*. Pynchon relates the story in his "Epilogue" to *V*.

V479.1, B558.27 next day was 1 September And the German *Wehrmacht* crossed the Polish frontier at dawn, beginning the war.

V479.10, B558.38 "Oh, pip, pip, old Jap" Bad pun on the British idiomatic farewell: "Pip, pip, old chap!"

V480.4–5, B559.37–38 "Hiroshima . . . a city on Honshu" First reference to the city, anticipating the atomic holocaust of August 6, 1945, the historical backdrop that marks the end of part 3 and the beginning of part 4 (see V588.8 and V693.36). Morituri's thoughts on "radioactivity" (V479.17) thus take on an edge of dramatic irony.

V480.20, B560.13 a black Italian maduro From the Latin *maturas* (ripe); thus a dark, very strong cigar.

V480.23, B560.17 "the face of a Jonah" Like the Old Testament figure, Slothrop is also an underwater, in-the-belly-of-the-beast traveler; and like Jonah he also flees his calling. As in the Book of Jonah, the storm that has arrived in this episode will eventually cause him to be pitched overboard.

V481.1, B560.38 "There's only one free ride" An old bit of colloquial wisdom whose completion is: "into hell" (which is where the Egyptian god Anubis conducts dead souls).

V481.5, B561.1 One of the General Orders In basic training, all newly recruited U.S. servicemen memorize the twelve "General Orders" pertaining to military conduct and discipline.

V481.21, B561.19 crystal birds Late sixties American slang. A "crystal ship" is a hypodermic syringe filled with any crystalline drug liquified for injection (such as methadrine or heroin); thus a "crystal bird" is the powdered form of a drug, when it flies up one's snoot.

EPISODE 17

Aboard the *Anubis*: this episode provides background on Greta Erdmann, her film roles, and the physical similarities between her child, Bianca, and Blicero's "young pet" (V484.17), Gottfried. Greta's recollections of Blicero and the last days at Lüneberg Heath add considerably to Slothrop's accumulating file on Rocket 00000 and the Schwarzgerät.

V482.15, B562.15 Gretel Diminutive form of Greta, from Margherita; it also links her to Katje Borgesius, who played the Gretel role (to Gottfried's Hansel) in part 1 of *GR*.

V482.18–19, B562.19 comatic From the Latin *comatus* (hairy) and the Greek *coma* (sleep).

V482.29, B562.31 *Weisse Sandwüste von Neumexiko* Literally, "White Sand-waste [Desert] of New Mexico," but associatively it's White Sands, New Mexico, the southwestern military base where the first atomic bomb was test-detonated in 1945 and where the one hundred captured V-2 rockets, and various German technicians, were brought in 1946.

V482.34, B562.37 an American horse named Snake Tchitcherine's central Asian mount from 1935 (see V342.11); and evidently the horse that Crutchfield rides in Slothrop's fantasy of episode 10, part 1.

V483.1, B563.2–3 the Sagittarian fire Sagittarius (the Archer, from November 22 to December 21) is a fire sign and ninth in the astrological year.

V483.25, B563.33 Lotte Lüstig Another onomastic pun, from the German *Lüstig*: gaiety and fun, or "lusty."

V483.28, B563.36 *Jugend Herauf!* "Youth Arise!" a National Socialist propaganda slogan from the period, with a grim pun on the command *Juden heraus!* (Jews out!).

V484.10–11, B564.21–23 **Double and Triple Protars . . . Grundlach Turner-Reichs** A list of turn-of-the-century lenses and cameras, all of them representing the best of American, British, and German optical engineering.

V484.25, B564.40 **Croix mystique** See V16.15–16n.

V484.33, B565.10–11 **The Eye at the top of the pyramid** See B470.18n.

V485.13, B565.32 **a Hannomag Storm** The name is short for Hannoversche Maschinenbau AG, a manufacturer of road vehicles from 1905 on (the company still builds trucks). The Sturm, or "Storm," was introduced in 1928: a very powerful, neatly appointed automobile popular with Germany's upper middle class.

V485.32–34, B566.14–16 **at the Schußtelle . . . bleeding with beads of gum** Kooy and Uytenbogaart (289) describe similar damage to trees at the rocket-firing sites in Holland.

V485.35, B566.18 **"Blicero was a local diety."** See V30.12n.

V486.1, B566.25 **"into the Heath"** That is, the Lüneberg Heath.

V486.2, B566.26 **"Jabos flew over"** The term was German slang for the American P-47 fighter plane. The source of this detail is Huzel (149–50), who recalls the harassment of American *Jabos* as the Peenemündans made their escape.

V486.3, B566.27–28 **"a werewolf"** We could see this change coming over Weissmann, who earlier "screamed at the sky" (V465.21) and whose totem has been the wolf. The motif will come up once more (V640.23n).

V486.7, B566.32–33 **" 'my Ur-Heimat' "** Primeval homeland.

V486.26, B567.16 **"I said, 'The Castle' "** The reference is to card sixteen of the Tarot deck, known as the Tower or Castle. In the Rider deck, the illustration on this card shows a white castle tower struck by lightning, its crown exploded off, fire belching from the windows, and its two occupants falling headlong to the ground. Waite (*Pictorial Key* 132) interprets the image as a portent of destruction in material creation: "the ruin of the house of life, when evil has prevailed therein."

V486.39–40, B567.32–33 **"I only recognized one: Generaldirektor Smaragd"** The IG Farben representative from the séance of part 1 (see V164.10n).

V487.24, B568.21–22 **"methyl methacrylate, a replica of the Sangraal"** See also Perspex, the light-bending plastic (V384.31n). Methyl methacrylate was synthesized during the thirties from acetone, methyl alcohol, cyanide, and sulfuric acid. Like polystyrene it is a rigid plastic, and its ability to "pipe" light makes it useful in fiber optics. The

Sangraal is the Holy Grail of Arthurian legend: a chalice containing Christ's blood, for the redemption of sin.

V488.2, B569.2 "costume of some black polymer" Donning the plastic suit of black Imipolex G designed for the white boy, Gottfried, Greta recalls the Qlippoth (see V176.14–15n and V197.1n).

EPISODE 18

As an evening storm tosses the ship, Slothrop slips from the decks of the *Anubis* and tumbles into the Oder Haff.

V488.36, B570.4 the clinometer bob The pendulum swings of this instrument indicate the angle of inclination of the ship as it rolls in the storm.

V489.3–4, B570.10 the pelorus Aboard ship, a device for taking one's bearings.

V489.6, B570.13 Corposants From the Latin signifying "holy bodies"; that is, the electrical phenomenon known as St. Elmo's fire (see V491.6).

V489.9, B570.16 the Oder Haff A bay formed where the river Oder dumps into the Baltic Sea, divided into the lesser or Kleines Haff to the west and the greater or Grosses Haff to the east. The pun on "other half" is coincidental.

V489.20, B570.29 Fort-Lamy Named for renowned French soldier-explorer F. J. A. Lamy (1858–1900), Fort-Lamy is the capital city of Chad, a protectorate in French Equatorial Africa after 1910. During World War II it was a stronghold for Free French activities against Rommel's desert troops.

V489.21, B570.31 high albedo See V152.24n.

V490.5, B571.18–19 The second dog watch That is, from 6:00 to 8:00 P.M.

V490.11, B571.25 Dramamine Registered American trademark of a mild sedative for relieving motion sickness.

V490.30, B572.5–6 the September afternoon Here, the afternoon of Friday, September 8, 1944, when the first V-2 rocket fell on London.

V491.21, B573.2–3 the Iron Guard . . . screaming *Long Live Death* See V11.35n.

EPISODE 19

A black-marketeer named Frau Gnahb (the name, a backward spelling of "bhang," suggests the Hindu term for marijuana) plucks Slothrop from the storm-tossed waters of the Baltic Sea, then puts him in touch with Der Springer, Gerhardt von Göll. For a price, Springer offers to recover the S-Gerät for Slothrop. They make their way westward along the Usedom coast to Peenemünde, where the Russians detain von Göll.

V493.7, B575.3   Bohnenkaffee   Bean coffee, the real article instead of the *ersatz-kaffee* of wartime.

V493.12–13, B575.9–11   See the sugar bowl . . . big, bad, Devil's food cake   Echoing Bianca's Shirley Temple song on board the *Anubis* (see V466.4n).

V494.21–22, B576.30   about Anton Webern   On the anachronism, see V440.31n.

V495.7–9, B577.19–21   the same Klaus Närrisch that aerodynamics man Horst Achtfaden fingered for the Schwarzkommando   See V456.33. The name Närrisch recalls the German for "foolish."

V496.23–24, B578.41–579.1   Ulcerous impresario G. M. B. Haftung   The German acronym GmbH stands for a *Gesselschaft mit beschränkter Haftung* (limited liability corporation).

V496.33, B579.11   "Deine *Mutter*"   "Your mother."

V497.8, B579.27   across the brow   Fowler mistakenly assumes this is a misprint for "prow." But in nautical terminology a "brow" is any inclined planking or gangway used in loading a ship, which is why Pynchon's boys and girls go "stevedoring" across one.

V497.15, B579.36   film, *Lucky Pierre Runs Amok*   One fictional night ten years later "Pig" Bodine will file these reels of film in his private collection of "depraved" movies stowed aboard his ship, the USS *Scaffold* (*V.* 219).

V497.26, B580.8   Crosscurrents tug at the boat   Another Bantam error: "tug a the boat."

V498.6, B580.30   the Flying Dutchman   According to seagoing legend, a Dutch captain named Vanderacken swore by the gods Donner and Blitzen that he would safely beat a dangerous storm into harbor. At the very moment of his oath, the ship foundered and was condemned to sail on eternally. Sailors believe that seeing his ship portends doom. In Richard Wagner's opera *Der Fliegende Holländer*, every seven years Captain Vanderecken is allowed a sabbatical to swim ashore and seek the woman whose love can redeem him from his eternal sailing.

V499.17, B582.9   "He's an OSS man"   That is, from the Office of Strategic Services, Wild Bill Donovan's precursor to the CIA (V268.6n).

V499.36, B582.32–33   Helen Trent, Stella Dallas, Mary Noble Backstage Wife   Slothrop's mother, Nalline, would float away in "nameful recapitulating" (V499.34) at the mention of these programs because they were her favorite radio soap operas. "Stella Dallas" ran from 1937 to 1955 and billed itself as "the true-to-life story of mother love and sacrifice, in which Stella Dallas saw her beloved daughter Laurel marry into wealth and society, and, realizing the differences in their tastes and world, went out of Laurel's life" (but not entirely; she was an eternal outsider looking in). John Dunning (568) has written that only "The Romance of Helen Trent" could ever match "Stella Dallas" in the "misery-per-episode quota." From 1933 to 1960 radio's Miss Trent was a model of purity, temperance, and equanimity in sinful Hollywood. The third program, "Backstage Wife", featured the character "Mary Noble . . . a lovely girl from the Iowa sticks" (ibid. 54) who marries a matinee idol other women are forever trying to seduce. This show had a long run too, from 1935 to 1959.

V500.26, B583.28 Dr. Mabuse In Fritz Lang's 1922 film, the people who show a "glacial smile" are those prospective victims whom the evil doctor has hypnotized.

V500.40, B584.3 Rocket Noon Recalls the "Evil Hour" (V374.39–375.2n), and it anticipates another detail: Rocket 00000 was fired from the Lüneberg Heath at noon (V667.3–4n).

V501.5–6, B584.10–11 scorched as Rossokovsky and the White Russian Army left it in the spring During March 1945 the Russian general Rossokovsky led his divisions out of White Russia (Latvia, Lithuania) and into Pomerania. By April Peenemünde was in his hands.

V501.6–7, B584.11 On the maps, it's a skull Just so, as the map in Irving's book (6) will show. Remember, too, that the "black scapeape" (V275.34), King Kong, originates from Skull Island.

V501.10, 584.15–16 a Wilhelm Busch cartoon face German artist Wilhelm Busch (1832–1908) was the country's best known and most beloved humorist. *Max and Moritz*, his illustrated children's book, appeared in 1865. These were also the names playfully assigned to two experimental A2 rockets fired from Borkum in 1934 (Klee and Merk 12). In addition, Blicero has two members of his firing crew named Max and Moritz (V757.26, 29).

V501.22, B584.30–31 Bicycle Rider in the Sky A vague and ambiguous allusion with at least three possible referents. First is the so-called Rider pack of Tarot cards manufactured by William Rider and Sons of London: A. E. Waite and P. D. Ouspensky both used the Rider images in their interpretations of the Tarot. Second is Rilke: in the eleventh of the *Sonnets to Orpheus* there appears a constellation called *Reiter* (Rider, Horseman), symbolizing human nature (the horse) guided by an unseen force astride it, and a constellation appearing in the sky over the newfound "Pain-Land." Third is the Norse god Odin: one of his frequent nicknames was "Atrithr," meaning "Rider" and signifying his role as a wind god galloping across the heavens. His horse, Sleipnir, was a gray with eight legs. In part 4 Blicero appears as the Knight of Swords, "the rider on a black horse" (V747.5–6).

V501.25–26, B584.35   In the Tarot he is known as The Fool   In most interpretations the card is the twenty-second and last card of the Major Arcana, though its number is zero. Ouspensky (17) reads the image as "ordinary man . . . separate man. The uninitiate lower consciousness. The end of a ray not knowing its relation to the center." As "Fool," Slothrop will approach his "Holy Center" in the next episode, but will not know the place. So "groweth his Preterition sure" (V509.37).

V501.40, B585.11   the Jonahs   See V480.23n.

V502.9–10, B585.21–22   stations of the cross   In Roman Catholicism there are fourteen stations symbolizing events in the Passion of Jesus. Here, out of historical and numerological necessity, there are ten, one for each of the test stands at Peenemünde. From Dornberger, we know that only stands VII (for A4 rockets) and X (for experimental rockets) were used in actual lift-offs; the rest were used in various types of static tests.

V502.20–21, B585.35–36   the red brick . . . cathedral in Wolgast   From Dornberger (3): "In the west the low hills on the far bank of the river Peene were dominated by the red brick tower of Wolgast Cathedral."

V503.35, B587.14   unslinging his Tokarev   An automatic pistol similar to the German Luger (V505.22n), and the weapon of preference among Russian officers during the war.

V504.28, B588.9   "Zu Befehl, Mutti!"   "At your command, Mommy!"

V505.22, B589.12–13   a Luger   A German officer's semiautomatic pistol, designed by Georg Luger for the German Parabellum Company and in service from 1900 until 1947.

V505.36, B589.29–30   the orchestra plays *Tristan und Isolde*   Wagner's 1865 opera. Perhaps they would play the "Deliverance by Death" theme from the last act, or perhaps Isolde's song as she falls dead on the prostrate body of Tristan—the "Liebestod" (Love-Death) theme.

EPISODE 20

The time is now July 30, 1945. Klaus Närrisch leads Slothrop on a commando raid, springing Der Springer from his Russian captors. This action supplies a pretext for touring the facilities at Peenemünde, a parody of the "Holy Center" in traditional mythology. In a scene that recalls the ending of *For Whom the Bell Tolls*, Klaus is left heroically behind as Slothrop and Springer escape. Details stem largely from Dornberger and Irving.

V506.37, B590.38   A sharp sickle of moon has risen   The moon entered its last quarter in late July, and on July 30 a sickle-shaped moon would have risen near midnight, the "twilight" of V505.37 having shown between nine and ten that evening.

V508.9, B592.14 Zitz und Arsch The narrator's German is slightly off. *Zitz* is the noun for any chintz or calico fabric, and *Zitze* the low German for an udder, teat, or dug. *Arsch*: the bum, backside, or ass.

V508.29–30, B592.39 a holy Center Mircea Eliade (17) describes such a place as "preeminently the zone of the sacred, the zone of absolute reality." Symbolically, the center is that navel or *omphalos* from which all reality is thought to have unfolded. It is the locale of objects having "absolute" significance, like the trees of life, knowledge, and death. It also exists as a meeting place for all three cosmic regions: hell, earth, and heaven. Test Stand VII is a fitting center because of its ellipsoid shape, as though it truly were a cosmic "Egg" (V510.31). For further discussion see Eliade (12–18).

V508.39, B593.8 Gauss curve will herniate toward the excellent That is, events will exactly correlate to the statistical formula for a "normal" or "Gaussian" distribution, which when graphed yields a perfect rainbow curve, a parabolic section (see also V709.33–35n).

V508.40, B593.9 tankers See V298.15n.

V509.33–34, B594.7 the terrible Rider See V501.22n.

V510.1–2, B594.19–20 forgive him his numbness, his glozing neutrality A condition that stems from his habit of always glossing, or interpreting, events occurring around him. Later the narrator will note: "Those whom the old Puritan sermons denounced as 'the glozing neuters of the world' have no easy road to haul down" (see V677.1–2n). Too studious of minor annotations on experience to recognize the "Egg the flying Rocket hatched from" (V509.41), Slothrop has the experience but not its meaning.

V511.22, B596.9–10 his Degtyarov See V377.11n.

V512.39, B597.36 the *budka* Russian for a sentry box.

V513.3, B597.41 "It's your Schwarzphänomen" Slothrop's "black phenomenon," the recurring presence of blackness in the "plot" of his being.

V513.9, B598.4 *pogoni* From the Greek *pogon*, for "beard"; the Russian for a fringed shoulder epaulet affixed, here, with gold stars.

V513.10, B598.6 a Kurt Weill medley Probably from the composer's best German operas: *Der Neue Orpheus* (1925) and *Die Dreigroschenoper* (1927). Weill fled Germany for the United States in 1935.

V513.15, B598.12 Suomi subs A Russian submachine gun. Below its barrel is a circular magazine that, here, seems to Slothrop as large as one of jazz percussionist Gene Krupa's "drums."

V514.39, B600.1 "Lebe wohl" "Farewell."

V516.3, B601.15   John Dillinger, at the end   Toland has related the story in *The Dillinger Days* (319–31). On July 22, 1934, Dillinger and Anna Sage went to Chicago's Biograph Theater to see *Manhattan Melodrama*. In the film Jim Wade (played by William Powell) wins the governorship after prosecuting a childhood friend, Blackie Gallagher (Clark Gable), who has shot and killed the man running against Wade in the gubernatorial election. There are some mitigating circumstances. Governor Wade therefore extends a commutation of sentence to Blackie, who refuses it and goes to the electric chair just as the narrator relates it here. Cigar-smoking Melvin Purvis and his FBI G-men were waiting outside the Biograph. When Dillinger stepped out, they opened fire. Anna Sage, the Judas goat and so-called lady in red, had relayed Dillinger's plans for the evening.

V516.22, B601.39   *Der Müde Tod*   Released with English subtitles as *Destiny* (though the German means "Tired Death"), this 1921 film was directed by Fritz Lang for Ufa. Kracauer (88–91) gives a synopsis: A young woman tries to save her lover from his mortal destiny by promising Death she will bring a substitute victim. She fails at the last moment and dies in a fire. As the film ends, "Death finally guides the dying girl to her dead lover, and, forever united, their souls wander heavenward over a blossoming hill."

V516.30, B602.8   east with the Institute Rabe   The name is short for Raketenbetreib Bleicheröde (Bleicheröde Rocket Operation), established by the Russians near Nordhausen during the summer of 1945. They lured former V-2 engineers and technicians with promises of fantastic salaries, the prospect of remaining together with their wives, and employment in Germany. In 1946 the Russians reneged and moved them all to the steppes of Kirghizistan. Von Braun, Dornberger, Huzel, and other top rocketmen all went "west," first to Cuxhaven (to assist with Operation Backfire), then to America, for the "$6 a day" salaries mentioned in *GR*. Their wives weren't allowed to join them until much later. The Russians' biggest catch was Helmuth Gröttrup, whose wife, Irmgard, recorded her memories of these days in *Rocket Wife*, Pynchon's source here.

V517.12, B602.34–35   "Cocaine—or cards?"   Dr. Mabuse's nightclub line to prospective victims in Fritz Lang's film *Doktor Mabuse der Spieler*.

V517.17, B602.41   a Wien bridge   In electronic terminology, a four-arm alternating-current bridge that measures capacitance or inductance. This device was used in the automatic steering of the rocket (Kooy and Uytenbogaart 353–59). In describing its use, the narrator adopts Pavlovian terminology (for instance, the "reflex arc") to characterize these events inside the rocket's "body" (V517.24, 23).

V518.6, B603.36–37 Driwelling, and Schmeil Unknown if not fictional
Peenemünde technicians.

V518.8, B603.39 elctro-decor A Viking error, corrected in the Bantam
to read "electro-decor." And it's just that: the narrator lists a series
of measuring devices manufactured by such German firms as Zeiss, Sie-
mans, and Gülcher.

EPISODE 21

In Hamburg, in late July, Enzian and the Zone Hereros move to block an
abortion. They also glimpse, in the seemingly ruined landscape, signs of
transnational economic interests (cartels) just waiting to leap back into operation. Pavel, one of Enzian's assistants, experiences this immanent design
during a gasoline-fume–induced hallucination. Enzian reasons that a quest
for the rocket will endlessly divert his people from tribal suicide.

V518.31–32, B604.23–24 coming on like Smith, Klein, 'n' French Not
a reference to some trio of "famous Prohibition agents" (Fowler),
this points to the famous Philadelphia drug firm (slightly misspelled)
of Smith, Kline, and French. For decades the company's best-selling
pharmaceutical product was the Thorazine brand of tranquilizer,
which Pynchon's character Steve Edelman keeps in his "family-size
jar" (V753.27–28). Thorazine is still prescribed for relief of psychotic
symptoms, but now the firm's best-seller is the Contac brand of
antihistamine cold capsules.

V519.1–2, B604.31 their signature, their challenge Another Bantam
error: "ther signature."

V519.14, B605.7–8 Washing-blue is the abortifacient of choice One
of the dyestuffs manufactured by IG Farben, "washing-blue" or Prussian
blue is a source for a deadly toxin, hydrocyanic acid. Pynchon's source
here, as earlier (see V317.30–33n), was the pamphlet by W. P. Steenkamp, as T. S. Tillotson first pointed out. Among the abortifacient substances that Steenkamp (29) identifies as being in use among Herero
women, "another remedy used by them also since the contact with the
white man, is washing blue," which causes "a strong stomach irritation"
leading up to "uterine stimulation" and contractions powerful enough
to expel the fetus.

V519.22, B605.17 British G-5 See V125.22n.

V519.27, B605.22–23 red-shifting, fleeing the Center Another reference
to the Big Bang theory of cosmic creation and the phenomenon of
red-shifting stars as they speed away from the center (see V396.33n).

V520.15, B606.15 Jamf Ölfabriken Werke AG The fictional Jamf Synthetic Oil Works, Inc.

V520.20, B606.21 the Kabbalists Knowledge of Kabbalistic wisdom derives from three texts: those rabbinical writings collected in the Talmud, the Sephir Yetsirah drawn up in the second century A.D. (though based on much older material), and the Sohar, which was composed somewhat later in the second century. The central doctrine of Kabbalistic theosophy is that divine wisdom can be received directly from the close, hermeneutical study of these three holy texts.

V520.24–25, B606.26–27 orururumo orunene the high, rising, dead, the blazing From Kolbe's grammatical introduction (xxxi–xxxii). *Orururumo* signifies "a flame," and *orunene* is an adjective signifying immensity of size. But note the shift in lines 25–26, where the narrator explains that the Zone Hereros have already begun dropping the inanimate prefix (*oru-*) and, instead, attaching the animate one (*omu-*) to the rocket, yielding *Omunene*. In sum, even as they begin to represent themselves as emptied, inanimate shells of being (see V316.38n), the Zone Hereros simultaneously represent the rocket as animate, a "brother."

V520.26–27, B606.29 our Torah Strictly speaking, the capital "T" signifies only those sacred writings collected in the Old Testament Pentateuch. With a small "t" it would signify the whole body of Judaic literature.

V520.36–37, B606.42 8th AF bombers The U.S. Eighth Air Force, while stationed in England, was instrumental in bombing areas of Germany where rocket components were manufactured. For example, Irving (123–24, 187–88, 242) reports that squadrons of Eighth Air Force bomber planes hit various liquid oxygen plants, manufacturing areas, and petroleum works.

V520.38, B607.1 Director Krupp That is, Gustav Krupp von Bohlen und Halbach (1870–1950), the German financier, steel magnate, and director of the Krupp Steel Works.

V521.17, B607.25–26 a Gaussian reduction In mathematics, a procedure used to find one solution, or a manifold of solutions, to a given set of complex linear equations. Also called Gauss's algorithm, it involves the systematic elimination of variables from the equations. Because of its purely mechanical and time-consuming nature, the reduction is now routinely handled by computer. Yet this explains why here, before computer days, the Schwarzkommando argument against technology has been "iterated, dogged and humorless": too much boring detail to cover.

V521.38, B608.10 Blohm & Voss They produced nose cones for the A4 rocket at their Hamburg manufacturing plant (Irving 136n).

V522.1, B608.14   Pervitins   Brand name of methamphetamine hydrochloride, or desoxyephedrine, known in the drug underworld as the "crank" variety of "speed" (amphetamines). From what the reader has seen earlier (V328.25), and from what's to come (V731.33), Enzian must have an endless supply of these tiny tablets.

V522.6–8, B608.20–22   Sort of a Hoagy Carmichael piano   American composer and jazz pianist Howard Hoagland ("Hoagy") Carmichael (1899–1981). While a student at Indiana University he met Bix Beiderbecke, recorded with him, then commenced a solo career that is remembered best for his slow, graceful melodies set to romantic texts: "Georgia on My Mind" (1930), "In the Still of the Night" (1932), and "Skylark" (1942), for example.

V522.12, B608.27–28   the Stars 'n' Stripes   Official magazine for servicemen in the U.S. armed forces.

V522.29, B609.7–8   Berliner Schnauze   Literally, the "Berlin Snout"; here, a nasal speech habit.

V523.13–16, B609.33–37   Leunagasolin . . . Moss Creature . . . Water Giant   The fuel is a brand of gasoline manufactured at the Leuna works of Hamburg, a subsidiary of IG Farben (Sasuly 56). The monsters are the sort of fantastic creatures often threatening Plasticman.

V523.34, B610.17   BVDs   Men's underwear manufactured by the American firm of Bradley, Vorhees and Day.

V523.39, B610.23   3–sigma white faces   That is, with lots of variation in the shades of white (see also V40.13–14n). Here, the white, green, and blue "faces" in this hallucination are directed by Bing Crosby.

V524.11, B610.39   Mukuru   The Herero god (see V321.40–322.1n).

V525.24, B612.20   Saint Pauli   The St. Pauli district of west Hamburg is, like London's East End, a haven for the preterite. Here is Baedeker (*Northern Germany* 150), who graciously neglects specific mention of the prostitutes renowned for working the Reeperbahn in St. Pauli: "principally frequented by sailors, for whose amusement booths and shows of every kind abound. The scene witnessed here on a Sunday or Monday afternoon . . . is a highly characteristic phase of Hamburg low life. Hawkers and itinerant venders of every kind also thrive here." The street comes up again at V652.19–20.

EPISODE 22

Around noon on July 31, off the coast of Rugen, Slothrop boards the *Anubis* one last time. Bound northward, evidently toward Copenhagen, the ship contains in its engine room not only a package of contraband but, as Slothrop discovers, the dead body of Bianca Erdmann, the Eurydice this Orpheus will not bring up from hell (see also V472.20–21n). Frau Gnahb puts him back ashore at Stralsund, where Slothrop begins a long trek across the Zone.

V526.13, B613.13   very Savile Row   See V184.14–15n.

V526.16–17, B613.17   Mitteleuropäisch   Middle-European.

V526.39, B614.1   Operation Backfire   Those connected with the British effort to test-fire several rockets from Cuxhaven (V272.32–34n).

V527.3, B614.6   the Dorum road   Leads to the village of Dorum, about one or two miles south of Cuxhaven. From subsequent details (V602.6ff.), we know that Slothrop and Springer arrange to meet on the night of August 5, about one week after this (V602.34).

V527.19, B614.24   Schmeissers   In World War II German infantrymen made widespread use of the Haenel MP38 and MP40 submachine guns, which the Allied troops dubbed "Schmeissers," after world-famous gunsmith Hugo Schmeisser, who designed the weapons.

V527.24, B614.29   Schilling's best man   None of the historical accounts mention this engineer from Peenemünde.

V527.25, B614.30–31   outside of Garmisch   That is, Garmisch-Partenkirchen, the Bavarian village where the Allies detained the German rocket experts. By this time, however, most had been released or offered positions with the Operation Backfire/Operation Hermes group.

V527.36–37, B615.1–2   *mythical Rügen off our starboard bow*   It is "mythical" because, as Baedeker explains in *Northern Germany* (204), this large island in the Baltic was initially inhabited by the ancient Germanic tribes of Rugii, then by Slavonic peoples who "resisted the influences of Christianity and civilization down to the middle of the 14th century." A residue of the Teutonic and Slavonic mythologies remains in the place-names scattered along the coast (see V528.9–10n, V528.13–15n). Heading west, Frau Gnahb steers them between the main coast and Rugen Island, encountering it off the starboard (right) bow.

V527.40, B615.5–6   *the Greifswalder Bodden*   A bay to the southeast of Rugen Island.

V528.9–10, B615.17–19   the Stubbenkammer . . . Cape Arkona   After searching several of the firths on the southeastern coast of Rugen, Frau Gnahb has turned northward, according to our mock tour guide, and these landmarks from the island's *"eastern coast"* (V528.5) slide by on the left, or port, side of the ship. The geographical details stem from Baedeker (*Northern Germany* 206–7), according to whom the island is dotted with mounds and altars used in ancient Slavic sacrificial rites. The Stubbenkammer is a set of rock steps in the chalk cliffs; further west is the Königstühl, or "King's Seat," a chalk precipice rising over four hundred feet above the Baltic; last there is Cape Arkona, the island's northernmost point, site of an old Slavonic temple "consisting of a circular intrenchment 20–40 ft. high, and containing the temple of their four-headed idol Swantewit" (ibid.).

V528.13–15, B615.21–24 *Svetovid . . . Triglav . . . Porevit . . . Rugevit* The sources here are Baedeker and Grimm. The latter (201) treats the Slavonic god Svetovid or Swantewit in several connections, equating him with the Teutonic god Tiw, a war god analogous to Mars. Interestingly, the Saxon rune for Tiw was an arrow pointing heavenward, rocketlike. The other names are variants, or nicknames, for this god.

V528.19, B615.28–29 the Wissow Klinken The source once again is Baedeker's *Northern Germany* (206), who describes the place as "a series of chalk cliffs resembling those of the Stubbenkammer." *Klinken* are latches or latchkeys, so this white promontory might be said to metaphorically probe "the wards of Slothrop's heart" in this passage.

V529.38, B617.13–14 Guy Lombardo . . . "Running Between the Raindrops" A song written by Gibbons and Drenforth, but a great hit for Guy Lombardo and His Royal Canadian Orchestra in 1931.

V530.29, B618.9 three bells strike The ship's bells strike every half hour, the number of strokes increasing with every half hour, up to eight bells for each four-hour watch. Since it is afternoon, and the cook aboard the *Anubis* is "peeling potatoes" for supper (V529.21), the time must be 1:30.

V531.27–40, B619.12–27 His hand closes on stiff taffeta. . . . the smell of . . . *of* The smell of death, and all the details of dress (the taffeta and satin garments with their "hooks and eyes"), as well as the long hair, identify it as Bianca's corpse.

V532.7, B619.35 what's dancing dead-white The girl has become her name: Bianca/White. As if she were the sacrifice presaged by the references in this episode to Teutonic and Slavonic custom, she dances the dance of death.

V532.28, B620.19 the wet Hafenplatz The "harbor plaza" of Stralsund.

EPISODE 23

Back to England. Except for the remark that "Brigadier Pudding died back in the middle of June" (V533.10), the time of this episode is indistinct, but probably it is contemporaneous with episode 22 (July 31). Here Katje watches a reel of film that Osbie has left behind especially for her. The film images constitute a code, an allegorical call for her to leave "The White Visitation" for an as yet undefined "counterforce" (V536.23).

V532.32, B620.25 Where is the Pope whose staff will bloom for me? The reference, again, is to the Tannhäuser myth (V364.22n);

and this question becomes line 1 in a Petrarchan sonnet written,
it appears, by Brigadier Pudding. Its details (the "whips," the "call"
of its Lisaura at night, its speaker having "knelt" before her in confession) all recollect Pudding's coprophagic ritual of episode 4, part 2.

V532.33, B620.26   vamps me   See V320.12n.

V533.9, B620.38   No pentacles, no cups, no holy Fool. . . .   The ellipses
are Pynchon's and suggest the modernity of this sonnet, for a traditional
one would require closure at the end of its sestet. In Tarot symbolism,
Pentacles and Cups are two of the four suits in the Lesser Arcana. Pentacles (five-pointed stars) are generally associated with monetary motifs,
Cups with matters of the heart and pleasure. On the Tarot Fool see
V501.25–26n.

V533.10–11, B620.39–40   a massive *E. coli* infection   See V236.32n.

V533.11, B620.40–621.1   "Me little Mary hurts"   Soules identifies
this as the argot of British children complaining of stomach ache, from
J. M. Barrie's play *Little Mary* (1906).

V533.13, B621.3   demobbed   That is, "demobilized" (British service
slang).

**V533.31–32, B621.24–25   the day Osbie Feel was processing the Amanita
mushrooms**   December 22, 1944 (in episode 14 of part 1).

V534.2, B621.38   "with Nelson Eddy in the background"   With singer/actress Jeanette MacDonald, Eddy (1901–67) crooned his way
through a fistful of movie musicals in the thirties: *Naughty Marietta*,
Rose Marie, *Rosalie*, and so on.

**V534.9–10, B622.5–6   "Basil Rathbone and S. Z. ('Cuddles')
Sakall"**   Actor Rathbone played Karenin to Greta Garbo's Anna Karenina, the son of Baron von Frankenstein in *The Son of Frankenstein*
(1939), and the villainous Mr. Murdstone in *David Copperfield* (1934).
But most of all Basil Rathbone (1892–1967) was known for his portrayals
of Sherlock Holmes during the thirties and forties. A more unlikely
cowboy cannot be imagined, unless it is Sakall, who fled Europe and
Hitler's madness in 1939. Hungarian by birth, Sakall (1888–1955)
appeared in his first English-speaking role in a Deanna Durbin film
of 1940, *It's a Date*. He learned his lines by means of phonetic transcriptions, but his thick Eastern European accent always remained. He
is best known as the plump desk clerk in *Casablanca* (1942).

V534.11, B622.7–8   the Midget who played the lead in *Freaks*   This
was Harry Earles, who starred with his wife, Daisy, in several other Tod
Browning films before *Freaks*, his 1932 masterpiece of horror. In
Freaks, Earles played "little Hans," a midget who marries a beautiful
but devious trapeze artist called Cleopatra. She only wants his money.
For that, the other "Freaks" give her a fearful beating and Hans marries
"little Frieda" (Daisy). In *Freaks*, a grotesque allegory on the theme

of the beautiful and the damned, life's preterite get in their licks. See earlier references at V106.36, V125.3, and V151.1–11.

V536.12, B624.8–9   the windmill called "The Angel"   See V106.12n.

V536.18, B624.29   *An Introduction to Modern Herero*   Fictional book.

EPISODE 24

The time is as unspecified as the place. Katje and Pirate make an allegorical tour of a rather pleasant hell, an inversion of Dante's Inferno with its deeper levels of greater punishments. The version here is horizontally arranged, plastically changeable, and certainly not frightening. It does involve elements of tedium, as with the long list of illicit sexual encounters, but Pirate and Katje break into joyous dance at episode's end.

V537.1–4, B625.10–13   Dear Mom, I put a couple of people in Hell today . . . (Oxyrhynchus papyrus number classified)   The Oxyrhynchus papyri were named for the Nile River village where they were discovered, near the turn of the century. They consist of forty-plus volumes of fragments, three of which (numbers 1, 654, and 655) include sayings ascribed to Jesus, sayings eventually found to resemble other sayings contained in the Gospel of Thomas, a coptic Gnostic manuscript uncovered at Nag Hamadi. However, there is also an apocryphal Gospel of Thomas, commonly referred to as the "Infancy Story" of Jesus. It exists in four recensions, one each in Greek and Latin, two in Syriac. In it are narratives of Jesus' boyhood from his fifth to his twelfth years, narratives abounding with miracles: Jesus restores the dead to life, inflicts death on some who thwart his will, makes birds out of clay, and (like Satan in Mark Twain's *Mysterious Stranger*) causes them to fly. Pynchon may well have had this background in mind here. This epigraph, however, appears in neither of the gospels of Thomas, though it is consistent with the motif of youthful magic. Indeed, this episode of *GR* does "put a couple of people [Katje and Pirate] in Hell" for the day. On the Gnostic and apocryphal backgrounds to this bit of satirical play, see M. R. James (14–15, 49–69).

V537.33–34, B626.12–13   like Route One . . . through the heart of Providence   As the narrator says, the road does provide a scenic tour. Entering Providence, Rhode Island, from the south, Route 1 arcs to the right over the Woonasquatucket River, turns left under George M. Cohan Boulevard, and then motors one past the campus of Brown University.

V538.14, B626.33   Beaverboard Row   Beaverboard, formerly a trademark, is that form of building material made from compressed wood chips and commonly used to divide cubicles of offices.

V539.12, B627.33 Teilhard de Chardin A Jesuit father, paleontologist, and philosopher, Pierre Teilhard de Chardin (1881–1955) wrote his best-known work, *The Phenomenon of Man*, while serving as a missionary in China during the early years of World War II. His philosophy attempts a synthesis of evolutionary science and mystical Christianity. The question of a "return" thus arises here because, in Teilhard's view, the evolution of material forms up to man is an evolution of spirit; and man is the "omega point" of a linear progress that Teilhard sees as an escape from entropy, a transcendence founded on love and unity. For mankind he projects no "return" to repressed, primitive forms but rather a continued evolution of that divine spirit.

V539.21, B628.4 "Critical Mass" This is the smallest amount of fissionable material necessary to sustain a nuclear chain reaction. But the date is late July or very early August of 1945, and the first A-bomb (or "Cosmic Bomb," as the news media dubbed it) will not become common knowledge until after August 6, the day of the Hiroshima blast. So the idea, here, is still "trembling in its earliness."

V540.23, B629.13–14 Charley-Charley, Hits 'n' Cuts, and Rock-Scissors-and-Paper Children's games, mostly English. The Opies (*Children's Games* 133–35) describe Charley-Charley as a "Catching Game" in which one child, the odd man out, stands to one side of a street. To him, the other children call out "Charley-Charley, may we cross your golden river?" The child who is "Charley" replies: "You mayn't cross my river unless you have *blue*." Anyone wearing something blue may safely cross. Those who don't must rush across while Charley tries to catch them, assisted by the ones with blue. It goes on this way until the colors are exhausted or none are left; and the last one caught is the new "Charley." In the same book (25) the Opies also describe hits-and-cuts as a game that involves the drawing of lots or straws, the loser becoming the chaser in a game of catch. Rock-scissors-and-paper is universally known, and the Opies (ibid. 26–27) suggest that it may well have come from the Orient. After chanting in unison with three thrusts of their fists, the players (three in all) expose an image made with their fingers. The winner is determined according to a circular formula: the "rock" (fist) blunts the "scissors" (a V-shape), which cut "paper" (flattened palm, held down), which enfolds the "rock."

V540.28, B629.19 Sammy Hilbert-Spaess The double agent of part 2 (see V217.18n).

V540.38, B629.32 sitrep A "situation report" or, as Noel's *Naval Terms Dictionary* puts it: "a report required when prescribed conditions exist without reference to the time lapse between occurrences." Exactly.

V541.23, B630.23 Say a prayer for the common informer This song by character "Merciful" Evans riffs on the Rolling Stones' 1970 anthem to the preterite, "Salt of the Earth," from their *Beggar's Banquet* album:

Let's drink to the hard-working people,
Let's drink to the lonely pervert;
Raise your glass to the good and the evil,
Let's drink to the salt of the earth.

Say a prayer for the common footsoldier,
Spare a part for his backbreaking work;
Say a prayer for his wife and his children,
Who burn the fires and who still till the earth.

When I search a faceless crowd,
A swirling mass of gray and black-white;
They don't look real to me,
In fact they look so tame . . . (etc.)

V541.24, B630.24 a quim Old-timey British vulgarism for the female genitalia.

V541.27, B630.27 Kilkenny to Kew Kilkenny is a poor county of southwestern Ireland; Kew, an aristocratic district west of London, home of the Royal Botanic Gardens.

V542.13, B631.17 Gallaho Mews Fictional London mews (alley) that is home to the fictional Twelfth House (V217.24n).

V542.39, B632.5–6 Smithfield Market Famous as an execution site and as the home of the Bartholomew Fair from 1150 until 1855. Today the square is surrounded by fish, meat, poultry, and produce markets.

V544.8, B633.26 living in St. John's Wood Pirate imagines his lost love, Scorpia Mossmoon, living in this upper-crust London district.

V544.33, B634.15 sufficient unto the day Is the evil thereof (Matt. 6:34).

V545.4–5, B634.30–31 young Porky Pig holding out the anarchist's ticking bomb Porky Pig was a regular feature (with Donald Duck and nephews, Bugs Bunny, and Woody Woodpecker) of *Walt Disney's Comics and Stories*, a comic book in continuous publication after 1940. The three-color animated films of Porky began appearing on screen one year earlier, and the anarchist's bomb was a standard cliché in both formats.

V546.24–25, B636.25–26 Rexist meetings . . . Degrelle In Belgium, in the late thirties, French separatists under the fanatical leadership of Léon Degrelle organized a fascist brotherhood known as the Rexists. The "realm of total souls" (V546.29) is actual rhetoric from Rexist propaganda, which emphasized a mystical nationalism.

EPISODE 25

Sometime in early August, Slothrop continues his trek across northern Germany, near Rostock. A short analepsis treats his Puritan ancestors, who are satirical representations of Pynchon's own. Slothrop is joined by a young boy looking for his lost lemming, and at episode's end Major Marvy once more crosses his path.

V549.1, B639.16   the narrow gassen   German "alleys."

V550.7, B640.29–30   pale green farmworker triangles   As the Allied occupying force began to organize war-torn Europe after May 8, they devised a system of designating the occupational status of displaced persons with colored triangular cloth patches.

V550.14–15, B640.38–40   stripped by the SS ... every fucking potato field ... alcohol for the rockets   A bit of detail whose source was Dornberger (111). He describes the general concern, in 1943, that the SS would be unable to meet the army's need for alcohol to fuel nine hundred rockets per month: "How much alcohol we should have depended on the potato harvest." See also V640.25–26.

V550.34, B641.21   Allgeyer soldiers   Johann Baptiste Allgeier (1763– 1823) was an Austrian chess master whose writings on the game, and whose designs for the chess pieces (described in this line and the next), became nineteenth-century standards. Pynchon gives the correct spelling at V675.34–35.

V550.38–39, B641.27   Vorsetzer rolls   Rolls for the Vorsetzer brand of player piano, produced in Germany.

V550.40, B641.29   Jugendstil cups   Literally, "youth-style," a German artistic movement of the early twentieth century. Its principal tenets were a strict economy of line and a return to classical forms. After 1918 its precepts were largely absorbed by German expressionism.

V552.4, B642.40   "where've you *been*, gate?"   Here and throughout *GR*, "gate" is American forties slang indicating a person especially sensitive to swing music. It derives from the expression "to swing like a gate" (to have a sense of jazz). On Bob Hope's wartime radio show, comedian Jerry Colonna used the expression in a variety of rhyming slang greetings, as in "Greetings, gate! Let's deliberate."

V553.4, B644.7   bleaching that to paper   Recall the etymology of *Blicero*, the "Bleacher" (see V30.12n).

V553.27, B644.32   Ludwig   The kid's name recalls mad, suicidal King Ludwig II of Bavaria (V394.23n).

V553.31, B644.37   Pritzwalk   A town eighty miles south of Rostock.

V553.34, B644.41   "*One lemming*, kid?"   A fitting question for Slothrop to ask, given the motif in his sodium amytal nightmare of episode

10, part 1: "One each of everything" (V67.36). Remember also the quotation from Rilke's Ninth Elegy: "Once, only once" (V413.15–16n).

V554.31–32, B646.3–5 "what Jesus meant . . . venturing out on the Sea of Galilee" Jesus has just been informed that John the Baptist's head has been delivered to Herod, as the king ordered. Thronged by grief-stricken crowds, Jesus works several miracles, healing the sick and feeding the five thousand. That night, his walking on the water terrifies the disciples, who think he's a ghost. Peter tries it and, seeing "the wind" on the water, sinks to the bottom, whereupon Jesus upbraids his faithlessness: "O man of little faith, why did you doubt?" (*Oxford Bible*, Matt. 14:31).

V554.40–555.5, B646.13–21 William Slothrop was a peculiar bird . . . and his son John got a pig operation going Here Pynchon begins a fairly close satire of his own seventeenth-century ancestors, William and John, originally of Writtle, Essex County, England. William Pynchon (1590–1662) was a moderate sort of Puritan, one who preferred to continue his worship in accord with the Episcopal Book of Common Prayer. He was learned in Latin, Greek, and Hebrew; was prominent in the business affairs of Essex; and, in 1629, became one of the original patentees of the Massachusetts Bay Company. With Winthrop, Saltonstall, and others, Pynchon signed the famous Cambridge Agreement of August 26, 1629, promising they would all migrate to the New World colony and establish a Christian commonwealth there. Interestingly, William Pynchon was assigned the task of supervising the purchase of weapons for the colonists, and he appears to have become enough of an expert on ordnance so that he offered a "narration" on the topic before Governor Winthrop.

William Pynchon did not come to America aboard the *Arbella*, as did his fictional counterpart William Slothrop. Nor did he amass a fortune selling pigs. He did, however, establish the village of Roxbury and then, in 1634–35, the village of Agawam, now Springfield, Massachusetts. At the time, he became the westernmost frontiersman of the colony. With his son John, he commenced to build a sizable wealth by trading for furs. Most sources agree that he was able to accomplish this by establishing policies of fair, humane dealings with the neighboring Indians. For further information, see McIntyre, Byington, Winston, and Morison.

V555.21–22, B646.41 a little early for Isaac Newton Indeed it was, for the famous physicist wasn't born until 1642, and the formulation of his second law of motion (the subject here) waited another thirty years after that.

V555.24, B647.2–3 his Gadarene swine The story of how Jesus exorcised the demons from a man of Gadara, sending them into a herd of pigs that promptly plunged over a hillside, appears in Mark 5:1–17 and Luke 8:26–33.

V555.29–31, B647.9–12   He wrote a long tract . . . called *On Preterition* . . . burned in Boston   Pynchon continues the satirical history of his own ancestors. While at Agawam, William Pynchon arranged for the private printing, in England, of a quarto volume 156 pages long entitled *The Meritorious Price of Our Redemption*. The book was published by James Moxon of London in 1650. Copies reached Boston in August of that year, and the General Court promptly declared that they "detest and abhorre many of the opinions and assertions therein, as false, erronyous, and hereticale." As punishment, they ordered "the said book to be burned in the market place, at Boston, by the common executioner" (Byington 200–201). The sentence was carried out in October, and one result was that William Pynchon's tract became exceedingly rare; only four copies are extant in U.S. libraries.

The crux of the matter was a rather technical point in Puritan theology. The orthodox view was that Christ suffered the full extent of hell torments because only thus could he fully discharge the debt of the elect, and so secure their heavenly place. The Puritans therefore held that *all* sins of the elect, including their original sin inherited from Adam, were "imputed" to Christ. Only in this way would Christ's punishment fully release the elect from their sinfulness. William Pynchon disagreed. In an elaborate argument set out as a dialogue laden with scriptural citation, he argued that Christ did not *need* to bear these sins by imputation and so did not suffer the hell torments of God's awful wrath. In closely argued chapters at the end, he held that Christ's obedience was, by definition, always and already perfect; therefore the question of punishing him was unnecessary. Christ's death on the Cross was the final test of his total obedience to the Father's will, and so it fully redeemed God's covenants established with Adam after the Fall. Simply put, no terrible harrowing of hell was required of Christ because he did God's will; by definition, his will was identical with that of God the Father.

In satirizing this technical point, Pynchon has to simplify. Still, he remains faithful to the perceived threat of his ancestor's writings. *The Meritorious Price of Our Redemption* was banned because it undercut the doctrine of Puritan sainthood, with its absolute separation of elect from preterite. William Pynchon's argument implied that anyone might have access to divine grace, that Christ died for elect and preterite alike. And in thus opening the doors, it might even be necessary, as Thomas Pynchon writes three hundred years later, "to love Judas too" (V555.40).

V556.1, B647.26   86 him out   See V21.36n.

V556.3–4, B647.29   he sailed back to Old England   Frustrated at the

legal proceedings against him, William Pynchon transferred the Springfield lands and businesses to his son John and, in 1652, sailed back
to England, where he retired to an estate in Wraysbury, Buck-
inghamshire. There he continued his theological writings. A 450–
page defense of the 1650 tract appeared in 1655. He also wrote tracts
on the Sabbath, another one entitled *The Jewes Synagogue* (1652),
and another describing in elaborate detail God's covenant of grace with
Adam (1662), a reprise of many of the arguments put forth in the
"hereticale" tract of 1650.

V556.19, B648.5–6   that anarchist he met in Zürich   This was Francisco
Squalidozzi (V263.16).

V557.19, B649.12   Michaeliskirche   The Church of St. Michael, but
since so many northern European towns have one by that name,
this particular one is unknown.

V557.20, B649.14   a Sterno fire   From the American brand of "canned
heat," the tiny tins of paraffin fuel doled out to servicemen.

EPISODE 26

Still early August. Slothrop, in his next disguise—that of a Russian officer—bluffs his way through an encounter with Maj. Duane Marvy and
a character from Pynchon's first novel, Clayton ("Bloody") Chiclitz (who
takes his name from the Chiclets brand of American chewing gum). Learning of Marvy's plans to raid the nearby encampment of Schwarzkommando,
Slothrop warns the Hereros away. He also gives Andreas Orukumbe a summary of what is known, thus far in the narrative text, about the firing of
Rocket 00000.

V557.30–31, B649.26–27   a Russian accent . . . like Bela Lugosi   Or,
more precisely, a voice with a molasses-slow, heavy Middle European
accent; American actor Bela Lugosi (1888–1956) was born in Hungary
and maintained an especially pronounced accent in his early roles:
as the count in Tod Browning's *Dracula* (1931) and as Legendre in his
White Zombie (1933).

V558.3, B649.38   old Bloody Chiclitz   A refugee from Pynchon's first
novels. In chapter 8 of *V.*, set in 1955, Chiclitz has become "president of
Yoyodyne, Inc., a company with factories scattered careless about
the country and more government contracts than it really knew what
to do with." By *The Crying of Lot 49*, set in 1966, Yoyodyne has
burgeoned from this (1945) toy factory into an international cartel.

**V558.15–20, B650.14–20   equator-crossing festivities. . . . the Royal
Baby. . . . the polliwogs' hair**   Aboard ship, those who have not
previously made an equatorial crossing, the "polliwogs," are subjected

to playful rites of humiliation, presided over by the gluttonous "Royal Baby," to whom they make obeisance.

V558.21, B650.21–22 the T-Force Military argot for the Technical Force; in this case the bureaucracy that includes SPOG, CIOS, and so on.

V559.11–14, B651.17–20 Cecil B. De Mille . . . rowin' old Henry Wilcoxon American film director Cecil B. De Mille spotted tall, rugged Henry Wilcoxon (b. 1905) on the English stage and brought him to Hollywood in 1934, when he played Mark Antony to Claudette Colbert's Cleopatra in the epical film *Cleopatra*. That is the referent of Marvy's allusion: "rowin' old Henry Wilcoxon away into th' sunset to fight them Greeks or Persians" is an image from De Mille's 1934 epic.

V559.16–17, B651.22–23 "For De Mille, young fur-henchmen can't be rowing!" The most elaborately staged pun in all of *GR*. Camouflaged within it is the declaration, "Forty million Frenchmen can't be wrong," itself a variation on a phrase attributed to actress, speakeasy owner, and dance girl Texas Guinan (see V657.10–11n). In 1931 she attempted to take a troupe of forty-two girls to Paris, where she hoped to open a nightclub free from Prohibitionism and the harassments of J. Edgar Hoover's G-men. However, French officials refused to let the troupe disembark. Legal proceedings commenced, during which it became clear from the popular outcry that French males were delighted to have the Americans. Nevertheless, after ten days Texas and her girls were deported. Arriving back in New York on March 21, 1931, they were met by throngs of well-wishers and reporters. Texas proclaimed: "*Fifty* million Frenchmen can't be wrong" about a sexy display of skin. Her saying stuck and has since been taken to comment in general on the (supposed) sexual preferences of Frenchmen. Note that Pynchon has fashioned an entire narrative digression about illicit trading in furs, oarsmen in boats, fur henchmen, and De Mille—all of it in order to launch this pun.

V559.30, B651.38 *da, da* "Yes, yes" (Russian).

V559.36–37, B652.4–5 Marvy bellowing "San Antonya Rose," his fav'rite song The lyric "San Antonio Rose" is a perennial hit. It was written in 1941 by Bob Wills, of Bob Wills and the Texas Playboys:

> Deep within my heart lies a melody,
> A song of old San Antone,
> Where in dreams I live with a memory,
> Beneath the stars all alone.
>
> It was there I found beside the Alamo,
> Enchantment strange as the blue up above;

A moonlit path that only she would know,
Still hears my broken song of love.

Moon in all your splendor, know only my heart,
Call back my Rose, Rose of San Antone!
Lips so sweet and tender, like the petals falling apart,
Speak once again of my love, my own.

Broken songs, empty words I know,
Still live in my heart all alone,
For that moonlit path, by the Alamo,
And Rose, my Rose of San Antone.

V560.5–6, B652.16–18 Everything's been stripped. . . . back to the hollow design envelopes of their earliest specs Yet another *hysteron proteron* figure in *GR*.

V560.21, B652.36 "the Soviet CIC" The All-Soviet Trade Union Council.

V560.25, B652.41–42 holding up the mandala, cross to vampire According to folk tradition, vampires will shrink away from a cross. In the Zone it is the KEZVH mandala, from the rocket, that works a spell against evil, like another sign of redemptive sacrifice.

V561.30–31, B654.12–14 Fred Astaire . . . reflecting on his chances of ever finding Ginger Rogers again Between 1933 and 1939, Fred Astaire and Ginger Rogers danced and acted their way through ten films, *Top Hat* and *Swing Time*, for example. They never teamed up again, and Astaire's career took a downward turn.

V562.7, B654.31 a thumb-harp Another name for the four-hole, eight-reed harmonica manufactured by the Hohner Company and marketed as its Little Lady model. A thumb harp measures about one and a half inches long. But this is wartime and Hohners, virtually the only harmonica manufactured, are "almost totally unavailable" (Glover 10). That's why this one has been constructed from scavenged materials.

V562.25, B655.13 Mukuru See V321.40–322.1n.

V563.6–11, B655.38–656.2 "In our villages the women lived . . . on the northern half . . . men on the south . . . in the center . . . the sacred cattle" On the traditional, mandala-like arrangement of the Herero village, see V321.3–4n.

V563.24–25, B656.19 A mezuzah In Judaism, a small roll of parchment inscribed with the words from Deut. 6:4–9 and 11:13–21, invoking faith in Jahweh as the one God. Inside its small container, a mezuzah was assumed to work as an amulet against evil.

EPISODE 27

L ater that evening, Marvy, Chiclitz, and Tchitcherine huddle in readi-
ness for their midnight attack on the Schwarzkommando encampment.
We get some technical information about Rocket 00000, and Marvy drops
the names of some prominent American businessmen-politicians.

V563.29, B656.24–25   Audie Murphy style   America's most decorated
  soldier (twenty-four medals) of World War II, handsome young Murphy
  became a Hollywood actor in 1948, played in a handful of cowboy
  and war films, and died in a plane crash in 1971.
V564.3, B656.38–657.1   More precious than Ravenna   The coastal
  city of northern Italy, here recalled for its beautifully intricate mosaics.
**V564.31–32, B657.36   visas to far Lemuria, to the sun-resorts of
  Sargasso**   Named for the *Lemures* of Roman myth (they were terrifying
  specters of the dead), Lemuria was, like Atlantis (V269.9–10n),
  thought to be a sunken land between East Africa and India. On the
  opposite coast, between the Azores and the West Indies, the calm expanse of Atlantic Ocean known as the Sargasso Sea grows vast, is-
  landlike masses of seaweed, sites of these fanciful "resorts" for dead
  sailors.
V565.11, B658.18   "Dillon, Reed . . . Standard Awl"   Pynchon's source
  for these references is Sasuly (chap. 9, esp. 197, 205). He details the
  economic forces that in the twenties brought IG Farben into a collision
  course with Standard Oil of New Jersey. Standard had a heavy stake
  in Europe, with subsidiary refineries in England, Denmark, Germany,
  and Italy. At the same time, the IG Farben cartel had developed a
  process for retrieving gasoline from hydrogenated coal, a process that
  might well have wrecked Standard's refining interests in coal-rich,
  oil-poor Europe. So the two monoliths struck an agreement: Standard
  Oil agreed to stay out of research into hydrogenation, while IG Farben
  agreed to shelve its plans for hydrogenation refineries. A crucial side
  effect, Sasuly argues, was a shortage of rubber goods in Allied countries
  during the first years of the war, a shortage that made no impact
  on Germany because IG Farben had continued with plans to manufacture butyl rubber from hydrogenated coal. And butyl rubber was vital for
  tires and other machine products necessary to conduct the Panzer
  Army's Blitzkrieg attacks. After V-E Day, the Truman Committee inves-
  tigating these and similar corporate agreements reported that the
  policies of Standard Oil made Germany's initial military successes
  possible. And even as the Truman Committee was opening its inquiry—
  indeed, as early as June 1945—Standard Oil was actively assisting
  IG Farben in its recovery from the war, evidence that the cartel arrange-

ments were in effect before, during, and after hostilities. One way
the Standard/Farben agreements were maintained was through the work
of Gen. William Draper, who had worked at the Wall Street firm
of Dillon, Reed and Company. As head of the Army Economics Division
in occupied Europe, Draper was to have directed efforts to "de-Nazify"
German industry. Instead, claims Sasuly, he probably headed the
effort to reaffirm the old cartel arrangements.

**V565.19–20, B658.27–28 "Herbert Hoover . . . He came over and *fed
you people"** When the United States entered the Great War, President
Wilson appointed Herbert Hoover to head the Food Administration,
where he oversaw the distribution of almost 19 million tons of
foodstuffs to famine-stricken areas of Western Europe. After the armistice was signed, he coordinated relief projects in Austria, Hungary,
Armenia, and Russia, raising over $250 million for food and aid.

**V565.24–26, B658.32–34 "Mister Swope was ace buddies with old
FDR . . . Electric Charlie's in there now . . . one-thim Brain Trusters.
Jews, most of'm."** Gerard Swope (1877–1957) worked first of all
for Western Electric, then for General Electric. In 1922 he became president of the company. But in fact there were two Swopes: Herbert
Bayard Swope was Gerard's younger brother, was the one-time head
of the New York *World* newspaper, and was more an "ace buddy"
to Roosevelt than Gerard. Franklin D. Roosevelt's "Brain Trust" was
formed during the 1932 campaign around a nucleus of Columbia
University professors: Rexford Guy Tugwell, Adolf Berle, and Raymond
Moley. Hugh Johnson, financial adviser to Bernard M. Baruch, was
added later; and Gerard Swope was loosely associated with the group.
In *GR*, Major Marvy's anti-Semitism stands out here; for Swope,
Moley, and Berle were Jewish, but mostly lapsed. "Electric Charley"
is a reference to the founder of General Electric, Charles Coffin (V332.5–
6n).

V565.36, B659.5 Carl Schmitz of the IG Unknown, or else fictional.
Sasuly (101, 165) does mention Hermann and Dietrich Schmitz, both associated with IG Farben for decades; but neither had any connection
to the German-based Siemens manufacturing company, mentioned here.

**V566.1–2, B659.13–14 his Eleanor Roosevelt routine . . . "my son
Idiot—uh, Elliot"** Elliot Roosevelt (b. 1910) was Franklin and Eleanor
Roosevelt's fourth child. He came out of the war a brigadier general
for his work with a photo-reconaissance squadron of the U.S. Army Air
Force. He had a reputation for being the family maverick; later he
wrote six books on the Roosevelt family and his father's presidency.

V566.14, B659.28 a very large white Finger Appears to be a reprise
of Adam Smith's "invisible hand" that guides the marketplace of
laissez faire capitalism (see V30.30n). This hand, however, also makes
an obscene gesture.

EPISODE 28

At a town "near Wismar" (V567.32) in northern Germany, Slothrop adopts the last of his disguises, or alter egos, before part 4, when he fragments. The time of this episode is Thursday and Friday, August 2–3, 1945. As Plechazunga, a (seemingly) fictional pig-hero, Slothrop finds himself in the midst of a raid. He escapes, leaves yet another young girl beneath a rainbow archway, takes up with Franz Pökler's pig, Frieda, and as the episode ends meets Pökler himself.

V567.20, B661.7–8   the Askania films of Rocket flights   See V407.3–4n.

V567.22, B661.10–11   Treppengiebel shapes   The "step-gables" of the houses.

V567.24–25, B661.13–14   playing Himmel and Hölle   Heaven and Hell, a popular German version of the children's game of hopscotch. Peesch, in his *Berliner Kinderspiel* (22–28) describes it as follows: the playing area is chalked out to form a cross, with ten squares in all; children start play from a zero area called *Erde* (Earth), hop through the numbered squares with increasingly more difficult moves, the ninth (*Hölle*) being the hardest; and the tenth square (*Himmel*) is home. It's a striking image, given the prevalence throughout *GR* of crosses, the number ten, and the desire to return "home."

V567.31, B661.21–22   singing Laterne, Laterne, Sonne, Mond und Sterne   The call in another German children's game, described again in Peesch. This game is hide-and-seek. The Sun (*Sonne*) must catch the other children, who are the Stars (*Sterne*), and bring them back to a holding area, usually a lantern post (*Laterne*). The Moon (*Mond*) is a player with the privilege of releasing those captives by invading the home base and pulling them out. The Opies mention the contest rules in *Children's Games* (173–74); Peesch (42–43) refers to the game as *Englische Versteckspiele*, or "English hide-and seek."

V567.33, B661.23–24   near Wismar   Slothrop has traveled to a point about fifteen miles southeast of Rostock. This town with its Peterskirche and Roland Statue—common features in many northern German towns—is otherwise unidentified.

V567.34, B661.25–26   Plechazunga, the Pig-Hero   Apparently was created from a page of etymological ramblings in Grimm (178): "The lightning's flash, which we name *blitz*, was expressed in our older speech both by the simple *plih* . . . and by *plechazunga* . . . derived from *plechazan*, a frequentive of *plechan*. A Prussian folk-tale has an expressive phrase for the lightning: 'He with the blue whip chases the devil,' i.e. the giants; for a blue flame was held especially sacred." In a footnote Grimm adds: "While writing *plechazan*, I remember *pleckan* (pateria, nudari, bleak), MHG [Middle High German] blecken, blacte ... which, when used of the sky, means: the clouds open, heaven opens, as we will say of forked and sheet lightning." Simply put, *plechazunga* belongs to a complex of Germanic words associated with Thor (Donnar, Thunar), whose weapon is the lightning. The "Pig-Hero" business is Pynchon's fiction, but note that this *Schweinheldfest* occurs on a Thursday (Thor's Day), which is consistent with the details in Grimm. Also, note that this hero was not "tamed," that is, was not translated from the pagan into a Christian context, "into St. Peter or Roland," even though the ceremony did occur near the Roland Statue and Peterskirche mentioned above.

V568.6, B661.38–39 Schraub the shoemaker Derives his moniker from the German noun *Schraub*, a screw.

V568.7–8, B661.40 drafted last winter into the Volksgrenadier Hitler's Home Guard or "People's Infantry," made up of old men and boys.

V568.36, B662.29 a Wilhelm Busch original Reminiscent of Busch's comic strip characters (see V501.10n).

V569.2, B662.38 "Well, Haferschleim is better than none, ho, ho" This is Slothrop punning in the manner of Groucho Marx. *Haferschleim* is a gruel or porridge made from oats.

V569.16, B663.13–14 Quark ... Gold-brown Kartoffelpuffer Respectively, curds packed sausage-style in tubes and fried potato cakes.

V569.26, B663.26–27 an hour's game of hammer-and-forge Probably a variant on Glocke und Hammer (bell and hammer), a German table game also known as *Schimmel* (white horse). Popular in cafés and taverns, the game uses eight special dice, a hammer, and five picture cards (bell, hammer, white horse, hotel, and bell & hammer). A game of chance, it is played auction-style, in three phases: first the determination of an auctioneer (highest roll of the dice); then the auctioning of the five cards, after which the auctioneer bangs the hammer and play commences; players throw the eight dice and are paid, or pay, according to the value of the roll and the value of a pool.

V569.41, B664.4 Plattdeutsch The north German dialect spoken in these low-country areas, Rostock or Lüneberg, for example.

V570.3, B664.8 Gemütlichkeit Cosiness, comfort.

V570.6, B664.10–11 charabancs full of bluegreen uniforms A parody of the Keystone Cop routines of silent film fame. The uniformed "coppers," with their "starburst" badges, show up in two open buses (the French *char à bancs* is an open carriage with bench seats). Brutal pandemonium ensues.

V570.28, B664.37 that erste Abreibung The noun *Abreibung* (rubdown) used figuratively—"the first beating."

V571.26, B666.2 dossed down In underworld cant, to "doss down" is to sleep somewhere; during the thirties, drifters through depressed

America would search out a cheap "doss-house" for the night (Partridge, *Macmillan Dictionary*).

V571.28–29, B666.5–6   *Die Welt am Montag* . . . the Buchdrucherverband   The first is a weekly news magazine published in Berlin. In both the Viking and Bantam editions the second item is in error: it should be *Buchdruckerverband*, literally, the "book-printer's union."

V571.31–32, B666.8–9   the German Wobbly traditions   In the early decades of this century, "Wobbly" was the slang term given to the International Workers of the World, a Socialist labor organization.

V572.30, B667.15   "There's no moon"   The moon entered its last quarter on July 31 (see V506.37n); by August 2 the thin sliver of a moon did not rise over Europe until after 1:00 A.M. Earlier in the evening, as here, one would see "no moon."

V572.39, B667.25   the Tauschzentrale   See V366.3n.

V573.11, B667.40–41   through the ogival opening   That is, under a vaulted arch, whose "stairsteps" recall the narrator's earlier discussion of projectile calculus (V567.13–24). Notice that the young woman "makes no move to step through the arch" (V573.13–14) with Slothrop. One inference must be that his is no quest "over the rainbow," no joint venture—as in *The Wizard of Oz*—founded, like skipping Dorothy's, on mutual risk and compassion. Instead, Slothrop's journey takes him *under* the rainbow, alone.

V573.19–20, B668.7   a Winkelhaken   Brand name of an Austrian printing press.

V573.21, B668.8   "You're a May bug"   An engaging metaphor for Tyrone Slothrop. The May bug, or cockchafer (*Melolontha melolontha*), emerges from its chrysalis in April or May, whence it commences to devastate the vegetation of Europe.

V575.14–16, B670.13–14   pines thick with shreds of tinfoil, a cloud of British window . . . to fox the German radars   This detail stems from Irving (88–89): "At noon [on July 24, 1943] Hitler raged at his Air Force experts for their incompetence; owing to the first use of *Window* by the R.A.F., their losses had been unusually low . . . the British had introduced a technique feared for a long time—dropping showers of metal foil; as a result, all radar except *Freya* had been jammed." Incidentally, the pig at Slothrop's side is named Frieda, for the Teutonic goddess Freya (see V398.19n).

V575.24–26, B670.24–27   They fall asleep . . . waiting for morning and a child to claim him   According to an old Germanic folk belief, to dream in a pigsty will cause the dream to come true (Grimm 1146).

V576.35, B671.40   "an aromatic polyimide"   Polyimides are also known as polypeptides. They are produced by reacting an aromatic diamine with anhydrous pyrometallic compounds. But this is little help in specifying what Imipolex G is, for the handbooks advise that there are approximately 6.4 × 10^{15} theoretically possible molecular products of such a reaction.

EPISODE 29

The time is Friday, August 3, 1945. In response to Slothrop's questions about Laszlo Jamf and Imipolex G, Franz Pökler launches on a lengthy digression concerning German expressionist cinema and recollections of chemistry lectures by Jamf while Pökler was getting his technical schooling at Munich. The episode concludes with Jamf's Fascist theories of chemical physics.

V577.10, B672.18 "On D-Day" June 6, 1944.
V577.28, B673.1 back at the T.H. The Technische Hochschule, in Munich.
V577.29, B673.2 "the lion" At this time in *GR*, action occurs under the astrological sign of Leo (July 22–August 21).
V578.7–9, B673.19–22 Klein-Rogge was carrying . . . Brigitte Helm in *Metropolis* A reference to Fritz Lang's film of 1927. Kracauer (162– 64) gives a helpful summary: In the film Lang creates an upper city of skyscrapers and lively streets, while underground the downtrodden workers tend mammoth machines. Brigitte Helm plays Maria, a young woman who—for the workers—stands as a symbol of saintly comfort, of heart. Rudolf Klein-Rogge plays an inventor, Rothwang, who constructs a robot-Maria, then uses it to incite the workers, giving the bureaucratic leaders a pretext to crush the nascent dissent. The film thus develops into an allegory of the higher mind triumphing over heart, of a Fascist and masculine reason coldly ruling over a feminine and irrational mass culture. In the key scene, Maria goes to the in- dustrialists' office complex high above the city and there attempts to mediate between management and the workers. But her compromise works mainly in favor of Freder, the industrialist. As Kracauer (164) puts it, "The whole composition denotes that the industrialist acknowl- edges the heart for the purpose of manipulating it." Pynchon's image of the "magnificent-looking suits" (V578.14–15) can be checked against a still photo that is illustration 27 in Kracauer's book.
V578.22–23, B673.39 whatever Käthe Kollwitz saw At the time of this fictional episode, she may have been seeing it (death) again, for the German artist Käthe Schmidt Kollwitz died on August 22, 1945, at the age of seventy-eight. She was known principally as a printmaker and a masterful draftsman, secondarily as a sculptor. Here Pynchon has in mind a series of sketches she did, from 1903 to 1935, on the theme of death. One of these she transformed into a poster com-

memorating the murder of Socialist Karl Liebknecht (see V621.40n).
Carl Zigrosser (xviii) describes the rest of the fifteen–drawing sequence
as "a process or dance of death in the grand tradition—visions of
death violent and death serene." The picture that Pynchon specifically
means, of "lean Death" swooping down "to hump Its women from
behind," belongs to the violent category. In the Zigrosser edition of her
work it is plate 71, "Death Seizes a Woman." The subject's one visible
eye is riveted ahead, her mouth open in the beginning of a scream.
The featureless, bony figure of Death is virtually sexless, an "It" that
has wrapped lean but muscular arms around her breast in a sure
embrace.

V578.25–26, B673.42–674.1   the Mare nocturnum   Latin for "night
mare."

**V578.31–33, B674.7–10   Attila the Hun . . . come west out of the steppes
to smash . . . the Burgundians**   The reference is to Fritz Lang's 1924
film *Die Nibelungen*, produced in two parts, *Siegfried* and *Kreimhild's
Revenge*. The first shows Siegfried's fight with the Fafnir, the dragon, his
proposition of marriage to Kreimhild (sister to the Burgundian king,
Gunther), the "magic hood" by which Hagen cheats Brunhild into
a marriage with Gunther, and Siegfried's death by another of Hagen's
greedy schemes. In the second film Kreimhild marries the barbarian
chieftain, Attila, and encourages him to sweep out of the east and
lay waste to the Burgundian stronghold. See Kracauer (91–93).

V579.9, B674.31–33   Klein-Rogge . . . as Dr. Mabuse   In Lang's 1924
film *Doktor Mabuse der Spieler*.

V579.10, B674.32   Hugo Stinnes   See V284.23n.

**V579.21–22, B675.3–5   Bernhardt Goetzke as State Prosecutor von
Wenk . . . Death in *Der Müde Tod***   As von Wenk in *Doktor Mabuse*,
actor Bernhardt Goetzke plays the public prosecutor charged with
tracking down the sinister hypnotist and criminal. Wenk enlists the
help of "the degenerate Countess Told, while Mabuse relies on his
mistress, Cara Carozza" (Kracauer 81–82). But Mabuse falls in love with
the countess and ravishes her, much as the narrator describes it here.
On Goetzke's role as Death in *Der Müde Tod* see V516.22n.

V579.30, B675.15   Agfa plate   A photographic plate manufactured
by Agfa of Berlin, a subsidiary of IG Farben. Note that Mabuse, as a
"savage throwback" unpicturable on that plate, stands as another
instance of *hysteron proteron*—here, a regression to primal savagery.

V579.36, B675.22–23   white light, ruins of Atlantis   The reference
is to Georg Wilhelm Pabst's 1932 film *Atlantis*, shot with the blazing
white sands of northern Africa as the backdrop (Kracauer 242).

V580.5–6, B675.34   they sang *Semper sit in flores*   The narrator translates the Latin a few lines further: "be he always in flower." It's a
line from the student song "Gaudeamus Igitur" (see V432.13n).

V580.12–13, B676.1   Stickstoff Syndikat   Nitrogen Syndicate.

V580.15–16, B676.4–5   scrawled C—H on his chalkboard . . . Si—N
The chemical notations for covalent bonds of carbon and hydrogen
and for silicon and nitrogen. As the narrator notes, silicon is just
below carbon on the periodic table of the elements, so it has the same
valence.

EPISODE 30

A flashback concerning Lyle Bland, Slothrop's uncle who conspired in
selling the child to Laszlo Jamf. Bland's connections with the Masons
and his attraction to Rosicrucian mysticism form, with pinball, the main
focus of this episode.

V581.24–25, B677.22   commodity and retail, Harriman and Weinberg
A contrast between old wealth and the nouveau riche, with hints of
anti-Semitism. Sidney James Weinberg (1891–1969) was an investment
broker and a member of the Business Advisory Council from 1933
to 1969. On Harriman, see below.

**V581.29–30, B677.27–28   Business Advisory Council . . . Swope of
General Electric**   During the Great Depression, the Business Advisory
Council was organized under the U.S. Chamber of Commerce, headed
by Henry I. Harriman of the venerable New England Harrimans.
Gerard Swope, then the president of General Electric (see V565.24–
26n), was also a member. In 1933 the council put forward a group
of proposals, known as "The Swope Plan," calling for industry-wide
controls on production and prices.

V581.34–35, B677.34   the Alien Property Custodian   This functionary
was empowered to seize and redistribute assets of aliens for reasons
of war, nonpayment of taxes, violations of immigration laws, and the
like. During World War I, the APC seized many German firms, the
IG Farben subsidiaries among them, shortly after the United States
joined the hostilities in 1917. However, as Sasuly argues (178–83),
seizure was one thing; not removing managers with ties to IG Farben
was another. By failing to replace upper-management figures at seized
firms, the APC made it easy for IG Farben to rebuild the old cartel
arrangements during the twenties and thirties.

V581.41, B677.42   Glitherius Paint & Dye, a Berlin firm   Entirely
fictional company, its name of unknown origin.

V582.5, B678.6–7   the same Pflaumbaum Franz Pökler worked for   See
V159.38–39. The Bantam contains a misprint: "Frank Pökler."

V582.28–29, B678.36   the annual Veiled Prophet Ball   During the
November to January "season," a debutante living in St. Louis would

hope to be presented at the Veiled Prophet Ball, the Midwest's most glamorous and exclusive cotillion. But there is more. In Masonry, the "Veiled Prophet" is Christ. According to Masonic scholar Albert Pike (839–40), Moses purified and "re-veiled" the "Occult Science of the Ancient Magi" when he brought down the tablets of stone: "He covered them with a new veil, when he made of the Holy Kabbalah the exclusive heritage of the people of Israel, and the inviolable secret of its Priests." But Jerusalem lost that occult wisdom through centuries of false gods imported by Syrians and Babylonians. So it remained until Jesus, "a Prophet announced to the Magi by the consecrated Star of Initiation, came to rend assunder the worn veil of the old Temple, in order to give the Church a new tissue of legends and symbols, that still and ever conceals from the Profane, and ever preserves to the Elect the same truths." In addition, these secrets are only fully revealed to Masonic adepts in their last or "Thirty-Second Degree" of initiation (recall that part 3 of *GR* has thirty-two episodes).

V582.39, B679.7–8   the Nieman-Marcus bowl, the Bauhaus-style furniture   The bowl is from Neiman-Marcus (misspelled in both editions), the Dallas-based chain of specialty department stores, with branches through the Mid- and Southwest. The furniture is a mass-produced version of the high modernist designs generated from the German Bauhaus Institut, founded in 1919 and dedicated to functional and experimental designs in architecture and household furniture and products.

V582.40–41, B679.9–10   little HO trains . . . cans 'n' reefers   The HO is a small gauge of toy railroad; and, in the lingo, "cans" are tank cars while "reefers" are refrigerator cars.

V583.3–4, B679.14–15   "Even Laurel & Hardy doesn't work"   To make him smile, that is. On this comic duo of American cinema, see V375.31–32n.

V583.13, B679.27   Mouthorgan, Missouri   Fictional town named after the harmonica.

V583.21–24, B679.36–40   Oh Boys, Grand Slams . . . a Folies-Bergères   The subject is pinball machines, and a bit of pop history will help. Michael Colmer fixes the beginning of the pinball game in 1931, when Raymond T. Moloney, a printshop owner, began manufacturing a purely mechanical game called Ballyhoo. It was a huge success, and before long the newly formed Bally Company was joined by a host of others: Chicago Coin, Keystone Novelty, and Gottleib among them. A Chicago Coin game, Beamlight, was the first electrically hopped-up machine, in 1938. But it ran on batteries; the first of the complex electrical boards was not designed until just before the United States entered World War II, and they were mass-produced only after V-E Day. Meanwhile, throughout the late thirties and early forties pinball games were vilified by civic leaders everywhere: Mayor Fiorello

La Guardia had them banned from New York City in 1942 and led the charge by personally sledgehammering a bunch of them into junk. Here is the main point: the scene is depression-era St. Louis, where Lyle Bland's friend, Alfonso Tracy, supposedly has a warehouse full of malfunctioning *electrical* pinball machines, which in the historical scheme of things haven't been invented yet. Still more anachronistic is the reference (at V584.31–32) to the drunken sailor playing an electrical machine (it has a "solenoid" at V584.36) at Virginia Beach on July 4, 1927. Of the machines listed here, the Oh Boy was produced by the Williams Company in 1964, its table featuring a pair of leggy bathing beauties showing plenty of cleavage. The others are unattested in the literature.

V584.1, B680.21   Katspiel   The background for this fantasy is Scholem (*Major Trends* 53), who explains that in the pre-Kabbalistic writings of many Merkabah mystics, the archons Domiel and Katspiel are "gatekeepers" of the sixth antechamber, the next-to-last stop for the adept during his ascent to the divine throne or *Merkabah.*

V584.9–10, B680.31   Keokuk and Puyallup, Oyster Bay, Inglewood   Thomas Pynchon graduated from Oyster Bay High School, on Long Island, in 1953; he lived in Seattle, just north of Puyallup, from 1960 to 1962; and he was living in the Los Angeles suburb of Manhattan Beach, near Inglewood, by 1965. Then we lose his public trail. The reference to Keokuk, Iowa, and its great pinball players ("thumbs"), is unknown.

V584.12–13, B680.34–36   dead on Iwo . . . gangrenous in the snow in the forest of Arden   The Pacific island of Iwo Jima, where U.S. Marines fought a fierce battle against Japanese defenders in the spring of 1945; and the forested area of the Ardennes, site of the Rundstedt offensive of December 1944. (An allusion to Shakespeare's "forest of Arden" in *As You Like It* is possible but doesn't fit the context.)

V584.14, B680.38   M-1   The standard service rifle of the U.S. armed forces during World War II.

V584.21, B681.4   some Offenbach galop   A galop is a quick, lively dance tune in 2/4 time; with the waltz, polka, and quadrille it was one of the nineteenth century's most popular dance forms. There is a parody of the form in Jacques Offenbach's *Orphée aux enfers* (1858). A French composer of German origin, Offenbach stood with Johann Strauss as the outstanding figure in nineteenth-century popular music and is best known for gay, exhilarating, and tuneful comic operettas, such as *La belle Hélène* and *La vie parisienne.*

V584.32, B681.17–18   ship went down at Leyte Gulf   Leyte is an island of the central Phillipines. The battle to retake it from the Japanese began in early October 1944, when Allied troops landed there. The Japanese counterattacked, sending a large fleet of ships and nearly half their available fighter aircraft. During the naval battle, American submarines and surface ships cut up the fleet, severely crippling the Japanese navy from then on. In desperation, the Japanese employed suicidal kamikaze attacks, and losses in the U.S. Seventh Fleet were also fairly steep.

V584.40–41, B681.27–28   check out the portrait of Michael Faraday in the Tate Gallery   Good luck! Museum director Norman Reid's 1967 catalog, *The Collections of the Tate Gallery*, lists no such portrait of British physicist Faraday (1791–1867). A red herring, apparently.

V585.17–18, B682.8–9   reprise of . . . "Bright Days for the Black Market"   See V495.26–36.

V586.17–18, B683.8   play morra   Also known as "mora." Of Italian origin, it's a game in which one player guesses the number of fingers another holds up, but obscures. Also, when applied to mules and horses, the Italian expression *giocare alla mora* (to play mora) means "to kick [somebody]."

V586.23, B683.14   or if it has happened   A Bantam error: "of if it has happened."

V586.40, B683.35   Last we saw of Fibel   See V454.39.

V587.17, B684.16   a Schnipsel   A shred or scrap.

V587.29, B684.32   the Illuminati   Closely tied to Masonic and Rosicrucian writings since the beginning of these movements in the late sixteenth and seventeenth centuries is the idea of an elect, secret group, the Illuminati, who are scholar-statesmen learned in the ancient mysteries and banded together in brotherly love. The term was given a certain millennial character in the writings of Masonic philosopher Francis Bacon, especially in his *Advancement of Learning* (1605) and *The New Atlantis*, published in 1627 shortly after Bacon's death. Frances Yates (125–29) has argued that the latter work, an allegory of the settlement of New England, is also a utopian representation of the Rosicrucian ideal, a state run by the Illuminati.

V587.32–33, B684.36   Bakunin, Proudhon, Salverio Friscia   In his 1840 tract "What Is Property?" Pierre Joseph Proudhon (1809–65) adopted the term "anarchy" to define his system of "mutualist" exchange, which would be devoid of interest rates and profits stemming from concepts of possession. Mikhail Bakunin (1814–76) was one of Karl Marx's bitterest opponents and, incidentally, a Mason during the 1840s. In the last decade of his life he promoted schemes for an "International Brotherhood" of anarchists divided into "National Families" and secretly controlled by an "International Family" opposed to all property ownership. Bakunin migrated to Italy in 1863, settling first in Florence and then (in 1865) in Naples, where three Italian anarchists became his devoted followers. Saverio Friscia (Pynchon has missspelled the first name) was one of them, and together with Alberto Tucci

and Giuseppi Fanelli he founded the International Brotherhood
in 1868.

V587.36, B684.41   Doctor Livingstone   Dr. David Livingstone (1813–
73) was the Scottish missionary who took his medical practice into
central Africa. He was instrumental to British exploration of the
region, and he *was* a Mason.

V587.40, B685.4   a Masonic high sign   The upraised left hand, palm
open and expanded: "a symbol of equity and fair-dealing, of which the
left hand, as slower than the right, and more void of skill and craft,
is therefore the appropriate emblem" (A. Pike 388). But *we* know better:
the left side is also the *sinister* side (see V137.20n).

**V588.1–2, B685.7–8   like Wernher von Braun, was born close to the
Spring Equinox**   See V237.1–2n.

V588.5, B685.11   Check out Ishmael Reed   The narrator pays homage to
Reed's 1972 novel, *Mumbo Jumbo*. In Reed's satire, Masonism par-
ticipates in a centuries-long effort to veil the real mysteries in racist, destructive visions. The original mysteries out of Egypt, his fiction
argues, had several revered black deities: Isis, Osiris, and others who are,
like Krishna, dark-skinned. Also, the real mysteries practice the magic
of the right hand, while, in Reed's satire, the evil "Atonists" (Knights
Templars and Masons, for example) practice the deceptive magic of the
left hand. Opposite p. 210 in the Avon paperback edition of *Mumbo
Jumbo* is a photograph worth noting: captionless, it nonetheless clearly
shows rocketmen Walter Dornberger and Wernher von Braun, his *right*
arm in a cast, shortly after the internment at Garmisch, in March 1945.

**V588.7–9, B685.13–16   Missouri Mason Harry Truman . . . this very
August 1945 . . . his control-finger poised right on Miss Enola Gay's
atomic clit**   On August 3, having just departed Europe from the
Potsdam Conference, Truman issued orders to send Col. Paul Tibbets
aloft on the night of August 5. Tibbets's plane, the *Enola Gay*, was
named for his mother. If Truman's finger is "poised," this must be during the period of August 3–5, and probably the fifth, because Truman
was capable of rescinding the mission down to the last hours. The
grotesque, anticipatory image of a "vapor-deposit of fat-cracklings"
(V588.11) from immolated Japanese will reappear in part 4 as a cloud circling the earth and "changing" the color spectra at sunset (V642.31–
41).

V588.27, B685.38   home to Beacon Hill   A residential district of Boston,
Massachusetts.

V588.40, B686.13   Belleau Wood   The forest near Château-Thierry,
France, where in 1918 the U.S. Marines stopped the German advance
on Paris. Bland is evidently a veteran of that battle.

V589.10, B686.26–27   State Street   Runs through the heart of Boston's
business and financial district.

254 In the Zone

V589.24–27, B687.2–5   the Pearys and Nansens . . . Sir John Franklin and Salomon Andrée   A short catalog of Arctic explorers. Franklin was one of the last mariners to believe in a Northwest Passage, and he died in 1845 while trying to locate it. In 1897 Swedish balloonist Salomon Andrée tried to navigate an airship over the Pole; a crash left the remains of Andrée and two assistants spread out over several miles of polar ice, to be discovered in 1930. Robert Edwin Peary (1856–1920) was the American naval officer who made it to the North Pole in 1909; Fridtjof Nansen (1861–1930) was a Norwegian arctic explorer.

V590.12–13, B687.38–39   having hugged to its holy center the wastes of dead species   The center of the earth as a (gravitational) "Holy Center." In the following paragraph of *GR* the idea becomes clearer: living beings "left on the outside of Earth," on its surface, blunder along; they are another instance of "Holy-Center-Approaching."

V590.28, B688.15–16   a power series   In mathematics, a function expressed as powers of a variable, multiplied by a coefficient. The formula for a Poisson distribution is a common example.

V591.3, B688.36   holding a red rose   With the cross, the red rose is a principal symbol of Rosicrucianism, and Lyle Bland's experiment with astral projection confirms that sense. The surrounding details ("before sunrise," and so on) all correspond with Albert Pike's interpretation (291) of the rose as a symbol "of *Dawn*, of the Resurrection of light and the renewal of life, and therefore the dawn of the first day, and more particularly the Resurrection; the cross and the rose together are therefore hieroglyphically to be read, the *Dawn of Eternal Life* which all nations have hoped for by the advent of a Redeemer." To achieve this eternal life is Bland's aspiration.

V591.10–11, B689.3–4   law firm of Salitieri, Poore, Nash, De Brutus, and Short   Outrageous pun on Thomas Hobbes's character- ization (*Leviathan*, pt. 1, chap. 13) of cultural desolation in times of civil disorder and war: "No arts; no letters; no society; and which is worst of all, continual feare and danger of violent death; and the life of Man, solitary, poore, nasty, brutish, and short."

V591.18, B689.13   Buddy left to see *The Bride of Frankenstein*   Univer- sal Pictures' big 1935 sequel to their hit of four years earlier. Boris Karloff played the monster, Elsa Lanchester was both "bride" and Mary Shelley. In any event Buddy Bland never sees the film; instead, we learn, he takes in *Dracula* (see V652.12n).

EPISODE 31

At around 10:15 P.M. on Sunday, August 5, 1945, in Cuxhaven, medical officers Muffage and Spontoon prepare to castrate Tyrone Slothrop surgically. At precisely this moment, in a different time zone near Japan, the *Enola Gay* is winging its way to Hiroshima, delivering the "Cosmic Bomb" anticipated in *GR* for some time. In this episode the circular dancing of the gathered preterite forms a symbolic counterpoint to the mushroom cloud that will form eight thousand miles to the east. The rosette pattern of the dancers also establishes a set of related allusions: to the Red Cross (or "rosy cross" of the Rosicrucians); to Maj. Duane Marvy's song, "San Antonio Rose"; and to Shirley, "the rose of no-man's land" (V601.15), in this episode. As for Slothrop, he beds down with Leni Pökler in a whorehouse located in Dorum, a village outside Cuxhaven. In a mix-up, Marvy dons the Plechazunga suit and suffers the sacrificial castration in Slothrop's stead.

V591.22, B689.19   Queen Anne salutes   Characteristic of the British Royal Guards, a snappy salute used by sentries.

V591.24, B689.20–21   deuce 'n' a halfs and civilian bobtail rigs   Slang terms for types of trucks: a two-and-a-half-ton model and a flatbed civilian truck.

V591.32, B689.32   junkie M.O.s   Drug-addicted medical officers.

V592.5, B690.6–7   stroking his full Imperial   A pointed beard grown only from the lower lip and chin.

V592.12, B690.16   Weltschmerz   World-weariness.

V592.21, B690.26   like James Mason   The voice of actor Mason (1909–1984) was a blend of Yorkshire dialect and transatlantic drawl.

V592.22–23, B690.29   Marston shelters   Half-cylindrical buildings also called "quonset huts." The picture of Britain's Operation Backfire headquarters at Cuxhaven, in Kooy and Uytenbogaart (268), clearly shows a row of these in the background.

V592.25–26, B690.32–33   the General Forces Programme features Sandy MacPherson at the Organ   Here, the "distant radio" playing in the background establishes the time of these events. BBC programming schedules in the *Times* of London list Mr. MacPherson on Sunday night, August 5, at 10:15 P.M., and at no other time during this month. See also V13.39–40n.

V592.32, B690.39–40   an American Bugs Bunny comic book   Like Porky Pig (V545.4–5n), Bugs was a regular fixture of *Walt Disney's Comics and Stories*, but he apparently had no book of his own before 1946.

V592.35, B691.1   M.I.6   The (British) Military Intelligence, in charge of overseas spying.

V592.36–37, B691.4   a Nayland Smith   See V277.34–38n.

V593.7–8, B691.17–18   "If they ever get one in working order"   "They" (the British) did. Three A4 rockets were launched from Cuxhaven in late September and October 1945 as part of Operation Backfire.

V593.15, B691.27   the same General Wivern   After Katje departed

Monte Carlo, Wivern took over Slothrop's rocket education (V237.27–29).

V594.7–8, B692.20–22   boys circle clockwise, girls anticlockwise . . . a rose-pattern   The choreography seems straight out of a Busby Berkeley musical. Moreover, it is richly symbolic. The "rose-pattern" is reinforced by the color of the dancers' faces: "ruddy" tending even toward an "apoplectic mauve" (V593.14–15). To a Jungian, their direction of movement is also noteworthy: the "boys" move in the direction of consciousness, rationality, and analysis; the "girls" move in the direction of unconscious mind and associative logic. Together, the movements give yet another image of opposites held in equipoise by a circular mandala. Also, General Wivern's erection and launch, stamen- and penis- and rocket-like, occurs at the center of this circle, as narratively glimpsed from above. This image suggests a target, or an atomic blast as seen from an airplane. August 5 came on the very eve of the atomic age; the morning blast over Hiroshima occurred on the Feast of the Transfiguration; and to a Rosicrucian, the rose is a symbol of such a transfigured being, from material to spiritual existence. Indeed, Lyle Bland just accomplished that transformation, rose in hand, at the end of the last episode.

V594.17, B692.32–33   the CBI theatre with . . . bhang   He's come back from the China-Burma-India theater of war operation, with a ton of Indian marijuana.

V594.20, B692.36   Runcible Spoon   Soules identifies their weapons: "Edward Lear coined *runcible spoon* in 1871. Sometime after that, the curved-like-a-spoon, single-cutting-edge pickle fork was either invented or rechristened."

V594.30, B693.5   "Greetings, gate, need an opiate?"   Here and following, an imitation of comedian Jerry Colonna (V552.4n).

V594.31, B693.7   Albert Krypton, corpsman striker   Derives his family name from the Greek for "hidden" and from the white, inert element that is number thirty-six of the periodic table. In U.S. Naval nomenclature, any enlisted man in training for one of the specific technical ratings, such as "radarman," is called a "corpsman striker."

V594.38, B693.15   the goat hole   Location of the ship's bilge pumps.

V595.14, B693.35   La Forza del Destino   "The Force of Destiny," an 1862 *opera seria* by Giuseppi Verdi. The plot: a story of illicit love (between young lovers named Alvaro and Leonora); the woman goes into seclusion, the man into a monastery, while her brother (Carlo) vows eternal revenge. In the last act Carlo has his chance for revenge when he finds Alvaro in the monastery, surrounded by hungry beggars. Lots of knifeplay, with speeches about *destino* mixed in, leaves everyone united in death.

V595.19, B693.42 **"I've OD'd"** Underworld acronym for an overdose of any potentially lethal drug.

V595.35–36, B694.18–19 **an old *News of the World*** See V215.29n.

V596.41, B695.27–28 **"Follow the yellow-brick road"** Krypton sings the lyric that the Munchkins teach Dorothy, as they send her Oz-ward in the film *The Wizard of Oz*.

V599.9–10, B698.8–9 **a Deanna Durbin hairdo** In the film *Mad about Music* (1938), she appears with her hair pulled tightly back from her forehead, parted on the left, its curls framing her face in guiches. Actress Durbin never changed that prim, cute, schoolgirlish look.

V601.1, B700.11 **snowdrops** See V247.8–9n.

V602.6, B701.20 **off the Dorum road** Their prearranged meeting place (see V527.3n).

V602.12–13, B701.28 **toward Helgoland** The tiny North Sea island off the Schleswig-Holstein coast, which the ancient Teutonics regarded as the home of dead souls.

V603.8, B702.31 **Solange** Plugging now into the triangle of Franz-Leni-Ilse Pökler, Slothrop beds down with Leni, under this assumed name.

V603.38, B703.26 **"San Antonio Rose"** Marvy's favorite song (V559.36–37n).

V603.39, B703.28 **reeling out the swinging doors** An interesting Bantam error: "realing out."

V603.40, B703.29 **the notorious Eisenkröte** An electrified "iron toad" in the urinal.

V604.39, B704.36 **"Call it a little lagniappe"** Louisiana creole (pronounced "lan-yáp"), from the Spanish *la ñapa*, meaning a gift or gratuity.

V605.1, B704.40 **"Boats"** Service slang designating a sailor.

V605.9, B705.6 **"It isn't the House of All Nations"** A legendary eighteenth- and nineteenth-century Paris brothel, catering exclusively to Europe's elite, operating in the Hôtel Chabanais Saint-Ponges.

V605.26, B705.27 **the Asturias** On October 1, 1936, two years before civil war erupted in Spain, the Socialist coal miners of the Asturias (mountains of Spain's northern coast) staged a revolt, quickly capturing each Civil Guard post in their separate valleys and cutting off all roadways. Their number has been put at sixty thousand. The government called in General Franco to suppress the miners, and he brought over his Moorish army troops stationed in Africa. The Moors took two weeks—of pillaging, rape, and random murder—to end the revolt. Estimates are that three thousand of the revolutionaries were dead by October 18, when an uneasy peace was declared. Two years later Franco was leading the Moors back into Spain as the civil war erupted in earnest (V234.7–8n).

V605.33, B705.35–36   the International Brigades   A collection of
leftist militia from various countries who joined the anti-Fascist Loyalist party during the Spanish civil war in an effort to defeat Franco.
American volunteers fought in the Lincoln Brigade.

V605.37–38, B705.40–42   *Ya salimos . . . otros frentes, ay, Manuela*   The
Spanish translates to "Now we've left Spain, to fight on other fronts,
yes, Manuela."

V607.1, B707.14–15   *puto* and *sinvergüenza*   Spanish slang for, respectively, a gigolo or "prick" (from *puta*, whore) and a rascal or scoundrel.

V608.40, B709.25   the small moon . . . at its zenith   The thinnest
sliver of a moon remained in the night sky of August 5–6, 1945. And
if the moon is this high up, the time would be early morning, perhaps 5
A.M. of August 6.

V609.6–7, B709.32–33   "We're catching the C-47 at one"   The American-made transport plane, known commercially as a Douglas DC-3;
the departure time for Muffage and Spontoon is presumably 1:00
P.M., August 6.

EPISODE 32

A prolepsis to some unspecified time *after* the botched castration of
Lieutenant Slothrop, part 3 closes with Tchitcherine arriving at the
Lüneberg Heath to find Gerhardt von Göll filming scenes for his movie
version of *Martín Fierro*. Then, in London, two lordly characters discuss
Pointsman's ignominy following the accidental castration of Marvy, which
has left Slothrop still on the loose.

V610.31, B711.24–25   copse of junipers   Another Bantam misprint:
"jumpers."

V610.32–33, B711.27   two men, one white, one black   Based on the
singing duel in *Martín Fierro* in cantos 29 and 30 of the "return"
half. This scene also duplicates the ajtys that Tchitcherine witnessed
ten years previously in Kirghizistan.

V611.13, B712.8   Since his illumination that night   With Major Marvy
and Clayton ("Bloody") Chiclitz, when the "large white finger" showed
Tchitcherine the existence of "A Rocket-cartel" (V566.14, 20).

V611.18, B712.14–15   Mravenko, one of the VIAM people   On VIAM
see V273.5n; Mravenko appears to be fictional.

V611.33, B712.32–33   "Molotov isn't telling Vishinsky"   Vyacheslav
Molotov was the Soviet foreign affairs commissar from 1939 to 1945.
Andrei Vishinsky was state prosecutor under Stalin and best known
as a ruthless leader of the great Soviet purges from 1934 to 1936.

V612.22, B713.26   estancieros   Ranchers.

V612.27–28, B713.32–33   Argentine legend . . . María Antonia Correa   Unknown.

V612.33, B713.39–40   M. F. Beal   Mary F. Beal (b. 1937) is a novelist (her first, *Amazon One*, appeared in 1973; a second, *Angel Dance*, in 1977) and a short story writer. She is married to novelist David Shetzline (mentioned earlier; see V389.23–24n). Here, the link to ideas of "mineral consciousness" calls to mind Beal's short story "Gold," included in Martha Foley's *Best American Short Stories of 1972.* The piece is a visionary allegory about mountain-dwelling ascetics who learn to create inwardly, and excrete, small nuggets of "calculi," or gold. Yet achieving this mystical power also brings with it premonitions of "the end"; that is, achieving the story's "mineral consciousness" is an allegory of death's final victory.

V613.30, B715.1–2   The boliche . . . the pulpería   Respectively, the tavern and the country store of the Argentine pampas, in Hernandez's epic poem.

V614.10, B715.26–27   Rin-Tin-Tin style   In 1918 Captain Lee Duncan of the U.S. Army found future canine star Rin Tin Tin (1916–32) cowering in an abandoned infantry trench. He brought the German shepherd to Hollywood, where the dog became a hero of silent films like *Rinty of the Desert* (1927) and serials like *Lone Defender.*

V614.12, B715.29   Hund-Stadt   "Dog City."

V614.18, B715.37   G-5   See V125.22n.

V615.15, B716.42   "in Portobello Road"   See V107.26n.

V615.27–28, B717.16   "if this show prangs"   Recalling Aaron Throwster's slang (V228.37n).

V615.28–29, B717.17–18   "Ginger Groupers jamming my switchboard"   Unknown.

V615.31–32, B717.21   "Bracken and Beaverbrook go *on*"   Sir Brendan Bracken was an influential member of Britain's Conservative party. He advised Churchill throughout the war, but Churchill and the Conservatives lost control of the government in the July 1945 parliamentary elections. William Aitken, Baron Beaverbrook, was another Conservative and a publishing magnate. After the election loss, Beaverbrook continued to argue in print for stiff dealings with the Soviets, whose ambitions, he felt, needed to be thwarted even at the expense of another war.

V616.4–5, B717.38   "ex Africa semper aliquid novi"   The Latin means "always something new out of Africa."

V616.31–32, B718.28–29   run . . . by no visible hands   Recalling Adam Smith's "invisible hand" running the laissez faire marketplace (V30.30n).

Part 4 *The*

Counterforce

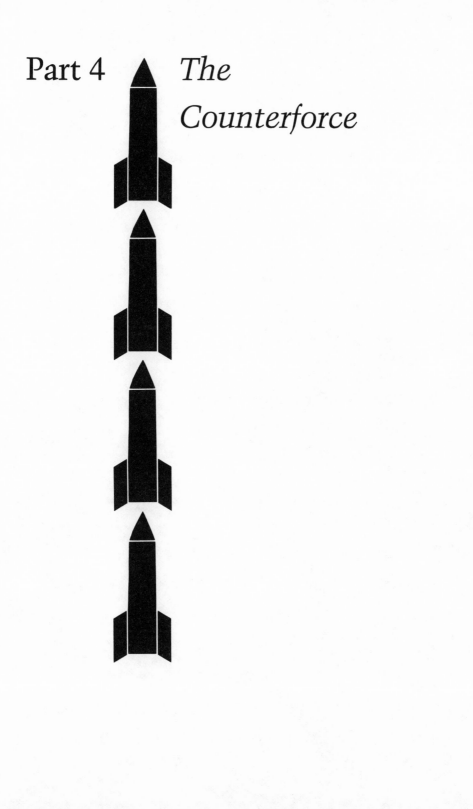

P ART 4, "The Counterforce," begins shortly after August 6, 1945, the Feast of the Transfiguration, though we also return to August 6 during an analepsis in episode 1, when Slothrop is shown miraculously recovering his long-lost mouth harp. This signals a transfiguration that inverts the Christian myth: here, Tyrone Slothrop becomes "The Fool" (V724.28–29), the eighth and last of his avatars in the novel. Stretched crosswise on the earth, he is Christ-like. With his ragged and ruddy appearance beneath the phallic sign of a "stout rainbow cock" (V626.17), he recalls Krishna, Vishnu's priapic avatar of fertility and dance. With his harp he is Orpheus, the dismembered Greek god. He embodies the acceptance of pain in Rilke's *Sonnets to Orpheus*, with their climactic expression of being and flux—"To the rushing water speak: I am." As "Fool," Slothrop is also the null or zero card of the Tarot deck, a card that shows a youth skipping near the edge of a precipice, oblivious to danger. And by part 4 of *GR*, Slothrop has completed the long descent of part 3 and fallen, the "fragments" (V742.25) of him scattering everywhere. For those in the burgeoning "Counterforce," who begin to organize around his memory, Slothrop and the rocket become central figures in a nascent polyglot mythology. And perhaps this is why part 4 consists of twelve episodes, for twelve is the number associated with discipleship. Appropriately, too, the dominant astrological sign of this part is Virgo, a common earth sign and symbolic of assimilation, the maneuvering of people into new and practical configurations. Twelve is also the number of the astrological signs, organized mandala-like around the astrological year.

In a minimal nod toward conventionally realistic narrative, part 4 brings most of the novel's other main characters to well-defined ends. Pointsman's career has become a mediocre disgrace, wrecked after his botched attempt at castrating Slothrop. Roger Mexico, Pirate Prentice, Katje Borgesius, Osbie Feel, and others form the loosely delineated Counterforce. With the war now safely past, Jessica Swanlake slides back into middle-class comfort with Jeremy. In episode 11, Geli Tripping wins Tchitcherine through a successful excercise in white magic. Enzian guides his Herero Schwarzkommando to Lüneberg Heath and the firing of Rocket 00001—a repetition, and a counterpart (as one to zero, autumn to spring, and black to white), of the quintuple zero fired months ago.

But the Herero rocket raising occurs in conjunction with another Christian feast day, September 14, the Exaltation (or Raising) of the Holy Cross. In episode 12, the last of seventy-three, this moment triggers an almost simultaneous prolepsis and analepsis. Out of its many and skewed narrative voices—Kabbalistic myth, comic book lingo, mock-etymologies, and history—part 4 finally represents Blicero's noontime sacrifice of Gottfried during the Easter/April Fool's weekend of 1945. But Weissmann/Blicero goes on after that, and the narrator advises us to look for him among the present-day heads of corporate America (V749.9–12). This validates the prolepsis to

Los Angeles and the Orpheus Theater, circa 1970. Its owner, a thinly disguised Richard M. Nixon, supplies the epigraph to part 4: a question, directed to no one in particular and perhaps most generally (and lamely) to the envisioned threat of nuclear winter—"What?"

This is how the published text of part 4 opens. Yet Clifford Mead, in a brief note, has commented that the galley sheets for *Gravity's Rainbow* did not have the Nixon epigraph but included instead the fourth verse of Joni Mitchell's 1968 song "Cactus Tree":

She has brought them to her senses,
They have laughed inside her laughter;
Now she rallies her defenses,
For she fears that one will ask her
For eternity
And she's so busy being free.

EPISODE I

Part 4 opens with Pirate Prentice flying southward toward the Harz Mountains of central Germany. The time is shortly after August 6, 1945. Slothrop plucks his recovered Hohner harmonica from where it has been soaking in a mountain stream. He begins to play. The narrative then moves back, by analepsis, to his recovery of that lost harp and his turning away from the quest for what Jamf and "the primal dream" (V623.31–32) of his infancy may mean. This occurred on August 6, "the day he became a crossroad" (V626.15–16) and a rainbow vision seemed to transform him forever. His transfiguration also alludes to the bombing of Hiroshima on August 6, and Slothrop will soon find a scrap of newsprint with a figure of that holocaust.

V619.1–4, B721.1–5   Bette Davis and Margaret Dumont . . . "Who Dat Man?" from *A Day at the Races*   The idea of dramatic heavy Bette Davis (b. 1908) appearing alongside comedy star Margaret Dumont (1889–1965) is the stuff of oneiric whimsy. So too with the backdrop of Slothrop's dream: François de Cuvilliés was the architect who, in 1734, designed the rococo pavilion for "Nymphenburg" (with lots of curlicues) outside Munich. In the film *A Day at the Races* (1937), Chico and Harpo Marx wander into the back lot of a horse track. They begin to sing and play. Soon all the black stableboys, grooms, and other menials (in fact, it is Hollywood's all-black Crinoline Choir) have joined in behind Harpo, who plays the pennywhistle, for a swing-time rendition of "Who Dat Man?" The lyric has mock-millennial overtones. To the question that recurs in the refrain—"Who dat man?"—the answer keeps coming back: "Ga-bri-el!" But Gabriel, ironically, is not God's trumpeter but Harpo, the foolish mute. In the film Margaret Dumont plays the wealthy Mrs. Upjohn, a hypochondriacal dowager. Groucho Marx plays Hugo Z. Hackenbush, the former horse doctor who—by a zany error—becomes her private physician. As the film ends, they all wind up at the racetrack again and everyone joins the Crinolines for one more chorus of "Who Dat Man?" As the narrator comments here, it is thus "a day at *the races*" in more ways than one.

V619.12, B721.15   P-47   A single-seat fighter aircraft, also called the "Thunderbolt" but affectionately known as the "Jug" because of its rotund shape. For its first year of service during the war, 1943 to 1944, P-47s had the "greenhouse canopy" (V619.16) Pynchon describes. After that, they appeared with a bubble canopy, giving pilots 360 degrees of visibility.

V619.23–25, B721.28–30   over Celle . . . Brunswick . . . an Immelmann over Magdeburg   Pirate flies an east-southeasterly course over towns situated just north of the Harz Mountains. In aeronautics, an Immelmann is a strategic maneuver, consisting of a roll combined with a loop, named for the German flying ace of World War I, Max Immelmann (d. 1916).

V619.33, B722.1   Tooting   Upper and Lower Tooting are, in Baedeker's description (*London* 196), two "uninspiring suburbs" outside London.

V619.36, B722.4   Kaiser Bill   That is, Kaiser Wilhelm II, German emperor from 1888 to 1918, when he abdicated and went into exile in the Dutch city of Utrecht. Hitler gave Wilhelm a full military funeral when he died in June 1941.

V620.25, B722.34–35   painted Kelly green   The U.S. Army's Eighth Air Force used grey on their "Thunderbolts." Pirate's plane has been repainted green, color of the Counterforce in part 4.

V621.11–13, B723.22–25   the Great Dying . . . northward march of black plague   The Black Death or plague of 1347–51 spread out of Turkestan (like Attila), then aboard ships to Mediterranean ports. Arriving in Sicily in 1347, it turned north: Spain and France were afflicted in 1348; northern Europe was devastated in 1349; and the plague moved on to England and Scandinavia in 1350–51. In its wake some one thousand villages and towns were virtually emptied.

V621.26, B723.39–40   Bakelite top . . . seal of Merck of Darmstadt   Bakelite is the trade name for a line of chemically and electrically inert plastics widely used for containers. D. Merck AG was a Swiss manufacturer of pharmaceuticals, now gone international. Its current seal: the letter "M" inside a shield.

V621.39, B724.14   smooth as a Jo block   The noun "joe" or "jo" is forties and fifties slang for a porcelain toilet; because he inhales copious quantities of cocaine, Bummer's nasal passages are as smooth as one.

V621.40, B724.15   the Liebknecht funeral   Karl Liebknecht was a
Socialist deputy in the Reichstag and an opponent of the Great War
from 1914 on. His resistance won him a prison sentence, together
with Rosa Luxemburg. From their cells they formed the Spartacus party,
in opposition to the majority Socialists. They were released in 1918
but imprisoned again on the fifteenth of January 1919, then supposedly
"shot while escaping." In fact, Liebknecht had been brutally beaten
before he was shot in the head at close range. His body was dumped off
a bridge into the Spree-Oder Canal in Berlin and not recovered until
the spring thaws. In 1922 a memorial was erected to his honor in
Luxembourg.

V622.3, B724.20–21   "why I listen to Spohr, Rossini, Spontini"   On
Gioacchino Rossini, see V440.4n. Louis Spohr (1784–1859) was a
German composer and violinist whose compositions were confined
mainly to violin pieces he wrote for himself. Known until Paganini's
heyday as Europe's best violinist, he passed most of his days as director
of the orchestra at the court theater of Kassel. Gasparo Luigi Pacifico
Spontini (1774–1851) was the son of a peasant and an Italian composer
whose early fame was built on comic operas performed in Rome,
then Paris. In 1814 Kaiser Frederick Wilhelm III of Prussia brought
him to Berlin, at an enormous salary. Thereafter he did little composing
and, rather like Rossini, lived his remaining decades in regal splendor.

V622.14, B724.34   the old Hohner   Focalized through Slothrop, the
narrative here recalls his miraculous recovery of the long-lost blues
harp, which fell down the toilet (in a vision) at Boston's Roseland
Ballroom in 1939. But why a Hohner? First, Slothrop's harmonica must
be a Hohner because the company holds a virtual lock on the market;
no one would think of challenging the company's happy worldwide
cartel. Hohner has offices and brand names scattered over the globe, but
Slothrop's Blues Harp, like any other, would have been manufactured
at the company's Black Forest factory in Trossingen, north of Zurich.
(Indeed, this must be the "harmonica factory" where Squalidozzi
and Gerhardt von Göll plan the filming of *Martín Fierro*, see V384.34n.)
In addition, Slothrop's Hohner is a sign of his identity with Orpheus,
the mythic harp player and dismembered holy Fool. The Hohner is thus
also a sign of Slothrop's preterition. In the coming pages the narration
describes how a harpist "bends" notes on the Hohner's reeds, describing
it as a transformation of pain: "you suck a clear note, on pitch, and
then bend it lower with the muscles of your face. Muscles of your face
have been laughing, tight with pain, often trying not to betray *any*
emotion, all your life" (V643.28–31). This kind of transformation might
well be taken as a synecdoche for the satire in *GR*. And so Slothrop's
harmonica must be a Hohner for yet another of the novel's etymological
puns: the German verb *höhnen* means "to deride or ridicule" (like

the character Minne Khlaetsch, of V683.23–684.24, we have to not hear
the umlaut); thus we have a *Höhner,* one who sneers or derides, a
figure in satire. The Hohner blues harp thus emerges as an instrument
of Slothrop's satirically transformed preterition. For such a "far-fallen"
character as he is (V569.33–34), the blues harp becomes an expression
of his being. Finally, the Hohner sound holes, numbered ten through
one, high through low, recall the significance of ten in Kabbalistic
myths and of the rocket with its countdown from ten. With its rainbow
of notes, the Hohner blues harp may thus be read as a narrative counterpart to the rocket.

**V622.17–21, B724.38–41   Like that Rilke prophesied, "And though
Earthliness forget . . . To the rushing water speak: I am"**   The narrator
quotes from the last of Rilke's *Sonnets to Orpheus* (pt. 1, no. 29).
Since details from it filter through the context of this episode, it will
help to have the entire lyric. Note also that while the copyright pages to
GR specify the Norton edition for translations of Rilke, here Pynchon
cribs his own version. Compare his three lines to the last three as translated by M. D. Herder Norton:

Silent friend of many distances,
feel how your breath is still increasing space.
Among the beams of the dark belfries let
yourself ring out. What feeds on you

will grow strong upon this nourishment.
Be conversant with transformation.
From what experience have you suffered most?
Is drinking bitter to you, turn to wine.

Be, in this immeasurable night,
magic power at your senses' crossroad,
be the meaning of their strange encounter.

And if the earthly has forgotten you,
say to the still earth: I flow.
To the rapid water speak: I am.

In several respects Pynchon's is the better and more interesting translation. His last line, with "rushing" in place of Herder Norton's "rapid,"
preserves the onomatopoeic sibilance of Rilke's *Zu dem raschen
Wasser sprich.* Pynchon's "And though Earthliness forget you" bends
the grammar of Rilke's *Und wenn dass Irdische vergass,* but preserves
the tightness of that line. And his translation of *der stillen Erde* as
"the still*ed* Earth" is striking: the participial adjective implies some
victimized subject, some paranoid striving to surmount others' efforts
to "perfect methods of immobility" (V572.20–21).

V622.30–31, B725.12–13   that dreamy tune Dick Powell sang   With his bright tenor voice, Dick Powell (1904–63) crooned "In the Shadows Let Me Come and Sing to You" to Ruby Keeler in *Footlight Parade* (1933).

V622.35, B725.18   Mangel-wurzels   A yellowish, rutabaga-shaped beet.

V624.1, B726.34   Werewolf stencils   The Werewolves were an underground group of Nazi resistance fighters who pledged to keep fighting after V-E Day. See also V640.23n.

V624.2–5, B726.35–39   WILLST DU V-2, DANN ARBEITE . . . WILLST DU V-4, DANN ARBEITE   The narrator translates the German in these supposed Werewolf slogans, but note also the (mindless, pointless?) puns: "Will you be, too? Then work!" and "Will you before? Then work." But before what?

V624.18, B727.12–13   Past Slothrops, say averaging one a day, ten thousand of them   Why not say so? If Slothrop is ten thousand days old on this August 6, 1945, and if we count backward, including the leap years, then Slothrop's birthday would fall on March 21, 1918. A coincidence? Perhaps, but if so he will have been born on "the great cusp," the "green equinox . . . dreaming fishes to young ram, watersleep to firewaking" (V236.36–37). There is remarkable symmetry in this. The young ram of Aries is, according to M. E. Jones, characterized by the assertion of individual being, the "I am." This would correspond with the great care Pynchon has taken over the Pisces/Aries cusp and explain why he also highlighted the birthdays of Wernher von Braun and Dr. Stanley Livingstone (see V588.1–2). Slothrop's being born on March 21, 1918, tallies with everything we know about him: his association with Jamf and Lyle Bland while an infant, his entering high school when Roosevelt was "starting out" as president (V373.39–40n), and his being at Harvard University in 1937. Slothrop would have been born as the Germans began their offensive in the Somme on March 21, 1918; and this narrative about his life opens with a parallel offensive, when the German Wehrmacht swept into the Ardennes forests during Advent 1944. Then there is, yet again, the numerological significance of ten: it's fitting that Slothrop should have counted down ten thousand days at this moment when he is transformed, when he says "I am."

If March 21, 1918, is indeed Slothrop's birthday (a wild surmise), then we may also cast his natal horoscope. We can use noon and the coordinates for Lennox, Massachusetts, as a basis for computing his sidereal time of birth. The results are also quite remarkable. The sun entered Aries at exactly 12:03 P.M., or noon, on March 21, 1918. This means that the *Medium coelum* or midheaven of Slothrop's chart would be a perfect zero degrees of Aries; the celestial equator would be directly overhead at birth, the sun's declination at zero. A striking pattern of balanced oppositions also occurs in the chart itself. Slothrop's sun is in Aries, his tenth house; while the moon counterbalances it in Libra, his fourth house. Similarly, Mercury in Pisces (his ninth) is neatly counterbalanced by Mars in Virgo (his third); Venus and Uranus in Aquarius (his eighth) are balanced by Neptune and Saturn in Leo (his second); and finally, Jupiter in Gemini (his twelfth) is balanced by Pluto in Sagittarius (his sixth). In sum, Slothrop's horoscope would demonstrate the motif of opposites held in equipoise that readers have noted in others of the novel's mandala images. Like the Fool, null card in the Tarot deck, Slothrop is astrologically zeroed out.

Or perhaps not. The one hitch in these naturalizing projections is that Slothrop's father, Broderick, laments having "a double Virgo" for a son (for further discussion, see V699.17n). The remark could easily refer to the presence of Mars in Virgo on Slothrop's natal chart. Or it could be that Slothrop *is* a Virgo (born between August 23 and September 22) and that chasing down these patterns sends one off on a fool's errand, another *poisson d'avril*. That uncertainty dogs the novel as a whole.

V624.20, B727.15   fifth-columnists   Originally the term applied to those residents of Madrid who sympathized with Generalissimo Francisco Franco during the Spanish civil war. Gen. Emilio Mora was leading four columns of troops against that city and hoping sympathizers inside would rise up as a "fifth column" in his aid. Ernest Hemingway defines the circumstances and the term in his Introduction to *The Fifth Column* (v–vi). In general use now, the phrase indicates any sympathizers, saboteurs, and secret supporters who assist enemies of a nation from within that nation's borders.

V624.31, B727.26–27   Frisch Fromm Frölich Frei   The Viking edition contains a misprint: "Frölich" should be "Fröhlich," as corrected in the Bantam. This Nazi motto might be translated "Fresh Faithful Frisky Free."

V625.3–4, B728.4–5   he becomes a cross himself, a crossroads   See V622.17–21n and lines 9–11 of Rilke's sonnet.

V625.5, B728.6–7   a common criminal . . . hanged at noon   This certainly recalls the noon execution of Jesus, flanked as he was by "common criminals." See also the discussion of "Rocket Noon" and "Evil Hour" at V500.40n and V374.39–375.2n.

V625.10, B728.13   gnädige Frau   "Merciful Mrs."

V625.17, B728.22   a mandrake root   This narrative digression stems from Jacob Grimm's discussion (1202–3) of the *Alraun,* or mandrake root:

> If a hereditary thief that has preserved his chastity gets hung, and drops water or seed from him, there grows up under the gallows

the broad-leaved yellow-flowered mandrake. If dug up, she groans and shrieks so dismally, that the digger would die thereof. He must therefore stop his ears with cotton or wax, and go before sunrise on a Friday, and take with him a black dog that has not a white hair on him, make three crosses over the mandrake, and dig round her till the roots hold by thin fibres only; these he must tie with a string to the dog's tail, hold up a piece of bread before him, and run away. The dog rushes after the bread, wrenches up the root, and falls dead, pierced by her agonizing wail. The root is then taken up . . . washed with red wine, wrapt in silk red and white, laid in a casket, bathed every Friday, and clothed in a new little white smock every new-moon. When questioned, she reveals future and secret things touching welfare and increase, makes rich, removes all enemies, brings blessings upon wedlock, and every piece of coin put to her overnight is found doubled in the morning, but she must not be over-loaded. When her owner dies, she goes to the youngest son, provided he puts a piece of bread and a coin in her father's coffin.

V625.18, B728.23   Heiligenschein   Saint's halo; also, a luminescence around the shadow of a person's head caused by light diffracting through vapor or dew.

V625.29, B728.36–37   Committee on Idiopathic Archetypes   Note this "CIA."

V625.38–39, B729.5   kif moirés   The kif is marijuana from the Maghreb region; a moiré involves the superimposition of one repetitive design on the same or a different pattern, which often results in a doubling effect where one image transforms, in the blink of an eye, into another—as, for example, in the work of M. C. Escher.

V626.2, B729.10   "Chapter 81 work"   Unknown argot.

EPISODE 2

The Counterforce begins to take shape. Roger Mexico learns that Jessica Swanlake has permanently deserted him for Jeremy, the "Beaver." Roger strikes back with a vulgar "commando raid" on one of "Their" board meetings. He urinates on their conference table. Also, more economic details treat the controls exercised on Slothrop when he was a child. Back at Pirate's Chelsea maisonette, Roger finds a host of other disaffected cast members joining him. The Counterforce now consists of Pirate and Katje, Roger, Stephen Dodson-Truck, Milton Gloaming, Osbie Feel, and Thomas Gwenhidwy.

V626.22, B729.35–36   a pre-Hitler Horch 870B   Horches were Germany's version of the SS Jaguar: powerful, relatively quiet, well-appointed touring cars. There is no mention in the literature of an 870 model. In fact, the Horch 800 line first appeared in 1933, and that is no longer "pre-Hitler."

V626.24, B729.38 Heidschnucken sheep From *Heide* (heath) and *Schnucken* (a little breed of sheep). These "little heath-sheep" are common only to the Lüneberg region of northern Germany.

V628.4, B731.28–29 8 May, just before the traditional Whitsun exodus Recall that part 2 ends with Pointsman and crew spending "Whitsun by the sea" (V269.26n). This traditional British holiday weekend fell on May 20 in 1945. On the significance of V-E Day, see V269.32n.

V628.23–24, B732.10–11 wide as a Fortress's wings Another reference to the B-17 "Flying Fortress" bomber (wingspan 104 feet).

V628.28, B732.16–17 her ATS brogans Jessica's high-top work shoes were issued for her assignment in the (women's) Auxilliary Territorial Services (V17.26n).

V628.36, B732.26 Woolworth's The department store chain (V114.19n).

V629.6–7, B732.41 *News of the World* London weekly news periodical.

V629.17, B733.13 ganged to In electrical terminology, the mating of two or more circuits to a common line, facilitating simultaneous control of them all.

V630.6–12, B734.9–16 Josef Schleim . . . to work for Imperial Chemicals Mr. Schleim (slime, mucous) is fictional, but the remainder of the detail here derives from Sasuly (95–108). Max Ilgner headed the industrial spy ring at IG Farben. His operating base was the Berlin office known as NW7, the largest section of which was innocently abbreviated VOWI, the Statistical Department of IG Farben. It was headed by a Dr. Reithinger, mentioned here in *GR*. His principal job was to gather financial and economic data on foreign countries, under cover of "scientific exchange," and to coordinate with the Army High Command (OKW) in disseminating that information. From the United States, data were funneled through the various IG subsidiaries: Chemnyco, General Aniline and Film (GAF), Ansco, and Winthrop Chemicals. From England, information came through Imperial Chemicals, the IG's main British contact.

V630.16, B734.20–21 Geheime Kommandosache Or "Secret Command-Matter," the same warning as appeared on earlier rocket documents (see V242.9–15n).

V630.23, B734.29 the Wehrwirtschaftstab The Wehrwirtschaftsabteilung, or Economic Warfare Staff.

V630.25, B734.31–32 Vermittlungsstelle W The Coordination Office. Sasuly (108) quotes from a 1935 memorandum outlining its strategic objectives: "To the field of work of the Vermittlungsstelle W belongs . . . the continuous collaboration with regard to armament and technical questions between the authorities of the Reich and the plants of the IG."

For the remainder of the details concerning this office, the source was Sasuly 106–10. Pynchon's representation of the *Sparte*, or "branch office" system, stems from the organizational outline from the Kilgore Committee Report on IG Farben submitted to the U.S. Senate and appended to Sasuly's book (esp. 274–75). An *Abteilung* is a staff or department.

V631.2, B735.10　some name like Mipolam　According to the *A-4 Fibel*, Pynchon's source, Mipolam was the name of a plastic sheeting used to protect rocket components.

V631.5–6, B735.13–14　"Ter Meer was a Draufgänger—he and Hörlein　The narrator here singles out two of the most notorious *Drauf gänger*, or go-getters, of IG Farben. Prior to World War I, Dr. Heinrich Hörlein headed the research laboratory of IG's Bayer (aspirin) subsidiary. He had the lab systematically testing *every* new coal-tar derivative and dye to determine if it had possible uses in medicine or industry. In 1909 the company obtained a patent on a brick-red dye that also turned out to have startling antibacterial properties: it was sulfanilamide. IG Farben hid the information. It was not until 1933 that an American IG subsidiary, Winthrop Chemicals, first marketed this sulfa-drug compound under the trade name of Prontosil. By this time, IG had a virtual lock on the sulfa-drug patents and stood to make a fortune on its worldwide monopoly over production and distribution. During World War II Fritz Ter Meer was, according to Sasuly (30–31), "one of the half-dozen most important men in the IG." He had knowledge of IG's development and use of Tabun gas in the death houses at Auschwitz. Questioned about the ethics of such "research," he answered that it stood to benefit IG Farben in the long run and, besides, "no harm had been done to these KZ [concentration camp] inmates, as they would have died anyway" (ibid. 125–26).

V631.10–11, B735.20　"rather thin chap with thick eyeglasses"　It was Weissmann/Blicero.

V631.25, B735.37–38　the Jaguar　Pointsman has withdrawn the use of his "vintage Jaguar" (V38.38n) from the PISCES motor pool, leaving it with the Morris, one of Britain's least expensive workingman's cars.

V631.29–31, B735.42–736.2　Nayland Smith campaign . . . Sax Rohmer's great Manichaean saga　See V277.34–38n. Pointsman's "visitation" on Whitsunday (episode 8, part 2) has blossomed into this "campaign."

V632.39, B737.20–21　Vereinigte Stahlwerke　United Steelworks, the Krupp firm.

V633.1, B737.24–25　"Miss Müller-Hochleben"　Punning on "Miller High Life," a postwar American brand of beer.

V633.40, B738.30　"the S.P.R."　Society for Psychical Research.

V634.22, B739.14 a Beardsley gown Such as British artist Aubrey Beardsley might have drawn for one of his imposing dames (see V71.27n).

V635.35, B740.37 what 3–sigma colors That is, colors with no norm, no similarity to each other (see V40.13–14n).

V635.37, B740.39 Atlantis See V269.9–10n.

V636.28–29, B741.34–36 Phi Beta Kappa keys . . . Dewey-for-President lapel pins An international catalog of badges of election. Phi Beta Kappa is an American honorary society, and the key its principal symbol. The Legion of Honour, Order of Lenin, Iron Cross, and Victoria Cross ("V.C.") are medals of valor awarded to soldiers by, respectively, the governments of France, Russia, Germany, and Britain, and only for consummate heroism. The Republican Thomas E. Dewey (1902–71) twice ran for the presidency of the United States: against Roosevelt in 1944 and against Truman (to whom he narrowly lost) in 1948. In 1944 his platform was raised on the promise that he would "get big government off the back of business."

V637.11, B742.21–22 Douglas Fairbanks scampering across that moon minaret The reference is to *Thief of Baghdad* (1924), a silent film in which Fairbanks (1883–1939) stars as a scimitar-wielding swashbuckler.

V637.13, B742.24 Roger dives under . . . to button his fly A misprint in the Bantam, which has Roger diving under the table "to unbutton his fly" (which is already unbuttoned).

V637.37–38, B743.11–12 *"Dick Whittington!"* . . . zooming down Kings Road A mercer, adventurer, and three-time lord mayor of London, Whittington (d. 1423) has a monument to his honor in Hampstead Heath, one of London's upper-crust neighborhoods. Kings Road runs southwest out of central London, nearly parallel to the Chelsea Embankment. It got its name in the seventeenth century when Charles II used it as his private route to Hampton Court and his mistress, Nell Gwynne.

V638.12, B743.29 "the Haig and Haig" Brand of Scotch whiskey.

V638.13, B743.31 "Chebychev's Theorem" In everyday life as in statistical investigations of a theoretical nature, it is important to know if the probability of an event—say, a bridge collapsing or a successful fissioning of nuclear material—will be nearer to zero or to one, respectively. Using large numbers as a model, the Russian mathematician P. L. Chebyshëv was able to create a formula for these types of calculations.

V638.33, B744.11 Jan Otyiyumbu The name means "firebrand" (Kolbe 57), appropriate for a spy or "liaison man" placed in London.

V638.37, B744.16 a Porky Pig tattoo Because the pig has been a totemic

sign of the preterite throughout *GR*. Also, because Porky last appeared
in a simile: Pirate looked like "Porky Pig holding out the anarchist's
ticking bomb" to Katje, during the "tour" of hell (V545.4–5n).

**V639.18–19, B744.42–43   Sabbatai Zvi's apostasy before the Sublime
Porte**   Amid the widespread messianism of seventeenth-century
Europe, Sabbatai Zvi (or Zevi) emerged as one of the most charismatic
and interesting figures. Despite his lowly origins (he was the son
of a Smyrna poulterer), Zvi became well schooled in Kabbalistic doctrine. During the mid-seventeenth century he began to gather around
himself a band of fanatical Jewish disciples who believed in him as
the messiah. Zvi preached that the Torah had been inscribed without
vowels and punctuation because of Adam's sin. As punishment, God arranged the letters into words treating only of earth and death. The
same letters, proclaimed Zvi, will be rearranged with the coming of
the true messiah, who will eliminate death altogether and thus interpret
a new Torah from the mortal chaos of the old. The new one, he
believed, would say nothing of death, uncleanness, and proscriptions
against animals such as swine. Like Jesus of Nazareth, Zvi was in
frequent danger. He was denounced by Jews and Muhammadans alike
as a false messiah and a heretic. Sources differ on the date, but it
appears that on September 14, 1666, Holy Cross Day, he was arrested
and brought before the Ottoman emperor, called the Sublime Porte
or "High Gate" (from the Turkish *Bab-i Ali*). The emperor, Mahomed
IV, demanded and got a complete renunciation out of Zvi, who became
a Muhammadan on the spot and descended into obscurity.

V639.39, B745.24–25   a rosewood crwth   A traditional Welsh instrument, stringed and fretless like a violin, and played with a bow.

EPISODE 3

A colonel from Kenosha gets a horrifying haircut. Above him is a light
bulb that has traveled widely throughout Europe, and also through previous episodes of *GR*. Outside his tent a harmonica player—evidently it's
Slothrop—plays a mortal blues. "The Story of Byron the Bulb" extends
Pynchon's paranoid conspiracies into the power and light industry. This
weird salmagundi concludes with Private First Class Pensiero (from the
Latin for deep, dark "thinking" and the Italian *pensiero*, "thought") poised
over the colonel's jugular with a pair of haircutting shears.

V640.23, B746.10   A certain lycanthropophobia or fear of Werewolves   A
Bantam error: the "or" is omitted. Recall that, as Greta Erdmann
said, Blicero in his last days "had grown on, into another animal . . .
a werewolf" (V486.3). There is also a historical precedent for the refer-

ence. In the last days of war and on into the summer of occupation, Allied troops clashed with so-called Werewolf Packs, German resistance fighters who refused to concede defeat. They had a song:

I am so savage, I am filled with rage—
Hoo, hoo, hoo!
Lily the werewolf is my name;
I bite, I eat, I am not tame—
Hoo, hoo, hoo!
My werewolf teeth bite the enemy,
And then he's gone, and then he's done—
Hoo, hoo, hoo!

An article in *Time* magazine for April 16, 1945 (40), describes the Werewolf threat and quotes this song. McGovern (159) also mentions the Werewolves' postwar activities.

V640.25–26, B746.12–14 Potato crops . . . all went to make alcohol for the rockets See V550.14–15n.

V640.30–31, B746.20 bright as dittany in July The *Dictamus albus*, also called "burning bush" or "fraxinella," is a summer-blooming plant with white flowers and leaves so aromatic that even their vapors may be ignited.

V640.33–35, B746.23–26 the divisional patch . . . all in black and olive-drab Pynchon's source was probably the *Life* magazine spread entitled "Shoulder Insignia," in the issue of August 6, 1945 (41–47). The patch for the Eighty-ninth Division, which fought in central Germany, could (to Pensiero's drug-addled vision) resemble a cluster of three rocket noses, "seen out of a dilating asshole."

V641.17, B747.8–9 Fourier-analyzed into their harmonics In the analysis of periodic wave forms, physicists use the Fourier series, developed in 1811 by the French mathematician Jean Baptiste Joseph Fourier (1768–1830). The series is a function involving the sines and cosines of multiples of a single variable, used to represent the values of that variable within the prescribed limits of the wave. The best example is a vibrating musical string, the length of which becomes variable when the player frets it to change the tone.

V641.20, B747.13–14 Howard ("Slow") Lerner Anticipating the title of Pynchon's 1984 collection of short stories, *Slow Learner*.

V641.30, B747.24 the "benny" habitué Eddie Pensiero is addicted to Benzedrine, a brand of amphetamine tablets known in the drug underworld as "bennies." Benzedrine is marketed by the Smith, Kline and French company, which appeared in part 3 (V518.31–32n).

V641.40, B747.37 *A Tree Grows in Brooklyn* This 1945 film was Elia Kazan's directorial debut. It won two Oscar awards, one for Peggy Ann Garner's portrayal of a sensitive girl growing up in the slums, another for James Dunn in a supporting role as her drunken father.

V642.32, B748.32–33   "something has exploded . . . in the East"   The atomic bombs used on Hiroshima (August 6) and Nagasaki (August 9). The island of Krakatoa was obliterated by volcanic eruption in 1883, and a cloud of ash and gases circled the earth for four years afterward. The A-blasts were thousands of times less powerful.

V643.1, B749.3   "I'm from Kenosha, Wisconsin"   So perhaps this colonel's "the Kenosha Kid" of episode 10, part 1.

V643.4, B749.7   "Graves Registration"   A division of the U.S. Army whose job it is to autopsy, identify, and ship home the bodies of the dead.

V643.11, B749.14   Atropos   In Greek myth, one of the three Fates. Clotho spins out the thread of destiny, Lachesis winds it onto spools, and Atropos cuts it. A figure, then, of death.

V643.24, B749.30   number 2 and 3 hole   Bass and mid-range notes on the harmonica.

V644.15, B750.28   dacoits   The robber bands of Burma, figures of terror in the stories of Arthur Sarsfield Ward (see V13.28n).

V644.25–26, B750.42   that A-sticker   Gasoline rationing, controlled through the Office of Price Administration, was imposed on the U.S. consumer beginning in the spring of 1942. The administrators devised a system of cards, later of stickers. An "A" sticker designated nonessential passenger use, "B" was for drivers who required an automobile for business, "T" for commercial transports, and so on. Throughout the war, "A" sticker allotments of gasoline averaged five gallons per week.

V646.8, B752.31   "I'm evading-room vino from Visconsin"   A pun: "I'm a waiting room wino from Wisconsin." This is why "the nurses run."

V646.12, B752.36   an ingenious Osmo-elektrische Schalterwerke   A *Schalterwerke* is a switch works, and Osmo-elektrische a trade-name designation of the German Siemens manufacturing cartel.

V646.14, B752.38   Beeman's licorice flavor   The American trade name of a laxative chewing gum.

V646.33, B753.18   the Schokoladestrasse   A fictional Zurich street (see V250.41n).

V646.38, B753.25   lieder   German for lyrical songs.

V647.5, B753.34   Osram light bulb   A European trade name, Osram light bulbs were available in England as well as on the Continent. Pynchon mentions others in the course of this digression: Tungsram (Hungary, Czechoslovakia, and Romania), Nitralampen and Azos (Germany and Austria), and Phillips (Canada).

V648.4, B754.40   this roach's abreaction   For a definition of this therapeutic term from psychoanalysis, see V48.14n.

V649.12–13, B756.17   Herbert Hoover, Stanley Baldwin   Respectively, the U.S. president from 1929 to 1933, and the British prime minister from 1923 to 1929 and 1935 to 1937, which would place these fantastical events in 1929.

V649.15, B756.20–21 "Phoebus," the international light-bulb cartel A fictional group named for the Greek sun god Apollo, nicknamed "Phoebus" (Radiant).

V649.27, B756.35–36 the statue of Wernher Siemens According to Baedeker (*Northern Germany* 184), this statue is located on Franklin Strasse in the Charlottenburg district of Berlin, in a park across the street from the Siemens factory. Siemens founded the company in 1847, discovered the dynamic principle of electricity in 1867, and invented the electric tramway in 1879.

V649.34, B757.2 prayers to Astarte and Lilith The Syrian goddess Astarte has been widely identified with Aphrodite and Venus, the Greek and Roman goddesses of love. In Hebrew mythology, Lilith was Adam's first wife. After her departure she became a demonic female spirit known for haunting children in forests and glades.

V650.38–39, B758.16 Committee on Incandescent Anomalies Yet another C I A.

V651.24, B759.6–7 young Hansel Geschwindig The German adjective *geschwindig* means "quick."

V652.12, B759.42–760.1 Buddy at the last minute decided to go see *Dracula* He started out to see *The Bride of Frankenstein* (V591.18).

V652.19–20, B760.10 a Reeperbahn *prostitute* The Reeperbahn is one of the principal thoroughfares in Hamburg's St. Pauli district, and famous for its thriving houses of prostitution.

V652.29, B760.22 he reaches Helgoland Again, the tiny island off the Schleswig-Holstein coast. Its name, "Holy Land," stems from the ancient Teutonic belief that it was a sacred home for dead souls. The *Hengst* (Stallion) and the *Monsch* (Monk) are two of the "rocks that have received fanciful names" on the island (Baedeker, *Northern Germany* 158).

V652.33–34, B760.27–28 a certain 1911 Hochheimer A fruity, mellow white wine from the Rheingau region of Germany, near Frankfurt; a high-quality wine, according to Lichine.

V653.6, B761.2 Mausmacher His moniker means "Mouse-maker."

V653.14, B761.12 "Die Fahne Hoch" "Banners Up," the Horst Wessel Song (see V443.2n).

V654.27, B762.35–36 the arrangement between General Electric and Krupp Pynchon's source is Sasuly (175): "In 1938 the Krupps made an agreement with the American General Electric Company concerning tungsten carbide. . . . In Germany tungsten carbide was produced in quantity and sold for prices ranging from $37.00 to $90.00 per pound. In the United States [it] was made in small quantities and sold at prices ranging from about two hundred dollars to four hundred dollars per pound." An antitrust action burst this bubble in 1940.

V654.38–39, B763.7–8 *Seele*, as the core of the earlier carbon filament was known in Germany In technical German *die Seele* (the soul) indicates the core of any object, for example, an electrical cable, the bore of a gun, or the filament of a light bulb.

EPISODE 4

K atje Borgesius meets with Enzian and discloses to him what she knows of Blicero's last days in Holland. Coming upon the Herero troops, she is startled to see them performing a dance in which she herself figures as the "Golden Bitch" (V658.21) of Blicero's sadoerotic fantasies. In short, she's already the stuff of legend and ritual. Blicero's continuation after the Easter launch of Rocket 00000 is disclosed to readers.

V656.34–35, B765.20   the Sprudelhof See V458.14n.

V656.36, B765.27   Pan The Greek god of woods and fields, half goat and half man. More significantly, however, Pan is the name applied to the "chief devil" during black magic rites.

V657.10–11, B765.34–35   Diamond Lil or Texas Guinan Guinan was the source of Pynchon's pun at V559.16–17. Born in 1884, she worked as a chorus girl, vaudeville trouper, and gun-girl heroine of numerous horse operas produced during the silent era of American cinema. With Prohibition, she opened a string of nightclubs (speakeasies), which brought rapid profits and fame. Prohibition agents were continually frustrated in their attempts to close down her businesses. One club, the Texas Guinan Club on West Forty-eighth Street in Manhattan, lasted for five tumultuous years, until a widely publicized 1929 raid forced its closure. By then, the term "Texas Guinan Clubs" applied to speakeasies in general. In 1930 she began touring with a troupe of forty dance girls; tried, and failed, to establish them in Paris; returned to the United States; and, during a tour of this continent, died unexpectedly of ulcerated colitis in 1933. Honora ("Diamond Lil") Ornstein (b. 1883) was a club dancer who achieved a certain notoriety in the early decades of this century. Her nickname derived from the diamond she had a dentist implant in one of her incisors and from the copious stones she wore about her person.

V657.17, B765.42   Even Goya, couldn't draw ya Francisco Goya (1746–1828) was, aside from his genius with paints, a master draftsman, and his drawings of the monstrous (as in his series "The Caprichios") are famous examples of the grotesque style. In short, *very* grotesque.

V657.22, B766.5 ENSA Acronym for the British Entertainers' National Service Association, a sponsor of shows and entertainments for servicemen stationed abroad.

V657.33–34, B766.18 an Isadora Duncan routine After the American dancer who died in 1927, at the age of forty-eight, when her long scarf caught on the axle of a sports car in which she was riding.

V658.26–27, B767.15 the great Kalahari rock painting of the White Woman All the Bantu-speaking peoples of the Kalahari region, the Hereros included, used to draw such petroglyphs. The "White Woman," however, remains a mystery. Pynchon's source may well be Parrinder (27), who includes an illustration and comments that "Bushmen were great engravers and painters on rock surfaces in red, black, yellow, white, and brown. The subjects are usually hunting, fighting or dancing. The practice of the art has almost completely died out, as there are only a few thousand Bushmen left and the survivors rarely know the meaning of the designs. This is clearly a hunting scene and the central figure is called the White Lady, though no more is known about it than the color."

V658.33, B767.23 leukemia of soul Physiologically, the disease involves an uncontrolled proliferation of the leucocytes, or *white* blood cells.

V660.26, B769.28 "All this I will give you, if you will but—" The completion of this biblical quotation is "fall down before me" (Luke 4:6–7): Satan's words to Jesus, when offering him the kingdoms of the world.

V661.27–28, B770.38 Pan's grove The meeting place of a witches' coven (see V656.36n).

V661.30, B770.41 the Qlippoth "Shells of the dead" in Kabbalistic lore (see V176.14–15n).

V661.39, B771.9–10 smooth as that Cary Grant See V13.34–35n, V240.41n.

V662.7, B771.19–20 this Suave Older Exotic Remember that Pirate Prentice was a commando with the SOE (Special Operations Executive).

V663.2–3, B772.16–17 "someone who was with Blicero in May. Just before the end" The timing is noteworthy. Blicero clearly goes his own way after launching Rocket 00000, before "the end" of hostilities on May 8, 1945. The mention is a key to Weissmann's fortunes after his Easter sacrifice of Gottfried, for Pynchon will soon disclose how we might look for him in positions of political and industrial power (see "Weissmann's Tarot," esp. V749.9–12). Weissmann's betrayal to the world, to mammon, may also be interpreted from an anagram given later (see V746.9n).

V663.6–7, B772.22–23 like mischievous Ophelia just having glimpsed the country of the mad A reference to Ophelia's madness and suicide in *Hamlet* (IV. vii).

EPISODE 5

The time of this episode is indistinct, as is its exact location in the occupied zone of Germany. The narrator opens with a haughty "You will want cause and effect. All right." Then he proceeds to clarify the rescue of Miklos Thanatz from the Baltic Sea, after he was swept overboard in the storm that tossed Slothrop from the *Anubis* in part 3. After Thanatz spent weeks wandering among Europe's preterite, the Schwarzkommando plucked him from a camp of homosexual displaced persons. To them Thanatz relates the story of Rocket 00000, fired from the Lüneberg Heath at noon.

V663.27, B773.8   He's a digital companion   A points-man?

**V663.37–664.1, B773.20–22   Benjamin Franklin was also a Mason
... practical jokesterism**   According to Van Doren (132), Franklin's biographer, the earliest known Masonic Lodge in America was St. Johns's in Philadelphia, and its records date back to 1730. Franklin (1706–90) joined in February 1731, drafted its by-laws, and eventually became grand master of the province of Philadelphia. He helped build the first Masonic temple in the United States (1755). Franklin was an accomplished literary satirist, and indeed given to practical joking. Van Doren tells (419) how he once hoaxed some French lords by promising to still some breeze-rippled waters. He walked around the pond and waved his cane three times over the water while mumbling some jibberish; within minutes all were amazed at its glassy surface. Franklin had released oil from a hollowed core in the cane.

V664.4–5, B773.25–26   a sinuous curve with first derivatives at every point   These are simple curves (or lifelines), Fourier analysis of which will yield a concise mathematical description of their shape and thus of each theoretical point on them (see V641.17n).

V664.13, B773.37   lammergeiers cruising there   Large predatory birds of Europe, the *Gypaetus barbatus*, called "lammergeiers" because they are said to swoop down on lost lambs, as upon these lightning-struck souls.

V664.19, B774.2–3   *Carmen Miranda* hats   Especially when she starred opposite Don Ameche in *Down Argentine Way* (1940), or in *That Night in Rio* (1941), actress Carmen Miranda's signature was her variety of extravagant high headgear, adorned with feathers and fruit.

V664.22, B774.5   Wilhelmets   Pynchon's portmanteau word for the spike-top parade helmets that Kaiser Wilhelm II (1849–1941) and his German soldiers wore in World War I.

V664.38, B774.25   monthly magazine *A Nickel Saved*   The allusion is to Benjamin Franklin's maxim: "A penny saved is two pence clear; a pin a day's a groat a year" (from *Necessary Hints to Those That*

Would Be Rich, 1736). But Franklin's was itself an inflated version of a still older, less greedy version: "A penny saved's a penny got" (anonymous).

V664.41–665.1, B774.28–30 Mark Hanna's: "You have been in politics long enough . . . owes the public anything" Mark Hanna—Cleveland capitalist, nickel magnate, campaign manager for William McKinley in the 1896 presidential race, and then McKinley's appointee to a vacant Ohio Senate seat—wrote this advice to a young Ohio prosecuting attorney. The date was May 8 (Pynchon's birthday, V-E Day) in 1890; the occasion, the attorney's trust-busting suit against Standard Oil of Ohio (Josephson 353).

V665.8, B774.38–39 got married Easter Sunday In 1945, April Fool's.

V665.15, B775.5 Hank Faffner Named for Fafnir, the monster guarding the hoard of Nibelung gold in Teutonic myth. Siegfried slays him, and Fafnir prophesies while dying (Grimm 370–71).

V665.34, B775.29 They are 175s On this numerical designation in the German Penal Code, and its application to homosexual inmates, see V289.29n.

V666.2–4, B775.40–776.1 Schutzhäftlingsführer to . . . Läufer In order of their appearance, these German nouns designate the Nazi warden and block leader at a concentration camp, then (among the inmates themselves) the camp head, block elder, trusty, foreman, house servant, and runner.

V667.3–4, B777.9–10 noon on the Heath when 00000 was fired This fixes the time of launch: "Rocket Noon," the "Evil Hour" (see V374.39–375.2n and V500.40n), the hour Christ was crucified.

V667.38, B778.7 Too bad, les jeux sont faits Once again the roulette croupier's call: "The bets are down."

V668.6, B778.18 the gassen Alleys.

V669.5, B779.20 anti-Lublin Persons opposed to the Russian-backed Polish Committee of National Liberation based in Lublin (V34.28–30n).

V669.23, B780.3 Soldbuch A German soldier's paybook.

V670.15–16, B781.2 black eyeball reflecting a windmill Various references—to London's Windmill Club (V39.1–2n) and the Dutch windmill called "The Angel" where Pirate makes his rendezvous with Katje (V106.12n)—now culminate in this visionary moment when Thanatz, who has been referred to as "Angel Thanatz," recalls the reflection of a nonexistent windmill in Blicero's eyes as Rocket 00000 was readied for launch.

V670.20–21, B781.8 snarling purple around a yellow Significant colors in *GR*. Yellow and purple are color opposites that appear in the first stage of the Brocken specter (see V293.17n). Earlier, the narrator

also identifies the colors with Weissmann's half-brother, Enzian,
the same name Weissmann gives to Gottfried during the Holland-based
rocket launchings, and the name of Rilke's purple-and-yellow flower
in the *Duino Elegies* (see V101.23–26). Then there is Margherita
Erdmann, whose sign is the "purple-and-yellow iris at her breast"
(V393.26).

V670.34, B781.25–26   Wandervogel-limp   For the pre-Hitler youth
movement in Germany, see V99.2n.

V672.8–9, B783.7   Hamburg to Bydgoszcz in a purloined P-51 Mustang
Bydgoszcz is a city in central Poland, eastward from Hamburg; the
"Mustang" was an American-made single-seat fighter aircraft.

V672.26, B783.28–29   Zeros bearing comrades away   The Japanese
Mitsubishi A6M8 fighter airplane (see V690.37–38n).

V673.37–38, B785.10–11   iya, 'kurandye   The source was Kolbe (203).
he gives *indyo 'kurandye* as "Come, my fellow." Pynchon appears
to have taken *iya* as a variant of *indyo* (to go, or to come).

V673.38–39, B785.11–12   the two palms do slide and brush, do touch
Here is that "miracle touch" which has appeared earlier (see V119.37n)
and which will recur at novel's end.

EPISODE 6

In this episode the narration begins to fragment. A variety of discourses,
modes, and forms are parodied in the twelve subsections, eleven of them
titled. Two ("On the Phrase 'Ass Backwards'" and "Shit 'n' Shinola") may be
read as parodies of the etymological/philological writing in Grimm's *Teutonic Mythology*, one of Pynchon's principal sources. Other subsections
parody comic books (the opening section treating the "Floundering Four"
and that treating "The Komical Kamikazes"), scientific writing ("Some
Characteristics of Imipolex G"), travel handbooks ("Streets"), poetic forms
(such as haiku and Miltonic verse), and letters ("Mom Slothrop's Letter to
Ambassador Kennedy"). In the midst of it all, Slothrop finds a scrap of newspaper announcing the atomic blast at Hiroshima. The time is therefore mid-
August, the action mainly occurring in northern Germany and Berlin, at
Säure Bummer's flat on the (fictional) Jakobistrasse.

V674.19–20, B785.38   the Radiant Hour   Phoebus (Radiant) was a
Greek kenning for the god Apollo. From prior references to the "Evil
Hour" and "Rocket Noon," "the Radiant Hour" is probably high noon
(see V374.39–375.2n).

**V675.10–11, B786.33–35   Club Oogabooga where Beacon Street . . .
with Roxbury winos**   The club, with the racist inferences of its name,

is a fictional Boston wateringhole. Running southwest out of central
Boston, Beacon Street skirts the Charles River and passes through
the upper-crust community of Brookline (former home of the Kennedys),
just southeast of which is Roxbury, founded by William Pynchon
and constituting the city's black ghetto at the time referred to here.

V675.15, B786.40 Stephen Foster music Perhaps "Old Black Joe"
or "My Old Kentucky Home," two songs by composer Stephen Collins
Foster (1826–64) that might fit the context.

V675.18, B787.1–2 the great conjurer Robert-Houdin He was the
renowned French magician of the nineteenth century, in whose honor
Erich Weiss (1874–1926) changed *his* name to Harry Houdini.

V675.23, B787.7–8 hi-de-hoing in . . . one finger jivin' in the air The
image refers to zoot-suited Cab Calloway in the film *Stormy Weather*
(1943). He dances and sings "Minnie the Moocher," with its refrain,
"hi-de-hi-de-hi-de-hay! hi-de-hi-de-hi-de-ho!"

V675.32, B787.18–19 the Floundering Four Patterned on Marvel
Comics' highly successful book series *The Fantastic Four*, first issued
in 1961, they are space-age types who ride a rocket into a belt of "cosmic radiation" and return to Earth transformed into superbeings.
Sue Storm becomes "the Invisible Girl"; her brother, Jimmy, becomes
"the Human Torch," capable of blazing up unannounced (with no
harm to himself); Ben Grimm becomes a super-strong "Thing,"
who looks like a cross between the Elephant Man and a stone fence;
and Reed Richards becomes "Mr. Fantastic," capable of stretching
and contorting himself much like Plasticman. Pynchon's Floundering
Four also owe a debt to *The Wizard of Oz*. Like Dorothy's three
traveling companions, Slothrop's also *lack* some essential quality:
Maximilian (like the Cowardly Lion) lacks bravery; Marcel (like the
Straw Man) lacks a "touch of humanity" (V675.37) in his brain; and
Myrtle (like the Tin Woodsman) lacks heart, the "miracle"(V675.41) of
love.

V675.34–35, B787.22 little Johann Allgeier The chess master and
designer of board pieces (V550.34n).

V676.4, B787.34–35 Mary Marvel and Wonder Woman In the early
forties the Fawcett Comics group added a new wrinkle to their highly
successful *Captain Marvel* series. The captain was known in everyday
life as Billy Batson, and in 1943 the Fawcett writers introduced Billy's
long-lost twin sister, Mary, who reasons that if brother Billy has magic
powers then so must she. Mary says the magic word—"Shazam!"—
and becomes Mary Marvel, in a red dress with a golden thunderbolt emblazoned across her ample chest. *Wonder Woman* was a comic book
created by "Charles Moulton," the pseudonym of psychology professor
William Moulton Marston. His superwoman was raised under the

aegis of Aphrodite (Venus) on Paradise Island. She made her debut in a December 1941 issue of *Sensation Comics*, released through the Superman-D.C. Publications group. Her costume: a red strapless longline bra, golden headband, red culottes emblazoned with stars, and red boots. Her major weapon is a magic lasso worn girdlelike. When captured in it, feckless (male) criminals become immediately helpless.

V677.1–2, B788.41–42 Those whom the old Puritan sermons denounced as "the glozing neuters of the world" As David Seed has pointed out ("Thomas Hooker"), this is another quotation from Hooker's collection of sermons, *The Soules Implantation* (1637). To "gloze," according to the OED, is to veil a true meaning with specious comments. In Hooker (238) there is an added dimension: between the "open enemies to Christ" and those who are merely "fawning hypocrites" lies a middle ground, where "all glozing Neuters of the world" defer any commitment. They are, he goes on (246), like "lukewarm water" that "goes against the stomacke, and the Lord abhors such lukewarme tame fooles." Hooker censures them, but in this passage (as Seed aptly notes) Pynchon pleads for the humanity of their uncertainty before conflicting and incomplete evidence. "When's the last time you felt *intensely lukewarm?* eh?" the narrator asks, concluding that "Glozing neuters are just as human as heroes and villains" (V677.5–7).

V677.26–27, B789.27 "time for that *Pause that Refreshes!*" As in, "A happy occasion is an occasion for a Coke, and the happy American custom, *the pause that refreshes!*" (1945 Coca-Cola advertisement).

V677.34, B789.36 Kelvinator Registered trademark of the Kelvinator Appliance Company of Grand Rapids, Michigan.

V677.36–37, B789.39 "like Mawxies, 'n' big Baby Rooths" Once again, Slothrop's favorite soft drink, Moxie; and Baby Ruth brand candy bars.

V678.14–15, B790.18 in *love* with Chiquita Banana The registered trademark of Chiquita Brands, Inc., a subsidiary of the United Fruit Company (see V678.26n). In the company's ads, she appeared as a leggy, south-of-the-border banana-girl.

V678.21–22, B790.26–27 the Spike Jones record of "Right in the Führer's Face" Actually, the song was titled "Der Führer's Face." Oliver Wallace wrote it for a Walt Disney cartoon, "In Nutzy Land," featuring Donald Duck. However, when Spike Jones and his City Slickers made the song an overnight hit in 1942, Disney changed the name of his cartoon to that of the song. Spike Jones did the vocal, and Willie Spicer played a honking-farting instrument called the Birdophone. Here is the lyric, with the honks:

Ven der Fuehrer says ve ist da Master Race,
Ve Heil! (honk), Heil! (honk) right in der Fuehrer's face.

Not to love der Fuehrer iss a great dis-grace!
So ve Heil! (honk), Heil! (honk) right in der Fuehrer's face.

Ven Herr Goebbels says ve own der World of space,
Ve Heil! (honk), Heil! (honk) right in Herr Goebbels' face.

Are ve not der Super-men, Aryan pure Super-men?
Jah ve iss der Super-men, Super-duper super-men!
Iss dis not zee land zo good?
Jah dis Nazi land iss good! Ve vould leave it if ve could!

Ve bring der world to order, heil Hitler's world to order (honk)!
Every one of foreign race will love der Fuehrer's face,
Ven ve bring der world dis-order (honk)!

V678.26, B790.32–33 United Fruit's radio commercials That is,
for Chiquita Bananas. United Fruit, the IG Farben of Central America
and the Caribbean basin, was formed in 1899 when Boston capitalist
Minor C. Keith unified two rival banana-importing firms. By 1940
the company not only handled almost 70 percent of the fruit and sugar
business from the region; it also controlled lucrative mail contracts
with the United States and other governments; several thousand miles
of railway; telephone, telegraph, and electrification contracts for
most of the region; a small navy, known as "The Great White Fleet";
and political influence that made it possible for UFC to remove and install governments almost at will. United Fruit lived by exploiting
cheap labor in Cuba, Jamaica, Nicaraugua, Panama, Santo Domingo,
Guatemala, and Mexico. Throughout the thirties and forties this
cartel's repressive wage practices fueled labor unrest in Central America.

V680.12–13, B792.33 a pack of Armies Service slang for packs of
generic, army-issue cigarettes.

V680.18, B792.40 station Metatron ... stall Malkuth On the angel
Metatron, in Kabbalistic lore, see V231.24–25n. Malkuth is probably
Malkoth, or Malakoth, the female genitalia as represented on the
Kabbalist Tree of Life (see V747.41–748.5n).

V681.20–21, B794.10 message ... back at the green edge of Aries The
"green" cusp of Aries would be at its end, around April 20–23, as
Aries moves further into springtime and Taurus. In part 2 Slothrop
takes the message from Squalidozzi, exchanges it, and returns to
Zurich, where he fails to relocate the Argentine anarchist. The timing
inferred here, April 20–23, jibes very well with chronological details
from episode 7, which discloses that Slothrop's escape from Monaco occurred during the week of April 20–27, 1945.

V681.23–24, B794.14 Rohr ... just out of the Ravensbrück camp
Located sixty miles north of Berlin, the Ravensbrück concentration
camp was built, in 1939, for the internment of women. By 1945 more

than 92,000 of its 132,000 prisoners had been cruelly executed. Victims included mainly Jewish, Gypsy, and Communist women and their children, but later in the war a number of male religious prisoners, including Catholic priests and Jehovah's Witnesses, were also shipped to Ravensbrück.

V681.26, B794.17   the local G-5   Political-administrative wing of the occupying U.S. Army (see V125.22n).

V681.30, B794.21–22   a War Crimes Tribunal . . . in Nürnberg   On August 8, 1945, British and Soviet delegates agreed on Nuremberg as a site for the War Crimes Tribunal. Trials didn't begin until November 20.

V681.32, B794.24–25   antisocial and mindless pleasures   Echoing the original title for *Gravity's Rainbow*.

V681.34–36, B794.27–30   28,000 meters (the distance . . . in Griefswald, where Slothrop . . . newspaper photo)   The distance is equal to 17.2 miles, and it roughly tallies with the scaled distances on David Irving's maps of the Peenemünde area (6, 96). Slothrop's discovery of the news photograph showing Hiroshima will occur at V693.39–41.

V682.8–9, B795.2–3   Nalline into ssshhhghhh . . . *What* was that word?   The word was doubtless *Shekhinah*, the black symbol of maternal punishment and death in Hebrew and Kabbalistic mythology. Wearing the black Imipolex G suit, Greta Erdmann "progresses into" (V682.7) the same archetype in part 3 (see V478.14–17n). On the moniker "Nalline" see V18.8–38n.

V682.10, B795.5   AMBASSADOR KENNEDY   Joseph P. Kennedy (1888–1969) was the U.S. ambassador to the Court of St. James from December 1937 until November 1940, when he stepped down to "keep America out of war." A great friend of British prime minister Neville Chamberlain, Kennedy was "Jolly Joe" to Londoners, who remembered him for calling (then) Princess Elizabeth "a cute trick" (Whalen 263). The ambassadorship came after his great successes as a financier, most notably his 1930 consolidation of Radio Keith Orpheum, the parent company of RKO Pictures. (Three years later the studio produced *King Kong*.)

V682.11, B795.6   Listen: Jew-zeppy   That is, Joseph. Yet Pynchon has put a sharp edge of irony on Mom Nalline's salutation, for Joe Kennedy was dogged by charges of anti-Semitism, as Whalen (387–90) points out. In a 1944 interview with two journalists, Lawrence Spivak and Joe Dinneen, Kennedy tried to respond to these long-standing charges and succeeded only in revealing the ambivalence and prejudice of his time. He said (ibid. 388): "It is true that I have a low opinion of some Jews in public office and in private life. That does not mean that I hate all Jews; that I believe they should be wiped off the face of the earth; or that I favor pogroms or persecutions. I don't. It was inevitable that I should find myself in conflict at times with Jews. I do, and have done, business with them."

V682.14–15, B795.10–11   what you said when . . . the PT boat   The story of John F. Kennedy's heroism in the South Pacific, from August 1 to 13, 1943, is widely known and available. Its most popular retelling was in Robert J. Donovan's *PT-109* (1962). Joseph Kennedy's remarks were widely quoted in news accounts of the time. The navy did not clear the story of Jack Kennedy's deeds until August 19, 1943, and a *New York Times* story from that day records what he said: "Former Ambassador and Mrs. Kennedy shouted in joy when informed of the exploit of their son. Mrs. Kennedy, first to hear the news by telephone at their summer home, expressed 'deep sorrow' for the two crewmen who lost their lives. 'That's wonderful,' Mrs. Kennedy said when told her son was safe. The former Ambassador then exclaimed: 'Phew. I think Mrs. Kennedy has said enough for both of us!'" In the fictional context, here, the most notable things about these remarks are their singular blandness and Joseph Kennedy's deference to his wife.

V682.20–21, B795.16–18   your wonderful speech at the GE plant over in Pittsfield the other week   Given the time of Pynchon's narrative *histoire*, this is slightly anachronistic. During the second and third weeks of September 1945, Joseph Kennedy, Sr., barnstormed the manufacturing towns of Massachusetts on a speaking tour. The GE Plant in Pittsfield, in Berkshire County, was one of his stops. The trip was his attempt to reenter public life after his 1940 break with Franklin D. Roosevelt over whether America should join the war against Nazism, and after two family tragedies (the deaths in action of Joe Junior and a son-in-law) and the much-publicized injuries to son Jack. In addition, the tour marked his return to Boston after living for some time in New York. *Time*, in a September 24, 1945, story (17), reported on the trip:

> In a midnight blue Chrysler, he rode like a Paul Revere through the textile, shoe, and machinery-producing towns in Middlesex, Essex, and Berkshire counties. All the way from Greenfield to Salem, in some 30 speeches within ten days, he spread the alarm: "I'm willing to come back [to Massachusetts] to live because this is where my heart is. But I don't expect to come back to stay until I think there has been change for the better. For the past 25 years Massachusetts has consistently been losing business—in that time 2,300 industries have left the state. . . . We haven't done a blessed thing to find out why they are leaving or to keep them here. During the next five years Massachusetts will have its last chance to keep itself out of the grave.

Kennedy thus argued for governmental intervention in the form of tax incentives, stricter labor laws, and the like. Whalen also reports on the trip in his biographical study (390–91).

V682.24, B795.21 the WLB Acronym for the War Labor Board, established in January 1942 to mediate labor-management disputes when they threatened production goals during the war.

V683.22, B796.30–31 a second-story man Also known in underworld argot as a cat burglar, because the perpetrator breaks into the upper stories while the occupants of a house are asleep.

V683.23, B796.32 Minne Khlaetsch From the Middle High German *Minne* (love) and the modern German *Klaetsch* (slap).

V683.26, B796.36 Hieropon Imaginary drug of the sacred (see V152.17n).

V683.28, B796.39 chess Läufer A bishop. But note that Minne cannot hear the German umlaut, so it would be *Laufer*, one who is "passed by," from the verb *laufen* (to pass).

V683.38, B797.10 "Hubschrauber!" As the German for "helicopter," the noun *Hubschrauber* does not enter the German lexicon until the later forties. As a compound, its etymology (here) is from the masculine noun, *Hub*, for the "lift" of a piston or valve, and from *schrauben*, the verb "to screw."

V684.4, B797.18 "Deutschland, Deutschland Über Alles" The harmonica player in this scene struggles to play the first bars of the German national anthem: "Germany, Germany above all, above all in the world!"

V684.15, B797.31–32 "Spörri" of Horst Achtfaden's confession See V455.35n.

V684.31–35, B798.9–13 William Bendix . . . Cagney . . . Sam Jaffe Before playing the lead in his television sit-com, "Life of Riley," William Bendix starred in *The Hairy Ape* (1944) and *A Bell for Adano* (1945), films that established his reputation as a character actor. In the film *City for Conquest* (1940), Arthur Kennedy made his screen debut as the younger brother of a prizefighter (James Cagney) blinded in a bout that was to have earned him enough money to support "little Danny" (Kennedy) in his music lessons. In *Gunga Din* (1939), the film based on Kipling's poem, actor Sam Jaffe played Din to Cary Grant's role as Cutter. Bodine thus specializes in the roles of "second sheep," those actors who wear "a white-hat in the navy of life" (that is, they are *not* officers).

V684.39, B798.18–19 some hypothetical Joachim Joseph Joachim (1831–1907) was Germany's most celebrated violin virtuoso of the nineteenth century. A prodigy who first performed at the age of seven, Joachim was a student of Mendelssohn and Schumann and was known principally as a quartet and solo player.

V684.40, B798.19–20   the long-suppressed Rossini violin concerto (op. posth.)   This is a Pynchon red herring. After his early retirement, Rossini did continue to score various types of musical works, many of them performed only for his friends. For almost a century these private pieces were generally unknown. In 1950 the Rossini Foundation began the task of editing them. Some scores were evidently unavailable, because lost, and the foundation knows of them only at second hand. Nevertheless, among all these later scores (the so-called *Péchés de viellesse*, or "Sins of age"), whether extant or known to be missing, there exists no violin concerto.

V685.21–22, B799.5–6   "My Prelude to a Kiss," "Tenement Symphony"   Unknown or fictional songs.

V685.29, B799.14   a "box"   Here, self-conscious slang for a guitar.

V685.36, B799.21   La Gazza Ladra   Rossini's opera, "The Thieving Magpie" (see V440.4n).

V685.38, B799.23   *opening of the Beethoven 5th*   The well-known "Victory" motif that begins Beethoven's Fifth Symphony.

V685.39, B799.26   Harry James   An orchestra leader and singer. His first big break came with a singing part in the film *Springtime in the Rockies* (1942). The following year James (b. 1916) married GI heartthrob Betty Grable.

V686.19–21, B800.14–17   morphine tartrate . . . amyl nitrite . . . tins of Benzedrine   Respectively these drugs are an opiate with depressant effects, a stimulant commonly prescribed for patients with heart trouble, and the brand name of a mild stimulant, in tablet form.

V687.25, B801.25   "Schitt"   This German has been crossbred with English: the infinitive verb *scheissen* means "to shit"; the imperfect indicative form (here, for instance) is *schitz*.

V687.31, B801.35   Schein-Aula   From the noun *Schein* (a blaze, a seeming, and in some contexts a halo); and from the noun *Aula* (an assembly hall, an auditorium).

V688.28, B802.39–40   Jack and Malcolm both got murdered   Malcolm X was assassinated on February 21, 1965, as he spoke in New York City's Audubon Ballroom; John F. Kennedy was killed fifteen months before that, in Dallas, on November 22, 1963.

V688.36–37, B803.8–9   Fay Wray . . . in her screentest scene with Robert Armstrong   In the film *King Kong*, actor Robert Armstrong plays Carl Denham, a director of jungle-adventure movies. He takes starlet Ann Darrow (Fay Wray) on a South Pacific cruise to Skull Island, home of Kong. Her screen test, a long take of overtly erotic mugging for the camera, occurs on board ship.

V689.4–20, B803.17–33   At that first moment . . . whisper me a line   Thus far in *GR*, Pynchon has parodied T. S. Eliot (V226.33n), the Italian sonnet (V532.32n), and the Rolling Stones (V541.23n). Shortly he will parody the Japanese haiku. Here, he takes up the Miltonic blank verse line and, indeed, has a fine time with it. Note how skillfully the caesural pauses are moved around, and the occasional spondee in this poem. Its colloquialisms, like the alliterative spondee in "best bum actor's way" and the feminine ending in the twelfth line of the page ("mooning sappy"), all work to lower the tone, underscoring the Miltonic "Fall" of the eighth line. It is all charged, in addition, with allusions to RKO Pictures' *King Kong*. The speaker of the poem is Ann Darrow (Wray), who recalls how the natives on Skull Island dragged her and tied her Christ-like to the posts outside their massive gate. Their "flight" occurs when Kong appears to return with her to his lair. The "Ravine," "tyrannosaurus," and "pterodactyl" are obstacles and opponents Kong meets on his way. He jumps over the first and defeats the second in a wrestling match, using the "flying-mare," or kick. In these lines Ann also remembers that while waiting for Kong she prayed, not for Jack (Bruce Cabot), the sailor pacing the decks of the anchored ship, but for her director, Denham, who has used her, brought her to this nightmare, and offered her up to this sexual symbol just as Miklos Thanatz offered up Greta Erdmann to the jackal-headed men of *Alpdrücken*. Finally, in the line "making the unreal reel" one hears an echo of French director Jean Cocteau's famous paean to film: "Long live the young muse, cinema, for she possesses the mysteries of a dream and allows the unreal to become real."

V689.26, B803.40–41   a round black iron anarchist *bomb*   Recalls the comic book and cartoon cliché, with Porky Pig left holding the round black bomb (V545.4–5n).

V690.2, B804.16   little Margaret O'Brien   She was five years old in 1942 when her film career began. At seven she won a special Oscar for her role in *Meet Me in St. Louis*, when she was widely hailed as a Shirley Temple for the forties.

V690.16, B804.34–35   "Your closet *could* make Norma Shearer's look like the wastebasket in Gimbel's basement"   Gimbel's is the New York City department store on Thirty-third and Broadway; its basement is famous for its bargain goods. Actress Norma Shearer (b. 1904) was mainly a clotheshorse during the early years of her film career. In *Slave of Fashion* (1925), for example, she plays a young woman who accidentally comes into possession of a fabulous wardrobe and uses it to pass herself off as a New York socialite.

V690.27–28, B805.4–5   Takeshi flies a Zero . . . Ichizo . . . an Okha   The Mitsubishi A6M8 was the main fighter aircraft of the Japanese arsenal. Official Allied code books identified it as "Zeke," but U.S. servicemen dubbed it the "Zero." Beginning in 1944 the planes were fitted up for long-range *kamikaze* suicide attacks (from *Kami kaze*, or "divine wind," after a famous storm that sunk an invading Mongol fleet in A.D. 1274). The Okha (Cherry Blossom) 11 was a much smaller aircraft, designed specifically as a suicide bomber and produced during the fall and winter of 1944–45. Built of flimsy wood and fabric, this stubby, rocket-propelled craft was fitted with a half-ton explosive charge and dropped from the belly of a bomber. It had no landing gear, and the charge was rigged to go off on any impact. In sum, no going home in this piloted version of the German V-1 (see Inoguchi and Najakima 132–34).

V690.36–37, B805.15–16 The fighting is . . . at Leyte . . . Iwo Jima, moving toward Okinawa The U.S. Marines invaded Leyte Island, in the central Philippines, in mid-October 1944. Iwo Jima was next, in February 1945. And in this northward march of death, Okinawa was invaded on April 1, Easter of 1945. The main chronological inference: just as Gottfried waits out the last terrible weeks of winter for the Easter weekend sacrifice, Takeshi and Ichizo simulta-neously await their calling. Inoguchi and Nakajima (135–38), Pynchon's source, report the first, unsuccessful use of Okha piloted bombs on March 21, 1945.

V690.40, B805.19 Cypridinae Family name of a tiny oceanic crustacean that phosphoresces when its surrounding waters are disturbed. The name stems from the Greek *Kypridios*, signifying that these little beings "belong to Aphrodite," the Cyprian Venus.

V691.16, B805.39–40 PPI scopes The acronym stands for "Plan-Position-Indicator," a radar device.

V691.19–20, B806.1–2 screened eight-fold in a circle On the radar screen. Note again the numerical and mandala symbolism.

V691.25–26, B806.9 an improvised haiku According to Japanese tradition, a haiku is supposed to express, in lines of five, seven, and five syllables, some distinct image that occasions spiritual insight. Old Kenosho's haiku adheres to the syllable rules, but his image puts across only a mundane irony.

V691.34–35, B806.20 *Paranoid . . . For The Day!* What follows is a mordant little parody of the fifties television show *Queen for a Day*, hosted by master of ceremonies Jack Bailey on the NBC (and later, ABC) network, from 1955 to 1964. The contest pitted four preterite women against each other, to see whose tale of woe and loss evoked the most audience approval, as registered on the "Applause-O-Meter."

V692.4, B806.29–30 exotic Puke-a-hook-a-look-i *Island!* See V635.14.

V692.19, B807.7 STREETS In this subsection of the episode we are given a list of streets and towns that Slothrop evidently has wandered through: Hafenstrasse (Harbor Street), Slüterstrasse (Dyer's Street), and Wandfärberstrasse (Painter's Street) among them. They are appar-ently all fictional.

V693.22–23, B808.20 the Ortsschutz The local constable.

V693.39–41, B808.40–42   The letters / MB DRO / ROSHI   A newspaper headline, from circa August 7, 1945, announcing "ATOM BOMB DROPPED ON HIROSHIMA." In a proleptic comment, we were told that Slothrop would find this scrap during his rambles (see V681.35–36).

V694.3, B809.3–4   3rd Armored treads 'n' triangle   Soldiers of the Third Armored Division of the U.S. Army wore a triangular shoulder patch with tank treads stitched in its center. Pynchon's source, again, is probably the article on "Shoulder Insignia" in the August 6, 1945, issue of *Life* (46).

V694.12–16, B809.16–21   the pale Virgin was rising . . . The sun was in Leo   These astrological details are accurate. The atomic bomb was dropped on Hiroshima at 9:15 A.M., Hiroshima time, on August 6. The constellation Virgo, usually represented as a maiden dressed in a white gown, was rising in the east, at the angle the narrator gives here. The sun was midway through the house of Leo (July 23–August 22). Readers with a star wheel can roughly verify the figures, though an ephemeris table gives the exact fixes.

V694.19, B809.25   cryptozoa   A biological term (from circa 1895) signifying any class of organisms that live hidden lives, for example, the planaria worm, which comes out from under its seaside rocks only at night.

V694.25, B809.33   Their Movieola   Brand name of a film editor's device, capable of rolling the film one frame at a time, backward or forward, for cutting and splicing.

V695.25–28, B810.38–42   Dungannon, Virginia . . . or Ellis, Kansas   The "Sound-Shadow" (V695.23) delineated by these ten place-names is another of Pynchon's fictions, or red herrings. No time zones are (of course) involved. Instead, plot these locations on a map and connect the points. The first five seem to sketch a sideways parabola, the second five a diagonal line. Put together, they seem to make something like a chalice (or Grail cup?) spilled toward Europe. Or maybe (again) it's all baloney.

V695.33–34, B811.7–8   thine-alabaster-cities   Echoing the last verse of "America the Beautiful":

> O beautiful, for patriot's dream,
> That sees beyond the years;
> Thine alabaster cities gleam,
> Undimmed by human tears.
> America, America! God shed his grace on thee;
> And crown thy good, with brotherhood,
> From sea to shining sea.

V696.28–29, B812.8–9   voices far away out at sea *our position is two* *seven degrees two six minutes north* Inoguchi and Nakajima, the source for these details, append tables detailing all known kamikaze sorties, including map coordinates of their point of contact with Allied warships. Only one sortie matches these coordinates: on April 30, 1945, two kamikazes attacked the U.S. destroyer *Bennion*, seriously damaging it (ibid., app. C, p. 209). These "voices" would apparently be from those doomed pilots, broadcasting on Walpurgisnacht (V293.19n).

V696.30–40, B812.11–21   a voice reciting in Japanese . . . the slogan of a Kamikaze unit . . . Power cannot conquer Heaven The source, again, was Inoguchi and Nakajima (138, n1), who report that the lieutenant commander of the first Okha squadron to attack American vessels, a Lieutenant Nonaka, had flown a white pennant over the bivouac of his unit. This meditation was inscribed on it. The footnote explains: "This is the *on* or Chinese reading of the five ideographs in the pennant. Their literal meanings are, respectively: Injustice, Principle, Law, Power, Heaven." Pynchon quotes the remainder of the note, verbatim. A photo of Nonaka's squadron, and their HI, RI, HO, KEN, TEN pennant, appears in *The Divine Wind* (opp. 49).

V697.29, B813.15–16   a Japanese Hotchkiss machine gun The American-born gunsmith Benjamin Berkeley Hotchkiss developed his first machine gun, capable of firing six hundred rounds per minute, in 1876. This was in Paris. Governments the world over quickly bought rights to the design of his gun: the U.S. Army used a Hotchkiss (as the narrator notes) against Sioux Indians at Wounded Knee, South Dakota, during the Christmas 1890 massacre there. Ichizo's "Model 92" is a latter-day Hotchkiss, from circa 1930.

V698.33, B814.29   "Keying waves" In electrical argot, waves that oscillate at frequencies corresponding to musical tones, for instance, the dialing tones of our contemporary phone system.

V699.17, B815.18–19   double Virgo fer a son The term "double" identifies this astrological sign as one of the four "bicorporal" or "double-bodied" signs, including Pisces, Gemini, and Cancer. The designation "double Virgo" could be Slothrop's sun sign, indicating that he was born between August 23 and September 22. This would of course contradict the inferences drawn, in an earlier note, from V624.18. On the other hand, such bicorporal descriptions are also applied to other aspects of a subject's natal chart. And Slothrop's possible chart— cast for noon of March 21, 1918—*does* contain one noteworthy aspect: the planet Mars in Virgo, a sign of foolish, selfish pursuit of satisfaction, for which one might pay any price. That seems to fit the context here.

V700.19–20, B816.29–30   Otyiyumbu Indeterminacy Relation Jan Otyiyumbu is the Schwarzkommando "liaison man" for London (V638.33n).

EPISODE 7

Under the influence of drugs, Tchitcherine discloses the reasons for his obsessive pursuit of his half-brother, Enzian. And it develops that Soviet agents let him track Enzian, just as Slothrop was allowed to escape into the Zone as a way of leading Allied agents to the Schwarzkommando. The time and setting of this episode are both indistinct.

V700.26–27, B816.38–817.1   Nikolai Ripov of the Commissariat for Intelligence Activities   Yet another fictional CIA. Ripov: from American sixties slang "rip-off," a verb form signifying "to steal" or "to defraud."

V700.36–37, B817.12   Fuder and Fass   Respectively, cask (of wine) and keg (of beer).

V701.1, B817.14   the Drunkards Three   The DTs, as in *delirium tremens?*

V701.18, B817.33   Opiates of the people   Echoes Karl Marx's sentence from the *Critique of Hegelian Legal Philosophy*: "Religion is the opiate of the people."

V701.30, B818.6   "natürlich"   Naturally, certainly.

V702.9, B818.31   a number 26 point   Hypodermic needle of .26 millimeters in diameter, one of the smallest in use (so Tchitcherine won't feel it).

V702.15–16, B818.39–40   recalling Tchaikovsky, salmonella . . . tunes from the *Pathétique*   Wimpe eyes the water tap "nervously" because *Salmonella* is the genus of pathogenic bacteria that causes stomach disease, especially when ingested in tainted water. Pëtr Ilich Tchaikovsky's last work was his Symphony No. 6, op. 74, also known as the *Pathétique*, a brooding, anguished, sorrowful work. Nine days after its first performance in 1893, Tchaikovsky committed suicide.

V702.24, B819.8   Polschuhen   Connecting terminals, in electrical jargon.

V703.13–14, B820.4   0.6 mg atropine subcut.   That is, a subcutaneous injection of six-tenths of a milligram of atropine, a central nervous system depressant derived from belladonna. The scholarly reference, to the *Journal of Oneiric Psycho-Pharmacology* (V702.40), is another of Pynchon's fictions.

V704.3, B820.37   "We lost twenty million souls"   The Soviet Union claimed an estimated 20 million dead as a result of German aggression, most of them dead peasants, or *dushi* (souls).

V704.41, B821.42   his Nagant   The Russian pistol (V293.26n).

V705.7–8, B822.8   One is to examine the recently dead   A Bantam error: "One is the examine."

V706.3, B823.7 "TsAGI" The Russian Central Aerodynamics and Hydrodynamics Institute (see V273.5n).

V706.4–5, B823.9–10 "**We'll be taking German rocket personnel out to the desert**" Just as the Americans took their captured rocketry experts out to the desert of White Sands, New Mexico, so the Soviets took theirs to Semirechie, in Kirghizistan. Irmgard Gröttrup narrates the story of their 1946 move in *Rocket Wife*.

EPISODE 8

L̲ate August, in Cuxhaven. Jessica tells Roger Mexico that she and Jeremy are planning marriage and a family. The Counterforce proposes that Rocket 00000 had to have been fired in a due-northerly direction, completing a mandala of compass bearings. Roger and "Pig" Bodine attend a dinner party, disrupting things with a boorish but zany verbal assault they have evidently learned from that connoisseur of indigestible delights, Brigadier Pudding, who has joined the Counterforce from the Other Side.

V707.4–5, B824.12–14 **a ghost-firing which, in the logic of mandalas, either has occurred, most-secretly, or will occur** The subject is mandalas, traditionally divided into four quadrants. The compass bearings of the V-2 test-firings were variously available to Pynchon in Kooy and Uytenbogaart (285), in Dornberger, and in Irving. The striking thing here, however, is the narrator's verb tenses: in the story time (or narrative *histoire*) the firing "has occurred" back on Easter weekend; but in the narration itself (the *discours*), it "will occur" in episode 12 of part 4.

V707.31, B825.2–3 **Der Grob Säugling, 23rd card of the Zone's trumps major** The narrator translates *Grob* as "gross," but more accurately it means "coarse" or "rude." A *Säugling* is a suckling pig. There are twenty-two cards in the Trumps Major (or Major Arcana) of the standard Tarot deck. This additional symbol seems analogous to that of a thirteenth house in the traditional zodiac (see V302.20–21n).

V708.31, B826.11 **the ENSA shows** The British servicemen's entertainment organization (V657.22n).

V709.18, B827.4–5 **Is this Noel Coward or some shit?** The British playwright (see also V134.40–135.1n).

V709.23, B827.10 **Operation Backfire** V272.32–34n.

V709.33–35, B827.21–23 "**Little sigma, times . . . little-sigma squared.**" In statistics, this is the equation for a "normal" or "Gaussian" distribution, a graph of which will yield a "normal" or parabolic curve (see V508.39n). The German mathematician Karl Friedrich Gauss (1777–

1855) developed the equation, which took on seminal importance in statistics when observations showed that many populations, or distributions of events, closely adhere to it.

V709.39, B827.27–28   the home of Stefan Utgarthaloki   He is named for the Teutonic god Utgarthaloki (Loki of Outgard), a giant and a personification of evil. Like Satan, Utgarthaloki lives far in the East. This is the simple importance of Roger's trip to "the Krupp wingding" (V711.16–17) at Stefan's house, but there is more. In Snorri Sturluson's tenth-century epic, *Gylfaginning* (chap. 44), we have a base text for the parody at work in this episode. That account of Utgarthaloki centers on a theme of deception. The god Thor journeys to Loki's castle in order to strive with the rival giant. First he challenges Loki to a drinking match, and loses. Loki then challenges Thor to pick up a cat, and again Thor loses; and he loses yet again at wrestling an old hag. Before sending Thor on his way, Loki sets the god a great feast. They eat most of the night, dining on strange delicacies from the world over. Next morning, with Thor too bloated to fight, Loki accompanies the great god to the gates of his stronghold, where he explains why Thor was so powerless the night before: Loki tricked him with three illusions. The drinking horn was connected to the oceans; Loki's cat was in reality the World Serpent, Ouroboros; and the old hag was really a great wrestler. Enraged, Thor seizes up his hammer, Mullicrusher, and swings at thin air, for Loki has vanished, a deceptive illusion like everything else in Outgard. Note that unlike Thor, however, Roger journeys to Utgarthaloki's stronghold with a friend.

V710.1, B827.31   "there're a lot of snazzy NAAFIs about"   See V17.26n.

V710.40–41, B828.37–38   "just a freckleface kid from Albert Lea . . . on Route 69 where the speed limit's lickety-split"   A crude pun on the old venereal slang term "69." Route 69 was once a major arterial running north-south, connecting Des Moines and Minneapolis. The town of Albert Lea, Minnesota, is ten miles north of the Iowa border.

V711.2, B828.38–39   "used a safety pin through a cork for a catwhisker"   In radio operator's slang, a "catwhisker" is an aerial.

V711.24, B829.23–24   at *your* door, Fred and Phyllis   Another reference to Fred Allen's radio program, *Allen's Alley* (V44.17–18n). Here, the format has been inverted: someone comes to knock on Fred and Phyllis's door.

V711.29–31, B829.30–32   suppressed quartet from the Haydn Op. 76 . . . *Largo, cantabile e mesto*   Composer Josef Haydn's opus 76 is a set of six quartets written in 1799 and dedicated to Count Erdödy, for whom they are usually named. The fifth quartet, in D, is a set of free variations in the middle of which is a *largo, cantabile e mesto* (a slow, sad song), meant to express a type of unearthly radiance. This middle movement of the quartet is scored in F-sharp major;

Pynchon's fictional, "suppressed" movement for kazoos is "in G-flat minor."

V711.34, B829.36–37 **"a spiccato to a détaché"** Bow strokes. A *spiccato* is a "thrown" stroke, when the bow bounces off the strings of the instrument, such as a violin. A *détaché* is a downstroke of some length—one continuous, downward stroke, perhaps *really* drawn out, in which case it is *le grand détaché*.

V712.4, B830.7–8 **song from the movie *Dr. Jekyll and Mr. Hyde*** In the 1932 version starring Fredric March, Miriam Hopkins in the role of Ivy Pearson sings a tavern song, "Champagne Ivy Is My Name." The lyric is a variation on an old song, "Champagne Charley Was His Name," from Boston circa 1867, written by H. J. Whymark and Alfred Lee.

V712.9, B830.14 **this feeb's pizzicato** Another violin stroke, this time a "plucked" instead of a bow stroke. "Feeb" is slang for any feeble-minded person.

V712.11, B830.16 **Reps from ICI and GE** Representatives from the British firm Imperial Chemicals Incorporated, the dyestuff and chemical manufacturer, and from the American General Electric company, keenly involved in Project Hermes, the operation to recover and export to the United States one hundred of the V-2 rockets.

V712.21, B830.29 **early Virgo** The sixth house of the astrological year, Virgo holds sway from August 23 to September 22.

V712.25–26, B830.34–35 **"the 'Hydra-Phänomen'"** "Hydra phenomenon," named for the monster of Greek myths. Heracles (or Hercules, to the Romans) won his immortality by performing twelve extraordinary labors, the second of which was to slay the Hydra, a beast that grew two heads for each one that was lopped off.

V712.26–29, B830.36–39 **Natasha Raum . . . *Proceedings of the International Society of Confessors to an Enthusiasm for Albatross Nosology*** Note Pynchon's continuation of the PISCEAN motif. Nosology is the study and classification of diseases. Fictional author Raum derives her moniker from the German for "space"; in addition, according to Waite (*Black Magic* 178), the angel Raum is one of the "throne Angels" who "appears in the form of a crow, but assumes human shape when bidden" and is capable of both destroying cities and bringing about love between foes.

V712.33–35, B831.2–4 **Pseudo-Goldstrassian . . . Mopp's Hebdomeriasis** Fictional diseases. The second stems from the Latin *hebdoma* (seven); thus *hebdomeriasis* is any pathology that manifests itself during the first week of life.

V713.10, B831.24 **Thermidor** The eleventh month of the French revolutionary calendar, corresponding to the period from July 19 to August 17, now part of Roger's memory.

V713.33, B832.12   a recco map   Produced from photographs taken by aerial reconnaissance.

V713.41, B832.22–23   according to the menu, full of relevés, poissons, entremets   Respectively, spiced dishes, fishes, and desserts.

V715.2, B833.33   Pappy Hod   Another refugee from Pynchon's first novel, *V.*, he's a shipmate of "Pig" Bodine's in 1955 aboard the USS *Scaffold*. A hod is a device slung over the shoulders for lugging bricks. Also, in Kabbalistic symbolism, *Hod* (Majesty, or Glory) are the thighs on the anthropomorphized tree of life (see Scholem, *Major Trends*, 213; and V747.41–748.5n).

V715.8, B833.39–40   They are not "sensitive flames"   In reference to the technique used to detect frauds in "table rapping" (V29.31n).

V715.14, B834.5   But is is through   An error in both the Viking and Bantam editions.

V716.38, B835.39   Lady Mnemosyne Gloobe   She takes her first name from the Greek goddess Mnemosyne (memory, mindful), the mother of all the Muses. Note that Mrs. Gloobe flees these "mindless pleasures."

V717.2–3, B836.4   "the Scrubs"   Again, London's Wormwood Scrubs Prison (V33.31–32).

V717.8–9, B836.10–11   Sixth Antechamber to the Throne   In Merkabah mysticism, the sixth antechamber is the next-to-last stop in one's ascent to the divine throne and is guarded by the archangels Katspiel and Domiel. It constitutes a supreme test of the mystic's faith; see also V231.24–25n, V584.1n, and V749.34–36n.

V717.18, B836.21–22   "a Storm Trooper . . . like Horst Wessel"   On Wessel's life and his murder at the hands of a rival Communist storm troop, see V443.2n.

V717.19–22, B836.23–26   "a Melvin Purvis Junior G-Man . . . For Post Toasties"   During the thirties Purvis was special agent in charge of the Chicago office of the FBI. At the time all agents were nicknamed "G-men" (short for "government men"). In 1935 the Post Cereals Company developed the "Junior G-Men" as a promotional gimmick, distributing badges and other paraphernalia in purchases of their Post Toasties cereal.

V717.24, B836.29   Tom Mix   The American cowboy-actor who made some sixty films and serials during his Hollywood career (see also V245.36n).

EPISODE 9

The time is late August or early September 1945. Geli Tripping continues her search for Tchitcherine in spite of reports that he has died. Her memories of kneeling before the chief devil, Pan, segue neatly into a key analepsis: Gottfried kneels before Blicero at the time of the spring equinox and just days before the launch of Rocket 00000.

V717.31, B837.1 Adam and Eve root Also known as "putty root," the *Aplectrum hyemale* is an orchidaceous plant with purple-and-yellow flowers and corms shaped like human bodies.

V717.35, B837.5 her gallant Attila Because Tchitcherine, like Attila, also swept down out of the steppes of central Asia.

V718.7, B837.14 Bauernfrühstuck A farm breakfast.

V718.33, B838.3 Hexes-Stadt "Witch City."

V719.10, B838.26 Beria's top man Lavrenti Beria was a member of Joseph Stalin's war cabinet (with Molotov and Malenkov). He headed the feared police agency in charge of Russian internal security, the NKVD (People's Commissariat of Internal Affairs).

V719.26, B839.1–2 scurvy lot of tommies British slang for "a lousy bunch of soldiers." "Tommies" are from "Tommy Atkins," a fictitious common soldier like the American GI Joe.

V719.39–40, B839.17–18 *the cross* the man has made on his own circle of visible earth Another mandala symbol. The cross in a circle is, in addition, the astrological symbol of earth. To Geli, moreover, this surveyor has just drawn a conjuring symbol in the dirt.

V720.2, B839.23 Pan The reference pertains less to the Greek mythological figure than to the chief devil of European witchcraft. Grimm (1071), for example, describes Pan as a goat-man who "sits silent and solemn on a high chair or stone table in the midst of the ring" of gathered witches. They approach and "do him reverence by kneeling and kissing."

V720.13, B839.36 it was the equinox March 21, the "great cusp."

V721.12, B840.42–841.1 his last ties The masculine pronoun refers to Gottfried, whose last memories, circa March 21, have been neatly segued into Geli's recollections. Gottfried "kneels at [Blicero's] feet" (V721.26) here, just as Geli and the other witches had knelt before Pan.

V721.21, B841.11–12 It's only a matter of weeks To be concise, seven weeks from the spring equinox to V-E Day.

V723.28–29, B843.36–37 "stories of us one day living on the Moon" Note that Gottfried's "stories" correspond with the bedtime stories that Ilse Pökler concocted with her father, Franz (V410.11n).

V724.21, B844.34–35 latest spring torn across rainy miles This comment, along with the "raw spring wind" (V724.11), confirms the time of Blicero's last firing: a matter of days after March 21.

V724.25–26, B844.40 a card: what is to come The tenth and last card drawn from the Tarot deck in a divinatory reading. It is the culmination of all influences brought to light through the previous nine cards. See, for example, "Weissmann's Tarot" (V746.30n).

V724.28–29, B845.1–2   like The Fool, no agreed assignment in the deck   As the zero card in the Major Arcana, the Fool's sequential place is disputed. Some Tarot handbooks put the card first, others put it last. Ouspensky makes the Fool a counterpart to the Magician, card number one in the sequence and a figure much like Blicero. Waite (*Pictorial Key*) places the Fool next to last, between the Last Judgment (number twenty) and the World (card twenty-one).

EPISODE 10

E arly September, approaching the Lüneberg Heath. Enzian has managed to keep his Zone Hereros together and has done it in spite of continued attacks by unidentified white forces. His troops press on toward Lüneberg to fire Rocket 00001, the "second in its series" (V724.34). Their undertaking is still suffused by a polyglot mythology.

V725.13, B845.28   you twelve struggled, in love, on this Baltic shore   Numerologically, recall that part 4 has twelve episodes and that Tchitcherine was rumored to have "a dozen" followers, even a "Judas Iscariot" among them (V719.19–20). Also, Enzian's group will soon be attacked by a "Dozen" hostile whites (V730.33). Here, there is a loose analogy to Christ's disciples struggling, "in love," on the shores of Galilee.

V725.23–24, B846.2–3   at Siemens . . . centaurs struggling high on the wall   Another reference to the statuary outside the Siemens Electrical Works of Berlin (V649.27n).

V726.6–8, B846.32–33   Constance Babington-Smith . . . at R.A.F. Medmanham discovered the Rocket back in 1943   The Royal Air Force office at Medmanham housed the Special Interpretations Unit. It was there, in the spring of 1943, that Mrs. Babington-Smith examined reconnaissance photos taken over Peenemünde. She identified the pencil-shaped, finned, A4 rocket cradled in its *Meillerwagen*. Her find supplied British intelligence with its first sure evidence that the rocket existed. Pynchon's source here was Collier (31–32).

V726.15, B846.43   toruses of Rocket range   In architectural usage, a "torus" is a convex, semicircular cross-section; in anatomy, it is a swelling or a tumorous bulge. Both meanings are at work here. The etymology of the word is similarly striking: in Hindu art, Shiva, the red god of destruction and waste, is frequently represented beneath a blazing *Torana*, a fiery arch symbolic of death and dissolution.

V726.19–20, B847.4–5   It Begins Infinitely Below The Earth And Goes On Infinitely Back Into The Earth   A reminder once more that the rainbow is not arch-shaped but is in its truest form a circle (see also V6.33–35n and V209.25–26n).

V726.41, B847.30–31   between quaternions and vector analysis in the 1880s   Vector analysis involves the description of motion in space when the particle has a known direction and force. Quaternions, on the other hand, are scalar quantities, hypercomplex numbers in which four components (such as the spin of a particle) are "scaled" together, so as to provide a much more accurate description of dynamic behavior. In physics, these hypercomplex numbers became crucial in early descriptions of atomic matter. But note: the reference is to "the 1880s," when motion was still thought to be a matter of distinct particles.

V727.6–10, B847.38–43   Gnostics . . . Kabbalists . . . Manichaeans   Gnosticism arose in the eastern Mediterranean during the early Christian centuries as a fierce opponent to Judaic mythology. Gnostics regarded the creation as a *pleroma*, a fullness that is hierarchically organized, each antechamber to the divine throne occupied by angelic beings: the potencies, aeons, archons, and dominions that were soon adopted by Kabbalistic Judaism and Christianity alike. The central belief of the Gnostics was in a hidden God, whose throne one approached at death, the moment of redemption. Gershom Scholem (*Major Trends* 73ff.) has shown that early Kabbalism rose from these Gnostic beliefs. The throne or Merkabah mysticism of the second through the fourth centuries, and the Neoplatonism of the medieval philosophers, combined to yield in thirteenth-century Europe the first two exemplary Kabbalistic texts: the writings of Abraham Abulafia of Italy and the anonymous *Sefer Ha-Zohar*, or "Book of Splendor" that was written in Spain. In the third century, the Manichaeans gathered around their Persian prophet, Manes. Their fundamental belief was in the divinity of the soul, which was thought to be imprisoned in terrestrial matter, symbolized by darkness and night. The soul's desire to seek the light is, however, checked by the jealousy of Venus, who wants to keep the soul locked up in dark matter. To be alive in the body is thus an absolute woe to the Manichaean, whereas death into a redeeming light is an absolute good. As Denis de Rougement has shown, it was from this Manichaean separation of divine and earthly love, the latter always connected with Venus, that the Tristan and Tannhäuser myths took shape among the Cathars of thirteenth-century Provence.

V727.11–12, B848.1–2   the sacred idiolalia of the Primal Twins   Enzian and Blicero are the Twins, and the "sacred idiolalia" will soon appear as an anagram concerning their fates (V746.9n).

V727.17–18, B848.9   the heretic's EEG   On the electroencephalograph see V146.1–7n.

V727.33–34, B848.29–30 fennel . . . mallow leaves Here Pynchon
lists a variety of medicinal herbs common to Europe; all are harvested
in late summer. Medieval Europeans believed that fennel would ward off
witches and evil spirits, and the herb is still used as a purgative. In
its most potent form, the stems are cut to draw off the resinous sap. Be-
tony is a woodland plant of England, also called bishopswort,
gathered in late-summer mornings after the dew has begun to evaporate.
It is used to treat headaches and neuralgia. Whitsun roses, also known
as guelder roses, grow in copses throughout England, producing snow-
white flowers around Whitsun (mid-May) and berries in late summer.
The berries and the bark are used as a nerve sedative and an anti-
spasmodic. Sunflowers are non–native European plants, introduced
from South America during the sixteenth century. The seeds quickly
became known for their diuretic properties. Mallow grows all over
Europe; its soft, velvety leaves have been widely used to treat inflammation and soreness in the throat and chest.

V728.39, B850.2 laager In Afrikaans, the language of South-East
Africa, a caravan.

V728.41, B850.4 a sonic death-mirror As early as 1941 British intelligence experts had picked up rumors of such a German "death ray,"
supposedly in development. The thing was nothing more than a rumor
(Irving 14).

**V730.4–6, B851.18–19 called "the Hare" . . . as in the old Herero
story** As a trickster, the hare (or Brer Rabbit, in Americanized versions)
could never get any messages across in the way they were meant
(V322.21n).

V730.30, B852.7 Orutyene dead. Okandio, Ekori, Omuzire wounded
The names of these dead and injured Hereros all stem from Kolbe's
lexicon: *Orutyene*, "steep" (471); *Okandio*, "little bell" (51); *Ekori*, "cap"
(75); and *Omuzire*, "shadow" (439).

V731.41, B853.28–29 how's the head Mieczislav A Bantam misprint:
"how the head."

**V732.22–24, B854.13–14 full of Cathar horror at the practice of im-
prisoning souls in the bodies of new-borns** The Cathars derived
the name of their Christian sect from the Greek *katharos* (spotless),
in honor of Christ, the "spotless" lamb. They flourished throughout
southern Europe, but especially in Provence during the thirteenth
century. The Roman church declared Catharist beliefs heretical, touching off their brutal extermination during the Albigensian crusades.
Denis de Rougement, who is surely Pynchon's source here, defines
Catharist doctrine as originating from the Manichaean sects of Asia
Minor, and before that from Gnosticism. The Cathars, or "Church
of Love," held that good and evil exist in absolute separation, in two
different worlds, one heavenly and the other earthly. Initiates to the

sect, called the "perfect" or the "elect," were required to renounce the world fully and to devote their lives wholly to God, never to lie, never to kill or eat of an animal, and to abstain completely from sexual love. A second group, the "believers" or "imperfecti," were the only ones allowed to marry. De Rougement argues that despite the fierce persecution of the Cathars, their otherworldly beliefs survived in codified forms, for example, in courtly love poems. The doctrines lived on in the works of Europe's troubadours and minnesingers. They can also be found in the opera librettos for *Tannhäuser* und *Tristan und Isolde*. A. E. Waite (*Pictorial Key*) has argued that Catharism was also preserved in the symbolic images of Tarot. He notes that the Hierophant, card seven in the Major Arcana, may correspond to the secret Catharist pope and that the Tower struck by lightning on card sixteen may represent the desired destruction of the Roman church.

V732.36, B854.30 Djuro Origin unknown.

EPISODE 11

The novel's penultimate episode ends, not in fulfillment of the anticipated revenge of Tchitcherine on Enzian, but in coincidence and peace. In early September, near Lüneberg, Geli Tripping is at last reunited with Vaslav Tchitcherine. Her magical spell blinds him at the moment of his long-awaited confrontation with his half-brother: they pass each other amicably, and even anonymously, at a roadside.

V733.24, B855.24 terrenity "Earthliness," from the Latin *terrenus* (of the earth) and by analogy with *serenus* (serenity).

V733.26, B855.27 Stretchfoot From the German *Streckefuss*, a nickname commonly applied to Lord Death, *Dominus Blicero*. Grimm (852) explains: "Death is called the pale *Streckefuss* or *Streckebein* (leg-stretcher) . . . because he stretches out the limbs of the dying."

V734.2, B856.5 the mystery word In this game of hangman the mystery word is not hard: "generator" (same meaning and spelling in English as in German). Probably it is meant to designate the LOX, or liquid oxygen generator (a turbo pump), a key piece of German rocket engineering (Irving 268–69).

V734.7–8, B856.12 someone is swinging an ax-blade into a living tree The "someone" is a member of Enzian's crew (V730.41), and the ax is yet another *saxum* or *Zaxa* (V218.10n).

V734.19–20, B856.27–28 the Angels Melchidael . . . great Metatron The spell Geli casts over Tchitcherine is Pynchon's variation on two spells described in Waite's *Book of Black Magic and of Pacts* (265–70), both of them designed to compel the presence and devotion of a beloved. In "The Experiment in Love" the practitioner makes a wax or clay figure of the beloved, inscribing it with a goose quill (Geli uses her fingernail). It is clothed (she uses "the silk crotch torn from her best underpants [V734.13–]") and conjured with; during those rites the angels (such as Melchidael, Yahoel, and Anafiel) are invoked, as well as the Names of Power.

V734.26, B856.35   the last Names of Power   In "Solomonic" or black magic rites there are, according to Waite (*Black Magic* 240), seventy-two "Names of Power" for God. The practitioner will recite them at the close of a conjuring spell to bring about his or her desired end. Waite lists the last five names as "CREATOR, REDEMPTOR, UNITAS, SUMMUM BONUM, INFINITAS."

V734.34, B857.8   mba-kayere   The Herero for "I am passed over" (V362.17n).

EPISODE 12

The last episode in *Gravity's Rainbow*. Like the sixth in part 4, this one is also subdivided: into sixteen subepisodes detailing Slothrop's dispersal (like the mythic Orpheus) and disclosing at last the sacrifice of Gottfried. The episode begins in early September and ends on September 14, when Christians celebrate the Feast of the Exaltation of the Holy Cross, and the Zone Hereros are poised, ready to raise (exalt) their recovered Rocket 00001. The day is especially appropriate because it occasions the analepsis to the Easter weekend when Gottfried was sacrificed. Yet there is more. That analepsis also triggers a prolepsis to Los Angeles and the Orpheus Theater, circa 1970, in the middle of the Nixon era.

735.19, B857.35   Queen of Cups   Here is Waite's reading of this Tarot card in his *Pictorial Key* (200): "Beautiful, fair, dreamy—as one who sees visions in a cup. This is, however, only one of her aspects; she sees, but she also acts, and her activity feeds her dream."

V735.30, B858.11–12   bleached colors of a September morning   Perhaps "bleached" because the spirit of Blicero rules.

V736.1, B858.22   "our own boundary layer"   On this aerodynamic concept see V222.32n.

V737.17, B860.7   It is the Lüneberg Heath, at last   Baedeker (*Northern Germany* 144) gives the place just one word: "dreary." The area is remembered in pre-1945 history for two things, however. In 1417, after centuries of wandering, the gypsies made their first European home here; some say they brought with them the methods of Tarot divination and that this is how Europeans learned of its occult powers (Waite, *Pictorial Key* 54). Also, on July 17, 1586, a secret meeting is supposed to have occurred here involving the kings of Navarre and Denmark, Elizabeth I of England, and a number of princes and electors. The object, supposedly, was to "form an 'evangelical' league of defense against the Catholic League" (Yates 34). It was at this meeting that Rosicrucianism is said to have been secretly founded.

V737.22–23, B860.14   the Messiah gathering in the fallen sparks   A reference to the Kabbalistic belief that the divine illumination was scattered in the form of "sparks" at the moment of creation. The Messiah, it was believed, would once more gather in these dispersed sparks of light. The image was frequently given a world-historical interpretation: the "sparks" were taken as symbols of Diaspora Jews who would be gathered together at the Apocalypse. Here, the narrator satirically inverts that moment: the sparks are drawn into the "singularity," the gravitational collapse, of a black hole. Note, in addition, the *hysteron proteron*.

V737.41–738.1, B860.37–38   the Kabbalists, the Templars, the Rosicrucians   On the Kabbalists, see V727.6–10 and passim. The Knights Templars are a Catholic secret society tracing its origin to the crusade of 1188, when the order was established in Jerusalem. The best source on the Rosicrucian fervor of seventeenth-century Europe is Frances Yates's *Rosicrucian Enlightenment*. She argues that the manifestos of the movement reveal it as a conflux of Kabbalistic, Hermetic, and alchemical theory and symbol. Yates sees the Rosicrucians—John Dee, Francis Bacon, and Frederick V, the elector of Palatine—as intermediaries between the Renaissance and the new science. She also sees the movement as decidedly antipapist and, after 1650, increasingly millennial in its beliefs—key aspects of its contextual use in *GR*.

V738.7–8, B861.4–5   His cards . . . in the order suggested by Mr. A. E. Waite   This is Slothrop's Tarot, done in what Waite (*Pictorial Key* 299–305) describes as the "Celtic Method" of divination. First a "significator" is chosen from the pack; it must correspond to the query at hand. For example, if a legal matter is to be decided then the cartomancer would probably select Justice, card eleven of the Major Arcana. The significator is laid down, then the ten divinatory cards are randomly chosen from the deck and laid down in the shape of a patriarchal cross. The first of these ten cards is said to "cover" the significator and to set the conditions affecting the inquiry at hand. Getting the three of Pentacles in this position, especially after two tries, would definitely mean "mediocrity in work and otherwise, puerility, pettiness, and weakness." This is why Slothrop's Tarot (though we know only three of its cards) is that of a "tanker and feeb," a loser and an idiot. Worse still, as his ninth card, which should indicate his "hopes and fears" (V738.17), he draws the Hanged Man, card twelve, but in a reversed position. This would signify "selfishness, the crowd, body politic." It is a card "of Martyrdom"; but its inverted position only underscores the satiric treatment Pynchon has given Slothrop's role as mock-Orpheus.

V739.3, B862.6–7   A Raketen-Stadt Charlie Noble   After the war, atomic engineer Charles Carmine Noble (b. 1916) was the chief military officer for the Manhattan Project at Los Alamos, or "Atomic City." Hence the analogy to this radium-illumined stream of urine in the "Raketen-Stadt" (Rocket City).

V739.6–7, B862.11   Typhoid Marys   Mary Mallon (d. 1938) was an Irish cook living in the United States. She was infamous as a carrier of the deadly typhoid virus.

V739.22–24, B862.30–32   why you see Gnostics so hunted . . . the Sangraal, is the bloody vehicle   The essence of Gnostic and Manichaeistic doctrine was to regard everything of flesh and blood as an absolute woe, the enemy of spiritual good. As de Rougement (65) has written, "The fundamental dogma . . . is that the soul is divine or angelic, and is *imprisoned* in created forms—in terrestrial matter, which is Night." The Grail cup, which for the Celtic hero Gwyon was made of stone, contains this blackness through the symbolic power of Christ's blood.

V740.14, B863.24   Humboldt County   On the northern California coast.

V741.6–7, B864.22–24   "I was there . . . down the street from the Biograph"   "Pig" Bodine was a recent enlistee in the navy ("just a boot") in 1934 when he saw John Dillinger ambushed outside the Biograph Theater in Chicago. John Toland (237) has described how the bystanders used handkerchiefs and articles of clothing to soak up Dillinger's blood from the sidewalk where Melvin Purvis's G-men gunned him down.

V741.17, B864.36   "gate"   See V552.4n.

V741.34, B865.15   "I'm out of the Dumbo stage now"   In the Disney cartoon feature, Dumbo needed his feather to fly (see V106.33–37n). Bodine no longer needs his totem, the blood-stained T-shirt, in order to secure physical grace.

V742.2, B865.26   Leverkusen   The west German city, near Cologne, that is home to the Bayer Works (below).

V742.5, B865.30   the Bayer factory   Another IG Farben subsidiary and the original patentee of aspirin (Sasuly 27).

V742.22–23, B866.7–8   Sprigs of woodruff . . . carried by the early Teutonic warriors   The woodruff, or *Asperula odorata,* has white flowers and fragrant leaves. Grimm (1199) mentions its use among Teutonic warriors.

V742.25, B866.10–11   downtown Niederschaumdorf   A fictional locality. The name translates to "Vulgar beerfroth village."

V742.29, B866.15–16   only record album ever put out by The Fool   Steven Moore (57) notes that "there was indeed a rock group called The Fool. It put out one record in the late sixties, but beyond that it doesn't fit the description of the group with which Slothrop eventually plays . . . in part because the real Fool (whose album jacket is covered with Tarot imagery) consisted of only four members—two men and two women—and are not posed 'in the arrogant style of the early Stones, near an old rocket-bomb site.' There is, however, an unidentified harmonica player on the album."

V743.11–12, B867.3   Maitrinke   Literally, "May drink"; the May Wine of V742.20–21.

V743.35, B867.32   too many Fortresses diving   Once again the American B-17 "Flying Fortress" bomber.

V744.1, B867.38   THE OCCUPATION OF MINGEBOROUGH   Appears to take place during the spring, when the "apple tree . . . is in blossom" (V744.7). Perhaps it is shortly after Slothrop's escape from Monaco and Nice, in April of 1945. Many of the details in this incident can be checked against the description of fictional Mingeborough in Pynchon's 1964 short story "The Secret Integration."

V744.21, B868.22   old Cord automobiles   Front-wheel-drive autos manufactured by the Auburn Automobile Company, of Indiana, from 1929 to 1937.

V745.5, B869.11   carburete   This is misspelled in both editions: there should be no "e" on the end.

V745.19, B869.28   Schadenfreude   The enjoyment of pain.

V745.35–39, B870.8–14   Part of a reverse world . . . the corpse comes to life to the accompaniment of a backwards gunshot   Another elaborate *hysteron proteron*. For a similarly elaborate example of this rhetorical figure see Vonnegut's 1969 novel *Slaughterhouse-Five* (63–64), where the guns "sucked bullets and shell fragments" from airplanes and corpses; there the scene is naturalized as a reversed film.

V746.9, B870.26–27   medoschnicka bleelar medoometnozz in bergamot   This is the "sacred idiolalia of the Primal Twins" mentioned at V727.11–12. Puzzled out, the anagram yields the following words, put them together howsoever one will: "the blicero enzian mammon gets zero black doomed." One possible reading: "Mammon doomed Blicero; the black Enzian gets zero." But any such efforts to discover benediction or malediction in the letters may of course be viewed as the imposition of system where none is invited. The bergamot, incidentally, is a small, spiny, citrus-bearing tree of southern Europe, the *Aurantium bergamia*, whose sour fruit yields an oil for use in perfumes.

V746.17–18, B870.37–38   devotees of the I Ching   Or "Book of Changes" (see V13.1n); and the trigger for an awful pun: "I Ching feet" (V746.20).

V746.21–22, B871.3   Qlippoth, Ouija-board jokesters   The "shells of the dead" from Kabbalistic lore, and those half-baked souls who believe in the Ouija board as a divinatory method.

V746.30, B871.13   WEISSMANN'S TAROT   Unlike Slothrop's Tarot, which is incomplete, Weissmann's is fully laid out. And while the narrator offers a reading, it will help to stand it alongside the comments of A. E. Waite, Pynchon's principal source. First, one would of course need to know the specific inquiry that Weissmann made; and there is one excellent clue: his significator, a Knight of Swords, which Waite identifies with chivalry and specifically with the Grail-quester, Galahad (*Pictorial Key* 230). Weissmann could well have chosen this card had he inquired about the future of his romantic quest. Next come the ten cards drawn at random from the Tarot deck. Weissmann's quest is "covered"—that is, limited or conditioned—by the Tower, a sign of "misery, distress, indigence, adversity, calamity, disgrace, deception, ruin" (286). This card symbolizes the chastisement of pride, the ruin of the "House of Life, when evil has prevailed therein" (132). Both Waite and Ouspensky speak of the card as a symbol of ruin coming to an entire body of doctrine, perhaps here the body of Weissmann's decadent romanticism.

Weissmann's query is also "crossed," or opposed, by the Queen of Swords, a sign of "female sadness and embarrassment, absence, sterility, mourning, privation, separation" (Waite, *Pictorial Key* 228). The narrator sees this as a sign perhaps of Weissmann himself, in drag" (V748.21–22), but one might as easily take it as a reminder of his defeat when Katje deserted him. The King of Cups "crowns" Weissmann's quest. That is, it represents the best he can expect to achieve from it. Interestingly, this card foretells equanimity and success in business (Waite, *Pictorial Key* 198), which will correspond with other cards to come. "Beneath" that card, representing events already past, is the Ace of Swords, signifying "conquest, triumph of force" (252). Its image, a sword skewering a crown from its bottom, suggests Weissmann's sexual dominion over Katje and Gottfried, as well as the phallic insertion of Gottfried into Rocket 00000. In the fifth and sixth cards, Pynchon has reversed Waite's ordering ("behind" and "before"). The Four of Cups coming "before" in this case implies fatigue: "weariness, aversion, as if the wine of this world had caused satiety only," is how Waite (218) puts it. "Behind" Weissmann, waning in importance in his life, is the Four of Pentacles, signifying that his "surety of possession" is through (274).

Weissmann's remaining four cards are displayed in a line to the right of the circular mandala formed with the first six cards. The Page of Pentacles, representing his insensibility to messages around him (260), comes up as the sign of his self-attitude at the moment. His

"house" card, showing the influence of his associates, comes up an
Eight of Cups: Waite (210) notes that "the card shows the decline of a
matter, or that a matter which has been thought to be important
is really of slight consequence—either for good or evil." One can take
this as yet another sign that Gottfried's sacrifice during the Easter/April
Fool's weekend is hopelessly equivocated: maybe a token of
redemption, or just a fool's quest. Surely it did not culminate with
the fulfillment Weissmann seems to have anticipated. This is confirmed
in the penultimate card, that of his "hopes and fears": the Two of
Swords shows a slide into conformity, equipoise, and business. The
narrator's comment is particularly striking: "If you're wondering
where he's gone, look among the successful academics, the Presidential
advisers, the token intellectuals who sit on boards of directors"
(V749.9–12). Something like that, incidentally, was the fate of Walter
Dornberger, who settled in the United States and sat on the Board
of Directors of the Bell Helicopter Corporation. Or of Wernher von
Braun, who wound up as head of NASA.

In the Celtic method of cartomancy, all these divinatory possibilities
are supposed to conclude in the last card—"what will come." In
Weissmann's spread, it's symbolized by the World, card twenty-one
of the Major Arcana. It is a sign of emigration (to the United States?), of
voyages, new beginnings. Indeed, this is what all Weissmann's previous
cards suggest *will* happen, now that his romantic quest has ended
in ambiguity. Here is Waite (157–59): "It represents the perfection and
end of the cosmos, the secret which is within it, the rapture of the
Universe when it understands itself in God. It is furthermore the state
of the soul in the consciousness of Divine Vision, reflected from
the self-knowing spirit. . . . But it is perhaps more especially a story
of the past, referring to that day when all was declared to be good,
when the morning stars sang together and the Sons of God shouted for
joy." The card is definitely also an apocalyptic sign. Ouspensky's
reading (27) is also noteworthy: "A circle not unlike a wreath woven
from rainbow and lightnings, whirled from Heaven to Earth with
a stupendous velocity."

How might readers interpret Weissmann's Tarot in its whole gestalt?
One powerful inference is that the World is what Weissmann, like
many other characters, is still left with: there is no transcendence, no
escape into the sublime empyrean. As the borrowed phrase from
Wittgenstein put it in Pynchon's first novel, "The world is all that
the case is." And (as Tatham aptly argues), the way to that world
is through the armed woman, the Two of Swords, a symbol of passivity
before the turbulent waters behind her. Surely, too, Weissmann's
Tarot points up the end of his romantic desire and its translation into
business, into conformity, into the cartelized state of postwar, into

the threat of nuclear winter. Recall that Weissman survived the April apocalypse and was seen as late as May. This effectively underwrites the denouement of *GR*, where the prolepsis to Los Angeles and the Nixon epoch infers a new transmogrification of Weissmann's apocalyptic desire. Blicero slips out of the Zone, but his spirit presides over contemporary America.

V747.33–34, B872.22–23   a Gnostic or Cathar symbol for the Church of Rome   On the Gnostics and Cathars, see V739.22–24n and V732.22–24n. Waite discusses the Tarot symbols as a secret code for antipapal Catharist messages in his Introduction to the *Pictorial Key* (8–11). The Tower, in his view (8–9), typifies "the desired destruction of Papal Rome, the City on the Seven Hills, with the pontiff and his temporal power cast down from the spiritual edifice when it is riven by the wrath of God."

V747.38, B872.27   the Order of the Golden Dawn   An organization of Christian Kabbalists centered around MacGregor Mathers, a reader at the British Museum. He attributed its origins to "secret sources" and to clairvoyant powers. In fact, he concocted it, in 1885, out of Rosicrucianism and Kabbalist symbolism. W. B. Yeats, the most famous member, joined in 1889 after a brief go-round with the Theosophist movement of Madame Blavatsky. Yeats got to the fifth of seven levels, or "Elements," that initiates were supposed to master. The rest of Mathers's followers were more common sorts of Londoners and very much prone to squabbling. One of their rows caused Mathers to disband the order twenty years after establishing it.

V747.41–748.5, B872.31–37   On the Kabbalist Tree of Life . . . Yesod, the sex and excretory organs.   Kabbalist myths of creation variously represent it as a downward, unfolding process, as a tree, and as a human body. At the peak, corresponding to the crown of the tree or the cranium of the body, is Kether, an infinite source that contains all material being within it. Hakemah and Binah, Wisdom and Understanding, are often interpreted as the two lobes of the brain. Gedulah and Geburah, Benignity and Strength, are represented as the arms or two main branches. Tephareth, Beauty, is the trunk of the tree or the torso of the body. Netzach and Hod, Victory and Glory, are identified with the thighs or roots; and they are joined in Yesod and Malakoth, Foundation and Dominion, which are also the male and female genitalia, respectively. In their descending order, each of these ten Sephira, or Vessels, is thought to contain all that lies below. Furthermore, corresponding to these ten levels are the ten Qlippoth, the empty shells of creation. Pynchon rightly identifies the two Qlippoth that correspond to Netzach and Hod; they are, respectively, Ghorab Tzerek, the Ravens of Death, and Samael, the Poison of God. His accuracy

on these obscure points confirms that Scholem's *Major Trends* was his
source in these matters.

V748.18, B873.11   the Amanita muscaria   Or so-called flycap mushroom
which supposedly gives visionary powers (see V93.2–3n).

V748.40, B873.38   taken as "concord in a state of arms"   The phrase
is quoted from Waite (*Pictorial Key* 250), on the Two of Swords.

**V749.21–22, B874.20–21   heathen Germans . . . in their old
ceremonies**   The source is Grimm (46–48), according to whom nothing
so offended proselytizing Christians as the pagan Teutonic practice
of propitiating their gods through the sacrifice of horses, the bodies of
which were eaten, while the heads were hung on trees.

**V749.34–36, B874.35–38   an Aggadic tradition . . . that Isaac . . . saw
the antechambers of the Throne**   The source once more is Sholem's
Major Trends (53, 61–63). He explains that of the major Judaic writings
two classes stand out: Halakah, those writings occupied with sacred
law; and Aggadah, which means "narrative" and indicates any writings
consisting of folktales, dramatic monologues, parables, allegories,
maxims, satires, wordplay, permutations of letters, acrostics, and so
on. (In this sense, *GR* may be read as an Aggadic text.) The Aggadic writings are pre-Kabbalistic, dating from the first century B.C. until about
the tenth century A.D. Among them is a fourth-century manuscript,
"The Apocalypse of Abraham," which Scholem connects with the
Merkabah mysticism of the time, for it is concerned with a sevenfold
ascent thorugh the antechambers to God's throne. However, Pynchon
has worked a significant inversion of the tradition. In "The Apocalypse
of Abraham" it is the patriarch and not his son who ascends
throneward at the moment of sacrifice. On his way, Abraham hears
a hymn "like the voice of the waters in the rushing streams" (*Major
Trends* 61). It is the singing of angels who guard the Merkabah, and
Abraham can hear them from the sixth antechamber. In Pynchon's version, it is "Isaac under the blade" (V750.9–10) who has this visionary
experience.

V750.13, B875.17   at Nymphenburg   See V619.1–4n.

V750.18–19, B875.24   mad Ludwig and his Spanish dancer   An error.
It was not "mad Ludwig" (the Second, who committed suicide) but
his father, Ludwig I, who fell in love with the so-called Spanish Dancer,
Lola Montez, an Irish beauty who was born Marie Gilbert.

V750.20–21, B875.26–27   ascent to the Merkabah   To God's throne.

V750.33, B876.2   the Hand of Glory   Derives from A. E. Waite's *Book
of Black Magic and of Pacts* (276–77). Why burglars, or "second-story
men," would want to employ such a monstrous device to "light their
way into your home" will be apparent from Waite's discussion:

The Hand of Glory is indifferently the right or left hand of a criminal who has been gibbeted. The sorcerer obtains it as he can, and in the days of Tyburn Tree [London's infamous Hanging Tree] such requisites might have cost nothing beyond the personal risk of the adventure; it is indispensable, however, that it should be wrapped in a piece of winding sheet, and this suggests that the criminal must have been previously cut down with a view to interment. Thus enclosed, the hand must be well squeezed so as to force out any blood which may possibly remain in the member, after which it must be placed in an earthen vessel, together with some zimort, saltpetre, common salt, and pepper-corns, all pounded. It should remain in this vessel for fifteen days, and when extracted should be exposed to the heat of the sun during the time of the dogstar until it is extremely dessicated. If solar warmth be insufficient, it may be placed in a furnace heated with bracken and vervain. The object is to extract all the grease from the member, and therefrom, in combination with virgin wax and sesame from Lapland, to compose a species of candle. Wheresoever this frightful object is lighted, the spectators will be deprived of all motion, and the sorcerer can do what he will. It is possible to destroy its influence by anointing the threshold of the door, or other places through which entrance may be gained to a house, with an unguent composed of the gall of a black cat, grease from a white fowl, and the blood of a screech owl. This should also be confected in the dog-days [i.e., in high summer].

Note also the color symbolism in this counter-spell: black, white, and red. These colors are standard in occult literature and have dogged the narrative of *GR* since part 1.

V751.11, B876.24   the Zündkreuz   Literally, a "spark-cross," a device affixed to a long pole and used to ignite the A4 rocket's fuels at the initiation of launch. Pynchon's source on the launch procedures is Kooy and Uytenbogaart (374–77).

V751.19, B876.33   Ochsen-Augen   These are "oxen eyes" or round dormer windows, made of isinglass, in upper stories of houses.

V751.33–34, B877.10–11   Sir Denis Nayland Smith   See V277.34–38n.

V751.35, B877.12   Superman will swoop boots-first   As a comic book, *The Adventures of Superman* was originally written by Jerry Siegal and drawn by Joe Schuster. The first issues were published by Action Comics in 1936. Two years later the Mutual Radio Network debuted the program.

V752.1–3, B877.17–20   Philip Marlow . . . the Bradbury Building   Perhaps the address stems from one of the film versions of Raymond Chandler's detective stories and novels featuring hard-boiled Philip Marlow, who operated out of the Condor Building for many of the early stories of the thirties, before moving into the fictional Cahuenga Building.

V752.4, B877.21–22 Submariner and his multilingual gang will run into battery trouble The Timely Comics company published *Submariner* from 1941 to 1949, and Atlas Comics picked it up for the period 1954–55. Since 1968 it has been available from Marvel Comics as *Sub-Mariner*. The hero was Prince Namore of Atlantis, the underwater kingdom of myth and fable. In gathering together the remnants of his scattered realm, he traveled far and wide on "the surface world" (as the writers of *Submariner* called it). During the war years, this search brought him into frequent conflict with the forces of evil—Nazis and Fascists. Submariner's costume consisted of a red cape and blue swim trunks.

V752.5, B877.22 Plasticman will lose his way Jack Cole's comic book (see V206.37n).

V752.7, B877.25–26 The Lone Ranger will storm in Here, the narrator parodies the CBS Radio program that ran from 1933 to 1955. Tonto was the "faithful Indian companion" who saved Texas Ranger Dan Reid after he was ambushed and left for dead in a dry gulch.

V752.12, B877.31 "Too late" was never in their programming Literally, it was not in the radio programs and comic books featuring these pop-cultural heroes. But note, as well, that *GR* has come full circle: in the first episode Pirate Prentice saves Teddy Bloat from a fearsome fall; now the heroes arrive "Too late."

V752.29, B878.11–12 Pavlov on his own deathbed, recording himself The subject here is Pointsman, ignominiously self-defeated; and the source once more is "The Book." In his Introduction to volume 2 of the *Lectures*, Horsley Gantt (35) recalls of Pavlov that "in every illness he studied himself as he did his dogs in a laboratory experiment. The day of his death, February 27, 1936, while suffering a collapse, with a pulse rate of 150, he summoned a neuro-pathologist to know whether his symptoms might not be interesting to science and to discuss them."

V753.5–8, B878.33–37 The countdown as we know it . . . Fritz Lang said The source is a footnote in Willy Ley's *Rockets* (284): After the "Viking Hall" at the Hayden Planetarium in New York had been opened with a count-down, Milton Rosen casually remarked that the countdown was a custom that had originated at the Raketenflugplatz. I assured him that we had not thought of it, but later I began to wonder who had. Thinking back, I realized to my surprise that it had first been used in the film *Frau im Mond*. This was a silent movie, and at one point the words "10 seconds to go" flashed on the screen, followed by numbers, "6–5– 4–3–2–1–0

Fire!" Knowing that Fritz Lang had been in the Austrian Army in the First World War, I asked him whether he had adapted some military practice which used a countdown. He replied that he had thought it up for dramatic purposes when working on the film; on a proving ground nobody would possibly *think* of that side effect! Note, once again, the *hysteron proteron* motif.

V753.9–21, B878.38–879.8   "At the Creation . . . the Tree of Life."   On the tenfold ordering of the creation, imagined as a tree of life, see V747.41–748.5n.

V753.23–24, B879.17   the Bodenplatte . . . axis of a particular Earth   The *Bodenplatte* (ground plate) was the portable steel launching pad, also called a "lemon squeezer" because of its shape, that was placed under the A4 while in the field to provide a stable base and to deflect the exhaust (see Irving 274). Here, it assumes symbolic importance as what Mircea Eliade has called the *axis mundi*, or world axis. In most mythologies, the *axis mundi* becomes a meeting place for all the cosmic regions: heaven, earth, and hell. In the Christian mythology it is the site where Adam and Eve were created and buried, as well as the site where Christ was crucified. Thus, the "blood of the Savior falls on Adam's skull," Eliade (14) notes, and that blood "redeems him." The symbolic play here, though part of the broader satire, is crucial. Finding the *Bodenplatte* (V754.3) stands as analogous to discovering the True Cross, celebrated on September 14, the day it was "Exalted" or "Raised" again, in the year 335.

V753.29, B879.22   Thorazine   A brand of tranquilizer (see also V518.31–32n).

V753.40, B879.37   for leads, mu's, numbering   Mu, the twelfth letter in the Greek alphabet, would show with its accompanying number the capacitance value of a "wafer capacitor," with its two wire leads projecting from it and identifying it as something *other* than a pill.

V754.34, B880.37   (PNS)   Fowler thinks PNS indicates a "Pynchon News Service," but during the sixties and early seventies the Pacific News Service supplied an alternative source of news to FM radio stations and underground tabloid-style newspapers, like the *L.A. Free Press*.

V754.38, B881.4   "the Adenoid"   As in the adenoid that terrorized London, in Pirate Prentice's fantasy (V14.30ff).

V755.3–4, B881.8–9   "our Bengt Ekerot / Marie Casarès Film Festival"   Swedish actor Bengt Ekerot played the role of Death in Ingmar Bergman's cinema classic *The Seventh Seal* (1956). Spanish-born Marie Casarès Quiroga sought asylum in France after Franco's victory in 1938 and subsequently played Death in Jean Cocteau's 1950 film *Orpheé*.

V755.6–8, B881.12–14   throwing his arms up into an inverted "peace

sign" . . . exposing . . . white French cuff   The pacifists' peace sign of the Vietnam era was an upside-down "V" divided in two by a vertical line, inside a circle; in a hand salute, this became the two-fingered "V" (a Victory sign in World War II). The gesture described here, with the white cuffs exposed, unmistakably identifies Richard M. Zhlubb as Richard M. Nixon, photographed just so in 1971.

V755.19, B881.26   in Atascadero   The California Penal Facility located just north, and inland, from San Luis Obispo. LSD guru Timothy Leary was incarcerated there after his arrest in 1969.

V755.28, B881.36   the black Managerial Volkswagen   Improbable as a managerial limousine, but implicated here perhaps because V W plants at Fallersleben and Magdeburg manufactured V-weapon parts (Irving 199, 291).

V755.33–36, B882.1–5   The Santa Monica Freeway . . . the Harbor.   A tally of some of the principal freeways in the Los Angeles basin.

V756.22–23, B882.37–38   dark Lincolns, some Fords, even GMCs, but not a Pontiac   If there is any logic to this list, perhaps it is that Pontiacs were named for the eighteenth-century chief of the Ottowa Indians, the likes of whom had to be pitchforked further west by whites like Abe Lincoln and Henry Ford.

V757.17–758.24, B883.39–885.11   "Räumen. . . . Steuerung klar? . . . Stecker 1 und 2 gefallen"   With these calls from Captain Blicero and Moritz on the launch crew, the ascent of Rocket 00000 begins. Pynchon's source on the launch sequence was probably the *A-4 Fibel* (see also V361.12–13n), though once again he appears to have put the terms back into the original German. Blicero and his launch assistants, Max and Moritz (see V501.10n), begin to call out a string of technical commands, warnings, and inquiries. They are, in order: "Räumen," Blicero's command to unnecessary members of the launch crew, ordering them to clear the space. With the question "Steuerung klar?" one of the boys asks if the controls or steering vanes are clear of obstructions. The "Treibwerk" is the fueling gear, and it must be cleared out of the area. The "Luftlage" is the launch site itself. Then the actual lift-off commences. "Durchschalten": Switch on. "VORSTUFE": First stage. "Entlüftung. 'Beluftung klar' ": Ventilation. "Take-off cleared." "Zundung": Ignition. "Hauptstufe": Main stage. At this point the "Stecker" or plugs would be blasted from the main engine nozzles and the rocket would have begun its ascent.

V759.24, B886.20   a Brocken-specter   On the unusual plays of light visible from atop the devilish Brocken, in Germany's Harz Mountains, see V293.17n.

V759.29, B886.26   Streckefuss   Again, Blicero's nickname, "Stretchfoot" (see V733.26n).

Bibliography

This is a bibliography of works cited or consulted. Textual evidence shows that many of them were sources Thomas Pynchon included in his reading for *Gravity's Rainbow*. Among these source materials, the *Times* of London, circa 1944–45, played a very large role indeed. The *Times* supplied so much background—in politics, military history, material and popular culture (household brands and pop bands, for example), even the weather—that the individual references are too numerous to list here. Source materials from the *Times* of London are cited, instead, within annotations. Pynchon also made use of such American periodicals as *Time, Life*, and the *New York Times*, and those items are listed in this bibliography when the text of *Gravity's Rainbow* shows a clear debt to the original.

A-4 Fibel [A-4 Handbook]. Trans. John A. Bitzer and Ted Woerner. Redstone Arsenal, Ala.: Army Ballistic Missile Agency, 1957.

Adams, Henry. *The Education of Henry Adams*. Ed. Ernest Samuels. Boston: Houghton Mifflin, 1974.

Adams, Henry, and Charles Adams. *Chapters of Erie*. 1871. New York: A. M. Kelley, 1967.

Adorno, Theodor. *Philosophy of the New Music*. New York: Seabury, 1973.

Alexander, Robert J. *The Péron Era*. New York: Russell, 1965.

Anastazi, Anne. *Psychological Testing*. 3rd ed. New York: Macmillan, 1968.

Angellucci, Enzo. *The Rand-McNally Encyclopedia of Military Aircraft*. New York: Rand-McNally, 1980.

Asquith, Margot. *More or Less about Myself*. New York: Dutton, 1934.

Baedeker's Handbooks Inc. *Belgium and Holland*. 14th ed. New York: Scribner, 1905.

———. *Berlin and Its Environs*. 4th ed. Leipzig: Karl Baedeker, 1910.

———. *Great Britain*. 5th ed. London: Dulau, 1901.

———. *London and Its Environs*. 21st ed. New York: Macmillan, 1955.

———. *Northern Germany*. 14th ed. Leipzig: Karl Baedeker, 1904.

———. *South-eastern France*. 3rd ed. London: Dulau, 1898.

———. *Southern Germany*. 12th ed. New York: Scribner, 1904.

Bakhtin, Mikhail. *The Dialogic Imagination: Four Essays*. Ed. Michael Holquist. Trans. Caryl Emerson and Michael Holquist. Austin: University of Texas Press, 1982.

————. *Rabelais and His World*. Trans. Helene Iswolski. Boston: M.I.T. Press, 1968.

Baring-Gould, S. *The Lives of the Saints*. 16 vols. New York: Longmans, Green, 1898.

Bercovitch, Sacvan. *The Puritan Origins of the American Self*. New Haven, Conn.: Yale University Press, 1975.

Blackett, P. M. S. *Fear, War, and the Bomb*. New York, McGraw-Hill, 1955.

Borges, Jorge Luis. *Ficciones*. Ed. Anthony Kerrigan. New York: Grove Press, 1962.

Branston, Brian. *Gods of the North*. New York: Thames and Hudson, 1955.

Braun, Wernher von. *Space Frontier* Greenwich, Conn.: Fawcett, 1969.

Braun, Wernher von, and Frederick Ordway. *History of Rocketry and Space Travel*. New York: Crowell, 1968.

Briggs, Katharine. *The Faeries in English Tradition and Folklore*. Chicago: University of Chicago Press, 1967.

Brincker, P. H. *Wörterbuch und Kurzgefässte Grammatik des Otji-Herero*. Leipzig: C. G. Buttner, 1886.

Brown, Norman O. *Life Against Death: The Psychoanalytical Meaning of History*. 1959. Middletown, Conn.: Wesleyan University Press, 1970.

Bullock, Alan. *Hitler: A Study in Tyranny*. New York: Bantam, 1961.

Byington, Ezra Hoyt. "William Pynchon, Gent." In *The Puritan in England and New England*. Boston: Roberts Bros., 1896.

Campbell, Lewis, and William Garnett. *The Life of James Clerk Maxwell*. 1882. New York: Johnson Corp., 1969.

Carman, W. Y. *A History of Firearms*. London: Routledge and Kegan Paul, 1955.

Clerc, Charles. "Film in *Gravity's Rainbow*." In Clerc, *Approaches* 103–52.

————, ed. *Approaches to "Gravity's Rainbow."* Columbus: Ohio State University Press, 1983.

Clouston, William Alexander. *Popular Tales and Fictions: Their Migrations and Transformations*. 2 vols. London: Blackwood, 1887.

Collier, Basil. *The Battle of the V-Weapons*. New York: Viking, 1965.

Colmer, Michael. *Pinball: An Illustrated History*. New York: New American Library, 1976.

Cooksley, Peter G. *Flying Bomb: The Story of Hitler's V-Weapons in World War II*. New York: Scribner, 1978.

Cooper, Peter. *Signs and Symptoms: Thomas Pynchon and the Contemporary World*. Berkeley and Los Angeles: University of California Press, 1983.

Cowart, David. *Thomas Pynchon: The Art of Allusion*. Carbondale: Southern Illinois University Press, 1980.

Cowke, L. W., and John Selwin Gummer. *The Christian Calendar.* Springfield, Mass.: Merriam, 1974.

D'Annunzio, Gabriele. *The Triumph of Death.* Trans. Arthur Hornblow. Boston: Page, 1917.

Dickinson, Emily. *The Poems of Emily Dickinson.* Ed. Thomas H. Johnson. 2 vols. Cambridge, Mass.: Harvard University Press, 1955.

Dictionary of American Regional English. Vol. 1 (A–C). Ed. Frederic G. Cassidy. Cambridge, Mass.: Belknap Press, 1985.

Donovan, Robert J. *PT-109: John F. Kennedy in World War II.* Greenwich, Conn.: Fawcett, 1962.

Dornberger, Walter. *V-2.* Trans. James Clough and Geoffrey Halliday. New York: Viking, 1955.

Drake, Francis S. *The Town of Roxbury.* Roxbury, Mass.: By the Author, 1878.

Dubois, Josiah Ellis. *Generals in Grey Suits: The Directors of the International "IG Farben" Cartel, Their Conspiracy and Trial at Nuremburg.* London: Bodley Head, 1953.

Dunning, John. *Tune in on Yesterday: The Ultimate Encyclopedia of Old-Time Radio.* Englewood Cliffs, N.J.: Prentice-Hall, 1976.

Ehrenburg, Walter. "Maxwell's Demon." *Scientific American* 217 (Nov. 1967): 103–10.

Eliade, Mircea. *The Myth of the Eternal Return.* Trans. Willard R. Trask. New York: Pantheon, 1963.

Ewen, David. *All the Years of American Popular Music.* Englewood Cliffs, N.J.: Prentice-Hall, 1977.

Federal Writers' Project. *The Berkshire Hills.* New York: Funk and Wagnalls, 1939.

Fifield, William, ed. *Alex Lichine's Encyclopedia of Wines and Spirits.* New York: Knopf, 1968.

Fitzgerald, F. Scott. *This Side of Paradise.* New York: Scribner's, 1920.

Fowler, Douglas. *A Reader's Guide to "Gravity's Rainbow."* Ann Arbor, Mich.: Ardis, 1980.

Frazer, James George. *Adonis, Attis, Osiris,* vol. 2. Part 4 of *The Golden Bough.* New York: Macmillan, 1935.

Frenssen, Gustave. *Peter Moor's Journey to Southwest Africa: A Narrative of the German Campaign.* Trans. Margaret Ward. Boston: Houghton Mifflin, 1968.

Georgano, G. N., ed. *The Complete Encyclopedia of Motor Cars, 1895–1965.* New York: Dutton, 1968.

Gibbon, Edward. *The History of the Decline and Fall of the Roman Empire.* 1776. London: Chatto and Windus, 1960.

Gibson, G. D. "Double Descent and Its Correlates Among the Herero of Ngamililand." *American Anthropologist* 58 (1956): 109–39.

————. "Herero Marriage." *Rhodes-Livingstone Journal* 24 (1959): 1–37.

Gilman, Alfred. *The Pharmacological Basis of Therapeutics.* New York: Macmillan, 1980.

Giovanetti, Len, and Fred Freed. *The Decision to Drop the Bomb.* New York: Coward-McCann, 1965.

Glover, Tony. *Blues Harp.* New York: Oak, 1965.

Goethe, Johann Wolfgang von. *Faust: A Tragedy in Two Parts.* Trans. Bayard Taylor. London: Oxford University Press, 1963.

————. *Goethe's Color Theory.* Ed. Rupprecht Matthei. Trans. Herbert Aach. New York: Van Nostrand Reinhold, 1971.

Goldblatt, Irving. *History of South-West Africa.* Cape Town: Juta, 1971.

Graham, F. Lanier. *The Rainbow Book.* Berkeley: Shambala, 1975.

Graham, Stephen. *Through Russian Central Asia.* New York: Cassell, 1916.

Graves, Robert. *The Greek Myths.* New York: Penguin, 1967.

————. *The White Goddess: A Historical Grammar of Poetic Myth.* New York: Farrar, Straus and Giroux, 1966.

Greene, Richard Leighton. *The Early English Carols.* Oxford: Clarendon, 1935.

Grimm, Jacob. *Teutonic Mythology.* Trans. James Steven Stallybrass. 4 vols. [Paginated consecutively.] New York: Dover, 1966.

Gröttrup, Irmgard. *Rocket Wife.* Trans. Susi Hughes. London: André Deutsch, 1959.

Hanson, Stephen, and Frank Magill. *Magill's Survey of Cinema.* Englewood Cliffs, N.J.: Salem, 1981.

Hardinge, Rex. *South-African Cinderella: A Trek through Ex-German South-West Africa.* London: Herbert Jenkins, 1937.

Harmon, Jim. *The Great Radio Comedians.* New York: Doubleday, 1970.

Harrison, Max. *Charlie Parker.* New York: Barnes, 1961.

Hayles, N. Katherine. *The Cosmic Web: Scientific Field Models and Literary Strategies in the Twentieth Century.* Ithaca, N.Y.: Cornell University Press, 1984.

Hayles, N. Katherine, and Mary B. Eiser. "Coloring *Gravity's Rainbow.*" *Pynchon Notes* 16 (Spring 1985): 3–24.

Haynes, William. *This Chemical Age.* New York: Knopf, 1942.

Heiber, Helmut. *Goebbels.* Trans. John K. Dickinson. New York: Hawthorne, 1972.

Hemingway, Ernest. Introduction to *The Fifth Column.* London: Cape, 1939.

Hernandez, José. *The Gaucho Martín Fierro.* Trans. Walter Owen. New York: Farrar and Rinehart, 1936.

Hite, Molly. "'Holy Center-Approaching' in the Novels of Thomas Pynchon." *Journal of Narrative Technique* 12, no. 2 (1982): 121–29.

———. *Ideas of Order in the Novels of Thomas Pynchon*. Columbus: Ohio State University Press, 1983.

Hogg, Ian V. *The Complete Illustrated Encyclopedia of the World's Firearms*. London: Quarto Editions, 1978.

Hollingsworth, Derek. *They Came to Mauritius*. London: Oxford University Press, 1965.

Hooker, Thomas. *The Soules Implantation into the Natural Olive*. 1637. London: AMS, 1981.

Hume, Kathryn. *Pynchon's Mythography: An Approach to "Gravity's Rainbow."* Carbondale: Southern Illinois University Press, 1987.

Huzel, Dieter. *Peenemünde to Canaveral*. Englewood Cliffs, N.J.: Prentice-Hall, 1962.

Inoguchi, Rikihei, and Tadashi Nakajima. *The Divine Wind: Japan's Kamikaze Force in World War II*. Ed. Roger Pineau. Westport, Conn.: Greenwood, 1978.

Irving, David. *The Mare's Nest*. London: William Kimber, 1964.

Jackson, Stanley. *The Sassoons*. New York: Dutton, 1968.

James, Montagu Rhodes. *The Apocryphal New Testament*. London: Nash and Grayson, 1924.

Jones, Marc Edmund. *Astrology*. London: Penguin, 1969.

Josephson, Mathew. *The Robber-Barons*. 1934. New York: Harcourt, Brace and World, 1962.

Jung, Carl Gustav. *The Collected Works of C. G. Jung*. Ed. G. Adler et al. Trans. R. F. Hull. 2nd ed. Vol. 9, *Mandala Symbolism*. Vol. 12, *Psychology and Alchemy*. Vol. 16, *Practice of Psychotherapy*. Bollingen Series. Princeton, N.J.: Princeton University Press, 1968–69, 1968, 1966.

Kármán, Theodore von. *The Wind and Beyond*. Boston: Little, Brown, 1967.

Kastrup, Edwin K. *Facts and Comparisons: A Pharmacological Handbook*. St. Louis: Facts and Comparisons, 1979.

Katz, Ephraim. *The Film Encyclopedia*. New York: Crowell, 1979.

"Kennedy Hits the Trail." *Time*, September 24, 1945, 17.

Klee, Ernst, and Otto Merk. *The Birth of the Missile: The Secrets of Peenemünde*. Trans. T. Schoeters. Intro. Wernher von Braun. New York: Dutton, 1965.

Kolbe, F. W. *An English-Herero Dictionary with an Introduction to the Study of Bantu in General*. Cape Town: Juta, 1883.

Kooy, J. M. J., and J. W. H. Uytenbogaart. *Ballistics of the Future: With Special Reference to the Dynamics and Physical Theory of the Rocket Weapons*. London: McGraw-Hill, 1946.

Kahn, Ely Jacques. *The Big Drink: The Story of Coca-Cola*. New York: Random House, 1960.

Kozminski, Isidore. *Numbers and Their Magic*. New York: Samuel Weiser, 1972.

Kracauer, Siegfried. *From Caligari to Hitler: A Psychological History of the German Film*. 1947. Princeton, N.J.: Princeton University Press, 1969.

Lake, Stewart M. *Wyatt Earp, Frontier Marshall*. Boston: Houghton Mifflin, 1931.

Larson, John A. *Lying and Its Detection*. Chicago: University of Chicago Press, 1932.

Lee, Stan. *Origins of Marvel Comics*. New York: Simon and Schuster, 1974.

Leiss, Andreas. *Carl Orff*. London: Calder and Boyers, 1966.

Levine, George, and David Leverenz, eds. *Mindful Pleasures: Essays on Thomas Pynchon*. Boston: Little, Brown, 1976.

Ley, Willy. *The Drifting Continents*. New York: Weybright and Talley, 1969.

_____. *Rockets, Missiles, and Space Travel*. New York: Viking, 1959.

Lichine, Alexis. *Encyclopedia of Wines and Spirits*. New York: Knopf, 1967.

Lueddecke, W. J. *Morituri*. Greenwich, Conn.: Fawcett, 1964.

Lugones, Leopoldo. *Obras Poeticas*. Madrid: Aguilar, 1959.

Luttig, Hendrik Gerhardus. *The Religious System and Social Organization of the Herero: A Study in Bantu Culture*. Utrecht: Kemink en Zoon, 1933.

Lykken, David T. *A Tremor in the Blood: Uses and Abuses of the Lie Detector*. New York: McGraw-Hill, 1981.

McGovern, James. *Crossbow and Overcast*. New York: Morrow, 1964.

McHale, Brian. "Modernist Reading, Postmodern Text: The Case of *Gravity's Rainbow*." *Poetics Today* 1, no. 1 (1979): 85–110.

McIntyre, Ruth A. *William Pynchon: Merchant and Colonizer*. Springfield, Mass.: Connecticut Valley Historical Museum, 1961.

Major, Clarence. *Dictionary of Afro-American Slang*. New York: International, 1970.

Malcolm X (Malcolm Little). *The Autobiography of Malcolm X*. New York: Grove, 1966.

Mangel, Anne. "Maxwell's Demon, Entropy, Information: *The Crying of Lot 49*." In Levine and Leverenz 87–100.

Marriot, David. "*Gravity's Rainbow*: Apocryphal History or Historical Apocrypha?" *Journal of American Studies* 19 (1985): 69–80.

Marriot, John A. *The Eastern Question*. Oxford: Clarendon, 1958.

Mead, Clifford. Untitled note. *Pynchon Notes* 11 (Feb. 1983): 64.

Mendelson, Edward. "Gravity's Encyclopedia." In Levine and Leverenz 161–96.

_____, ed. *Pynchon: A Collection of Critical Essays*. Englewood Cliffs, N.J.: Prentice-Hall, 1978.

Mesher, David. "Corrigenda: A Note on *Gravity's Rainbow*." *Pynchon Notes* 5 (Feb. 1981): 13–16.

Moore, Steven. "Pynchon on Record." *Pynchon Notes* 10 (Oct. 1982): 56–57.

Morison, Samuel Eliot. "William Pynchon, the Founder of Springfield." *Massachusetts Historical Society Proceedings* 64 (1931): 67–107.

Nabakov, Vladimir. *Pnin*. New York: Avon, 1969.

Nagel, Ernest, and James R. Newman. *Gödel's Proof*. New York: New York University Press, 1958.

Newman, Ernest. *The Wagner Operas*. New York: Knopf, 1963.

Newman, Robert D. *Understanding Thomas Pynchon*. Columbia: University of South Carolina Press, 1986.

Noel, John V. *Naval Terms Dictionary*. 2nd ed. Annapolis, Md.: U.S. Naval Academy, 1966.

Novikoff-Priboy, V. *Tsushima*. New York: Holt, Rinehart, 1948.

Nussenzweig, H. H. "The Theory of the Rainbow." *Scientific American* 236 (Apr. 1977): 116–27.

Opie, Iona, and Peter Opie. *Children's Games in Street and Playground*. Oxford: Clarendon, 1969.

_____. *The Lore and Language of Schoolchildren*. London: Oxford University Press, 1959.

Orff, Carl. *Carmina Burana: Cantiones profanae, cantoribus et chorus cantandae*. New York: Schott, 1937.

Ouspensky, Petr D. *The Symbolism of the Tarot*. Trans. A. L. Pogossky. New York: Dover, 1976.

Oxford Annotated Bible. Ed. Herbert G. May and Bruce M. Metzger. New York: Oxford University Press, 1962.

Oxford Dictionary of Quotations. 3rd ed. New York: Oxford University Press, 1979.

Ozier, Lance. "Anti-Pointsman/Anti-Mexico: Some Mathematical Imagery in *Gravity's Rainbow*." *Critique* 16, no. 2 (1974): 73–90.

_____. "The Calculus of Transformation: More Mathematical Imagery in *Gravity's Rainbow*." *Twentieth Century Literature* 21, no. 2 (1975): 193–210.

"Paris Black Market Robs U.S. Army." *Life*, March 26, 1945, 25–29.

Parrinder, Geoffrey. *African Mythology*. London: Paul Hamlyn, 1967.

Partridge, Eric, ed. *A Dictionary of Forces' Slang, 1939–45*. London: Secker and Warburg, 1948.

_____. *The Macmillan Dictionary of Historical Slang*. New York: Macmillan, 1974.

Pavlov, Ivan Petrovitch. *Conditioned Reflexes*. Trans. and ed. G. V. Anrep. Oxford: Clarendon, 1928.

————. *Lectures on Conditioned Reflexes.* Trans. W. Horsley Gantt. Vol. 1, *Twenty-five years of Objective Study of the Higher Nervous Activity of Animals.* Vol. 2, *Conditioned Reflexes and Psychiatry.* New York: International, 1928–41.

Pearce, Richard, ed. *Critical Essays on Thomas Pynchon.* Boston: Hall, 1981.

Pearsall, Ronald. *The Table-Rappers.* New York: St. Martin's, 1972.

Peesch, Reinhard. *Das Berliner Kinderspiel der Gegenwart.* Berlin: Akademie-Verlag, 1957.

Perle, George. *Serial Composition and Atonality: An Introduction to the Music of Schoenberg, Berg, and Webern.* 3rd ed. Berkeley and Los Angeles: University of California Press, 1970.

Petillon, Pierre-Yves. "Thomas Pynchon and Aleatory Space." Trans. Margaret S. Langford and Clifford Mead. *Pynchon Notes* 15 (Fall 1984): 3–46.

Pike, Albert. *Morals and Dogma: The Ancient and Accepted Rite of Freemasonry.* Richmond, Va.: L. H. Jenkins, 1906.

Pike, Nicholas. *Sub-tropical Rambles in the Land of the Aphanapteryx: Adventures in and Wanderings in and around Mauritius.* London: Sampson Low, Marston Low, and Searle, 1873.

Plater, William M. *The Grim Phoenix: Reconstructing Thomas Pynchon.* Bloomington: Indiana University Press, 1978.

Pynchon, Thomas Ruggles (1823–1904). *Introduction to Chemical Physics.* New York: Van Nostrand, 1881.

Pynchon, Thomas Ruggles, Jr. *The Crying of Lot 49.* New York: Lippincott, 1966.

————. *Gravity's Rainbow.* New York: Viking, 1973; New York: Bantam, 1974.

————. Introduction to *Been Down So Long It Looks Like Up to Me,* by Richard Fariña. New York: Penguin, 1983.

————. "Is It O.K. to Be a Luddite?" *New York Times Book Review,* October 28, 1984, 1, 40–41.

————. "Journey into the Mind of Watts." *New York Times Magazine,* June 12, 1966, 34–35, 78, 80–82, 84.

————. *Slow Learner.* Boston: Little, Brown, 1984.

————. "Under the Rose." *Noble Savage* 3 (1961): 233–51.

————. *V.* New York: Lippincott, 1963.

Pynchon, William (1590–1662). *The Meritorious Price of Our Redemption; or, Christ's Satisfaction Explained and Discussed.* London: Thomas Newberry, 1655.

————. *The Time When the First Sabbath Was Ordained.* London: Printed by R.G., and to be sold by T.N. at the Three Lions in Cornhill, 1654.

Pynchon & Co. *The Aviation Industry.* New York, 1929.

Qazi, Javaid. "Source Materials for Thomas Pynchon's Fiction: An Annotated Bibliography." *Pynchon Notes* 2 (Feb. 1980): 7–19.

Reed, Ishmael. *Mumbo Jumbo*. New York: Avon, 1972.

Reid, Norman. *Collections of the Tate Gallery*. London: Tate Gallery, 1967.

Rilke, Rainer Maria. *Duino Elegies*. Trans. J. B. Leishman and Stephen Spender. New York: Norton, 1967.

———. *Sonnets to Orpheus*. 1922. Trans. J. B. Leishman. London: Hogarth, 1957.

———. *Sonnets to Orpheus*. 1922. Trans. M. D. Herder Norton. New York: Norton, 1942.

Rougement, Denis de. *Passion and Society*. Trans. Montgomery Belgion. London: Faber and Faber, 1957.

Sacher-Masoch, Leopold von. *Venus in Furs*. Trans. Friedrich Schaffhausen. London: Sphere, 1969.

Sadoul, Georges. *Dictionary of Films*. Trans. Peter Morris. Berkeley and Los Angeles: University of California Press, 1972.

Safer, Elaine B. "The Allusive Mode and Black Humor in Pynchon's *Gravity's Rainbow*." 1980. In Pearce 157–68.

Sassoon, Siegfried. *Memoirs of an Infantry Officer*. London: Faber and Faber, 1931.

Sasuly, Richard. *IG Farben*. New York: Boni and Gaer, 1947.

Schaub, Thomas R. *Pynchon: The Voice of Ambiguity*. Urbana: University of Illinois Press, 1981.

Schauffler, Robert R. *Beethoven: The Man Who Freed Music*. New York: Doubleday, Doran, 1933.

Scholem, Gershom. *Major Trends in Jewish Mysticism*. 1941. New York: Schocken, 1954.

———. *On the Kabbalah and Its Symbolism*. Trans. Ralph Mannheim. New York: Schocken, 1965.

Schwab, Gabriele. "Creative Paranoia and Frost Patterns of White Words: Making Sense in and of Thomas Pynchon's *Gravity's Rainbow*." Working Paper No. 4. Milwaukee: Center for Twentieth Century Studies, 1985.

Seed, David. "Pynchon's Hereros." *Pynchon Notes* 10 (Oct. 1982): 37–44.

———. "Pynchon's Two Tchitcherines." *Pynchon Notes* 5 (Feb. 1981): 11–12.

———. "Thomas Hooker in Pynchon's *Gravity's Rainbow*." *Notes on Modern American Literature* 8 (1984): item 15.

"Shoulder Insignia." *Life*, August 6, 1945, 41–47.

Siegal, Jules. "Who Is Thomas Pynchon . . . and Why Did He Take Off With My Wife?" *Playboy* 34 (March 1977): 97, 122, 168–74.

Sillar, Frederick C. *The Symbolic Pig*. London: Oliver and Boyd, 1961.

Skinner, B. F. "Pigeon in a Pelican." In *Cumulative Record: A Selection of Papers,* ed. B. F. Skinner. New York: Appleton-Century-Crofts, 1972.

Slade, Joseph. *Thomas Pynchon.* New York: Warner, 1974.

Smith, Adam. *An Enquiry into the Nature and Causes of the Wealth of Nations.* Ed. Edwin Cannan. London: Methuen, 1981.

Smith, Joseph H., ed. *Colonial Justice in Western Massachusetts: The Pynchon Court Record.* Cambridge, Mass.: Harvard University Press, 1961.

Smith, Marcus, and Khachig Tololyan. "The New Jeremiad: *Gravity's Rainbow.*" In Pearce 169–86.

Soules, Terrill Shepard. "What to Think about *Gravity's Rainbow.*" *Esquire,* October 1980, 104–7.

Speer, Albert. *Inside the Third Reich.* New York: Macmillan, 1970.

Steenkamp, Willem Petrus. *Is the South-West African Herero Committing Race-Suicide?* Cape Town: Unie-Volkspers, 1944.

Stendahl. [Marie Henri Beyle]. *Life of Rossini.* 1824. Trans. Richard N. Coe. New York: Orion, 1970.

Tanner, Tony. *Thomas Pynchon.* London: Methuen, 1982.

Tatham, Campbell. "Tarot and *Gravity's Rainbow.*" *Modern Fiction Studies* 32 (Winter 1986): 581–90.

Taylor, A. J. P. *English History, 1914–45.* Oxford: Clarendon, 1965.

Taylor, A. Marjorie. *The Language of World War II.* New York: H. W. Wilson, 1948.

Thompson, Don, and Dick Lupoff. *All in Color for a Dime.* New Rochelle, N.Y.: Arlington House, 1970.

———. *The Comic-Book Book.* New Rochelle, N.Y.: Arlington House, 1972.

Thompson, Stith. *Motif-Index of Folk-Literätur.* 6 vols. Rev. ed. Bloomington: Indiana University Press, 1955–58.

Tillotson, T. S. Untitled Note. *Pynchon Notes* 5 (Feb. 1981): 29.

Toland, John. *The Dillinger Days.* New York: Random House, 1963.

Tölölyan, Khachig. "Fishy Poisson: Allusions to Statistics in *Gravity's Rainbow.*" *Notes on Modern American Literature* 4 (1979): item 5.

———. "War as Background in *Gravity's Rainbow.*" In Clerc, *Approaches* 31–68.

Twain, Mark. *Roughing It.* Ed. Hamlin Hill. New York: Penguin, 1981.

Van Doren, Carl. *Benjamin Franklin.* New York: Viking Press, 1964.

Vedder, Heinrich. "The Herero." In *Native Tribes of South Africa.* Cape Town: Cape Times Limited, 1928.

———. *Southwest Africa in Early Times.* Oxford: Clarendon, 1938.

Vonnegut, Kurt. *Slaughterhouse-Five; or, The Children's Crusade.* New York: Delacorte, 1969.

Waddell, Helen J. *The Wandering Scholars*. 1927. London: Constable, 1938.

Waite, Arthur Edward. *The Book of Black Magic and of Pacts*. Ed. I. W. Laurence. 1898. Chicago: de Laurence, 1940.

_____. *The Pictorial Key to the Tarot*. San Francisco: Harper and Row, 1971.

"Walpurgisnacht Is Celebrated by G-Is." *Life*, May 28, 1945, 122–24.

Ward, Arthur Sarsfield [pseud. Sax Rohmer]. *The Trail of Fu-Manchu*. New York: Doubleday, Doran, 1934.

Watson, John B., and Rosalie Rayner Watson. *The Psychological Care of Infant and Child*. New York: Norton, 1928.

Weber, Max. *The Protestant Ethic and the Spirit of Capitalism*. Trans. Talcott Parsons. New York: Scribner, 1958.

_____. *The Theory of Social and Economic Organization*. Trans. Talcott Parsons and A. M. Henderson. New York: Oxford University Press, 1947.

Weiser, Francis. *Handbook of Christian Feasts and Customs*. 2 vols. New York: Harcourt, Brace and World, 1958.

Whalen, Richard J. *The Founding Father: The Story of Joseph P. Kennedy*. New York: New American Library, 1964.

Wheeler, Fern. *The Thirteenth House: Lost Chapter in Spiritual Astrology*. Seattle: Lowman and Hanford, 1939.

Wiener, Norbert. *Cybernetics*. 1948. Boston: M.I.T. Press, 1961.

Wildgans, Friedrich. *Anton Webern*. Trans. Edith Roberts and Humphrey Searle. New York: October House, 1967.

Wilhelm, Richard, trans. *The I Ching; or, The Book of Changes*. Bollingen Series. Princeton, N.J.: Princeton University Press, 1967.

Winner, Thomas G. *Oral Art and Literature of the Kazakhs of Russian Central Asia*. Durham, N.C.: Duke University Press, 1958.

_____. "Problems of Alphabetic Reform among the Turkic Peoples of Soviet Central Asia." *Slavonic and East European Review* 31 (1952): 133–47.

Winston, Mathew. "The Quest for Thomas Pynchon." In Levine and Leverenz 251–64.

Wister, Owen. *Padre Ignacio; or, A Song of Temptation*. New York: Harper and Bros., 1900.

Wolfley, Lawrence. "Repression's Rainbow: The Presence of Norman O. Brown in Pynchon's Big Novel." 1978. In Pearce 99–123.

Wray, Fay. "How Fay Met Kong; or, The Scream that Shook the World." *New York Times*, September 21, 1969, Sec. 2, 17–18.

Yates, Frances Amelia. *The Rosicrucian Enlightenment*. Boston: Routledge and Kegan Paul, 1972.

Yule, George U., and M. G. Kendall. *Introduction to the Theory of Statistics*. 14th ed. New York: Hafner, 1950.

Zigrosser, Karl, ed. *Prints and Drawings of Kathe Kollwitz.* New York: Dover, 1969.

Zipf, George Kingsley. *Human Behavior and the Principle of Least Effort.* Cambridge, Mass.: Addison-Wesley, 1949.

———. *The Psycho-Biology of Language.* Boston: Houghton Mifflin, 1935.

"Zoot Suits and Service Stripes: Race Tension Behind the Riots." *Newsweek,* June 21, 1943, 35–40.

Index

This listing references the various allusions, brand names, characters, contexts, items, motifs, persons, place names, sources, subjects, substances, and texts in *Gravity's Rainbow*, as well as the principal texts consulted for notes in the *Companion*. Excepting a small percentage of items from introductory sections of the *Companion*, whose page-number references are given below in brackets, all other indexed items are to things discussed in the annotations, and use page- and line-number references to the Viking-Penguin editions. As such, this index may also double as an index to the novel. Readers with the Bantam edition may use it by turning from the index to the annotation, for example to "Aberystwyth" (at page 171, line 7 of the Viking-Penguin editions), and finding the corresponding Bantam location—in this case, B199.41—provided before the note for that entry.